WYOMING

CARTER G. WALKER

Contents

Wyoming

Embodied by the bucking bronco on its license plates, Wyoming is a child's cowboy fantasy come to life, with rodeos aplenty and dude ranches where even city slickers can try their hand at riding and roping.

But what strikes people most about Wyoming is its authenticity. The harsh climate and isolation that make Wyoming the least populated state in the union result in an uncommon grace in its residents. It's expressed not just in the weathered creases on their faces but in the way they do business and welcome visitors. There is glitz here too, in places like Jackson Hole and Cody, but it doesn't distract from the essence of Wyoming. Those towns are but a flash of silver, the shiny buckle on a well-worn belt.

The landscape—from soaring mountains and narrow valleys to sweeping plains—was carved over eons by water, wind, fire, and ice. The culture was also shaped by conflict: between those who were from here and those who were not; those who valued the land itself and those who sought its riches. Its distinct histories—both natural and cultural—are evident everywhere, not just tucked away in dusty museums, as the state continues to redefine itself.

Clockwise from top left: mountain goat; cowboy; Yellowstone's Old Faithful; Million Dollar Cowboy Bar in Jackson Hole; cutthroat trout; Mormon Row in Grand Teton National Park.

7 TOP
EXPERIENCES

1 **Spot Wildlife in Yellowstone National Park:** Yellowstone is a wonderland of wildlife. Visit **Lamar Valley** (page 57) for the chance to see bears, bison, and bighorn sheep. This is also the best place to look for **wolves** (page 56).

2 **Go on an Adventure in Grand Teton National Park:** With the towering Tetons a near constant backdrop, the land here lends itself to superb hikes, bike rides, rock climbing, horseback adventures, fishing, and boating expeditions (page 79).

>>>

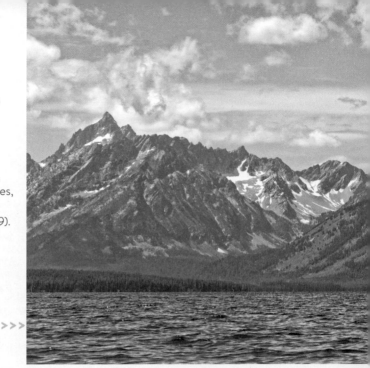

3 **Go Skiing:** Skiing in Wyoming means phenomenal terrain and true ski towns like **Jackson Hole** (page 119).

>>>

4 **Take to the River:** An abundance of enviable rivers offer fishing, boating, and both flat and whitewater river rafting. Kayak or canoe on **Oxbow Bend** (page 92) or go rafting on the **Snake River** (page 118).

5 **Learn about Indigenous Cultures:** There are many ways to explore Native American heritage (page 23).

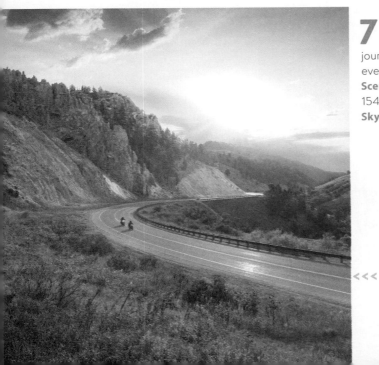

6 **Soak in the Hot Springs:** From resort-style pools and thermally heated rivers to entire towns built on hot springs, this region offers infinite ways to take a dip (page 22).

7 **Take a Scenic Drive:** The journey is the main event on **Chief Joseph Scenic Highway** (page 154) and **Cloud Peak Skyway** (page 184).

Planning Your Trip

Where to Go

Yellowstone National Park

This magnificent park is constantly in motion; nothing here is static. See abundant wildlife, including **bison, elk, bears, and wolves;** marvel at geothermal features like **Old Faithful;** and stay in historic lodges like the **Old Faithful Inn** and rambling **Lake Yellowstone Hotel.** Perimeter communities, including **West Yellowstone, Gardiner,** and remote **Cooke City,** should not be missed.

Grand Teton National Park

Grand Teton packs a punch, particularly when it comes to **mountain splendor.** Twelve peaks in the Teton Range soar above 12,000 feet (3,600 m). While there are only 100 miles (161 km) of roads in the park, there are twice as many **miles** of trails, leaving hikers endless options for adventure. Favorite landmarks include picturesque **Jenny Lake,** vast **Jackson Lake,** drive-to-the-summit **Signal Mountain,** and serene **Oxbow Bend.**

Jackson Hole, Cody, and the Wind Rivers

Wyoming's northwest corner is far more than a gateway to Yellowstone and Grand Teton National Parks. **Jackson Hole** is a destination in and of itself, with **glitzy galleries** and boutiques, gourmet eateries, **luxe accommodations,** and a sensational art scene in immediate proximity to world-class **ski resorts** and **white-water rafting.** The **National Museum of Wildlife Art** and the **National Elk Refuge** are major

Jenny Lake

Medicine Wheel National Historic Landmark

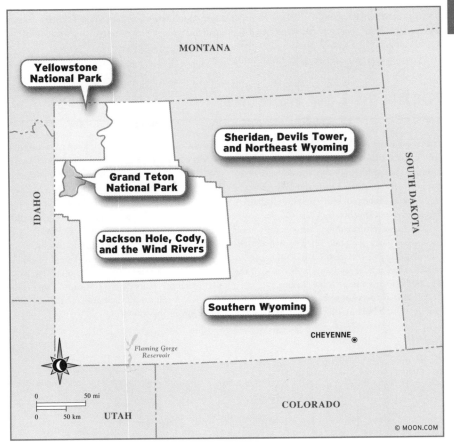

MONTANA

Yellowstone
National Park

Sheridan, Devils Tower,
and Northeast Wyoming

Grand Teton
National Park

IDAHO

SOUTH DAKOTA

Jackson Hole, Cody,
and the Wind Rivers

Southern Wyoming

CHEYENNE

Flaming Gorge
Reservoir

0   50 mi

0   50 km   UTAH

COLORADO

© MOON.COM

draws for animal enthusiasts. In **Cody** the cowboy is still king, and the sun rises and sets on the **Buffalo Bill Center of the West** and its five museums. Farther south, outdoors enthusiasts will find **hot springs** and **mountain meccas.**

Sheridan and Northeast Wyoming

Where the prairies meet the mountains, cowboy culture comes alive. This is where you'll find **dude ranches** and **Sheridan,** one of the most charming and authentic Western towns in the state. The spectacular **Cloud Peak Skyway Scenic Byway** climbs into the mountains

toward the pictograph-rich **Medicine Lodge State Archeological Site** and more mysterious **Medicine Wheel National Historic Landmark.** The isolated and enigmatic **Devils Tower National Monument** draws climbers, geologists, and Native Americans who consider it a sacred site.

Southern Wyoming

Southern Wyoming contains everything from **sweeping deserts, sand dunes,** and **wild mustang herds** to **lush river valleys** and **green mountains.** The southwestern corner is noted for fabulous recreational opportunities along the Green River and in the **Flaming Gorge National Recreation Area.** And the southern part of the state is also home to three of Wyoming's largest cities: capital **Cheyenne,** synonymous with its legendary **Frontier Days** rodeo; college town **Laramie;** and onetime frontier town **Casper.**

High and Low Seasons

Summer is the easiest, and by far the busiest, time to travel the roads, both front- and backcountry. Thoughtful planning and advance reservations, particularly for hotels and campgrounds, are essential. Hotel rooms are particularly hard to find during local events.

Rates for accommodations are generally lower and rooms more available when snow is on the ground, except around ski areas, but **winter road travel** can be challenging because of the inevitable storms and possible closures.

The **shoulder seasons** can be a delightful time to visit. The **national parks** are slightly less crowded in **autumn,** but keep in mind that winter comes very early at high elevations. There are also little-known ways to enjoy the parks by bicycle in the **spring,** before they open to cars. Opening and closing times for the parks can vary by year (weather and federal budget too), so make sure to check with the parks before travel.

Don't try to see too much in too short a time; this cannot be overstated. Don't spend so much time on the road that you miss the small details— idyllic hikes, roadside burger joints, the locals who give small towns their true character—that make Wyoming what it is.

Grand Tetons in winter

Yellowstone and Grand Teton

Don't get stuck behind the wheel. See and experience this breathtaking region without exceeding 200 miles (320 km) of travel in a single day.

Day 1
Cody

After breakfast, head out on the hour-long **Cody Trolley Tour,** which can include tickets to the **Buffalo Bill Center of the West.** Spend most of the day exploring its five museums. Before dinner at the celebrated **Irma Hotel,** grab a cocktail and step outside to watch the **Cody Gunfighters.** After dinner, head over to the **Cody Nite Rodeo** for a two-hour action-packed show with local cowboys and cowgirls.

Day 2
Cody to Tower Junction
111 MILES (179 KM), 3 HOURS

On your way out of town, stop by **Old Trail Town.** Then head farther west on the **Buffalo Bill Scenic Byway** toward the east entrance of **Yellowstone National Park.** Stop for a bite at Buffalo Bill Cody's historic **Pahaska Tepee** resort. Once inside the park, check out the phenomenal **Grand Canyon of the Yellowstone** and the wildlife-rich **Hayden Valley** on your way to **Tower Junction** and the classic **Roosevelt Lodge Cabins.** Arrive in time to ride horseback (or travel by covered wagon) to the **Old West Dinner Cookout.** Then retire to your rustic cabin under the stars.

Day 3
Tower Junction to Paradise Valley
59 MILES (95 KM), 1.5 HOURS

Early birds will delight in a sunrise drive through the famed **Lamar Valley** for amazing opportunities to spot wildlife, including wolves and bears, depending on the season. Consider a hike up to **Trout Lake** or maybe meander along the trout waters of **Slough Creek.**

Don't go without bear spray! Turn around and head north to **Mammoth and the Mammoth Hot Springs Terraces,** where you can amble around the colorful geothermal features. For lunch, try the bison burger or elk sliders at the **Mammoth Hotel Dining Room,** just below the geothermal terraces. On your way out of the park, perhaps you'll want to soak in the **Boiling River** between Mammoth and Gardiner, or just wait until you arrive at **Chico Hot Springs Resort** to enjoy the naturally heated waters. After a gourmet dinner in the Chico dining room, settle in for the night and listen for Percy, the resident ghost.

Day 4
Paradise Valley to Lake, Wyoming
91 MILES (147 KM), 3 HOURS

Backtrack through the park's northern entrance. River rats should take a morning **raft** trip on the Yellowstone River through Yankee Jim Canyon. Inside the park, head to **Norris Geyser Basin** for another education in geology and supervolcanology. Then head to **Canyon—** check out the canyon or the falls from another angle, or even on a trail like **Uncle Tom's Trail,** which will take you to the spectacular **Lower Falls.** Wind up your day with a cocktail on the porch and a relaxing dinner at the idyllic **Lake Yellowstone Hotel.**

Day 5
Lake to Jackson
95 MILES (153 KM), 2.5 HOURS

After a morning stroll at water's edge, head down to **West Thumb Geyser Basin,** an incredible selection of geothermal features. From there, continue south to **Grand Teton National Park.** You'll pass this way again in two days, so don't feel pressured to stop at every scenic turnout. Grab lunch along the way and try a hike along the gentle **Lakeshore Trail** at

Colter Bay. Continue down to Jackson and settle in at the **Anvil Motel**. Walk just a few blocks for small plates and communal seating at **Bin 22**, or sit down to a long and sumptuous meal at the **Coelette**. Before tucking in for the night, stop for a nightcap at the famous **Million Dollar Cowboy Bar**.

Day 6
Jackson Hole

Hit the old-school favorite—**The Bunnery**—for a hearty breakfast. White-water enthusiasts will have no shortage of options on the **Snake River**. Mountain bikers and hikers can hit the alpine slopes at either **Snow King** in town or off the fabulous **gondola** at **Jackson Hole Mountain Resort**, or consider **horseback riding**. If you have the energy in the afternoon, visit the **National Museum of Wildlife Art** before grabbing a margarita and some Mexican fare at **Hatch Taquería & Tequilas**. Wednesday and Saturday nights you can catch the **Jackson Rodeo**.

Day 7
Jackson to Old Faithful
98 MILES (158 KM), 2.5 HOURS

After breakfast at **Persephone Bakery**, head north toward Grand Teton and Yellowstone. Stop at **Jenny Lake** for a hike to **Hidden Falls and Inspiration Point**, a boat ride, or just a picnic. Continue north through **Grand Teton**, checking out the sights you missed on the way down. Once in **Yellowstone**, drive north and west to Old Faithful and stay at the **Old Faithful Inn** for the night. There are great trails along the way, including an easy jaunt to **Lone Star Geyser**. Explore the area before settling in for dinner and a bed at the inn. If you can keep your eyes open, Old Faithful eruptions in the moonlight are pretty unforgettable.

Day 8
Old Faithful to West Yellowstone
32 MILES (52 KM), 0.75 HOUR

After a leisurely morning, head north and then west to the town of West Yellowstone. Enjoy this small but dense section of the park on your way

Lower Falls in Yellowstone National Park

rafter on the Snake River

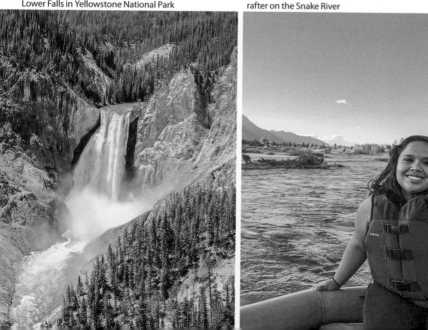

Where the Wild Things Are

Appreciating wildlife is as much a part of the culture as mountains are part of the landscape. The most obvious choice for prime wildlife-viewing is Yellowstone National Park, where animals have the right-of-way; just try telling a herd of rutting bison that you have to be somewhere. Grand Teton National Park is also a great bet, although the restricted roads and dense forests can limit visibility. Wyoming has seven national wildlife refuges that offer prime habitat to any number of species.

- Just outside **Jackson,** the **National Elk Refuge** is home to 6,000-7,000 elk or more throughout the winter months.

- In **Dubois,** the **National Bighorn Sheep Interpretive Center** offers winter tours of the nearby **Whiskey Mountain Habitat Area.** Self-guided tours take visitors into prime sheep country, where waterfowl, raptors, and moose can often be seen as well.

- Just north of **Rock Springs,** the **White Mountain Herd Management Area** is home to 1,100-1,600 wild mustangs, which can sometimes be seen on a 24-mile (39-km) self-guided driving tour. Pronghorn, sage grouse, coyotes, and eagles also frequent the region.

- North of **Green River,** the wetland habitat

bighorn sheep

of the **Seedskadee National Wildlife Refuge** hosts some 200 bird species, including Canada geese, great blue herons, nighthawks, and swans.

out. Don't miss the opportunity to swim in the thermally heated waters of the **Firehole River.** In West Yellowstone, check out the **Grizzly and Wolf Discovery Center** and the adjacent **Yellowstone Giant Screen Theatre.** Grab some brisket or pork ribs at **Firehole Bar-B-Que Company** or a gourmet meal at **Bar N Ranch** before calling it a night in a cozy safari tent at **Under Canvas Yellowstone.**

Get Yourself in Hot Water

In the middle of winter, when the cold works its way into your bones, there's nothing quite like soaking in a natural hot spring to restore your energy and wellbeing. Thanks to the geothermal and hydrothermal activity that put Yellowstone National Park on the map, most can be enjoyed year-round. Options range from middle-of-nowhere holes in the ground to well-known natural features and developed pools in resort-like settings. In general, the closer you get to Yellowstone, the more options there are. The Wyoming state tourism site (www.travelwyoming.com), which also has a page on hot springs (navigate to Things to Do, then Hot Springs).

Located between Jackson Hole and Pinedale, Wyoming, Granite Hot Springs (page 131) was built in 1933 by the CCC and boasts a lovely mountainous setting and a family-friendly ambience. Access in winter is limited to skiers, snowmobilers, and dogsledders, and there's a campground nearby.

The entire town of Thermopolis, Wyoming, is built around natural hot springs, and Hot Springs State Park (page 145) is a wonderful place to enjoy them. Originally part of the Wind River Indian Reservation, the area was sold to the U.S. government in 1896 with the stipulation from Shoshone chief Washakie that the waters would always be freely available so that anyone could benefit from their healing properties. Today, the park houses a variety of developed pools, including State Bath House, which offers the only free thermal pools in the park.

Cowboys, Hot Springs, and Wide-Open Spaces

This 10-day road trip includes two tried-and-true cowboy towns, a geological wonder, an outdoors mecca, four days at a working ranch, and all the beautiful and historical sights in between. As is true of the other itineraries, the goal is to minimize driving time while maximizing wonderful stops along the way.

Day 1
Sheridan

Ease into your cowboy experience with a visit to the Trail End State Historic Site. Check out the Western duds at the legendary King's Saddlery, and don't leave without a King Ropes baseball cap, which is de rigueur in the West. Wander around town, nosing into some of the shops and galleries along Main Street. Then enjoy an upscale American supper at the popular Frackelton's. Wind things down at the classic Mint Bar and find a comfy bed at the historic Sheridan Inn.

Day 2
Sheridan to Thermopolis
160-205 MILES (260-330 KM), 3 HOURS

To get from Sheridan to Thermopolis, there are a couple of starkly beautiful drives, both offering access to interesting sights and countless trails in the Bighorn National Forest.

The Bighorn Scenic Byway (about 205 miles/330 km) climbs up and over the mountains past such sights as the Medicine Wheel National Historic Landmark and Bighorn Canyon National Recreation Area, where mustangs can be spotted. This route follows Highway 14 to Lovell and then south toward Thermopolis.

Indigenous Heritage

The culture and history of Indigenous people have powerfully defined the identity of Wyoming. The state offers great opportunities for those interested in learning about and experiencing Native American history, traditions, and contemporary culture.

WIND RIVER RESERVATION

Wyoming's only reservation is home to about 9,000 Northern Arapaho and some 4,400 Eastern Shoshone. Sights of interest include the **Shoshone Tribal Cultural Center** and the gravesites of the two most prominent Shoshone, **Chief Washakie** and Lewis and Clark's guide **Sacagawea**.

The best time to visit is during the annual three-day powwows. The largest Shoshone powwow is the **Eastern Shoshone Indian Days Powwow and Rodeo,** held the fourth weekend in June. The largest Arapaho powwow is the **Ethete Celebration,** usually held in late July.

MEDICINE WHEEL NATIONAL HISTORIC LANDMARK

This mysterious carved stone wheel has spiritual but unexplained significance to many Native American tribes. Interpretive tours are offered by local Native American guides.

DEVILS TOWER NATIONAL MONUMENT

This iconic rocky sentinel, the first national monu-

performer at Eastern Shoshone Indian Days Powwow and Rodeo

ment in the country, is considered sacred by numerous tribes, all of whom have unique origin stories for it. A voluntary climbing closure is in effect each June out of respect for various Native American ceremonies.

The shorter route (about 160 miles/260 km) is higher but no less scenic. It heads south to **Buffalo** past the impressive **Fort Phil Kearny State Historic Site,** then over the **Cloud Peak Skyway Scenic Byway** through Ten Sleep to Worland and eventually south to Thermopolis.

As you pull into Thermopolis, head to the colorful and otherworldly **Hot Springs State Park.** Stroll along the **Spirit Trail** or stop into the historic **State Bath House** for a swim before checking in to the **Best Western Plaza Hotel.** For

dinner, grab a burger at the **One Eyed Buffalo Brewing Company.**

Day 3
Thermopolis to Lander
80 MILES (128 KM), 1.5 HOURS

Spend the day in Thermopolis, exploring the park and soaking in the medicinal waters. Arrange for a tour of the **Wyoming Dinosaur Center and Dig Sites.** You can even participate in their **archaeological digs.** Fill your belly at the **Black Bear Café** before heading

It's hard to drive through Wyoming without running into rodeo action somewhere. Stop. Buy a ticket. The bleachers are fine. These small-town rodeos offer a unique window into life here: Locals wear their Sunday best, and no one seems to mind the dust. Sitting on a sunbaked wooden bench, cold beer in one hand and a bag of popcorn in the other, is the best first date in small towns, where they show off their best without hiding what's real.

THERMOPOLIS COWBOY RENDEZVOUS (WEEKEND AFTER FATHER'S DAY)

From tailgate parties and a Western dance to a pancake breakfast and parade, the small-town rodeo in Thermopolis ushers in the pro rodeo circuit for the Big Horn Basin with plenty of action and family fun.

CODY STAMPEDE RODEO (JULY 1-4)

With all the showmanship one would expect from a town named after Buffalo Bill Cody, this professional rodeo lets the town shine with all the classic events, including bareback riding, roping, steer wrestling, barrel racing, and saddle bronc and bull riding. The rest of the summer, visitors can get a true sense of small-town rodeo at the Cody Nite Rodeo.

TEN SLEEP FOURTH OF JULY RODEO (TWO DAYS OVER FOURTH OF JULY)

With a rodeo history that dates back to 1908 and includes some of the biggest names in the sport, Ten Sleep boasts rodeo action throughout the summer. Special events at the annual Fourth of July shindig include a Pony Express Ride from nearby Hyattville, a Main Street parade, an old-fashioned rodeo, fireworks, and a sometimes-bloody wild horse race.

SHERIDAN WYO RODEO (USUALLY THE SECOND WEEK IN JULY)

This is the biggest week of the year for Sheridan. Events include a golf tournament, art show, rodeo royalty pageant, carnival, relay races, a parade, and a street dance on top of four nights of pro rodeo action.

---

south through some of the oldest rock formations on the planet. If time allows, consider planning a white-water excursion with Wind River Canyon Whitewater and Fly Fishing, the only outfitter licensed to operate on the Wind River Reservation. Keep your eyes peeled for bighorn sheep. At Shoshoni, head south toward Lander.

If it's early enough when you arrive, drive south 6 miles (9.7 km) to Sinks Canyon State Park for a nice walk or to wet a line in the Popo Agie River. Don't miss the canyon where the Middle Fork of the Popo Agie rushes into a cave, only to emerge 0.5 mile (0.8 km) away in a place called the Rise, after what geologists have learned is an inexplicable two-hour journey. Back in town, enjoy a gourmet dinner at Cowfish or

Gannett Grill/Lander Bar right next door. Settle in for the night at the convenient Holiday Inn Express & Suites.

Day 4
Lander to Casper
158 MILES (254 KM), 2.5 HOURS

Take the opportunity to explore the 2.2-million-acre Wind River Indian Reservation—just beyond the edge of Lander—home to both Northern Arapaho and Eastern Shoshone. If your timing allows, be sure to attend either the Eastern Shoshone Indian Days Powwow and Rodeo (late June in Fort Washakie) or the Ethete Celebration (late July in Ethete)—or tour the Shoshone Tribal Cultural Center and visit the gravesites of both Chief Washakie

Top 5 Hikes

The best way to see this place and to know it is to get out and hike. Explore the wilderness. Climb the mountains. Run your fingertips along the bark of trees. Feel the whisper of high grasses on your legs. Earn the best view you've ever seen in Wyoming.

YELLOWSTONE NATIONAL PARK

- Starting with a steep descent to a suspension bridge over the rushing Yellowstone River, the backcountry **Hellroaring Trail** is beautiful but strenuous. Enjoy a 6.2-mile (10-km) stretch through scenic sagebrush plateau to the confluence of Hellroaring Creek and the Yellowstone River.

GRAND TETON NATIONAL PARK AND THE WIND RIVER RANGE

- The **Taggart Lake-Bradley Lake Loop** takes hikers to two glacially formed lakes at the base of the Tetons. With only 585 feet (178 m) of elevation gained over 5.5 miles (8.9 km), this moderate trail along water and through forest offers up views of Nez Perce peak, Middle and Grand Tetons, and Teewinot Mountain.

hiking the Taggart Lake-Bradley Lake Loop

- **Hidden Falls Trail** offers the best of the park—access to Jenny Lake, pristine conifer forests, rushing creeks, soaring alpine views, and a chance to encounter wildlife. The moderately challenging trail is 4.9 miles (7.9 km) but can be shortened to 1 mile (1.6 km) by taking the shuttle across Jenny Lake.

SHERIDAN AND NORTHEAST WYOMING

- Hiking is a great way to appreciate the stark

beauty of Devils Tower. The 1.5-mile (2.4-km) **Joyner Ridge Trail** takes in beautiful views of the tower, particularly at sunset, and can be linked to the 2.8-mile (4.5-km) **Red Beds Trail**, which is steep, but lovely.

SOUTHERN WYOMING

- In the Vedauwoo climbing area near Laramie, **Turtle Rock Loop** is an easy 2.8-mile (4.5-km) loop with plenty of options for more mileage. The trail winds through aspen forests, across open country, and around dramatic rock formations.

and Sacagawea. On the way, you could also stop at the **Wind River Wild Horse Sanctuary** to learn about and see wild mustangs. Hikers will do well around Lander with places like the 3.3-mile (5.3-km) **Popo Agie Falls Trail.** By late afternoon, get back on the road and head toward Casper by backtracking north, then east, on Highway 26,

or on the southern route through Jeffrey City and Alcova, which is just a few minutes longer than the northern route. In Casper, enjoy a thick steak at the **Silver Fox Steakhouse** or hearty southern Italian fare at **Racca's Pizzeria Napoletano**, and find your hard-earned pillow at the comfortable all-suite **Residence Inn.**

Day 5
Casper to Buffalo
115 MILES (185 KM), 1.5 HOURS

Nature lovers will want to rise early to get to the well-recovered **North Platte River** for a chance to fish; or for a morning trip up **Casper Mountain,** where an opportunity to learn about local folklore at the **Crimson Dawn Museum** is requisite when it's open. For a more cultural experience, head to the **Nicolaysen Art Museum and Discovery Center** and wonderful **National Historic Trails Interpretive Center.** Lunch at **The Cottage Café** or **Sherrie's Place,** and then get back on the road to Buffalo.

Head north on I-87, which runs parallel to the old **Bozeman Trail.** This is stark open country, with the Thunder Basin National Grassland sweeping out east of the highway. In Buffalo, belly up to the bar in the historic **Occidental Hotel** for a meal and a cozy room for the night. For a little exercise, hit the 13-mile (20.9-km) **Clear Creek Trail System.** If you're lucky, you'll be able to catch the weekly **Cowgirl Rodeo,** on Tuesdays June through August, at the Johnson County Fairgrounds.

Day 6
Buffalo to TA Guest Ranch
14 MILES (22.5 KM), 0.5 HOUR

Rise early and hightail it to the historic **TA Guest Ranch,** south of Buffalo off Highway 196, where you'll spend the next four days. This is where cowboy culture comes to life.

Days 7-9
TA Guest Ranch

Spend the next three nights enjoying an **authentic ranch experience.** Activities range from riding to fly-fishing, hiking, biking, and golf. You'll visit tipi rings and Bozeman Trail sites on the property, plus important battlefields nearby. Expect to work and play hard.

Day 10
TA Guest Ranch to Sheridan
61 MILES (98 KM), 1 HOUR

Trade your saddle for a bucket seat and head north to Sheridan. Consider a stop at **Fort Phil Kearny State Historic Site** and the tiny town of **Big Horn** to see **The Brinton Museum.** Enjoy a beautiful last meal—Wyoming gourmet—at the elegant, farm-to-table **Birch.**

The Clear Creek Trail System begins in downtown Buffalo.

Yellowstone National Park

Yellowstone National Park is at the heart of our country's relationship with wilderness. It's also the largest intact ecosystem in the Lower 48—all of the species that have roamed this plateau are still (or once again) in residence. For now.

Yellowstone was our nation's first national park, signed into being by President Ulysses S. Grant after a series of important and legendary scouting expeditions through the area. The region's history is lengthy and very much alive, from its prehistoric volcanic eruptions, to its occupation by the U.S. Army in the 1880s, to the controversial reintroduction of wolves in the 1990s and the more recent snowmobile usage, bison, and grizzly delisting quagmires. The stories, both far-fetched and true, and characters that have emerged from the park

Highlights

Look for ★ to find recommended sights, activities, dining, and lodging.

★ **Boiling River:** In a stretch of the Gardner River at the park's north entrance, hot water flows over waterfalls and via springs, mixing with the river water to create a perfect soaking temperature (page 43).

★ **Mammoth and the Mammoth Hot Springs Terraces:** The travertine terraces here look like an enormous cream-colored confection. Since the springs shift and change daily, a walk around the colorful terraces is never the same experience twice (page 48).

★ **Grand Canyon of the Yellowstone:** The sheer cliffs and dramatic coloring of this canyon have inspired millions of visitors. In the summer, get a rare bird's-eye view of several osprey nests (page 49).

★ **Watching the Wolves:** The wolves put on a spectacular show—with at least one reported sighting daily since 2001. The sagas of the 11 packs are dramatic, heart-wrenching, and captivating (page 56).

★ **Lamar Valley:** Known as the "Little Serengeti of North America," this scenic, glacially carved valley offers spectacular wildlife-watching year-round (page 57).

★ **Yellowstone Lake:** This beautiful lake was touted by early mountain men as perhaps the only place where you could catch a fish and cook it without ever taking it off the line (page 63).

★ **Old Faithful:** One of nearly 500 geysers in the park, and undoubtedly the most famous, this natural wonder erupts every 45-90 minutes (page 64).

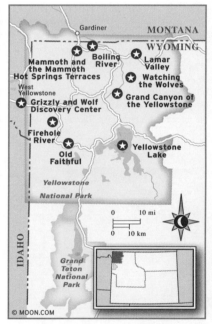

★ **Firehole River:** This river offers a stunning, heated swimming area surrounded by cliffs. The twists and turns of the cascading canyon are worth seeing even if you don't get wet (page 66).

★ **Grizzly and Wolf Discovery Center:** You're guaranteed an up-close look at two of the park's biggest and most fascinating predators at this home to grizzly bears and wolves that can't survive in the wild (page 71).

are as colorful and compelling as the landscape itself.

A vast 2.2 million acres, Yellowstone is indeed a wonderland, filled with steaming geysers and boiling mud pots, packed with diverse and healthy populations of wildlife, and crisscrossed by hundreds of miles of hiking and skiing trails. A stretch of the park called the Lamar Valley is known as the "Little Serengeti of North America," and for good reason: At certain times of the year, in a single day visitors can spot grizzly and black bears, moose, wolves, bison, elk, coyotes, bald eagles, and the occasional bighorn sheep or mountain goat. In fact, the opportunities for viewing wildlife in the park are unparalleled anywhere in the United States, and although Yellowstone may not be as picturesque as Glacier or the Tetons, it is magnificent in its wildness and uniquely American.

Seeing Yellowstone from the back of a cramped station wagon—or these days, a decked-out Winnebago—is almost a rite of passage in this country. What parent doesn't dream of hauling their children out West to see Old Faithful erupt or to catch a glimpse of a grizzly bear? And what kid doesn't want to swim in the Boiling River or lie awake in a sleeping bag, listening to the howl of coyotes? It's not exactly the last frontier it once was—there are convenience stores, beautiful old hotels, major traffic jams, and even places to get a decent latte—but Yellowstone still occupies its own corner of our national imagination; classified somewhere between American wilderness and family vacations, it conjures up foggy but perfect memories.

PLANNING YOUR TIME

One could quite literally spend a lifetime in Yellowstone without being able to cover every last corner of this magnificent wilderness, but the reality is that most visitors only have a couple of days, at best, to spend exploring the park. Something like 98 percent of visitors never get more than a mile from the road, but it's easier than you might think—and incredibly worthwhile. Three days in the park is ideal, but if you have less time, there are ways to maximize every minute.

One important consideration in planning your time in Yellowstone is to know the season you'll be traveling. Summer offers magnificent scenery, usually good weather, and the inevitable "bear jam," when drivers hit the brakes as soon as someone spots anything resembling a brown furry creature. Summer visitors to Yellowstone need to plan for traffic and often for road construction delays. Fall and spring are fantastic times to see wildlife, but the weather can change in a heartbeat—at Yellowstone's high elevation, blizzards can strike nearly any month of the year. Winter is a magical time in the park, but cars are only permitted on one road in the northeast corner. All other travel is done via snow coach, guided snowmobile tour, or on skis and snowshoes. There is no wrong time to visit the park, but knowing the advantages and disadvantages of the various seasons will help you manage your expectations.

Assuming you'll be in Yellowstone when the roads are open to car traffic, there are five entrances and exits to Yellowstone, making loop trips relatively easy. From Montana, you can enter or exit the park from the northeast at Cooke City, from the north at Gardiner, or from the west at West Yellowstone. From Wyoming, you can enter the park from the east entrance nearest Cody or from the south through Grand Teton National Park. If you're going from one state to the next, there is no more spectacular route than through the heart of Yellowstone.

A cursory glance at a Yellowstone map will reveal the main roads, which form a figure eight in the heart of the park, and the access roads leading to and from the entrances. The majority of the park's big-name highlights—**Old Faithful, West Thumb Geyser**

Previous: Grand Prismatic Spring; view of Lower Falls; a wolf in Yellowstone in winter.

Yellowstone National Park

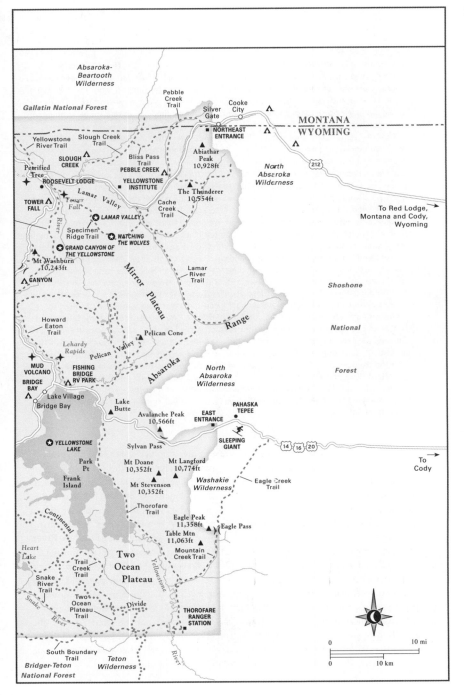

The Sheep Eaters of Yellowstone

During the early 18th century, the horse was introduced to many of the Native American tribes that frequented the Yellowstone area. With the acquisition of this new, strong, and agile animal, people were able to spread out across the plains, traveling farther and longer to follow the bison. Hunting and warfare became more efficient almost overnight. A small group of Shoshone chose not to use horses or guns, however, and instead remained committed to their traditional mountain living.

The Sheep Eaters, also known as the Tukudika, were forest dwellers considered to be the only Native Americans to have inhabited Yellowstone year-round. They lived in *wikiups*—temporary shelters made of aspen poles, pine boughs, and other brush—rather than animal-hide tipis, and they traveled the mountain ridges rather than the river paths as their counterparts on the plains did. Living in small bands of 10-20 people, they relied on their wolf dogs to help them move provisions up and down the mountains. They were named for the animal whose migration they followed: the bighorn sheep. The Sheep Eaters developed highly effective sheep traps, the remains of which can be seen around Dubois, Wyoming, and they utilized the animal for both food and tools. They heated the sheep's horns in the hot springs of Yellowstone to mold them into exquisite and strong bows, powerful enough to drive an arrow through a bison. The reputation of these bows spread to other tribes and were highly sought-after. The European outsiders who made their way into the park during the early and mid-1800s described the Sheep Eaters as destitute and forlorn, not owning or seeming to want the modern trappings of the Plains Indians. Contemporary views suggest that these people revered their environment and ancestors' way of life and were more intent on maintaining their customs than competing and conquering.

Unfortunately, their traditions did not allow the Sheep Eaters to escape the same fate as other Native Americans. Devastated by smallpox and considered an obstacle to westward expansion, the Sheep Eaters fought the U.S. Army in the last Indian war in the Pacific Northwest. Unfairly accused of murdering five Chinese miners, the last remaining Sheep Eaters, a group of 51 people that included woman and children, were relentlessly pursued in the Idaho wilderness along the Middle Fork of the Salmon River in the fall of 1879. When the army purportedly captured a woman who had just given birth, the remaining members of the tribe surrendered to save her and were sent to the Wind River Shoshone Reservation in Wyoming and Fort Hall Shoshone Bannock Reservation in Idaho.

Basin, Fishing Bridge, Grand Canyon of the Yellowstone, Norris and Mammoth Geyser Basins—are accessible from the main loops. Depending on your time and your plan for accommodations, you could easily spend a full day driving each of the two loops. A third day would permit an opportunity for deeper exploration—perhaps a hike—and a leisurely exit from the park.

If time won't permit even one night in the park, it is still well worth driving through, just to get a sense of this tremendously diverse place. Consider choosing one feature and pursuing it. To give yourself the best chance of seeing wolves, traveling between the north and northeast entrances is an excellent route during non-summer months. Geothermal aficionados will have no shortage of choices for seeing the park's impressive features, but to swim in them, try the **Boiling River,** a stretch of the Gardner River near Mammoth, which is swimmable year-round except during spring and early summer runoff. The **Firehole River** also offers excellent summer swimming not far from Old Faithful. Landlubbers might prefer a short hike into a less-famous geyser like **Lone Star,** just a few flat miles from Old Faithful.

The best advice is this: Get off the road, get out of your car, be smart, and come prepared to give yourself the opportunity to see and understand what makes Yellowstone America's first wonderland.

INFORMATION AND SERVICES

The best resource to familiarize yourself with the park and to help plan your trip is the National Park Service (307/344-7381, www.nps.gov/yell). On the website, click on the link titled Plan Your Visit. The site also posts information about the different Ranger Programs being offered, including educational lectures and hikes.

Two official free apps can help with trip planning. The NPS Yellowstone App gives users live updates on the status of lodging, campgrounds, roads, and geyser predictions when in cell service. It also provides downloadable interpretive stories and self-guided audio tours that can be played when you are out of coverage areas. A more general app, the NPS Parks App, offers downloadable information for all the national parks in the U.S., including Yellowstone and Grand Teton. It does not provide live updates on lodging, roads, or geyser predictions.

Park Fees and Passes

Admission to the park is $35 per vehicle for seven days, $30 for motorcycles and snowmobiles, and $20 for hikers and bicyclists. An annual pass to the park costs $70. In 2021, entrance fees to the park were waived on 6 days, including Martin Luther King Jr. Day on January 18, April 17 to celebrate the start of National Park Week, August 4 to celebrate the one year anniversary of the Great American Outdoors Act, September 25 for National Public Lands Day, and Veterans Day on November 11. Check the Yellowstone website before you travel to see if any fee-free days are on the horizon. The park is open year-round, but during the winter, cars can only access the park through the north and northeast entrances.

Visitor Centers

There are 10 visitor centers in and around the park. Since days and hours vary seasonally, and all of them have been shortened due to the pandemic and staff shortages, it's a good

idea to check the website (www.nps.gov/yell) before you go into the park.

The Albright Visitor Center at Mammoth Hot Springs (Grand Loop Rd., 307/344-2263, 9am-5pm daily) is open year-round and houses a bookstore, wildlife and history exhibits, and films on the park and its early visitors. Free Wi-Fi is also available in the visitor center. Fishers and backcountry campers can get permits in the basement backcountry office. And there are restrooms, perhaps the last for a while depending on your adventure.

The Canyon Visitor Education Center (Canyon Village, 307/344-2550, 9am-5pm daily summer) offers the best overview of the park's geology, including phenomenal volcanic exhibits and a dynamic film. During the season, the bathrooms remain open 24 hours a day.

The Fishing Bridge Visitor Center (East Entrance Rd., 307/344-2450) is home to a museum, bookstore, bird and wildlife exhibits, plus information on the lake's ecology. The building was opened in 1931 and is a beautiful example of the "parkitecture"-type architecture seen in parks across the nation. The visitor center was closed throughout COVID, so check the website for hours.

The Grant Village Visitor Center (west shore of Yellowstone Lake, 307/344-2650, 8am-5pm daily Memorial Day-early Oct.) offers an outstanding exhibit on the integral role of fire in the Yellowstone ecosystem.

The Madison Information Station and Trailside Museum (307/344-2821) at Madison Junction provides a bookstore as well as detailed information on the Junior Ranger program. Another prime example of "parkitecture," the Trailside Museum was opened in 1930 for early travelers to the park. It was closed in 2021, so check the website for hours.

The Museum of the National Park Ranger (307/344-7353) is 1 mile (1.6 km) north of Norris Geyser Basin and gives a good history of the park ranger profession.

The beautiful log building was built in 1897 after a fire destroyed the original building, and modified in 1908 to be used as soldier stations. The building was rebuilt again, log by log, after the 1959 earthquake. It was closed for 2021, so check the website for hours.

The **Norris Geyser Basin Museum & Information Station** (east of Norris Junction, 307/344-2812, 9am-5pm daily late May-early Oct.) offers visitors an excellent overview of the hydrothermal features in the park.

The **Old Faithful Visitor Education Center** (Upper Geyser Basin, 307/344-2751, 9am-5pm daily mid-Apr.-early Nov. closed winter/spring of 2022 due to staffing issues) includes exhibits, information, and films on the park's hydrothermal features, plus a bookstore and geyser eruption predictions. A Young Scientist room with hands-on exhibits is a hit with young people.

The **West Thumb Information Center** (307/242-7690, 9am-5pm daily late May-early Oct.) offers information about the West Thumb Geyser Basin on the shore of Yellowstone Lake. You can also sign up for ranger programs.

In West Yellowstone, the **West Yellowstone Visitor Information Center** (30 Yellowstone Ave., 307/344-2876, 8am-5pm daily May-Labor Day, 8am-4pm daily Labor Day-early Nov., 8am-5pm Mon.-Fri. early Nov.-mid-Apr.) hosts a National Park Service desk, plus information and publications.

Entrance Stations

Yellowstone National Park is open 365 days a year, 24 hours a day. There are five entrance stations, three in Montana and two in Wyoming.

- The **North Entrance,** at Gardiner, Montana, is the only one open year-round to wheeled vehicles.
- The **Northeast Entrance** is near the small communities of Cooke City and Silver Gate, Montana, and generally open late May to mid-October, depending upon weather and road conditions.
- The **West Entrance,** in West Yellowstone, Montana, is open to wheeled vehicles generally from the third Friday in April until the first Sunday in November.
- The **South Entrance,** 49 miles (79 km) north of Jackson, Wyoming, at the border between Grand Teton National Park and Yellowstone, is open to wheeled vehicles typically the second Friday in May through the first Sunday in November, and to snow coaches and snowmobiles mid-December to mid-March.
- The **East Entrance,** 53 miles (85 km) west of Cody, Wyoming, is generally open to wheeled vehicles from the first Friday in May to the first Sunday in November.

All entrances can be closed at any time due to weather and unscheduled changes. Visit www.nps.gov/yell before your trip for up-to-date road information, or call 307/344-2117 for recorded road and weather information.

Services

Yellowstone National Park Lodges (307/344-7311, www.yellowstonenational parklodges.com) is the official concessionaire of Yellowstone, and all reservations for lodging, dining, and special activities in the park can be made through them.

If you encounter an **emergency** when traveling through the park, dial 911, but be aware that cell coverage is spotty. Emergency medical services are attended to by rangers. There are three **urgent care facilities** inside Yellowstone. The clinic at **Mammoth** (108 Grand Loop Rd., 307/344-7965, 8:30am-5pm Mon.-Fri. June-late Sept., 8:30am-5pm Mon.-Thurs., 8:30am-1pm Fri. late Sept.-May) is open year-round, and the clinics at **Lake** (1 Lake Station, 307/242-7241, 8:30am-8:30pm daily mid-May-mid-Sept., 10am-6:30pm daily mid-Sept.-late Sept.) and **Old Faithful** (307/545-7325, 7am-7pm daily mid-May-mid-Sept., 8:30am-5pm daily mid-Sept.-early Oct.) are open in prime visiting season.

Avoid the Crowds

In September of 2021, Yellowstone National Park topped 4 million visitors in the first nine months of the year for the first time ever. In September alone, the park saw 882,078 recreational visits, up 5 percent from the year before and up 27 percent from 2019. Annual statistics echo the pattern. Visits between January and September 2021 were up 32 percent from 2020 and up 17 percent from 2019. There is nothing to suggest that the influx of visitors will slow down anytime soon, if ever. "Never in Yellowstone's history have we seen such substantial visitation increase in such a short amount of time," said Park Superintendent Cam Sholly in October 2021.

The best advice anyone can offer is to manage your expectations. Instead of hoping for solitude, expect long lines at entrance stations, extremely busy facilities and destinations, and delayed travel times due to traffic and wildlife jams. Remember that you are a visitor and act responsibly and with thoughtfulness, for your own benefit, for your fellow visitors, and for the inhabitants of the park. If you come prepared and follow a few suggestions, you can lessen your time amongst the hordes and give yourself the opportunity to enjoy the wonders of the park.

- **Buy your park pass ahead of time online** at www.recreation.gov to avoid long waits at entrance stations.

- **Avoid the park's busiest areas,** including Old Faithful, Midway Geyser Basin, Norris, and the Canyon rims. Instead stick to areas that have **fewer attractions and fewer parking lots.** It's still true that the vast majority of Yellowstone visitors never get more than half a mile from the road. If you must visit the busiest attractions, time it early or late, **before 9am or after 4pm,** when the bulk of visitors are out and about.

- As has always been true, planning a trip to Yellowstone in months other than June, July, and August is a good start. The shoulder months are busier than they've ever been, but still the **peak summer months are the busiest.** Consider a spring trip in **April or May** when the park is coming awake after a long, cold winter, and some of the animals are just starting to have their babies. Or, plan a **winter trip** when snow and ice cover everything and hide nothing. Thermal features and wildlife are more visible than ever. Plus moonlight and snow is a pretty magical combination here.

- Stay informed about **weather, road conditions, and campground availability** by checking the park website (www.nps.gov/yell). Webcams can give you an idea of the lines at North and West entrance stations. The NPS Yellowstone app will give you park alerts and road closures in real time, which can be helpful when you are figuring out where to go, or where to not go.

TRANSPORTATION
Getting There
BY AIR

Yellowstone is about 90 miles (145 km) from the airports in Bozeman and Billings, 49 miles (79 km) from the airport in Jackson Hole, and 52 miles (84 km) from the airport in Cody. The **Yellowstone Airport** (WYS, 607 Airport Rd., West Yellowstone, www.yellowstoneairport.org, 406/646-7631) is served by Delta and United and is only open late May-late September.

BY CAR

The North Entrance at Gardiner, which is the only entrance open year-round to cars, is 83 miles (134 km) south of Bozeman and 170 miles (275 km) southwest of Billings. The Northeast Entrance at Cooke City is 124 miles (200 km), including the spectacular Beartooth Highway, from Billings. The West Entrance at West Yellowstone is 90 miles (145 km) south of Bozeman. The East Entrance is 53 miles (85 km) west of Cody. The South Entrance is 49 miles (79 km) north of Jackson.

BY BUS

Shuttle service with **Karst Stage** (800/287-4759 or 406/556-3540, www.karststage.com) is available from Bozeman to West Yellowstone year-round and to Gardiner during the winter and summer seasons.

Getting Around

PRIVATE VEHICLES

Your best bet to see the park on your own terms is to go by car. The nearest car-rental agencies are **Budget** and **Big Sky Car Rentals** (406/646-9564), available in West Yellowstone. Cars can also be rented from airports in Billings, Bozeman, Cody, and Jackson Hole.

When planning your drive through Yellowstone, it is best to fill up your tank outside the park. Once inside, the gas prices you'll encounter tend to be extremely high, and options are quite limited. Gas stations are located within the park at Canyon, Fishing Bridge, Grant Village, Mammoth, Upper and Lower Old Faithful, and Tower Junction. They are generally open late spring-early fall.

One of the things that makes Yellowstone so wild and enchanting is its utter unpredictability—something that relates to wildlife, weather, and, unfortunately, road conditions. A 20-year $300-million plan is currently afoot to address the structural deficiencies of Yellowstone's roads. Keep a close watch on road closures and delays that can happen at any time of year because of construction, bad weather, or even fire. For a 24-hour road report, check **Road Construction Delays and Closures** (307/344-2117, www.nps.gov/yell). Information on state roads is available from the **Montana Department of Transportation** (800/226-7623, www.mdt511.com) and **Wyoming Department of Transportation** (888/996-7623, www.wyoroad.info). **National Weather Service** (www.crh.noaa.gov) reports are available for Yellowstone and Grand Teton National Parks.

TOURS

Xanterra/Yellowstone National Park Lodges (307/344-7311 or 866/439-7375, www.yellowstonenationalparklodges.com) offers a variety of bus tours of the park during the summer, including historic Yellow Bus tours that range 1-12 hours. The **Yellowstone in a Day** tour ($130.50-138.50 adults, $65.25-69.75 kids 3-11) departs daily from Gardiner, Mammoth, and the Old Faithful Inn and covers the entire park in one day. Other options include early morning or evening wildlife tours, lake sunset tours, geyser gazers, Lamar Valley wildlife expeditions, photo safaris, boat tours, fishing trips, and custom guided tours.

Depending on your particular interests, a range of companies outside the park offer specialized tours of Yellowstone. The only one inside the park, and an outstanding option, is the **Yellowstone Forever Institute** (406/848-2400, www.yellowstone.org). Courses are broken into summer and winter semesters, and single-day field seminars fees begin around $195. Multiday tours with lodging are also available. The courses are engaging and are taught by experts in their fields. Using Yellowstone as their classroom, the instructors concentrate on "individual aspects of the ecosystem." During the summer, you can take the "Introduction to Wolf Management and Ecology" course led by a wolf biologist or "Mammal Signs: Interpreting Tracks, Scat, and Hair" with an animal tracker. There are several naturalist guide certificate programs offered in both summer and winter. Winter field seminars include "Yellowstone Block Printing," "Wilderness First Aid," "Wolves, Dogs, and Humans," and "Art of Winter Landscape Photography." The institute can provide unique (and inexpensive) lodging in its two field campuses, in Gardiner and the Lamar Valley. Or it can include standard hotel lodging at park hotels. If you take the time to browse through the course catalog, you will likely find something geared to your interests. The Yellowstone Forever Institute tours are one of the best ways to get an in-depth insider's view of Yellowstone.

The Ecology of Fire

In 1988, wildfires blazed through Yellowstone National Park. To quell the flames, the largest fire-fighting effort in U.S. history was organized, involving 25,000 people and $120 million, but it was the first snowfall of the season that would eventually rein in the fire. The fires began at the end of June and burned until November. More than 793,000 acres (roughly one-third of the park) were affected, 67 structures were destroyed, and 345 elk and 63 other large mammals died as a direct result of the fire. The entire nation watched in horror as the first national park burned. The park's fire management plan consequently came under intense scrutiny. The question on everyone's lips was, "How could this have happened?"

During the first half of the 20th century, it was widely believed that nothing good came of wildfire. In the 1940s and 1950s, all fires in Yellowstone were immediately suppressed. During the 1960s, however, the tide shifted as studies showed that fire was a natural condition helping to clean out understory and residual dead plant matter, creating less competition between tree species for important nutrients and natural elements. In addition, it was discovered that serotinous pine cones only open and release their seeds in extreme heat that can only be generated by fire. In fact, several plants and trees rely on fire for germination. It was determined that wildfires had always been a part of the ecosystem and were necessary to preserve healthy and continuous life cycles of plants and trees.

By the 1970s, the park allowed wildfires caused by lightning to burn under controlled conditions. Until 1988, 235 fires had burned; only 10 were larger than 100 acres. In June 1988, the driest year in the park's history, early summer storms produced lightning that ignited 20 fires. Eleven self-extinguished, and the rest were monitored; by mid-July only 8,500 acres had burned. Within a week, park managers agreed to extinguish all fires due to extremely dry conditions. Strong winds made that impossible, and within a week 99,000 acres had burned. By September, in order for emergency workers to battle the blaze, the park had to close to visitors for the first time in its history.

By spring, the earth was green and vibrant amid the fire-blackened swaths. With the exception of moose, which lost a significant portion of their forested habitat, the animal populations appeared as if nothing had ever happened. Elk were even reported munching on the burned bark. Yellowstone, it seemed, was different—better and healthier.

Other tour operators that offer excursions in the park include **See Yellowstone** (800/221-1151 or 406/646-9310, www.seeyellowstone.com), a full-service travel agency in West Yellowstone that can book everything from accommodations and tours to complete packages, and **Yellowstone Wild Tours** (Gardiner, 406/224-0001, www.yellowstonewildtours.com, from $650), which offers a fantastic array of private single- and multiday tours year-round. The company is owned by a wildlife biologist and staffed by naturalists, so the focus will be on finding and observing wildlife. They offer special bear and wolf tours, family wildlife tours, hiking, thermal features, and winter tracking tours. Since all tours are private, the day can be customized with pickups and meals. They also offer to document the day with a professional photographer (from $689).

PLANTS AND ANIMALS

Yellowstone is a living, breathing, evolving ecosystem that is home to a diversity of high-alpine, subalpine, and forest plants (more than 1,000 native species of flowering plants) and an extraordinary number of animals (including 67 mammal species). It is fascinating to understand how the flora and fauna relate—and react—to one another throughout the park.

Plants

What makes the plantlife in Yellowstone so interesting is neither the abundance nor the variety but rather the relationship between the plants and their environment and the way they are determined and shaped by forces of geology, climate, fire, insect infestation, drought, flood, and not least of all, wildlife. In various places throughout the park, for example, visitors will notice small fenced areas where grazing animals like elk, deer, and bison do not have access. The flora is decidedly different when it is protected from herbivores. The massive burns of 1988 and, more recently in 2016, have given rise to a plant lover's paradise where hot pink fireweed is among the first to recolonize the blackened areas. The geothermal areas have their own rare and unique plant communities. And the reintroduction of wolves caused the movements of elk to be more sporadic as they tried to avoid being eaten, which led to an increase in the number of willows and a resulting increase in various animals, including beavers, that thrive on willows. These chains of events linking plants, animals, and the natural forces that control the park are endless and fascinating.

Animals

For many, the fauna in Yellowstone is the main event. With large mammals such as elk, bison, bighorn sheep, pronghorn, bears, wolves, and mountain lions, Yellowstone is among the best areas in the country to see wildlife in its natural habitat. For those willing to get up early and be patient enough to wait, sometimes for hours, Yellowstone is like the Discovery Channel brought to life.

There are a few species of reptiles and amphibians known to inhabit the park—11 in all—thanks to Yellowstone's cool, dry climate, and some 330 species of birds have been documented since the park's 1872 founding, ranging from tiny calliope hummingbirds to majestic trumpeter swans.

But it's the big animals that draw more than 4 million people to the park annually. The omnipresent bison are the largest animal in the park, with males (bulls) weighing upward of 1,800 pounds (817 kg) and females (cows) averaging about 1,000 pounds (454 kg). Yellowstone is the only place in the Lower 48 where wild bison have existed since prehistoric times. The herd dropped to near-extinction levels at the turn of the 20th century with only 50 animals within the park boundaries. The importation of 21 bison from private herds and the subsequent 50 years of repopulation efforts led to a marked increase in numbers. By 2006 some 3,500 of these wild, woolly behemoths once again roamed the high prairies of Yellowstone, but significant population fluctuations occur,

bison along the Firehole River

primarily because of fears surrounding the disease brucellosis. In a given year, the bison population in Yellowstone ranges 2,300-5,000 animals, with the population in summer 2020 hovering around the high end at 4,680.

The most recent count in 2019 placed the number of grizzly bears in the park at around 150, with another 728 living within the Greater Yellowstone Ecosystem, and likely three to four times as many black bears. Gray wolves were reintroduced to the park (after being entirely killed off in the area) in 1995, and in January 2021 there were at least 123 wolves in nine packs living primarily within the park boundaries, and more than 500 living in the Greater Yellowstone Ecosystem. Wolverines and lynx live within the park but are rarely seen. Coyotes are plentiful and often visible from cars, and somewhere between 34-42 mountain lions inhabit the northern range. Elk populations soar in the summer months to 10,000-20,000 animals in six or seven herds, compared to the fewer than 4,000 elk that winter in the park, while moose, hard hit by the fires of 1988, number fewer than 200. In the northern Yellowstone ecosystem, there are 345 bighorn sheep, with 131 counted inside the park. There are also 200-300 nonnative mountain goats in and around Yellowstone.

Finding the animals means knowing their habitats, being willing to wait during the edges of daylight, and oftentimes just plain getting lucky. Excellent wildlife-spotting guides are available through **Yellowstone Forever** (www.yellowstone.org), but the most obvious place to start is by asking any of the rangers at the park's various visitor centers. They can tell you about recent predatory kills, bear and wolf activity, elk and bison migrations, and the most up-to-date sightings of any number of animals.

As is true with nearly every feature of the park, the importance of safety in the face of wildlife cannot be overstated. Just check out YouTube for any number of videos highlighting ill-advised visitor interactions with wildlife. Be certain to stay at least 25 yards/meters away from bison and elk and at least 100 yards/meters away from bears, wolves, and other predators. If the animals change their behavior because of your presence—if they stop eating to look at you, for example—you are too close and are creating a significant and perhaps even life-threatening hazard for both the animal and yourself. Always remember that you are the visitor here and they are the residents; show proper respect.

GEOTHERMAL FEATURES

If the animals are what bring people to Yellowstone, the geothermal features are what transfix them and lure them back year after year.

The world's largest concentration of thermal features—more than 10,000 in all—Yellowstone bursts to life with geysers, hot springs, fumaroles (steam vents), and mud pots. There are six grand geysers, of which **Old Faithful** is the most famous, and some 500 lesser geysers. Throughout the park are a number of basins where visitors can see all four types of thermal features, including **Norris Geyser Basin.**

The thermal features in Yellowstone are an indication of the region's volcanic past, present, and future, and as such they are in constant states of change. Small but daily earthquakes cause shifts in activity and temperature. The travertine **Mammoth Terraces** are literally growing and changing on a daily basis to the point that the boardwalks have had to be altered to protect visitors from different flows of searing hot water.

As miraculous as these water features are to see—with dramatic color displays and water dances that put the Bellagio fountains in Vegas to shame—and to smell (think rotten eggs), what you can't see is perhaps even more compelling: thermophiles, heat-loving microorganisms that inhabit the geothermal features throughout the park. A source of

Yellowstone's Volcano: Waiting for the Big One?

It's always interesting to watch visitors' expressions when you tell them that in Yellowstone National Park they are standing atop one of the world's largest active volcanoes . . . and that it is overdue for an apocalyptic eruption. While those two facts are true, the reality is much less threatening. Indeed there have been three super eruptions—Mike Poland, the scientist-in-charge at the Yellowstone Observatory, explains there is no such thing as a super volcano, only super eruptions—over the course of the last two million years, and the patterns do indicate that the volcano is overdue to erupt. But scientists agree that the chances of a massive eruption in the next 1,000 or even 10,000 years are very slight. For the time being, anyway, the volcano that gives rise to Yellowstone's extraordinary geothermal features is all bark and no bite—thankfully.

AN EXPLOSIVE HISTORY

The first super eruption 2.1 million years ago was 6,000 times more powerful than the 1980 eruption of Mount St. Helens, spouting rock and ash in every direction from Texas to Canada, Missouri to California. The eruption emptied the magma chamber located just underneath the park and caused a massive sinking of the earth, known as a caldera, within the confines of what is now the park. Small lava flows filled in the perimeter of the Huckleberry Ridge Caldera over the course of hundreds of thousands of years.

The second major eruption occurred 1.3 million years ago and created the Henry's Fork Caldera. The most recent massive eruption took place roughly 640,000 years ago and created the Yellowstone Caldera, which is 30 by 45 miles (48 by 72 km) in size. The perimeter of the Yellowstone Caldera is still visible in places throughout the park. Hike up Mount Washburn on Dunraven Pass between Canyon and Tower, look south, and you will see the vast caldera formed by the most recent eruption. The caldera rim is also visible at Gibbon Falls, Lewis Falls, and Lake Butte. As you drive between Mammoth and Gardiner, look at Mount Everts to the east and you will see layers of ash from the various eruptions.

TODAY'S EARTHQUAKES ARE HINTS

But volcanic activity is not a thing of the past in Yellowstone. The magma, which some scientists think is just 5 miles (8 km) beneath the surface of the park in places as opposed to the typical 40, has created two enormous bulges, known as resurgent domes, near Sour Creek and Mallard Lake. The Sour Creek Dome is growing at an impressive rate of 1.5 inches (3.8 cm) per year, causing Yellowstone Lake to tip southward, leaving docks on the north side completely out of the water and flooding the forested shore of the south side. In addition, there are roughly 1,500 earthquakes every year centered in Yellowstone, most of which cannot be felt. In 2014, however, a 4.8-magnitude quake occurred 4 miles (6.4 km) from Norris Geyser Basin. The earthquakes shift geothermal activity in the park and keep the natural plumbing system that feeds the geyser basins flowing. They also suggest volcanic activity. In early 2010, a series of more than 3,200 small earthquakes (the largest registered 3.8 on the Richter scale) rocked the park, with 16 quakes registering a magnitude greater than 3.0. A 1985 swarm recorded more than 3,000 earthquakes over three months, with the largest registering at 4.9 on the Richter scale.

DON'T WORRY!

Still, the scientists at the Yellowstone Volcano Observatory have no reason to suspect that an eruption, or even a lava flow, is imminent. For more than three decades, scientists have been monitoring the region for precursors to volcanic eruptions—earthquake swarms, rapid ground deformation, gas releases, and lava flows—and although there is activity, none of it suggests anything immediate or foreboding. Current real-time monitoring data, including earthquake activity and deformation, are available online at http://volcanoes.usgs.gov. The bottom line is that the volcano is real and active, but certainly not a threat in the immediate future, and not a reason to stay away from this awe-inspiring place.

ongoing scientific study, these thermophiles are modern examples of the earth's first life-forms and responsible for the discovery of DNA fingerprinting.

As spellbinding as they are, particularly in winter when the warm steam beckons, it is critically important to stay on boardwalks in geothermal areas and never touch the water. In addition to being boiling hot, many features are highly acidic or alkaline and could cause extreme chemical burns. The ground around the features is often thin and unstable, occasionally allowing animals to break through and be cooked. Twenty-two people have died in Yellowstone's thermal features, including one man who strayed off the boardwalk in 2016 to get a closer look and broke through the thin crust; the water was so hot that by the time help arrived, there were no remains to collect.

HISTORY
Tracing Human History

Evidence from archaeological sites, trails, and even oral histories suggests that humans inhabited the region of Yellowstone as far back as 11,000 years ago. And although the land is rich with history, not much has changed since the park was created in 1872, the invaluable blessing of having been protected as the nation's first national park. The unique geothermal features, pristine lakes and waterfalls, abundant wildlife, and the different ecosystems have endured through the years.

Yellowstone was traversed by various Native American tribes, including the Crow, Blackfeet, Nez Perce, and Shoshone, whose oral history teaches that they originated in this area. Although these nomads passed through the area, only a branch of the Shoshone, known as the "Sheep Eaters," made Yellowstone their home. The first Europeans to have visited the area were most likely fur traders and trappers who seem to have missed the unusual geothermal activity. Lewis and Clark's expedition bypassed the region completely. On their return voyage in

1806, however, John Colter separated from the group and ventured alone into the region. He is considered the first non-Native American to have seen the thermal features in the park. When Colter returned home three years later, his stories were considered suspicious. His tales of "bubbling ground," "mountains made of glass," and rivers where you could catch a fish and cook it without ever removing it from the water seemed preposterous to Easterners. Colter's descriptions of fire and brimstone quickly earned the place the nickname of "Colter's Hell." However, as more fur traders moved into the region, the stories of boiling mud, steaming land, and hot pools of water continued. Jim Bridger explored the area in 1856 and is considered by some the "first geographer" of the region. He too shared wild descriptions that were met with similar skepticism.

Expeditions into Yellowstone

The first organized expeditions into the Yellowstone area were made in 1869 and 1870. It was the 1871 government-sponsored expedition into the region led by Ferdinand Vandeveer Hayden, however, that produced a detailed account of the area. The Hayden Geological Survey was accompanied by William Henry Jackson photographs and artwork by Henry W. Elliott and Thomas Moran. Photographs and spectacular paintings and drawings were splashed across magazines and newspapers around the East so that people could see the wonders of the region for the first time. It was this report, coupled with the earnest pleas of the men who had seen the area, that prodded Congress to grant the region national park status in 1872. That year, the park had 300 visitors.

Nathaniel Langford was the park's first superintendent, but without proper funding and staff he had difficulty protecting the land. Poachers and vandals exploited the park's natural resources, creating a state of general lawlessness. By 1886 the U.S. Army had entered the park to help regain control of the region. They built park structures, strengthened and enforced regulations, encouraged visitors, and made sure the land and wildlife were protected. Transportation infrastructure improvements also helped attract more visitors to the park. The Northern Pacific Railway extended to the town of Cinnabar, north of modern-day Gardiner, near the northern entrance of the park, and in 1915 automobiles were allowed into Yellowstone, making it more accessible to the masses. Following World War II, car travel exploded, and more than a million visitors came to the park in 1948.

Shaping Park Policy

The army's leadership was not a long-term solution to managing the new national park, and in 1916 the National Park Service was created. (The birthday of the National Park Service is still celebrated every year on August 25 with a smattering of hilariously decorated Christmas trees around the park.) Since then, the park's boundaries have been redrawn to encompass 2.2 million acres (roughly equivalent in size to the state of Connecticut), and wildlife management has been continuously refined as new science emerges. One fundamental change came as a result of the 1963 Leopold Report, which suggested that "natural regulation" was superior to the long-held unnatural management in which park managers controlled animal populations and altered the course of naturally occurring events like fire. Ecological Process Management, as it has come to be called, is still the core philosophy behind park management today.

Both the grizzly bear and the gray wolf (reintroduced to the park in 1995) have seen enormous improvements to their endangered status due to Yellowstone's wildlife policies. In 1988 the park experienced the largest wildfires in its history, affecting more than a third of its land, and once again sparking furious debates about management of public resources and the value of natural ecosystems. In the spring of 2016, the U.S. Fish and Wildlife Service proposed removing grizzlies from the endangered species list in the Greater Yellowstone Ecosystem, a controversial decision that has been tied up in courts ever since.

Modern-day Yellowstone is every bit as spellbinding as it was for John Colter and Jim Bridger and the scores of Native Americans who had traveled through the park long before them. But it is increasingly complex. Issues like bioprospecting, bison management in the face of the disease brucellosis, and the delisting criteria of endangered species loom large. Despite the fact that, thankfully, the physical features of Yellowstone—its mountainscapes, geothermal features, and wildlife populations—remain largely untouched, an area of this size with more than 4.5 million visitors annually (nearly three times the populations of Montana and Wyoming combined!) cannot be immune to human influence. The challenge as we move forward is to determine a way to let Yellowstone age and evolve in its own way, on its own time, while giving people around the world access to this unique and spectacular place. It is we, the visitors, who have an opportunity to be changed forever by time spent in Yellowstone, and not the other way around.

Gardiner

Named rather inauspiciously for a mountain man who was described in the local paper in 1903 as "an outlaw and in general a worthless, dissolute character," Gardiner (pop. 879, elev. 5,314 ft/1,619 m) is actually a cute little town with plenty of places to stay, eat, and stock up and has ideal proximity to the park. The only year-round entrance to Yellowstone for automobiles, this scrubby little tourist town has a charm and an identity all its own. The Yellowstone River cuts a canyon beside the main drag, which allows for plenty of river-runner hangouts. Few other places in the world have elk congregating in the churchyard or on the front lawns of most of the motels in town. And where else do high school football players have to dodge bison dung as they're running for a touchdown? The town's architecture is a combination of glorious wood and stone "parkitecture" buildings alongside old-school Western-style buildings complete with false fronts. The towering **Roosevelt Arch,** built in 1903 and dedicated by Yellowstone champion Teddy Roosevelt himself, welcomes visitors to the park with its inspiring slogan, "For the Benefit and Enjoyment of the People." Yes, Gardiner is built around its proximity to the park, but the town has maintained its integrity by preserving its history and making the most of its surroundings.

SIGHTS
★ Boiling River

Halfway between Gardiner and Mammoth Hot Springs, straddling the Montana-Wyoming border and the 45th parallel, the halfway point between the equator and the North Pole, is the Boiling River, one of only two swimmable thermal features in Yellowstone. From the clearly marked parking area, visitors amble upstream along a 0.5-mile (0.8-km) rocky path running parallel to the Gardner River. Where the trail ends and the steam envelops almost everything, a gushing hot spring called the Boiling River flows into the otherwise icy Gardner River. The hot and cold waters mix to a perfect temperature that can be enjoyed year-round. The area is open during daylight hours only, and all swimmers must wear a bathing suit. The Boiling River is closed each year during spring and early summer runoff, when temperature fluctuations and rushing water put swimmers at risk. Alcohol is not permitted.

Kids and adults alike marvel at the floating Day-Glo green algae. The water should not be ingested. Bison and elk frequent the area, and despite the regular crowds of people (note that 20 people constitute a crowd in this part of the West), this is one of the most unforgettable and unique ways to enjoy a few hours in Yellowstone.

SPORTS AND RECREATION
Fishing and Boating

The Yellowstone is the longest free-flowing river in the Lower 48, and as such it offers excellent boating and fishing opportunities. With the river plunging through town on its way to Yankee Jim Canyon, Gardiner is home to several outfitters that can whet your appetite for adventure, trout, or both. The **Flying Pig Adventure Company** (511 Scott St., 888/792-9193 or 406/848-7510, www. flyingpigrafting.com, 2-hour scenic floats from $59 adults, $49 children 6-12, 2-hour whitewater trips from $69 adults, $59 children 12 and under, full-day trips $135 adults, $115 children) and **Montana Whitewater** (603 Scott St., Gardiner, 406/763-4465, www. montanawhitewater.com, half day from $66.50 adults, $56.50 children 12 and under, full day from $102.50 adults, $92.50 children 6-12) both offer scenic and white-water floats on the Yellowstone River. Both companies offer add-ons like ziplining, horseback riding, and more. **Yellowstone Raft Company** (212 W. Park St., 406/848-7777 or 800/858-7781, www.yellowstoneraft.com, May-Sept., half-day raft trip from $59 ages 6 and up, full day trips from $95 ages 6 and up) was established in 1978 and has an excellent reputation for experienced guides and top-of-the-line equipment.

For anglers eager to wet a line in or out of the park in search of native cutthroats or brown trout, **Parks' Fly Shop** (202 2nd St. S., 406/848-7314, www.parksflyshop.com, 8am-6pm daily summer, 9am-5pm Mon.-Sat., 10am-4pm Sun. fall-spring) is the best place to start. This is an old-school shop with a 1920s cash register—nothing fancy here. It offers half-day trips for two people starting around $475, and full-day trips for two from $575. Anglers can pick up their licenses and any supplies in the retail shop, which stays open year-round. And since Parks' has been serving the area since 1953, its guides are keenly aware of the spots where the fish greatly outnumber the anglers. And after Thanksgiving, half of the shop becomes a **cross-country ski and snowshoe rental** shop.

Hiking

Yellowstone is a hiker's paradise, and unless you have a pet that needs to stretch its legs, hiking just outside the park is like spending the day in the Disney World parking lot. Not that there isn't stunning country in every direction, but there is something particularly alluring about hiking within the boundaries of the park.

That said, some 4.7 miles (7.6 km) south of the terraces at Mammoth Hot Springs, on the left-hand side after the Golden Gate Bridge, is the **Glen Creek Trailhead** and a small dirt parking lot. A range of wonderful hikes start from this point. Across the street on the west side of the road, a trail leads through **The Hoodoos,** massive travertine boulders that look otherworldly in this setting, and down the mountain 3.8 miles (6.1 km) back to Mammoth. If you cannot arrange either a drop-off at the trailhead or a shuttle, the return trip, another 3.8 miles (6.1 km), climbs constantly for nearly 1,000 vertical feet (305 m). Another more ambitious hike is the 9.2-mile (14.8-km) round-trip to **Osprey Falls.** The first 4 miles (6.4 km) are easy and flat, following an abandoned roadbed popular with mountain bikers. A blink-and-you'll-miss-it spur trail off the south side of the road leads hikers down into Sheepeater Canyon and the remaining 0.6 mile (1 km) to the mesmerizing 150-foot (46-m) falls. Relax, have a snack, and save your energy for the 800-vertical-foot (244-m) climb back up to the road. **Bunsen Peak** offers hikers an interesting walk through an entirely burned forest and all of its colorful rebirth, as well as a stunning view from the 8,500-foot (2,591-m) summit. The climb is steep: 1,300 vertical feet (396 m) over 2.1 miles (3.4 km). Try to ignore the hum of the radio tower near the summit—easily accomplished when the summit view fills your senses.

ENTERTAINMENT AND EVENTS

The biggest event of the year in this gateway community is the annual **Gardiner Rodeo** (406/848-7971, $12 adults), usually held in June over Father's Day weekend. The rodeo is held in the Jim Duffy arena at the northern end of town off US 89 and includes the usual competitions such as bull riding and bareback bronc riding. Women and juniors compete in barrel racing and breakaway roping. The first night of the rodeo is followed by a dance at the Gardiner Community Center, and the following day the chamber of commerce hosts a parade downtown. This is a great small-town rodeo.

But Gardiner is far from a one-event town. In late February, the **Jardine Ski Run** (406/848-7971) is a 5-mile (8-km) groomed track race where outlandish costumes are appreciated as much, if not more than, speed. With a $7 "grazing permit" you can help yourself to chili, chili dogs, baked goods, and more. Another worthwhile pursuit for the active is the **Park to Paradise Triathlon**

(406/848-7971) in late April or early May, which includes a 17.5-mile (28.2-km) bike, 4-mile (6.4-km) run, and 7-mile (11.3-km) river paddle. The much less demanding and very family-friendly **Annual Brewfest** (406/848-7971, $20 in advance or $25 at the gate) happens in mid-August and raises money for the local chamber with live entertainment, food, crafts, microbrews, and fun kids' activities like soda-tasting, face-painting, horseshoes, and kites. For more information on these events, contact the **Gardiner Chamber of Commerce** (406/848-7971, www.visitgardinermt.com).

FOOD

Known since 1960 for its "Hateful Hamburgers" and the huge personality of its owner, Helen, this fabulous burger joint was sold to the Wild West Rafting Company and is now known as ★ **Wild West Corral** (711 Scott St. W., 406/848-7627, 11am-10pm daily May-Oct., burgers $7-17). Even without Helen, this is still the kind of place you might easily drive 100 miles (161 km) to for the burgers, shakes, and old-school ambience. The limited seating is mostly outside, and there is often a line of people waiting to order. But none of that will matter when you take your first bite of a bison bacon cheeseburger or a perfectly grilled elk burger. Wild West Corral even managed to improve on Helen's by expanding the menu and cleaning the place up a bit. This is still a little slice of hamburger paradise—if you like that sort of thing.

For a good, hearty breakfast, excellent pastries, fresh Mexican food, and burgers, the **Yellowstone Grill** (404 Scott St., 406/848-9433, call ahead for hours after a temporary pandemic closure, breakfast $8-15, lunch $13-17) is sure to please. Remember though, this is small-town Montana. Sometimes the place closes when short-staffed. Or when the owners' youngest son has a Legion baseball game. Be glad for that; the important stuff still matters here. You can always have a late lunch. Another great place for a grab-and-go

meal, with fantastic book browsing while you wait, is **Tumbleweed Bookstore & Café** (501 Scott St. W., 406/848-2225, www.tumbleweedbooksandcafe.weebly.com, 7am-3pm Wed.-Mon., $3.50-9.50, sack lunches $12). They have great breakfast burritos, grilled sandwiches, wraps, soups, salads, and baked goodies. Vegetarians, vegans, and gluten-free people will be delighted with the broad offerings.

For a hearty meal almost anytime, try **Wonderland Café & Lodge** (206 Main St., 406/223-1914, www.wonderlandcafeandlodge.com, 7am-8pm Tues.-Sun., 7am-11am Mon., lunch $12-20, dinner $12-45), which serves coffee and baked goods all day, plus excellent lunch and dinner items including elk chili, trout, rib eye, pasta, and burgers. They also have free Wi-Fi and charging stations if you're in need. If pizza is what you're craving, head to **Yellowstone Pizza Company** (210 E. Park, 406/848-9991, www.yellowstonepizzaga.wixsite.com, noon-8pm daily May-Oct., $16-20), which serves 13-inch pizzas, plus pastas, salad, and appetizers.

ACCOMMODATIONS

Gardiner is built to accommodate the overflow from the park, but in reality, many of the little motels have more charm and much better value, particularly in non-summer months, than those inside the park. For the most part, it's hard to go wrong in Gardiner. There are plenty of small cabins and larger vacation rentals in the area. The folk Victorian ★ **Gardiner Guest House** (112 Main St. E., 406/848-9414, $100-165 summer, $75-115 winter) welcomes both children and pets and offers three modest but comfortable guest rooms and a cabin. Owners Richard and Nance Parks are longtime residents and an extensive source of information on the area. His fly shop and guiding company, **Parks' Fly Shop** (202 2nd St. S., 406/848-7314, www.parksflyshop.com), is one of the oldest businesses in town.

Yellowstone Park Riverfront Cabins (550 Old Yellowstone Trail S., 406/570-4500, www.cabinsontheyellowstone.com, $375/ night for up to 4 people) offers comfortable cabins that can accommodate up to six people in a quiet location above the river. There is a five-night minimum. Another option for small, basic, and reasonably priced cottages right in town is **Hillcrest Cottages** (400 Scott St., 406/848-7353 or 800/970-7353, www.hillcrestcottages.com, early May-mid-Oct., $95-187). The cottages come in various sizes that can sleep 1-5 people. The **Flying Pig Adventure Company** (511 Scott St. W., 866/264-8448, www.flyingpigrafting.com) offers a host of higher-end vacation rentals ranging from cozy canvas wall tents on a nearby ranch (from $200) and cabins ($175-400) to an enormous private lodge (from $599) that can sleep up to 15. Minimum nights apply.

For more standard hotels, there is a decent selection including the riverfront **Absaroka Lodge** (310 Scott St., 406/848-7414, www.yellowstonemotel.com, $130-210), where each room has its own balcony looking into the park. And there is the barebones but clean and pet-friendly **Super 8** (702 Scott St. W., 406/848-7401, www.wyndhamhotels.com, from $62), which offers a free breakfast and Wi-Fi.

CAMPING

The difference between camping outside the park and inside Yellowstone is simply that you need to focus on reservations and availability instead of permits and regulations. There are six campgrounds in Gardiner—four national forest campgrounds and two private ones.

The private **Yellowstone RV Park & Campground** (121 US 89 S., 406/848-7496, www.rvparkyellowstone.com, May-Oct., 46 sites including pull-through and tent sites, tent sites from $48, RV sites from $91) is ideally situated on the Yellowstone River just 1.3 miles (2.1 km) north of the park entrance. They have plenty of full-service riverfront sites, plush a wash house for campers. The other private campground is **Rocky Mountain RV Park & Cabins** (14 Jardine Rd., 406/848-7251, www.rockymountainrvpark.com, May-Sept., standard RV sites $89, deluxe RV sites $99, premium RV sites $109, discounts for seniors and military, cabins $80-215), just four blocks from the park entrance.

Those in search of a more rustic experience might enjoy checking out a national forest campground. The pack-in, pack-out **Bear Creek Campground** (Forest Rd. 493, 10.5 mi/16.9 km northeast of Gardiner, 406/848-7375, 4 sites with no services, mid-June-late Oct. depending on weather, free) and the **Timber Camp Campground** (Forest Rd. 493, 9.5 mi/15.3 km northeast of Gardiner, 406/848-7375, no services, mid-June-late Oct. depending on weather, free) are both small, isolated, and pleasantly rustic. The other Forest Service campgrounds in Gardiner are Eagle Creek Campground and Canyon Campground, both of which charge $15 per night single, $30 double (plus $5 per additional vehicle) and are about 15 minutes outside of town.

INFORMATION AND SERVICES

For information on Gardiner and the area around it, the **Gardiner Chamber of Commerce** (216 Park St., 406/848-7971, www.visitgardinermt.com, 9am-5pm Mon.-Fri., 1pm-4pm Sat.-Sun., extended summer hours) is an excellent and welcoming resource. Just a couple of doorways down, the headquarters of **Yellowstone Forever** (308 Park St., 406/848-2400, www.yellowstone.org, 8am-8pm daily) offers information about the park, as well as its own phenomenal educational tours. A great gift shop is on-site, as well as the nicest bathrooms you have likely seen in a while.

1: the Roosevelt Arch 2: Canary Spring at Mammoth Hot Springs Terraces

The Northern Loop

With striking panoramas, wonderful thermals, plentiful wildlife, and year-round vehicle access between the North and Northeast Entrances, this is one of the most underappreciated parts of the park. The accommodations and dining are not as fancy as elsewhere, but the crowds are more manageable, and the experience is just as good or better. Phenomenal highlights include Mammoth Hot Springs, the Lamar Valley, Tower Falls, Dunraven Pass, the Grand Canyon of the Yellowstone, and Norris Geyser Basin.

SIGHTS

★ Mammoth and the Mammoth Hot Springs Terraces

Just 5 miles (8 km) into the park and up the road from Gardiner, Mammoth is the primary northern hub of Yellowstone National Park. It is also an interesting little community in its own right, with a small medical center, the most beautiful post office in the West, and a magnificent stone church. The town of Mammoth, once known as Fort Yellowstone, was essentially built by the U.S. Army during its 1886-1918 occupation. Thinking they were on a temporary assignment, the soldiers erected canvas wall tents and lived in them through five harsh winters. In 1890, Congress set aside $50,000 for the construction of a permanent post, a stately collection of stone colonial revival-style buildings, most of which are still in use today.

The 2015 renovated **Albright Visitor Center** (Grand Loop Rd., 307/344-2263, 9am-5pm daily) is a must-see. There are films, history and wildlife exhibits, and a small but excellent selection of books and videos in the shop run by **Yellowstone Forever** (406/848-2400, www.yellowstone. org). While at the center, don't miss seeing some of the artwork produced during the 1871 Hayden Geological Survey of the park, including quality reproductions of painter Thomas Moran's famous watercolor sketches and original photographs by William Henry Jackson. Rangers on staff can usually give you up-to-date animal sightings and activity reports. The flush toilets downstairs are the last for a while.

The primary ecological attraction in Mammoth (other than the elk often seen lounging around and nibbling on the green grass) can be found on the **Mammoth Hot Springs Terraces.** Since the days of the earliest stagecoach trails into the park, they have been a visual and olfactory marvel for visitors. The Hayden Expedition named the area White Mountain Hot Spring for the cream-colored, steplike travertine terraces.

Beneath the ground, the Norris-Mammoth fault carries superheated water rich in dissolved calcium and bicarbonate. As the water emerges through cracks in the surface, carbon dioxide is released as a gas, and the carbonate combines with calcium to form travertine. The mountain is continuously growing as travertine is deposited and then shifted as the cracks are sealed and the mineral-laden water emerges somewhere else. For frequent visitors to the park, vast changes are noticeable from one visit to the next. In addition to changes in shape and water flow, the colors at Mammoth can vary dramatically from one day to the next. Not only does travertine morph from bright white when it is new to cream and then gray as it is exposed to the elements, the cyanobacteria create fabulous color shifts too—from turquoise to green and yellow to red and brown, depending on water temperature, available sunlight, and pH levels.

Liberty Cap, at the base of the terraces, is an excellent example of a dormant spring, where all but the core cone has been eroded away. **Minerva Terrace** and **Canary Spring**

are two other springs worth seeing. Their temperatures average around 160°F (71°C), and when they are flowing, they often put on marvelous color displays.

Tower Falls

Eighteen scenic miles (29 km) down the road from Mammoth Hot Springs—past **Undine Falls** and **Blacktail Plateau,** where you can see deer, elk, and bison along with some impressive lookouts—is **Tower Junction** and the breathtaking Tower Falls. The waterfall itself cascades 132 feet (40 m) from volcanic basalt. A popular spot with visitors and just steps from the parking lot, this is not a place for solitude, but it is lovely to see.

Dunraven Pass

Between Tower and the dramatic Grand Canyon of the Yellowstone is one of the most nerve-racking and perhaps most beautiful drives in the park. Climbing up the flanks of **Mount Washburn,** Dunraven Pass is the highest road elevation in the park. The spectacular summit of the road tops out at 8,859 feet (2,700 m) and offers impressive views of Yellowstone's caldera rim. Eagle eyes can also spot the nearby Grand Canyon of the Yellowstone. Hikers will have no shortage of trailheads to start from. The whitebark pines that grow along the road are a critical and dwindling food source for grizzly bears, so keep your eyes open. Because of its extreme altitude and relative exposure, Dunraven Pass is one of the last roads to open in the spring and one of the first to close when bad weather hits. For current road information, call 307/344-2117.

★ Grand Canyon of the Yellowstone

Yellowstone's most recent volcanic explosion, some 600,000 years ago, created a massive caldera and subsequent lava flows, one of which was called the Canyon Rhyolite flow, in the area that is now known as the Grand Canyon of the Yellowstone. This particular lava flow was impacted by a thermal basin, which altered the rhyolite and created the beautiful palette of colors in the rock through constant heating and cooling. Over time, lakes, rivers, and glaciers formed in the region, and the relatively soft rhyolite was easily carved away. Roughly 10,000 years ago, the last of the area's glaciers melted, causing a rush of water to carve the canyon into the form it has today. The 20-mile-long (32-km-long) canyon is still growing thanks to the forces of erosion, including water, wind, and earthquakes. A number of terrific lookouts are on both the North and South Rims of the canyon.

Before setting out for the canyon itself, visitors are advised to visit the **Canyon Visitor Education Center** (Canyon Village, 307/344-2550, 9am-5pm daily summer), which has an outstanding and vast exhibit on Yellowstone's volcanic and geothermal activity, plus other natural history. In fact, this should be a mandatory stop for every visitor who might otherwise have no appreciation for the region's fascinating geology.

On the **North Rim,** don't miss **Inspiration Point,** a natural viewing platform that gives a bird's-eye view both up and down the river. Nathaniel Langford, who would go on to be the park's first superintendent, stood in the same spot with the Washburn Expedition in 1870. He wrote:

Standing there or rather lying there for greater safety, I thought how utterly impossible it would be to describe to another the sensations inspired by such a presence. As I took in the scene, I realized my own littleness, my helplessness, my dread exposure to destruction, my inability to cope with or even comprehend the mighty architecture of nature.

Look down, if you dare, among the nooks and crannies of rock to try to spot nesting ospreys.

Another phenomenal viewing platform can be found at **Lookout Point,** where visitors can gaze from afar at the thundering Lower Falls of the Yellowstone. Visitors who want to get closer to the spray of the falls and don't

mind a long hike down, and back up again, can head toward the base of the falls at **Red Rock Point.** It's a 0.5-mile (0.8-km) trip one-way that drops more than 500 vertical feet (152 m). There is another platform at the top of the 308-foot (94-m) falls aptly named the **Brink of the Lower Falls.** This lookout also involves a 0.5-mile (0.8-km) hike and a 600-foot (183-m) elevation loss. The **Upper Falls** are just over one-third the size of the lower falls, at 109 feet (33 m), but they are worth a gander and can be easily accessed at the **Brink of the Upper Falls.** Mountain man Jim Bridger purportedly regaled friends with tales of the Upper Falls as early as 1846 and urged them to see it for themselves.

From the **South Rim,** visitors can see the Upper Falls from the **Upper Falls Viewpoint.** A trail that dates back to 1898, **Uncle Tom's Trail** still takes hardy hikers to the base of the **Lower Falls.** The trail down loses 500 vertical feet (152 m) through a series of 300 stairs and paved inclines, but what goes down must come up again. From **Artist Point,** one of the largest and most inspiring lookouts, visitors get a glorious view of the distant Lower Falls and the river as it snakes down the pinkish canyon. It was long thought that Artist Point was where painter Thomas Moran made sketches for his 7- by 12-foot (2.1- by 3.7-m) masterpiece *Grand Canyon of the Yellowstone.* More likely, say historians, he painted from a spot on the North Rim now called **Moran Point.**

Norris Geyser Basin

Both the hottest and the most unpredictable geyser basin in the park, Norris Geyser Basin is a fascinating collection of bubbling and colorful geothermal features. A 2.3-mile (3.7-km) web of boardwalks and trails leads visitors through this remarkable basin. From the **Norris Geyser Basin Museum** (east of Norris Junction, 307/344-2812, 9am-5pm daily late May-early Oct., free), which

carefully unravels the geothermal mysteries of the region, two loop trails guide visitors safely through the basin. The 1930s log and stone building that houses the museum has been designated a National Historic Landmark, and it also holds an information desk and a Yellowstone Association bookstore.

Porcelain Basin is a stark, barren setting with a palette of pink, red, orange, and yellow mineral oxides. Some of the features of note include **Africa Geyser,** which had been a hot spring in the shape of its namesake continent and started erupting in 1971. When it is active, **Whirligig Geyser,** named in 1904 by the Hague Party, erupts in a swirling pattern for a few minutes at irregular periods with a roar and hiss. The hottest steam vent in the hottest geothermal basin in the park is **Black Growler,** which has measured 280°F (138°C). The second-largest geyser in Norris, **Ledge Geyser** erupts irregularly to heights up to 125 feet (38 m).

In Norris's **Back Basin** you'll find the world's tallest geyser, **Steamboat Geyser,** which can erupt more than 300 feet (90 m) in the air. Minor eruptions of 10-40 feet (3-12 m) in height are more common. The eruptions can last 3-40 minutes and be separated by days or decades (in the past, Steamboat has gone more than 50 years without an eruption, but in 1964, it erupted 29 times). A major eruption in September 2014 happened at 11pm and was witnessed by a park ranger. Prior to that, the last major eruption occurred in 2013, and before that in 2005. In 2018, Steamboat entered an active phase with eruptions starting in March (after 3.5 years of silence), followed by two in April, four in May, three in June, and one in July. In total, there were 32 eruptions in 2018, 48 eruptions in 2019, and 48 again in 2020. As of September 2021, there had only been 14 eruptions that year. Just down the boardwalk, **Cistern Spring** is linked to Steamboat Geyser and drains in advance of a major eruption. The color is a beautiful blue, enhanced by as much as 0.5 inch (1.3 cm) of gray sinter deposited annually. By comparison, Old Faithful only

---

1: Norris Geyser Basin **2:** Lower Falls **3:** view from Inspiration Point

Be Safe and Smart in the Backcountry

Hiking and camping in the Yellowstone backcountry is undoubtedly the best way to understand and appreciate this magnificently wild place. But with this opportunity comes the responsibility to keep yourself safe, protect the animals from human-caused altercations, and preserve this pristine environment.

When hiking, **prevent erosion and trail degradation** by hiking single file and always staying on the trail. Don't take shortcuts or cut corners on switchbacks. If you do have to leave the trail, disperse your group so that you don't inadvertently trample the vegetation and create a new, unwanted trail.

Chances are good that you will encounter some kind of wildlife in the backcountry, so you need to be prepared to react. **Never approach an animal:** Remember to always stay at least 25 yards/meters away from all wildlife, and at least 100 yards/meters away from predators, including bears. Make noise as you hike along to give animals the opportunity to depart before an encounter. Do not hike at the edges of day—dawn or dusk—or at night, as these are the most active times for bears and other predators. Always be aware of your surroundings and pay attention to wind direction. Look for overturned rocks and logs, dug-out areas, and, of course, carcasses, all of which suggest bear activity.

If you do **encounter a bear,** know what to do. If there is some distance between you and the bear, give the bear an opportunity to leave, or take the opportunity to redirect your own party. If you run into a bear at close range, be as nonthreatening as possible. Talk calmly and back away. Never turn your back, and never run. Make sure you have your bear spray accessible. If the bear charges, stand your ground. Bears will often bluff charge to determine whether you will run and are thus prey. If the bear does attack, keep your pack on, fall to the ground on your belly, protect your head and neck with your arms, and play dead. When the bear leaves, get up and retreat. In the very uncommon circumstance that a bear provokes an attack or enters a tent, fight the bear with every resource you have.

Go to great lengths to **avoid attracting bears** by hanging all food, cooking utensils, and scented items (toothpaste, deodorant, other toiletries, menstrual supplies, and trash) in a bear bag in a tree or atop a bear pole. Designate a separate cooking and eating area away from the sleeping tents. Dispose of your trash and personal waste properly.

You need to plan your trip carefully and secure all **permits** and **backcountry campsites** through any one of nine backcountry permit offices: Bechler Ranger Station, Canyon Visitor Center, Grant Village Visitor Center, Bridge Bay Ranger Station, Mammoth Visitor Center, Old Faithful Ranger Station, South Entrance Ranger Station, Tower Ranger Station, and the West Yellowstone Visitor Information Center (307/344-2160, www.nps.gov/yell, permits available 8am-4:30pm daily June-Aug., $25 annual backcountry pass, $3 pp over 9 years old per night, $5 pp for stock parties). Some of Yellowstone's roughly 300 backcountry campsites can be reserved in advance either in person, by fax, or through the mail. Backcountry use permits are required for all overnight stays and can only be attained in person no more than 48 hours before your trip. A park booklet titled *Beyond Road's End* is available online and will help familiarize you with the backcountry regulations and restrictions.

deposits 0.5-1 inch (1.3-2.5 cm) of sinter every century. **Echinus Geyser** is the world's largest acid geyser and is almost as acidic as vinegar. Eruptions since 2007 have been rare and unpredictable, typically lasting about four minutes, but large ones have been known to reach heights of 80-125 feet (24-38 m).

SPORTS AND RECREATION

Yellowstone is indeed a hiker's paradise, with ubiquitous brown signs pointing to trailheads. Look for them anytime your legs need a stretch. In the northern loop, there are some fantastic trails in an otherwise nondescript stretch between Norris and Canyon. Drive east of Norris Junction 3.5 miles (5.6 km) or 8.5 miles (13.7 km) west of Canyon Junction to the **Ice Lake Trailhead** on the north side of the road. It is a fairly popular 4.5-mile (7.2-km) loop with minimal elevation gain. In fact, the entire trail to Ice Lake is wheelchair accessible and leads to the only wheelchair-accessible backcountry campsite in the park. Avid hikers will want to continue on to **Little Gibbon Falls,** a 25-foot (7.6-m) waterfall that is not even on the U.S. Geological Survey topographic map. Another way to see this hidden gem is to find the Little Gibbon Falls Trailhead 0.4 mile (0.6 km) east of the Ice Lake Trailhead. There is a small pullout on the south side of the road. The trail starts about 100 feet (30 m) east of the pullout on the north side of the road. From here, Little Gibbon Falls is a 1.2-mile (1.9-km) out-and-back hike.

A lengthier hike in the vicinity of Tower Junction is along the **Hellroaring Trail,** a beautiful but strenuous hike through wide open sagebrush and along fishable water. The trailhead is 3.5 miles (5.6 km) west of Tower Junction and starts with a steep descent to a suspension bridge over the Yellowstone River. Day hikers can enjoy a 6.2-mile (10-km) there-and-back hike through scenic sagebrush plateau to the confluence of Hellroaring Creek and the Yellowstone River. This is Yellowstone, so best to come prepared: Bring bear spray and a fly rod!

FOOD

By far the most unusual meal option in the park is the ★ **Old West Dinner Cookout** (307/344-7311, www.yellowstonenationalparklodges.com), which operates daily early June to mid-September from the Roosevelt Lodge and is served in Yellowstone's wilderness. The hearty steak-and-potatoes dinner with all the cowboy trimmings can be attended on horseback (1-hour rides from $98 ages 12 and over, $81 children 8-11, 2-hour rides from $110

ages 12 and over, $97 children 8-11) or via covered wagon (from $70 ages 12 and over, $55 children 3-11, free for children under 3).

Breakfast, lunch, and dinner are served daily throughout the season in the **Roosevelt Lodge Dining Room; Canyon Lodge Eatery, Canyon Lodge Falls Café,** and **Canyon Lodge M66 Grill;** and the **Mammoth Hotel Dining Room** and **Mammoth Terrace Grill** (866/439-7375, www.yellowstonenationalparklodges.com). Each restaurant has its own flair—Roosevelt Lodge tends to be heartier, with options like barbecue beef, bison chili, and Wyoming cheesesteak, while Mammoth is known for elaborate buffets and inventive small plates like goat cheese sliders, mini trout tacos, and Thai curry mussels. Canyon offers a wok station and slow food fast, with ready-made entrées like barbecued ribs, country-fried steak and rotisserie chicken. Breakfasts include entrées ranging from pancakes and eggs to biscuits and gravy ($6-14). Lunches range $9-18, and dinners are generally $14-42. Generally, breakfast is served 6:30am-10am, lunch 11:30am-2:30pm, and dinner 5:30pm-10pm. Hours vary seasonally by restaurant and are subject to change. Call ahead for reservations, where available, or to check on hours.

ACCOMMODATIONS

There are three accommodations in the northern loop. The largest is the **Mammoth Hot Springs Hotel and Cabins** (late Apr.-early Oct. and mid-Dec.-early Mar.), which has 79 rooms, each with private bath, and another 116 cabins, four with hot tubs. The rustic cabins, two-room cabins, and deluxe hotel rooms range $124-345. Suites start at $664. Set amid historic Fort Yellowstone, Mammoth provides convenient access to restaurants, gift shops, a gas station, and the visitor center, so guests may forget they're somewhat out in the wild. Despite human and car traffic in Mammoth, wolves have been known to sneak onto the green watered

Camping in Yellowstone

As accommodations cannot meet the demand of Yellowstone's four million visitors each year, camping is an excellent option, particularly for those spontaneous souls who want to see the park without planning months in advance. More than 2,000 campsites spread over 12 campgrounds are located in the park. The five largest—Bridge Bay, Canyon, Fishing Bridge RV Park, Grant Village, and Madison—are run by Xanterra/Yellowstone National Park Lodges; all inquiries and reservations should be made by calling Xanterra (same-day reservations 307/344-7901, advance reservations 307/344-7311); these campgrounds have additional sales and utility tax fees. The other sites are assigned on a first-come, first-served basis. Try to arrive early to secure your spot; sites often fill up by 11am, especially in the busy summer months. Yellowstone also has more than 300 backcountry campsites, which require permits. Camping fees are discounted for bicyclists and hikers.

Campground	Number of Sites	Dates (Approx.)	Fees	RV Sites
Bridge Bay	432	late May-mid-Sept.	$28	call for availability and reservations
Canyon	273	late May-mid-Sept.	$33	call for availability and reservations
Fishing Bridge RV Park	310	early May-early Sept.	$52	call for availability and reservations
Grant Village	430	mid-June-mid-Sept.	$33	call for availability and reservations
Indian Creek	70	mid-June-mid-Sept.	$20	10 for 35-foot (10.7 m); 35 for 30-foot (9.1 m), walk through to assess site
Lewis Lake	85	mid-June-early Nov.	$20	25-foot (7.6-m) limit
Madison	278	late Apr.-mid-Oct.	$28	call for availability and reservations
Mammoth	85	year-round	$25	most pull-through, 30-foot (9.1-m) limit
Norris	111	late May-late Sept.	$25	2 for 50-foot (15.2 m), 5 for 30-foot (9.1 m)
Pebble Creek	27	mid-June-late Sept.	$20	some long pull-throughs
Slough Creek	16	mid-June-early Oct.	$20	14 for 30-foot (9.1 m), walk through to assess site
Tower Falls	31	late May-late Sept.	$20	all 30-foot (9.1 m) or less; hairpin turn

lawns at night to take down an unsuspecting well-grazed elk. You can imagine the surprise when early risers spotted the carcass on their way to get a breakfast burrito.

Named for Yellowstone champion Theodore Roosevelt, the ★ **Roosevelt Lodge Cabins** (early-June-early Sept.) offer a timeless rustic setting reminiscent of a great old dude ranch in a quieter corner of the park. The Roughrider Cabins (from $114) usually offer double beds and a wood-burning stove. What they lack in amenities they make up for with charming authenticity. Toilets and communal showers are available nearby. The Frontier Cabins (from $182) are slightly larger and include a private bathroom with a shower, toilet, and sink.

Set adjacent to the spectacular Grand Canyon of the Yellowstone, **Canyon Lodge & Cabins** (early June-late Sept.) is the largest single lodging property in the park. The facilities were built in the 1950s and 1960s, then added onto and renovated significantly in 2016 to bring the total to 590 rooms and cabins. Options include standard rooms, deluxe rooms, and Western cabins, which are basic motel-style units with private full bathrooms, starting at $242-500. Suites start at $940.

Reservations for all hotels inside the park should be made through **Yellowstone National Park Lodges** (307/344-7311, www.yellowstonenationalparklodges.com). Nature is the draw here: There are no televisions, radios, or air-conditioning. Internet access can be purchased in the public areas of some hotels in the park.

CAMPING

The only campground in the park's northern loop that can be reserved in advance, operated by Xanterra, the park's concessionaire, is the 270-site **Canyon** (307/344-7901 for same-day reservations, 307/344-7311 for advance reservations, late May-early Sept., from $34 nightly rate includes two showers/night), which has both tent and RV sites, 15 public restrooms with flush toilets, faucets with cold running water, and pay showers. The other six sites—at Mammoth, Tower Falls, Slough Creek, Pebble Creek, Indian Creek, and Norris—are available on a first-come, first-served basis and cost $20-25. These sites fill up quickly; your best bet is to arrive before 11am. Mammoth is the only campground open all year; all the campgrounds have some RV sites. A great feature on the Yellowstone app and website shows current availability and also what time any given site closed the day before (www.nps.gov/yell).

In addition to the campgrounds, more than 300 backcountry campsites are scattered throughout the park. Overnight permits, which are available at all ranger stations and visitor centers, are only issued in person up to 48 hours in advance; they are required for all the sites. Backcountry campsites can be reserved January-October by paying a $25 reservation fee. All requests to reserve sites must be made in person, faxed, or mailed in. Pertinent forms and information for backcountry camping in Yellowstone are available online at the National Park Service Backcountry Trip Planner (www.nps.gov/yell).

The Northeast Corner

With arguably the best wildlife-viewing in the park, especially in winter, this region is known as the "Little Serengeti of North America." The wide-open spaces of the Lamar Valley and much of the northeast corner of the park also offer some pretty dramatic mountain vistas. There is excellent fishing and hiking in the region, and just outside the park's northeast entrance is Cooke City, a cool little community with tremendous appeal to backcountry skiers, snowmobilers, and other outdoors enthusiasts.

TOP EXPERIENCE

★ WATCHING THE WOLVES

When visitors list the animals they most want to see in Yellowstone, wolves rank second, right behind grizzly bears. Since their return to Yellowstone in 1995, wolves have surprised parkgoers and wildlife experts alike by being much more visible than anyone anticipated. In fact, since their reintroduction, wolves have been spotted in Yellowstone by at least one person nearly every day. Much of that is thanks to wolf researchers, including the indefatigable Rick McIntyre, who is out in the field an average of 11 hours per day seven days per week, and the ever-passionate wolf watchers (who tend to follow Rick), armed with massive scopes and camera lenses that look strong enough to spot wildlife on other planets.

The bad news is that there are roughly 123 wolves in nine packs, plus a few lone wolves, roaming throughout Yellowstone, an area that is approximately the size of Connecticut. It's always a good idea to bear those figures in mind when you have only a couple of hours and a keen desire to spot one of these majestic canines.

But there's good news too. If seeing the wolves is a high priority for you, here are five ways to improve your odds:

- **Visit in winter.** Wolves are most active and most visible (nearest to the roads and against a white backdrop) in the winter when they have significant advantages over their prey, including elk and bison. Spring and fall can offer viewing opportunities as well, but summer visitors are at a disadvantage because the wolves are often way up in the high country, far from roads. Whenever you go, don't forget your binoculars or a scope if you have one.

- **Do your homework or hire a guide.** Stop at the visitor center in Mammoth in winter (or any of the visitor centers at other times of year) and inquire about recent activity. Rangers can often tell you where packs have been spotted, if kills have recently occurred, and so forth. You could also consider hiring a guide that specializes in wolf-watching. **Yellowstone Wolf Tracker** (406/223-0173, www.wolftracker. com, $700/day for up to 3 people, $800 for up to 5 people, $900 for up to 10 people) offers 6- to 8-hour tours led by wildlife biologists. The **Yellowstone Forever Institute** (406/848-2400, www.yellowstone.org) offers multiday courses that focus on wolves.

- **Visit the Lamar Valley.** The only road open to car traffic year-round, the stretch of asphalt that winds through the Lamar Valley takes visitors through the heart of some of the park's best winter wolf terrain. There are numerous pullouts along the road for viewing, but be sure to park safely out of traffic without blocking other visitors. In the summer, along the stretch of road near the confluence of the Lamar River and Soda Butte Creek, the road is often closed to stopping thanks to a wolf-denning site not far from the pavement. Your chances to see a wolf—even pups—are good.

- **Wake up early.** Like most wildlife, wolves are most active at the edges of day. Putting

Cinderella: The Real-Life Fairy Tale of Wolf 42

In 1926 the last known wolf in Yellowstone was killed, bringing to a conclusion a decades-long campaign to rid the region of an animal widely considered a worthless pest. The murderous eviction was a tragic end to a noble creature. It took near y 70 years for wolves to be seen not only for their intrinsic worth but their value in making the Yellowstone ecosystem whole again. This was their home, after all, and they had been unnaturally removed. Thirty-one Canadian gray wolves—*Canis lupus*—were reintroduced to the park in 1995-1996 with loud cheers and simultaneous objections.

Among the wolves brought into the park from Canada was a female who would come to be known as wolf number 42. Her sister, wolf 40, was the alpha female of the Druid Peak pack and known to rule the pack with an iron paw. She was suspected of running off her mother, number 39, and her sister, number 41. Number 42, the pack's beta female, managed to stay in the group, likely as a result of her unmatched speed and excellent hunting ability, but she could not get into her sister's good graces. The two fought constantly for four years. Both bred with wolf 21, the pack's alpha male, and wolf 40 reportedly killed her sister's first litter of pups in 1999. Wolf watchers nicknamed 42 "Cinderella" and flocked to the Lamar Valley to watch the drama unfold. Much of Cinderella's life was captured on film by Bob Landis for two *National Geographic* specials.

In a story that plays out like a fairy tale, wolf 42 got her nieces to den with her in 2000 when she had another litter of pups with 21, and after researchers saw wolf 40 approaching the den just before the pups were weaned, ostensibly to kill this second litter of pups, 42 and her nieces attacked. Wolf 40 was found dying of her wounds, and 42 not only rose to alpha status overnight and paired for life with wolf 21, but also moved into 40's den and adopted her dead sister's seven pups as her own. That year 42 and 21 raised 20 pups.

Over the course of her life—eight years, which is more than double wolf lifespan averages—she birthed 32 pups and held her alpha-female status over the Druid Pack, which climbed to 37 members in 2000, becoming one of the largest wolf packs ever recorded. She was known for her faithful and patient parenting, even coaching younger wolves in the middle of an elk hunt.

After receiving a mortality signal from 42's radio collar in February 2004, chief park wolf biologist Doug Smith hiked up Specimen Ridge on a blustery winter day. There he found Cinderella dead, killed by another pack. Wolf watchers noted wolf 21, her constant companion, atop a ridgeline howling for two days straight. The wolf watchers mourned along with him.

Cinderella was the last remaining member of the 31 wolves imported from Canada, but her legacy and story will be forever entwined with the Yellowstone wilderness and the saga of *Canis lupus* finally coming home.

yourself in the heart of the Lamar Valley before sunrise greatly improves your odds of seeing the wolves. The same is true at sunset. In this game, patience pays.

- **Watch for the wolf watchers.** They often have significant advantages, including radio telemeters that allow them to track collared wolves. These people know much about the wolves and can regale you with dramatic sagas of individual animals and entire packs. Don't be shy about pulling over when you see them; they are often willing to let you peer through their scopes.

But do be safe and courteous; turn off your engine and remain quiet.

TOP EXPERIENCE

★ LAMAR VALLEY

One of my favorite corners of the park, the Lamar Valley is stunningly beautiful with wide valleys carved by rivers and glaciers as well as views to the high rugged peaks around Cooke City. It's generally less crowded than other parts of the park (save for the ever-growing number of bespectacled and bescoped wolf watchers), and some of the best hiking, fishing, and camping can be had at Slough Creek. And the wolf-watching, particularly in the winter, is unrivaled anywhere else in the world. There are also grizzlies, black bears, mountain lions, coyotes, red foxes, elk, bison, bighorn sheep, and pronghorn in the area. In early summer, on occasion, there can be as many as 2,000 bison dotting the wide green expanse; it's a miraculous sight.

Lamar Buffalo Ranch

The **Lamar Buffalo Ranch Field Campus** of the **Yellowstone Forever Institute** (406/848-2400 or 307/344-8826, www. yellowstone.org/lamar-buffalo-ranch) is located away from the large crowds (of two-legged creatures, anyway) in the idyllic Lamar Valley. The institute offers field seminars at this private and unique campus year-round. If you bring your own sleeping bag and pillow, you can stay at the ranch in one of its shared or private log cabins. Propane heaters, a communal bathhouse with individual showers, and a fully equipped kitchen are housed in the common building. It's quite comfortable but not fancy. The best part is waking up each morning in the Lamar Valley, an opportunity very few people have. You can

also stay in a nearby campsite or hotel while taking a course at the ranch. Field seminars also take place at hotels throughout the park. The institute holds rooms in various lodges until 30 days before the course.

COOKE CITY

Before it was renamed for a miner and populated by hard-core modern-day prospectors in search of snow, **Cooke City** (pop. 63, elev. 7,600 ft/2,316 m) was called Shoefly. Today the town is a jumble of old buildings and some fairly salty characters, all with true Western flavor. At the end of a one-way road for most of the year (except during the height of summer when the Beartooth Highway leads visitors up and over the towering peaks), Cooke City has a remarkable sense of community, unlimited recreational opportunities, plenty of accommodations, and some excellent places to fill your belly. Nearby **Silver Gate** (pop. 29, elev. 7,608 ft/2,319 m) is equally scenic and even quieter, the Connecticut to Cooke's New York City. Pilot, Index, and Beartooth Peaks are three of the impressive summits that loom over these twin settlements, beckoning adventurers.

bison on the move in Lamar Valley

The Brucellosis Problem

Yellowstone is the only place in the continental United States where bison have existed since prehistoric times. Current policy mandates that the animals stay within the park's unfenced boundaries, and how best to enforce this is a matter of constant debate.

The park's management of the bison has changed throughout the years, just as bison numbers have fluctuated. Prior to 1967, park authorities would trap and reduce the herd to keep it manageable. After 1967, however, the guiding philosophy changed, and the bison were managed by nature alone. By 1996 the number of bison in the park had grown to 3,500. The size of the herd, coupled with winters that brought significant snowfall, led many of the bison to migrate out of the park in order to find better grazing and calving grounds. The problem of brucellosis played out on the national stage.

Brucellosis is a bacterial infection present in the bison and elk in the Greater Yellowstone area. The disease can cause spontaneous abortions, infertility, and lowered milk production in the infected animal, but the Yellowstone elk and bison populations seem relatively unscathed by the disease, despite the number of animals infected. The same tolerance of the disease is not common among cattle, however. The overwhelming fear is that bison exiting Yellowstone could infect neighboring cattle; this would be gravely detrimental to Montana, Wyoming, and Idaho beef production. Brucellosis cannot be treated in cattle and can be passed on to humans in the form of undulant fever. The government created a fairly simple inoculation program to eradicate the disease in cattle as early as 1934, but brucellosis has never been eliminated from wildlife.

Starting in the 1980s, when more than 50 percent of the park's bison tested positive for the disease, the park's approach was to control the borders with hazing to limit the number of bison that left the park. When hazing was unsuccessful, the bison were shot. The winter of 1996-1997 brought record cold and snow, and bison left the park in large numbers to forage for food; 1,079 bison were shot and another 1,300 starved to death inside the park's boundaries. This incident magnified the problem of maintaining a healthy herd while preventing the spread of brucellosis.

The National Park Service, the U.S. Department of Agriculture, and Montana, Wyoming, and Idaho are working together to see how brucellosis can be eliminated and free-roaming bison protected. A vaccination program has been implemented, with a 65 percent success rate, and the use of quarantine has proven fairly successful. Local bison rancher and wildlife advocate Ted Turner has agreed to accept some of the quarantined bison on his property. A small and highly regulated hunting season on bison is carried out each winter just outside the park boundaries.

But while there are no easy or obvious solutions, there are questions: What about elk, which also carry the disease and have been identified as the source of brucellosis outbreaks among horses in Wyoming and cattle in Idaho? No efforts to limit their natural migration in and out of the park have ever been attempted. Why are bull bison—who can carry the disease but cannot spread it through milk or birthing fluids as females do—quarantined and killed? For now, it seems, we watch, wait, and hope for a healthy, wild, and free-roaming bison population.

Sports and Recreation

The northeastern corner of the park and the area just outside it are a natural playground for fishing, hiking, cross-country and back-country skiing, and snowmobiling.

HIKING AND FISHING

One short but worthwhile hike can be found 1.8 miles (2.9 km) west of the Pebble Creek Campground at **Trout Lake.** The hike itself is short and steep, just 1.2 miles (1.9 km) round-trip, and leaves from the Trout Lake Trailhead on the north side of the road. Anglers can bring a rod after July 15 when it opens to catch-and-release fishing for native cutthroats. In late spring and early summer, trout can be seen spawning in the inches-deep inlet, a fairly miraculous sight. There is an excellent trail around the 12-acre lake and shallow inlet and a decent chance of spotting playful otters, but hikers should take great care not to disturb the fish, especially during spawning. Bear awareness and a can of bear spray are necessary, as the bruins like fish too.

Another great place to combine fishing, hiking, and wildlife-watching—perhaps the perfect Yellowstone trifecta—is along the trail at **Slough Creek.** East of Tower Junction 5.8 miles (9.3 km) or west of the northeast entrance is an unpaved road on the north side of the road leading to Slough Creek Campground. The trailhead is 1.5 miles (2.4 km) down the road on the right side, just before the campground. The trail itself is a double-rutted wagon trail that leads to Silver Tip Ranch, a legendary private ranch just outside the park. The trail is maintained for 11 miles (17.7 km) one-way and only gains 400 feet (122 m) in elevation. All along the trail there is world-class fishing in slow-moving Slough Creek, home to a healthy population of native cutthroat trout. You may meet elk, bison, wolves, and even grizzlies along the trail, so be prepared and be safe.

MOTORIZED RECREATION

With an average of 194 inches (493 cm) of snowfall each year, mountainous terrain with elevation that ranges 7,000-10,000 feet (2,134-3,048 m), and a nearly interminable winter, Cooke City is a winter mecca with 60 miles (97 km) of groomed snowmobile trails and endless acres of ungroomed terrain for skiing and snowmobiling. Some favorite trails are **Daisy Pass, Lulu Pass,** and **Round Creek Trail.**

A number of places in town rent snowmobiles and all the necessary gear. Most important, you'll need to talk with experts about local conditions, trail closures, and avalanche dangers. **Cooke City Motorsports** (203 Eaton St., 406/838-2231, www.cookecitymotorsports.com, snowmobiles $325-385) and **Cooke City Exxon** (204 Main St., 406/838-2244, www.cookecityexxon.com, call for prices and reservations) are obvious choices in town. When the snow melts, you can rent ATVs and side-by-sides from **Bearclaw Sales and Service** (309 E. Main St., 406/838-2040, www.bearclawsalesandservice.com, for 2-6

passengers from $125/hour, $280/half day, $345-385/full day) as another way to get out and cover a lot of ground. They also rent sleds when snow is on the ground ($285-360/day). They rent all the equipment needed in any season, and you can—and should!—buy ($40) or rent ($15/day) bear spray.

Entertainment and Events

Among the biggest events of the year in Cooke City is the annual **Sweet Corn Festival,** a gathering for backcountry skiers and snowboarders usually held in late April on the weekend after the nearby ski hills have closed for the season. The weather is often sublime—think blue skies, cold nights, and warm afternoons—and the snow is like, well, sweet corn. Accommodations are not easy to come by this weekend (even floor space is pretty much spoken for), so plan ahead or bring a tent. Plenty of snowmobilers are on hand to act as taxis, enabling backcountry skiers not to have to earn their turns for once. With some of the best backcountry skiing in the West when the conditions are right, this is a welcome event.

The **Annual Hog Roast** happens in mid-March and attracts a throng of hungry snowmobilers, backcountry skiers, and, more recently, a healthy number of cross-country skiers to Cooke City. The event includes an auction, dinner, and live music.

The popular **Firemen's Picnic** is held annually on July 4, just east of town, with a good old-fashioned parade on Main Street, food, kids' games, and fireworks after dark. Another great small-town event, the **Mount Republic Chapel Bazaar**—where you can buy tools, equipment, winter and summer sports gear, clothing, books, games, and more—is held annually on a Friday and half day Saturday in mid-July.

For some culture on the periphery of Yellowstone's wilderness, check out **Montana Shakespeare in the Parks** in Silvergate Park in July or August.

For more information on any of these events, call or visit Donna—who is as knowledgeable as she is friendly—at the chamber-run **visitor center** (206 W. Main St., 406/838-2495, www.cookecitychamber. org, year-round, hours change seasonally), on the west end of town on the north side of the street; the center also has flush toilets.

Food

There are a million ways to work up an appetite in and around Cooke City. Be assured you won't go hungry (or thirsty, for that matter). ★ **Beartooth Café** (211 Main St., 406/838-2475, www.beartoothcafe.com, 9am-4pm and 5pm-9pm daily late May-late Sept., $13-27) offers excellent mountain fare—think steak and trout—with just a hint of Asian flair. The front-porch outdoor dining is a treat. Another great spot for a quick bite anytime (except April, May, October, and November when it's closed) is the **Bearclaw Bakery** (309 E. Main St., 406/838-2040, 5am-10:30am daily, rolls and coffee served from 5am, hot breakfasts from 6am), which makes from-scratch baked goods, full hearty breakfasts from chorizo toast to breakfast burritos, and light lunch. The bakery also offers a full coffee bar.

The **Prospector Restaurant** (210 US 212, 406/838-2251, www.cookecity.com, 7am-10pm daily, breakfast $6-13, lunch $13-15, dinner $13-28), inside the Soda Butte Lodge, is open year-round and particularly known for steak and prime rib—not a stretch in these parts. The Soda Butte Saloon in the lodge serves standard bar snacks.

Finally, for those wanting to pick up some supplies, the bright red ★ **Cooke City Store** (101 Main St., 406/838-2234, www. cookecitystore.com, 8am-7pm daily mid-May-Sept., hours may vary slightly based on customers and local activity) is as much a local museum and community center as it is a place to pick up some bread and a bottle of sunscreen. At the fly shop inside, **Trout Rider Fly Shop,** you can get fishing licenses for Montana, Wyoming, and Yellowstone National Park as well as pick up some flies and other supplies. It's a wonderful place and worth a visit; plus the nearest grocery store is 90 minutes away.

Accommodations

For a town with a population that hasn't made it to the triple digits yet, Cooke City has an impressive number of places to hang your hat. Lodging runs the gamut from cabins and vacation rentals to roadside motels, chain hotels, and small resorts, although not all of them are open year-round. Most of the photo galleries on the accommodations' websites are images of moose and bears or snowmobiles buried in powder rather than pictures of beds and baths. Clearly, Cooke City has morphed from a mining town into a tourist destination.

Big Moose Resort (715 US 212, 406/838-2393, www.bigmooseresort.com, from $135) is 3 miles (4.8 km) east of town and a great place to set up a base camp if you want to explore the region's trails and rivers. Open year-round, the lodge has a collection of seven old and new cabins, all of which are quite comfortable and can accommodate up to four people. There are no phones in the cabins (and no cell service in the area), but free Wi-Fi is provided, and you can schedule a Swedish massage on-site. The website gets buggy, so sometimes calling or reaching out through Facebook is the better option.

The **Cooke City Super 8** (303 E. Main St., 406/838-2070, www.wyndhamhotels.com, from $101) has rooms that are basic and clean, and the service is exceptionally friendly.

In the heart of bustling Cooke City is the **Soda Butte Lodge** (210 E. Main St., 406/838-2251, www.cookecity.com, $89-189), a full-service hotel with 32 guest rooms, a saloon, and a restaurant. The guest rooms are basic, but you didn't come to Cooke City to hang out in your hotel room.

In nearby Silver Gate, ★ **Silver Gate Lodging** (109 US 212, 406/838-2371, www. silvergatelodging.com, $150-505) offers 29 great cabins, plus motel rooms and a big lodge that can accommodate up to 10 people. Some of the accommodations are pet-friendly, but be sure to ask ahead. The setting is both quiet and communal, with barbecue grills, horseshoe pits, and a playground. And because this is Yellowstone, you can also rent scopes, which will come in plenty handy. The staff know the park backward and forward, so don't hesitate to ask about their favorite places.

Camping

Three Forest Service campgrounds are in the vicinity of Cooke City. **Soda Butte** (406/848-7375, www.fs.usda.gov, June-Labor Day depending on weather, $20/vehicle) is 1 mile (1.6 km) east of Cooke City on US 212. It has 27 sites, restrooms, food boxes, drinking water, and fishing is available nearby. Please note that due to bear activity, this is a hard-sided campground only, and advance reservations are not accepted. Also strictly a hard-sided campground, **Colter Campground** (406/848-7375, www.fs.usda.

gov, June-Labor Day depending on weather, $20/vehicle) is just 2 miles (3.2 km) east of Cooke City and gives campers access to 18 sites, restrooms, food boxes, picnic tables, drinking water, and nearby fishing and hiking trails. Reservations are not accepted, so arrive early and have a backup plan in place.

Fox Creek Campground (307/527-6921, www.fs.usda.gov, July 15-Sept. 7 depending on weather, $20-60) is a larger, newly remodeled 33-site campground 6.7 miles (10.8 km) east of Cooke City on the Beartooth Highway with awesome views of Pilot and Index Peaks. Water is available, as are vault toilets, but cell service is not. Maximum spur length is 32 feet (9.8 m). The campground was closed due to construction on the highway through summer 2021. Reservations are not accepted.

The Southern Loop

Some of the park's biggest highlights are found in the southern loop, along with a significant number of visitors and plentiful wildlife. There are a lot of trees, many of them burned, and not as much dimension to the land as elsewhere, but the southern loop is what many people picture when they think of Yellowstone. From the sweeping Hayden Valley and the otherworldliness of West Thumb Geyser Basin to the sheer size of Yellowstone Lake and the well-deserved hubbub around Old Faithful, this section of the park has an abundance of dynamic features—some world-famous, others hidden gems—for every visitor.

SIGHTS
Hayden Valley

South of Canyon is the expansive and beautiful Hayden Valley, a sweep of grassland carved by massive glaciers named for the famed leader of the 1871 Hayden Expedition and occupied by copious wildlife that includes grizzly bears, wolves, and, in summer, thundering herds of bison. The Yellowstone River weaves quietly

through the valley, and because the soil supports grasses and wildflowers instead of trees, this is one of the most scenic drives in the park, especially during the bison rut and migration in late summer. Besides driving, hiking is an excellent way to explore the valley, either on your own (pay very close attention for signs of bear activity) or with a ranger on weekly **guided hikes** (4-5 hours, early July-late Aug., free). The hikes are limited to 15 people, and reservations must be made in advance at the **Canyon Visitor Education Center** (307/344-2550, 9am-5pm daily in summer) in Canyon Village.

Fishing Bridge

What was once the epicenter of Yellowstone fishing is today a relic of the past and a touchstone for the ongoing struggle between nature and human meddling. Fishing Bridge was built in 1937 and for years considered the best place to throw a line for native cutthroat trout. Humans were not the only ones fishing in the area, and human-grizzly encounters led to 16 grizzly bear deaths. To protect the bears and the fish, fishing in the vicinity was banned in 1973. Today, because of the sharp decline of cutthroat as a direct result of the introduction of nonnative lake trout, grizzlies are not seen as often fishing in the river.

There are some services—an RV park, a gas station, and a general store—and a 1931 log and stone structure that serves as the **Fishing Bridge Visitor Center** (East Entrance Rd., 307/344-2450, closed throughout COVID, so check the website for hours). On the National Register of Historic Places, the visitor center has a collection of stuffed bird specimens worth seeing and an exhibit on the lake's geology, including a relief map of the lake bottom.

★ Yellowstone Lake

Covering 136 square miles, Yellowstone Lake is North America's largest freshwater lake above 7,000 feet (2,134 m). In addition to being spectacularly scenic—both when it is placid and when the waves form whitecaps—the lake is a fascinating study in underwater geothermal activity. Beneath the water—or ice, much of the year—the lake bottom is littered with faults, hot springs, craters, and the miraculous life-forms that can thrive in such conditions. There is also a rather large bulge, some 2,000 feet long, that rises 100 feet above the rest of the lake bottom. The uplift is related to the ever-present geothermal activity beneath Yellowstone. Whether the bulge is gaseous or potentially volcanic in nature is the subject of ongoing research.

Aside from its geological significance, Yellowstone Lake also offers plenty of recreational opportunities, primarily in the form of boating and fishing. The water is bitter cold, though, typically 40-50°F (4-10°C), and not suitable for swimming. Eighteen-foot, 40 horsepower outboards ($62/hour) can be rented mid-June to early September at **Bridge Bay Marina** (307/344-7311 or 866/439-7375), just south of Lake Village or 21 miles (34 km) north of West Thumb. There is great fishing for native cutthroat trout as well. It's worth mentioning that early visitors to the park loved to tell stories about catching fish at the edge of the lake and then dipping their catch in the hot springs at West Thumb Geyser Basin to cook them without taking the fish off the line—a practice that would be seriously frowned upon today. Not to mention, what about the guts?

The rambling pale-yellow **Lake Yellowstone Hotel** was built in 1891 and is an elegant reminder of Yellowstone's bygone era. The lobby and deck, which overlook the

the vast Hayden Valley in summer

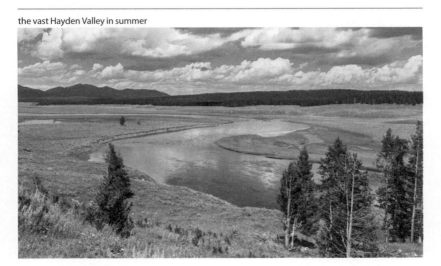

lake, are worth seeing, even if you are not staying here. Grab an iced tea and soak in the views; this is a stunning spot. If you can, stay for a meal and enjoy the live piano music. The crowds will fade as you gaze on the scenery.

West Thumb Geyser Basin

On the western edge of Yellowstone Lake is the eerie West Thumb Geyser Basin, a collection of hot springs, geysers, mud pots, and fumaroles that dump a collective 3,100 gallons of hot water into the lake daily. An excellent boardwalk system guides visitors through the area, but there have been injury-causing bison and bear encounters on the boardwalk, so keep your eyes open.

Abyss Pool is a sensational spring, some 53 feet deep, that transforms in color from turquoise to emerald green to brown and back, depending on a variety of factors. Similarly beautiful, **Black Pool** is no longer black because the particular thermophiles that caused the dark coloration were killed in 1991 when the water temperature rose. **Big Cone** and **Fishing Cone,** surrounded by lake water, are the features that led to the stories of fishing and cooking the catch in a single cast. Called "Mud Puffs" by the 1871 Hayden Expedition, **Thumb Paint Pots** are like miniature reddish mud volcanoes (depending on rainfall, after which they can get soupier) and are an excellent example of mud pots. Throughout the last several years, the mud pots have been particularly active, forming new mud cones and even throwing mud into the air. **Surging Spring** is fun to watch as the dome of water forms and overflows, unleashing a torrent of water on the lake.

Grant Village

On the West Thumb of Yellowstone Lake, Grant Village is a fairly controversial development dating to the 1970s and built in the heart of grizzly bear habitat and among several cutthroat spawning streams. The architecture is ugly, and the location is better suited to wildlife than visitors. In addition to the **Grant Village Visitor Center** (west shore of Yellowstone Lake, 307/344-2650, 8am-5pm

daily Memorial Day-early Oct.), which houses an exhibit dedicated to fire in the Yellowstone ecosystem, accommodations, a campground, and food services are available.

★ Old Faithful

Though often crowded, the **Old Faithful** complex brings together so many of the phenomena—both natural and human-made—that make Yellowstone so special: the landmark geyser and the incredible assortment of geothermal features surrounding it, the wildlife, the grand old park architecture of the Old Faithful Inn, and even the mass of people from around the world who come to witness the famous geyser.

An obvious stop at the Old Faithful complex is the **Old Faithful Visitor Education Center** (Upper Geyser Basin, 307/344-2751, 9am-5pm daily mid-Apr.-early Nov. closed winter/spring of 2022 due to staffing issues), which showcases Yellowstone's hydrothermal features. The $27 million facility hosts 4 million visitors annually. Efficient travelers (who are fighting an uphill battle here most of the time) can call ahead for a recorded message about daily geyser eruption predictions (307/344-2751) or check the NPS Yellowstone App.

Known as the **Upper Geyser Basin,** the area surrounding Old Faithful is the largest concentration of geysers anywhere in the world. By far the most famous is Old Faithful because of its combination of height (although it is not the tallest) and regularity (although it is not the most frequent or most regular). Intervals between eruptions are generally 60-90 minutes and can be predicted according to duration of previous eruptions. Eruptions can last anywhere from 90 seconds to five minutes. It spouts 3,700-8,400 gallons of hot water at heights of 106-184 feet. Signs inside the nearby hotel lobbies and the visitor center, a Twitter feed (@GeyserNPS), and the NPS Yellowstone App keep visitors apprised of the

---

1: Black Pool in West Thumb Geyser Basin **2:** crowd at Old Faithful

next expected eruptions, of which there are an average of 17 in any 24-hour period. Keep in mind that Old Faithful doesn't stop being predictable just because people go to bed or the weather turns cold—some of the most magical eruption viewings can happen without crowds. Choose a full-moon night, any time of year, and be willing to get up in the middle of the night. The vision of Old Faithful erupting in winter with snow and ice, frost, and steam in every direction is unforgettable.

If you take the time to come to Yellowstone to see Old Faithful, take the time—an hour or more is ideal—to walk through the other marvelous features of the Upper Geyser Basin. **Giantess Geyser** can erupt up to 200 feet high in several bursts. The irregular eruptions happen 2-6 times each year and can occur twice hourly, continuing 4-48 hours, and changing the behavior of many of the other geysers in the region. **Doublet Pool,** a colorful hot spring with numerous ledges, is lovely and convoluted. You can actually hear Doublet vibrating and collapsing beneath the surface. Looking something like a fire hose shooting 130-190 feet in the air, **Beehive Geyser** typically erupts twice daily, each eruption lasting 4-5 minutes. **Grand Geyser** is the world's tallest predictable geyser, erupting every 7-15 hours, lasting 9-12 minutes, and reaching heights up to 200 feet. Visible from the road into the Old Faithful complex if you look back over your shoulder, **Castle Geyser** is thought to be the park's oldest. It generally erupts every 10-12 hours, reaches 90 feet in height, and lasts roughly 20 minutes. A 30- to 40-minute noisy steam phase follows the eruptions.

★ Firehole River

Since swimming in Yellowstone Lake is not an option unless you are a trained member of the polar bear club, a dip in the heated (but far from hot!) waters of the Firehole River is one of the nicest ways to spend an afternoon. The designated and somewhat popular swimming area is surrounded by high cliffs and some fast-moving rapids both upstream and downstream, so the area is not recommended for new or young swimmers. The water temperature averages 80°F (27°C), but this avid swimmer would argue that the temperatures feel more like the 70s (about 24°C). Though quite limited, parking is accessible from Firehole Canyon Drive, which leaves the main road south of Madison Junction, less than 1,000 feet (305 m) after crossing the river. There is a toilet available but no lifeguards, so you will be swimming entirely at your own risk.

Midway and Lower Geyser Basins

Between Old Faithful and Madison Junction, along the pastoral Firehole River, are the Midway and Lower Geyser Basins, technically considered part of the same basin. In 1889, Rudyard Kipling dubbed Midway Geyser Basin "hell's half-acre" for its massive hot springs and geysers. Among the most significant features at Midway is **Grand Prismatic Spring,** a colorful and photogenic spring that was immortalized by painter Thomas Moran on the Hayden Expedition. It releases some 560 gallons of water into the Firehole River every minute. At 250 by 380 feet, and 160 feet deep, Grand Prismatic is the third-largest hot spring in the world and the largest in Yellowstone. Now dormant, **Excelsior Geyser Crater** was once the largest geyser in the world, soaring up to 300 feet high. Major eruptions in the 1880s led to a dormancy that lasted more than a century. In 1985, Excelsior erupted continuously for two days but never topped 80 feet. Today, acting as a spring, it discharges more than 4,000 gallons of heated water every minute.

Compared to the much smaller Midway Geyser Basin, the Lower Geyser Basin is enormous, spanning 12 square miles and including several clusters of thermal features. Among them are the notable **Fountain Geyser,** a placid blue pool that erupts on average every 4.5-7 hours for 25-50 minutes and sprays up to 50 feet high, the temperamental **White Dome Geyser,** the almost-constant **Clepsydra,** and the **Pocket Basin Mud Pots,** which are the largest collection of mud pots in the park. **Great Fountain Geyser** in the Firehole Lake area is the only predictable geyser in the Lower Geyser Basin and erupts every 10 hours and 45 minutes, give or take two hours, for up to an hour, reaching heights of 70-200 feet.

SPORTS AND RECREATION

Fishing and Boating

Some 50,000 anglers are lured to Yellowstone each year by the promise of elusive trout, and they are seldom disappointed by the offerings at **Yellowstone Lake.** In addition to the prized native cutthroat, the lake is home to a population of nonnative lake trout that is devastating the cutthroat trout population and threatening all the animals that eat the cutthroat trout. Introduced in 1890 into Lewis and Shoshone Lakes by the U.S. Fish Commission, the lake trout were first documented in Yellowstone Lake in the mid-1990s; scientists believe they were illegally introduced from a nearby lake in the 1980s. The average lake trout live and spawn in deep waters, feeding on as many as 40 cutthroat each year. By comparison, cutthroat trout spawn in the shallow tributaries of the lake, making them an important food source for

a variety of creatures that include eagles and bears. Since the lake trout have no enemies in the deep waters of Yellowstone Lake, they are creating a serious food shortage by devouring the cutthroat. As a result, the eagles are having to eat other birds instead of fish, and Yellowstone is facing the complete elimination of some nesting bird species. All lake trout caught in Yellowstone Lake must be killed. Pick up your **fishing permit** at one of the visitor centers along with a copy of the Yellowstone fishing regulations.

You can see Yellowstone Lake by boat. Scenic or fishing boat tours as well as outboard motor rentals ($62/hour) are available from **Bridge Bay Marina,** south of Lake Village or 21 miles (34 km) northeast of West Thumb. Hour-long cruises on the *Lake Queen* ($19.50 adults, $11.50 children 3-11, free for children under 3) depart regularly from the marina mid-June to mid-September. Reservations can be made through **Xanterra** (307/344-7311 or 866/439-7375, www.yellowstonenationalparklodges.com).

Hiking

The southern loop of the park offers plentiful hiking opportunities, most of which can be combined with other interests. The **Hayden**

Grand Prismatic Spring

Valley has great trails for wildlife lovers, but precautions against bear encounters must be taken. The **Alum Creek Trail,** 4.4 miles (7.1 km) south of Canyon at the north end of the Hayden Valley, is a good hike. Wide open and relatively flat, the trail offers a 10-mile (16.1-km) out-and-back trip through prime bison and grizzly habitat. There are also some thermal features along Alum Creek.

Among the geysers in the Upper Geyser Basin is **Lone Star Geyser,** named for its lonely location 5 miles (8 km) from Old Faithful. An old once-paved road leads to the geyser and makes a nice level hike or bike trip. The entire out-and-back trip is 4.6 miles (7.4 km). There is parking at the trailhead on the south side of the road, 3.5 miles (5.6 km) east of the Old Faithful interchange. Lucky viewers will get to see a 30- to 50-foot eruption, which happens every 2-3 hours and tends to last 10-15 minutes.

FOOD

As the southern loop is generally the most heavily traveled section of the park, there are plenty of dining opportunities. In the park restaurants, breakfast and lunch are on a first-come, first-served basis, but reservations are strongly recommended for dinner, particularly if 5pm or 9pm is not your ideal dining hour. In almost all the venues, you will find some good vegetarian options and many items made with sustainable or organic ingredients; these are identified on each menu. If you are planning a day activity away from the center of things, the restaurants or cafeterias offer box lunches for travelers to take with them. Place your order the night before, and it will be ready in the morning. The Yellowstone General Stores at Grant Village, Lake Village, and Old Faithful also have fast-food service, groceries, and snacks.

The **Grant Village Dining Room** (866/439-7375, check website for hours but generally open daily for breakfast, lunch, and dinner, late May-Sept.) offers a pleasant view of the lake, good service, and a nice variety of American cuisine. In addition to the à la carte menu for breakfast, a buffet is available. Lunch and dinner include dishes such as prime rib sliders, smoked bison bratwurst, or spinach ravioli. Reservations are required for dinner.

The **Lake House** at Grant Village (check website for hours but generally open daily for breakfast, lunch, and dinner, late May-Sept., with shortened hours early/late seasons) sits right on the lake, with great views and a casual ambience. Breakfast is buffet only, and the dinner menu consists of regional fare like huckleberry chicken, wild game meat loaf, prime rib, and lemon pepper trout.

The ★ **Lake Yellowstone Hotel Dining Room** (307/344-7311 or 866/439-7375, check website for hours but generally open daily for breakfast buffet, lunch, and dinner, mid-May-early Oct., reservations required for dinner) is the most elegant dining room in the park, with a gorgeous view of the lake. The restaurant is committed to creating dishes with fresh, local, organic, and sustainable ingredients. Lunch is a good way to sample some of the gourmet fare without putting too large a dent in your pocketbook. Try the delicious organic lentil soup or blackened wild Alaska salmon wrap. Dinner at the hotel is sure to be a memorable experience with options like Montana elk chops, bison tenderloin, and lamb sliders.

Directly inside the hotel is the **Lake Hotel Deli** (check website for hours but generally open all day daily, mid-May-early Sept., shortened hours early/late seasons), which serves a nice selection of soups, salads, and sandwiches. The **Lake Lodge Cafeteria** (check website for hours but generally open daily for breakfast, lunch, and dinner, early June-late Sept., shortened hours early/late seasons) is a casual place for a quick bite. It serves basic breakfast standards, plenty of kids' favorites, and comfort food dishes ranging from spinach pie and fried chicken to apple-glazed pork loin.

Five eateries are located in the Old Faithful complex, but by far the most desirable is the **Old Faithful Inn Dining Room**

(307/344-7311, check website for hours but generally open daily for breakfast buffet, lunch, and dinner, early June-early Sept., shortened hours in May, Sept., early Oct.), which offers a buffet for each of the main meals daily as well as an à la carte menu. You can dine in the historic inn while enjoying its distinct rustic architecture and Western-style ambience. Lunch is a "Western buffet" with items such as farm-raised pan-fried trout, pulled pork, and wild game sausage. If you don't opt for the dinner buffet (featuring prime rib and trout), you could try pork osso buco, penne with local lamb ragout, wild Alaska sockeye salmon, and New York strip steak. Reservations are required for dinner.

The **Bear Paw Deli** (6am-9pm daily late May-early Sept., shortened hours early/late seasons), also inside the inn, is perfect for on-the-go meals. It offers a continental breakfast including bagel sandwiches, and sandwich and salad deli fare for lunch, as well as serving up several flavors of ice cream. In addition to these two eateries at the inn, there is a cafeteria and bakeshop in the lodge and a dining room and grill in the Old Faithful Snow Lodge.

ACCOMMODATIONS

★ **Lake Yellowstone Hotel** (mid-May-early Oct., rooms $285-822, suites from $1,114) is both grand and picturesque, perched on the shores of Yellowstone Lake. Originally built in 1891 and completely renovated in 2014 to celebrate its colonial revival influences, the hotel houses the nicest rooms in the park. As is true everywhere in the park, though, the appeal comes from the location and the views. If you are staying in the hotel, request a room with a view of the lake. An adjacent building, **The Sandpiper Lodge** (from $350) also offers recently renovated rooms. Individual cabins, called Lake Cottages, are behind the hotel but part of the Lake Lodge operation. These duplexes were remodeled in 2004 and are simple and modest.

There are 186 **Lake Lodge Cabins** (mid-June-early Oct., $178-276), which are clean and simple; many were renovated in 2018. Located just off the lake, the cabins are clustered around the main lodge, which is an inviting common area for guests to gather. It has a large porch that beckons guests to take a seat in one of the rocking chairs and soak in the view, as well as two fireplaces, a gift shop, and a cozy lounge. The Western cabins are a bit more spacious, with two queen beds and a shower-tub in each bathroom. The Pioneer cabins are older and more spartan, with shower-only bathrooms and 1-2 double beds. The setting is tranquil and quiet, and early risers may spot a herd of bison wandering through the property.

The ★ **Old Faithful Inn** (early May-early Oct., Old House rooms, standard West Wing rooms, deluxe West Wing rooms and deluxe East Wing rooms $193-506, suites from $942) is the most popular lodging inside the park, and for good reason. The original part of the lodge, known as the Old House, was built in 1903-1904 by acclaimed architect Robert Reamer. Situated close to the Old Faithful geyser, the lodge epitomizes rustic beauty, originality, and strength. It has a large front lobby that houses a massive stone fireplace. The larger rooms are in the wings of the inn, built in the 1910s and 1920s, while the more modest rooms are in the Old House. The inn has a wide assortment of guest rooms and rates, ranging from two-room suites with sitting rooms and fridges to simple rooms without individual baths. Since this is the most sought-after lodging in the park, make reservations well in advance.

Close to the inn are the **Old Faithful Lodge Cabins** (mid-May-late Sept., $116-192), offering much simpler and rustic lodging. If you are looking for budget-friendly accommodations that put you in the center of park activity, these are a good option. The cabins are small motel-style units that vary in condition. Many of them were renovated in 2016. The lower-priced cabins do not come with baths, but there are communal showers nearby. The cabins are scattered around a main log cabin-style lodge. Built in the 1920s, the main lodge has a large cafeteria, bakery, and fully stocked gift shop, making it popular with park visitors throughout the day.

The **Old Faithful Snow Lodge and Cabins** (late Apr.-mid-Oct. and mid-Dec.-late Feb., $146-365) are among the newest accommodations in the park. The original lodge was torn down and a new structure was built in 1999. Its architecture is intended to complement, though not duplicate, the Old Faithful Inn, and the lodge won a Cody Award for Western Design. It offers comfortable, modern rooms decorated with Western flair. It also has a few motel-style cabins, built in 1989. The Western cabins are a good value for the money; they're large rooms with two queen beds and a full bath. This is one of only two lodges (the other is Mammoth Hot Springs Hotel) open during the winter season in Yellowstone.

Grant Village is about 20 miles (32 km) southeast of Old Faithful on the West Thumb of Yellowstone Lake. Although the accommodations do not have the same rustic feel or character of the other lodges, they do offer a comfortable and modern place to stay away from the crowds. The complex is made up of six small condo-like buildings. Each building has 50 nicely furnished hotel rooms (from $306) that come with either two double beds or one queen and full baths. The rooms and exteriors were renovated in 2016.

Reservations for all hotels inside the park should be made through **Xanterra/Yellowstone National Park Lodges** (307/344-7311 or 866/439-7375, www.yellowstonenationalparklodges.com). Note that there are no televisions, radios, telephones, or air-conditioning.

CAMPING

Five of the 12 campsites in the park are in this southern region: **Bridge Bay** (between West Thumb and Lake, late May-early Sept., flush toilets, $28); **Fishing Bridge RV Park** (at Fishing Bridge north of Lake Village, early May-late Sept., flush toilets and pay showers, $50), the only campground offering water and sewer, for hard-sided vehicles only; **Grant Village** (at Grant Village south of West Thumb, late June-mid-Sept., flush toilets, $33); **Lewis Lake** (at Lewis Lake south of Grant Village, early-June-early Nov., vault toilets, $20); and **Madison** (at Madison Junction between the west entrance and Old Faithful, late Apr.-mid-Oct., flush toilets, $28). Advance reservations (307/344-7311 or 866/439-7375) or same-day reservations (307/344-7901) can be made at Bridge Bay, Fishing Bridge RV Park, Grant Village, and Madison.

West Yellowstone

West Yellowstone (pop. 1,376, elev. 6,667 ft/2,032 m) has something of a split personality—hard-core athletes training for the Olympics next to hard-core snowmobilers aiming for high-marking honors; get-too-close tourists alongside bison activists who try to put themselves in the line of fire. The winters are huge, with snow that buries everything but this town's spirit. The region shines with sensational recreational opportunities, from guided snow coach and cross-country skiing excursions to snowmobiling and dogsledding. The winters look interminable with piles of snow still scattered around town well into May and sometimes June, but with so much sun and so much to do, residents never complain about the cold.

The summers tend to be crowded as most people going to Old Faithful come through "West," as the town is known locally. With crystal-clear alpine lakes and rivers in every direction, there is no shortage of summer recreation—fishing opportunities are phenomenal, and there are plenty of places to cycle. As the hub of the region and the busiest entrance to Yellowstone National Park, West Yellowstone has plenty of good grub plus lots of comfortable beds in and around town.

SIGHTS
★ Grizzly and Wolf Discovery Center

If you have your heart set on seeing a grizzly or a wolf in Yellowstone, here's my advice: Get it out of the way before you even go into the park, like a first kiss on a first date before you order dinner. The **Grizzly and Wolf Discovery Center** (201 S. Canyon St., 406/646-7001 or 800/257-2570, www.grizzlyctr.givecloud.co, 9am-4pm daily but hours may change with the season, year-round, $15 ages 13 and over, $14 seniors 62 and over, $10 children 5-12, free for children under 5, admission valid for two consecutive days) is a nonprofit organization that acts something like an orphanage, giving homes to problem, injured, or abandoned animals that have nowhere else to go. Although there is something melancholy about watching these incredible beasts confined to any sort of enclosure, particularly on the perimeter of a chunk of wilderness as massive as Yellowstone, there is also something remarkable about seeing them close enough to count their whiskers. Watching a wolf pack interact from a comfy bench behind floor-to-ceiling windows in the warming hut is a worthwhile way to spend an afternoon. The naturalists on staff are excellent at engaging with visitors of all ages and have plenty to teach everyone.

One fantastic opportunity for curious children ages 5-12 is the **Keeper Kids** program, which is offered twice daily during the summer season. For roughly 30 minutes, the kids learn about grizzly eating habits and behavior. They get to then go into the grizzly enclosure, while the bears are locked away obviously, and hide buckets of food for the bears. When the kids exit and the bears come racing out to search for their treats—overturning massive logs and boulders in the process—the kids (and their parents!) are mesmerized. Enrollment is first-come first-served, and signup happens at the admissions counter at least 15 minutes ahead of the program.

There are also educational programs like **Raptor Rap**, about the raptors, as well as bear spray demonstrations and other programs on the wolves and bears. The center has gone to great lengths to share the personal story of each animal and why it cannot survive in the wild. They also give the bears all sorts of games and tasks—aiding in the design of bear-proof garbage cans is one example. Since these bears do not hibernate, this is a stop absolutely worth making any time of the year. Ultimately, this is a really nice place to learn a lot about bears, wolves, and raptors before heading into the park to look for them in the wild.

Yellowstone Giant Screen Theatre

Montana's first giant screen, the **Yellowstone Giant Screen Theatre** (101 S. Canyon St., 406/646-4100 or 888/854-5862, www.yellowstonegiantscreen.com, premium seating for feature films $15.75 adults, $15.25 seniors, $13 children 4-12; regular seating for feature films $11.75 adults, $11.25 seniors, $9 children) boasts a six-story-high screen with stereo surround sound that makes any subject larger than life. Nature-oriented movies rotate in and out, as do popular movies like the *Dune* and the newest Marvel Studio and other action or sci-fi flicks that benefit from the massive screen, but *Yellowstone* (premium seating $13.75 adults, $13.25 seniors, $11 children, regular seating $9.75 adults, $9.25 seniors, $7 children) is frequently on the playlist and offers an extraordinary introduction to the park's history, wildlife, geothermal activity, and mountainous beauty with giant screen grandeur. The biggest bargain in town is the 50-cent soft-serve ice cream available daily at the theater.

SPORTS AND RECREATION
Fishing

The fishing around West tends to be as plentiful as it is phenomenal. In addition to the

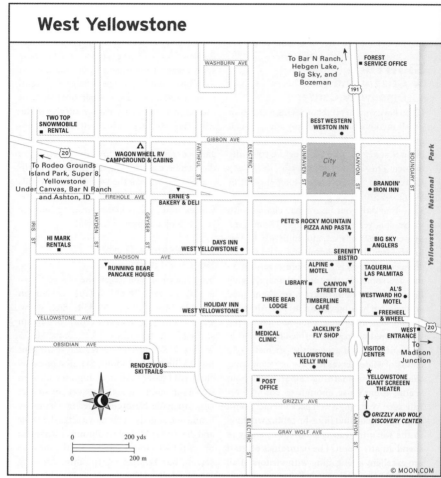

West Yellowstone

WASHBURN AVE

To Bar N Ranch, Hebgen Lake, Big Sky, and Bozeman

191

■ FOREST SERVICE OFFICE

TWO TOP SNOWMOBILE ■ RENTAL

BEST WESTERN WESTON INN ●

GIBBON AVE

20

To Rodeo Grounds Island Park, Super 8, Yellowstone Under Canvas, Bar N Ranch and Ashton, ID

WAGON WHEEL RV CAMPGROUND & CABINS

FAITHFUL ST

ELECTRIC ST

DUNRAVEN ST

City Park

CANYON ST

BOUNDARY ST

Yellowstone National Park

FIREHOLE AVE

ERNIE'S BAKERY & DELI

BRANDIN' ● IRON INN

IRIS ST

HI MARK RENTALS ■

HAYDEN ST

GEYSER ST

DAYS INN WEST YELLOWSTONE ●

PETE'S ROCKY MOUNTAIN PIZZA AND PASTA

BIG SKY ANGLERS ■

MADISON AVE

SERENITY BISTRO

RUNNING BEAR PANCAKE HOUSE

ALPINE ● MOTEL

TAQUERIA LAS PALMITAS

LIBRARY ■

CANYON STREET GRILL

AL'S WESTWARD HO ● MOTEL

HOLIDAY INN WEST YELLOWSTONE ●

THREE BEAR LODGE ●

TIMBERLINE CAFÉ

■ FREEHEEL & WHEEL

YELLOWSTONE AVE

MEDICAL CLINIC

JACKLIN'S FLY SHOP

■ WEST ENTRANCE

20

OBSIDIAN AVE

YELLOWSTONE KELLY INN ●

VISITOR CENTER

To Madison Junction

RENDEZVOUS SKI TRAILS

■ POST OFFICE

★ YELLOWSTONE GIANT SCREEEN THEATER

GRIZZLY AVE

ELECTRIC ST

CANYON ST

✪ GRIZZLY AND WOLF DISCOVERY CENTER

GRAY WOLF AVE

0   200 yds

0   200 m

© MOON.COM

big-name rivers like the **Madison, Firehole, Yellowstone,** and the nearby **Henry's Fork** across the border in Idaho, there are all sorts of small streams and beautiful lakes of all sizes. **Hebgen Lake** and **Quake Lake** are two favorites for year-round fishing.

You won't have any difficulty finding guides and gear in the town of West Yellowstone. Among the best is **Big Sky Anglers** (formerly Bud Lilly's Trout Shop, 39 Madison Ave., 406/646-7801, www.bigskyanglers.com, 7am-10pm daily during the season, 9am-5pm daily in the off-season, from $649 full-day walk/

wade or float trip for 2 anglers, $299 walk/wade clinic for 1-2 anglers), which has been outfitting and guiding anglers for 60 years. They also offer guided interpretive tours into the park. Another pretty famous name among anglers is Bob Jacklin of **Jacklin's Fly Shop** (105 Yellowstone Ave., 406/646-7336, www.jacklinsflyshop.com, 7am-10pm daily in summer, 8am-6pm daily in the off-season, $550 full-day guided float for 1-2 people; $450 half-day guided walk/wade for 1-2 people). Both outfitters are licensed to guide in and out of Yellowstone National Park, and both carry an excellent assortment of top-of-the-line gear. Bob is also happy to give private casting lessons for beginning anglers; call for rates. Anglers do not need state fishing licenses in Yellowstone, but a Yellowstone fishing permit—available at any of the visitor centers in the park—is required.

Mountain Biking and Cross-Country Skiing

Sandwiched between Yellowstone and the Gallatin National Forest on a high plateau, West Yellowstone offers excellent terrain for mountain biking. Because of its high altitude and location at the top of a reasonably flat plateau, West Yellowstone is also known for its cross-country ski trails. The town's excellent **Rendezvous Ski Trails** (look for the archway at the south end of Geyser St., 406/646-7701, www.skirunbikemt.com, passes required Dec.-Mar., $15 day pass, $30 3-day pass, children 12 and under ski free) offer roughly 22 miles (35 km) of gently rolling terrain, groomed for both skate and classic skiers, which easily converts to a single-track for mountain bikers and trail runners when the snow melts. Athletes from around the world come to train in West thanks in large part to this trail system. And it should be noted that the proximity to Yellowstone opens up a whole new world of opportunity for both mountain bikers and skiers.

The best bike and ski shop in town—which also has surprisingly stylish clothes, great gear, a Pilates studio, and killer coffee—is the **Freeheel & Wheel** (33 Yellowstone Ave., 406/646-7744, www.freeheelandwheel.com, 9am-7pm Mon.-Sat., 9am-6pm Sun. summer, 9am-5pm daily fall-spring). It rents, sells, and services bikes and skis and can offer any advice you could possibly need on the region's best rides and trails. Front suspension kid and adult mountain bikes and road bikes can be rented ($40/day) and come with a helmet and water bottle. Skate skis, classic waxable skis, and backcountry touring skis are all rentable for $35/day. Touring ski packages (for machine groomed or skier groomed trails) and snowshoes are available for $30/day. Pull sleds can be rented for $25/day. Any of this gear can be delivered to your hotel for $5/package. For those who want to rent e-bikes, **High Mark Rentals** (633 Madison Ave., 406/646-7855, www.highmarkrentals.com, $69/day) is the place. They also rent bear spray for $5/day—no money was ever better spent—and backpacks ($5/day).

Other Winter Recreation

Although snowmobiling inside the park has shifted with the four-stroke engine and guide requirements along with daily entry limits, West Yellowstone is still considered the snowmobile capital of the world for its proximity to the 200 miles (320 km) of groomed trails in the park as well as hundreds of miles of groomed terrain in the national forests surrounding West.

There are numerous places in town to rent a snowmobile, and since the park mandates that all snowmobilers within park boundaries use a guide, several outfits also offer guiding services both in and out of the park. **Two Top Snowmobile Rentals** (645 Gibbon Ave., 800/522-7802 or 406/646-7802, www.yellowstonevacations.com) has rentals for self-guided tours outside the park for $155-190 for single-riding machines and $200 for double-riding machines. Guided tours into the park start at $270 for a single-riding machine and $290 for a double-riding machine. They also have licensed guides, Yellowstone-mandated four-stroke engines, and other rental equipment, including clothing. Another outfit in town offering snowmobile, ATV, electric bike, and bike rentals is **High Mark Rentals** (633 Madison Ave., 406/646-7855, www.highmarkrentals.com, touring sleds $190-210, mountain sleds $230-260, high performance sleds for experts only $350-400). They rent Polaris, Ski-Doo, and Arctic Cat machines, and are the only place in town to rent SLP Stage 2 snowmobiles for experienced riders who want extra power for climbing and speed. Importantly, they also rent avalanche packs, beacons, and radios.

Spring Biking Through the Park

For a few magical weeks between the end of the snowmobile season and the onset of the summer car traffic, Yellowstone's roads are open exclusively to nonmotorized users. This means that bicyclists, walkers, runners, inline skaters, and roller skiers can cruise through the park in near silence with eyes focused on bison traffic as opposed to wide Winnebagos. Depending on the seasonal snow, the road between the West Entrance and Mammoth Hot Springs typically opens the last Friday in March and stays open to nonmotorized users until the third Thursday in April. Opening can be delayed in heavy snow years due to the need for plowing.

Sometime in May there is normally a brief period of bicycle-only traffic permitted from the East Entrance to the east end of Sylvan Pass, and from the South Entrance to West Thumb Junction. The roads between Madison Junction and Old Faithful, and Norris Junction to Canyon, remain closed to all traffic during this spring season for human safety and bear management.

There is something truly spellbinding about being on the open road in the park, the wind whistling through your helmet. The relative silence allows some unrivaled wildlife-viewing and necessitates great care. As nerve-racking as it can be to get engulfed by a herd of bison while driving in your car, coming across them on your bike is an entirely different scenario. Still, if you are cautious and respectful, being on your bike can allow you to feel somewhat less like an intruder and more like a resident. You can fall into sync with the flow of the rivers, the movement of the breeze, and the calls of the animals. It is an unforgettable way to experience the park.

With that said: Respect, restraint, and absolute caution are of vital importance to your safety and the well-being of the animals. Keep a good distance from all wildlife—25 yards/meters from ungulates and 100 yards/meters from predators. Remember that bison can run at speeds topping 30 mph (48 kph), and they can jump a 6-foot fence. Harbor no illusions about your immunity from an attack. The fact that you have approached silently allows for more of a startle factor for the animals and increases the likelihood of a conflict. Wear a helmet, and dress in layers: Yellowstone in spring can go from blue skies to blizzard conditions in a staggeringly short period of time. Be prepared for anything, and understand that there are no services in the park at this time. Enjoy this unique opportunity to savor the park up close. For specific information about road conditions, call 307/344-2109 (8am-4:30pm Mon.-Fri.).

For those who want to explore the backcountry outside Yellowstone National Park in a slightly quieter way, dogsledding might be the perfect choice. **Yellowstone Dog Sled Adventures** (406/223-5134, www.yellowstonedogsledadventures.com) offers half-day "Learn to Mush" tours ($235 adults, $150 children 5-12) where guests get to drive their own sled, which are appropriate for ages 5 and up. Other offerings allow guests to cuddle up in a sled while an experienced musher does the driving ($135 adult, $75 kids 12 and under).

Another amazing way to see the park is on a guided snow coach tour. Transportation between Old Faithful and Mammoth ($137 adult, $68.50 child), and an array of guided tours, can be arranged through **Yellowstone National Park Lodges** (307/344-7311, www.yellowstonenationalparklodges.com). Day tours of the Grand Canyon (from $237.50 adults, $118.75 children) include the Hoodoos, Swan Lake Flats, Obsidian Cliff and Roaring Mountain; night tours focus on steam, stars, and winter soundscapes (from $64.50). Other tours whisk visitors through a winter wonderland to destinations like West Thumb Geyser Basin (from $87 adults, $43.50 children) and the Firehole Basin (from $80 adults, $40 children).

1: a grizzly in Yellowstone 2: West Yellowstone

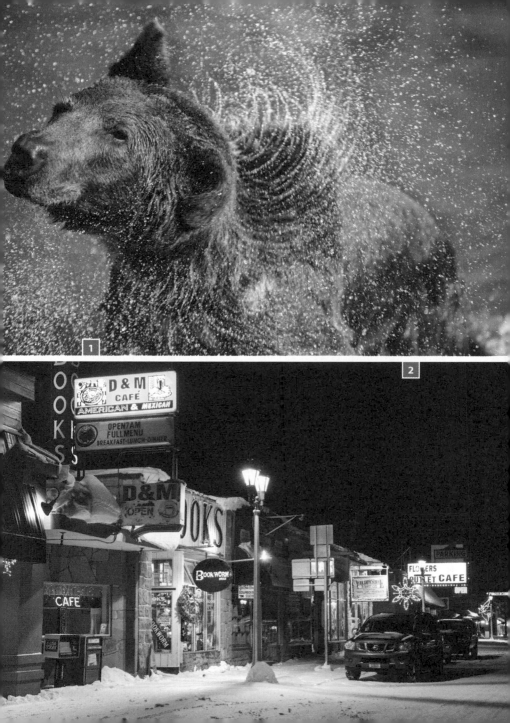

ENTERTAINMENT AND EVENTS

There is plenty for visitors to do year-round in West Yellowstone. Before you arrive, you may want to visit the chamber of commerce **events calendar** (www.destinationyellowstone.com) to scope out the current happenings. The **West Yellowstone Visitor Information Center** (30 Yellowstone Ave., 406/646-7701) also has information on programs like ranger-led educational Yellowstone National Park afternoon and evening programs and snow-shoe walks through the park in winter, free Music in the Park evenings, and weekly West Yellowstone rodeo shows in summer.

The **Yellowstone Rendezvous Race** (www.rendezvousskitrails.com or www.skirunbikemt.com), a one-day cross-country ski competition, is the largest event of the year. It usually takes place in early March, and 600-900 skiers come to participate. Six races are held concurrently, based on age and ability, over distances of 2-50 kilometers (1.2-31 mi). The **Kids 'N' Snow Youth Ski Festival** (www.kidsnsnow.org) is a newer event held the day after the Rendezvous Race. To encourage families to stay after the race, there are ski events (including a relay race, an obstacle course, and even musical chairs) for children 13 and younger. Throughout the ski season, look for such fun events as the monthly **Moonlight Skiing & Snowshoeing, Free Ski Day and Try It Biathlon** (Jan. 2), and **Taste of the Trails** (mid-Feb.).

The **Annual Mountain Bike Biathlon** (406/599-4464, www.skirunbike.com) takes place in June or July. There are two divisions, and first-timers are welcome to participate. The Match Class is for participants with experience and their own rifles; the Sport Class is for novices. The race covers 7.5 kilometers (4.7 mi) with two bouts of shooting. If you'd like to get some practice in before the event, you can sign up for the **Biathlon Shooting Camp** (406/599-4465) in August.

The **Wild West Yellowstone Rodeo**

(175 Oldroyd Rd., 406/560-6913, www.yellowstonerodeo.com, $15 adults, $8 children) is another summertime event that runs June-August. Shows begin at 8pm and are held Tuesday-Saturday June-August; tickets are available online or at the gate.

FOOD

A great spot for a full breakfast, hot lunch, or terrific sack lunches is the long-standing **Ernie's Bakery & Deli** (406 Hwy. 20, 406/646-9467, www.erniesbakery.com, 7am-3pm daily summer, 7am-2pm daily winter, breakfast $8-13, lunch $9-14, box lunch $9-19). **Running Bear Pancake House** (538 Madison Ave., 406/646-7703, www.runningbearph.com, 6:30am-2pm daily, $8-16, box lunch $11.50) offers family-style dining for breakfast and lunch.

For the best soup, salad, and potato bar in town, try the **Timberline Café** (135 Yellowstone Ave., 406/646-9349, 6:30am-4pm and 5pm-10pm daily mid-May-early Oct., breakfast and lunch $7-16, dinner $11-38), an old-school establishment that has been feeding Yellowstone visitors and locals during the summer season since the early 1900s. Don't miss the homemade pie.

Canyon Street Grill (22 N. Canyon St., 406/646-7548, 8am-8pm daily May-Oct., reduced off-season hours, $6-17) is a 1950s-style diner with delicious burgers, fries, onion rings, sandwich baskets, and milk shakes. **Pete's Rocky Mountain Pizza and Pasta** (112 Canyon St., 406/646-7820, www.petesrockymountainpizza.com, 4:30pm-10pm summer, seasonal hours vary, delivery available after 5pm, entrées $13-18, large pizzas $20-27) serves up good pizza and hearty pasta dishes like elk sausage spaghetti and Italian buffalo ravioli. They do have gluten-free pizza offerings too.

Firehole Bar-B-Que Company (120 Firehole Ave., 406/641-0020, www.fireholebbqco.com, look online or call ahead for seasonal hours, closed November-April) smokes their meats daily, and the flavor comes out in this Central Texas style barbecue. From pulled pork and brisket to ribs and buffalo sausage, these folks serve up the real deal and they're open summer and fall, but only until they sell out the day's meat, which can often be well before sunset.

If you like Mexican street food, the best place within a day's drive from Yellowstone is, without a doubt, ★ Taqueria Las Palmitas (21 N. Canyon St., 208/760-8174, 11am-10pm daily early Apr.-mid-Oct., $5-15), known locally as "The Taco Bus." We're talking soft tacos, beans, and more, piled onto paper plates and served in an old school bus. It couldn't be less fancy or more satisfying.

For a more gourmet experience, Serenity Bistro (38 N. Canyon St., 406/646-7660, 11am-3pm and 5pm-10 daily May-Oct., $10-36) is undoubtedly the place. It serves excellent, fresh meals utilizing local ingredients whenever possible. Entrées include the bistro burger, Panang chicken, seafood pasta, trout, buffalo tortellini, elk tenderloin, and twice-cooked quail. Pasta lovers won't want to miss the butternut squash. The bistro offers gourmet salads and sandwiches for lunch and boasts the most extensive wine list in town.

Six miles (9.7 km) outside of town is the Bar N Ranch (890 Buttermilk Creek Rd., 406/333-0534, www.bar-n-ranch.com, 7am-10am and 5pm-10pm daily mid-May-mid-Oct. and mid-Dec.-early Mar., $15-45), a wonderful place for a meal. With beautiful views all around, you can indulge in terrific Western gourmet cuisine including game burgers, bison stir-fry, steaks, and pasta. One favorite is the campfire tacos with pulled pork, jalapeño slaw, and barbecue aioli. Gourmet picnic lunches are available too.

ACCOMMODATIONS

In the summer months there are more than 2,000 hotel rooms to be found in West and about 1,300 when the snow covers the ground. Guest ranches, bed-and-breakfasts, and cabin rentals are also available. See Yellowstone (800/221-1151, www.seeyellowstone.com) is a full-service travel agency in West Yellowstone that can book everything from accommodations and private tours to complete packages. The West Yellowstone Chamber of Commerce (406/646-7701, www.destinationyellowstone.com) also has an excellent website that shows all lodging availability.

Open year-round, the Three Bear Lodge (217 Yellowstone Ave., 406/646-7353 or 800/646-7353, www.threebearlodge.com, $69-329) offers 44 guest rooms in its recently remodeled pet-friendly motel unit and 26 in the lodge, where no two rooms are alike. All guest rooms have a refrigerator, a microwave, an LCD TV, handmade furniture, and fluffy duvets.

The Alpine Motel (120 Madison Ave., 406/646-7544, www.alpinemotelwest yellowstone.com, May-Oct., $85-215) is a budget-friendly choice with a variety of units, some including kitchens, just two blocks from the park entrance. The service by owners Brian and Patty is noticeably good. Another good independent property, open mid-May to mid-October, is Al's Westward Ho Motel (16 Boundary St., 888/645-7331, www.alswestwardhomotel. net, $119-225), which has newly remodeled double queen rooms and air conditioning. It's just across the street from the park entrance and the Yellowstone Giant Screen Theatre. A couple of blocks farther from the entrance, but a long-standing and reliable choice in town, is the 79-room, pet-friendly Brandin' Iron Inn (201 Canyon, 406/646-9411 or 800/217-4613, www.brandiniron. com, $79-319).

Larger chain hotels in town include three Best Western options, the nicest of which is probably the Best Western Weston Inn (103 Gibbon Ave., 406/646-7373, www. bestwestern.com, from $290). Other options include Holiday Inn West Yellowstone (315 Yellowstone Ave., 406/646-7365 or 800/315-2621, www.ihg.com, $123-487), Days Inn West Yellowstone (301 Madison, 406/646-7656, www.daysinn.com, from $99), Yellowstone Kelly Inn (104 S. Canyon, 406/646-4544, www.yellowstonekellyinn.

com, $90-424), and, 7.5 miles (12.1 km) from town, **West Yellowstone Super 8** (1545 Targhee Pass, 406/646-9584, www. wyndhamhotels.com, $89-269).

CAMPING

With nearly two dozen private and public campgrounds in the vicinity of West, campers have plenty of choices, although most are geared to RV campers. The nearest U.S. Forest Service campground is **Baker's Hole Campground** (US 191, 3 mi/4.8 km northwest of West Yellowstone, 406/823-6961, www.hebgenbasincampgrounds.com, May 15-Sept. 30 depending on weather, $20 for 2 vehicles, $8 for each additional vehicle, $28 for electrical sites), with 73 sites (33 with electricity) set on a scenic oxbow of the Madison River. Basic services such as water and trash pickup are provided, there is firewood for sale ($6), and the fishing is excellent.

Right in town, just six blocks from the park's west entrance, is **Wagon Wheel RV Campground & Cabins** (408 Gibbon Ave., 626/848-3080, www.yellowstonerv.com, mid-May-mid-Oct., $59-79 full-hookup pull-through sites), offering a forested and quiet setting for RV camping only. Free Wi-Fi is available in some public areas.

For a truly unique experience outside of town, ★ **Under Canvas Yellowstone** (890 Buttermilk Creek Rd., 406/219-0441, www.undercanvas.com, Memorial Day-Labor Day) offers "glamping" (glamour-camping) options ($229-779) ranging from modest tipis and safari tents to luxury safari suite tents with king-size beds, private baths with freestanding tubs, and woodstoves. A variety of options are available, from shared bathrooms (the hot water showers are provided by a generator that runs from 6am to 11pm and is not quiet) to private but separate baths, influencing the price. But all of these tents and tipis are set in a mountain-ringed meadow with a creek running through. And the bedding is nothing short of luxurious. The guests are largely international, and it can be a treat to listen to campfire or next-tent pillow talk in several different languages. The only downside is that snoring is universally annoying, and with all but the most expensive tents situated so close together, light sleepers are bound to hear plenty of snorers. Still, this is comfortable camping without the work.

INFORMATION AND SERVICES

The **West Yellowstone Chamber of Commerce** (406/646-7701, www.destination yellowstone.com), **Montana State Visitor Center,** and **Yellowstone Park Visitor Center** (307/344-2876) are all housed under the same roof at 30 Yellowstone Avenue. You can get all the information you need about the city and the state, and you can even buy your park permits. The visitor center also has a lot of information about the regular and special events held in town.

The **West Yellowstone Public Library** (23 N. Dunraven St., 406/646-9017, 10am-6pm Tues.-Fri., 10am-2pm Sat. mid-May-Sept.; 10am-5pm Tues.-Fri., 10am-1pm Sat. Oct.-mid-May) is between Yellowstone and Madison Avenues. It offers free Wi-Fi and has three computers with Internet access. Residents 18 and older with a library card can check out a hot spot for 14 days, and a telescope for up to a week.

The town's only **post office** (209 Grizzly Ave., 406/646-7704, 8:30am-5pm Mon.-Fri.) is at the corner of Electric Street and Grizzly Avenue.

Swan Cleaners (520 Madison Ave., 406/646-7892, 8am-8pm daily) is just east of the Running Bear Pancake House. It has coin-operated machines and wash-and-fold laundry services (9am-3pm Mon.-Fri.).

For nonemergency medical care, you can walk into the **Community Health Partners-West Yellowstone Clinic** (11 Electric St., 406/646-9441, www.chphealthmt.org, 9am-6pm Mon. and Thurs., 8am-5pm Tues.-Wed. and Fri. in high season, winter hours start Oct. 30). There is 24-hour paramedic emergency service available in town by calling 911.

Grand Teton National Park

Just south of Yellowstone, Grand Teton National Park is even more dazzling in alpine splendor than its more prominent neighbor. The Tetons soar skyward, three in a sea of 12 peaks topping 12,000 feet (3,658 m).

The mountains are young—still growing, in fact—and utterly spectacular, perhaps the most dramatic anywhere in the Lower 48. The park itself contains approximately 310,000 acres (roughly 15 percent the size of Yellowstone), 100 miles (161 km) of paved road, and much to the delight of hikers, some 200 miles (320 km) of trails.

Like Yellowstone, Grand Teton is home to healthy populations of wildlife—this is among the best places in the West to see a moose—but the rugged terrain and limited number of roads afford the animals

Highlights

Look for ★ to find recommended sights, activities, dining, and lodging.

★ **Cruise to Elk Island:** Lure yourself out of bed and into this wonderland with an early morning cruise (page 90).

★ **Oxbow Bend:** This hairpin curve of slow-moving backwater from the Snake River is perfect for novice boaters, wildlife watchers, and photographers (page 92).

★ **Signal Mountain:** Follow this exciting drive with expansive views of the entire valley (page 92).

★ **Jenny Lake:** Resting like a mirror at the base of the Tetons, this alpine lake is a gem for hikers, boaters, and picnickers (page 98).

★ **Hidden Falls and Inspiration Point:** The glorious views along this popular hike are worth every step (page 99).

★ **Craig Thomas Discovery and Visitor Center:** This architectural gem—complete with video rivers running beneath your feet and walls of windows that showcase the Tetons—offers a stunning introduction to the park (page 103).

★ **Laurance S. Rockefeller Preserve:** The longtime summer home of the Rockefeller family, this lovely preserve exemplifies the family's commitment to stewardship (page 104).

Yellowstone National Park

Grand Teton National Park

0   5 mi

0   5 km

Cruise to Elk Island

Oxbow Bend

Jenny Lake

Moran

Hidden Falls and Inspiration Point

Signal Mountain

Moose Junction

Kelly

IDAHO
WYOMING

Teton Village

Craig Thomas Discovery and Visitor Center

Laurance S. Rockefeller Preserve

Jackson

© MOON.COM

better places to hide. Still, you always need to be prepared for bear encounters in the park. Beyond the fascinating natural and geological history of the region, Grand Teton offers some interesting human-built attractions—including the historic and elegant Jenny Lake Lodge, the Chapel of the Transfiguration, and the Laurance S. Rockefeller Preserve—that are well worth seeing. At the end of the day, though, Grand Teton is a place for nature lovers and outdoors enthusiasts. The vistas are unparalleled, as are the recreational opportunities.

PLANNING YOUR TIME

Grand Teton National Park is smaller, and in some ways more manageable, than its northerly neighbor. There are only 100 miles (161 km) of paved road, all of which can be driven easily in less than a day's time. With fewer accommodations than Yellowstone, Grand Teton lends itself to easy day trips from various locations in Wyoming, such as **Jackson Hole** or **Dubois,** 65 miles (105 km) from the east entrance. **Cody** is about a three-hour drive from the park, via Yellowstone, so overnighting there is an option when rooms cannot be found any closer. A destination in its own right, Grand Teton is a paradise for outdoors enthusiasts. Hikers, bikers, boaters, and, in winter, cross-country skiers will have no problem coming up with marvelous weeklong itineraries. Still, for those on a time budget, you can get an excellent sampling of the park in two days, but even if you are just driving through, there are a few places that should not be missed.

While summer is by far the busiest time in the park, spring and fall can be magnificent with wildflowers, golden aspens, and more active wildlife. **Hiking** and **climbing** in the Tetons is best done in summer and early fall, after the winter snow has melted and before it starts flying again. Still, snow squalls and bad weather can surprise hikers at any time of year, so come prepared. Park rangers offer educational programs throughout the year that are an excellent way to make the most of the time you have. In the fall, for example, drivers can join ranger-led **wildlife caravans** from the Craig Thomas Discovery and Visitor Center that guide visitors to the best places to see wildlife that day. **Ranger-led hikes and eco-talks** are geared to the seasons and offer visitors an insiders' look at the park.

The National Park Service offers an excellent **trip-planning tool online** (www.nps. gov), or you can order a booklet by mail by calling 307/739-3600.

INFORMATION AND SERVICES

Visit the website of the **National Park Service** (www.nps.gov) to help plan your trip to Grand Teton. In the section titled Plan Your Visit, you'll find answers to most of your pressing questions. When you enter the park, you will receive a copy of the park newspaper, *Grand Teton Guide,* which has a lot of useful information about park facilities, hours of operation, and programs and specific activities offered daily or weekly. If you need additional information before you go, you can call the **visitors information line** (307/739-3300, ext. 1). For campground information, call the **Grand Teton Lodge Company** (307/543-3100 or 307/543-2811) or check www.recreation.gov; for **backcountry** information, contact the permits office (307/739-3309) or book backcountry sites online (www. recreation.gov) in advance.

Park Fees and Passes

Single-entry entrance fees are $35 per vehicle, $20 per person for hikers or bicyclists, and $30 per motorcycle for seven days in both Grand Teton National Park and Yellowstone National Park. Entrance permits are also required for the multi-use pathway and are available for purchase at an automated fee station next to

---

Previous: Grand Teton National Park; canoes at Jenny Lake; Hidden Falls.

Grand Teton National Park

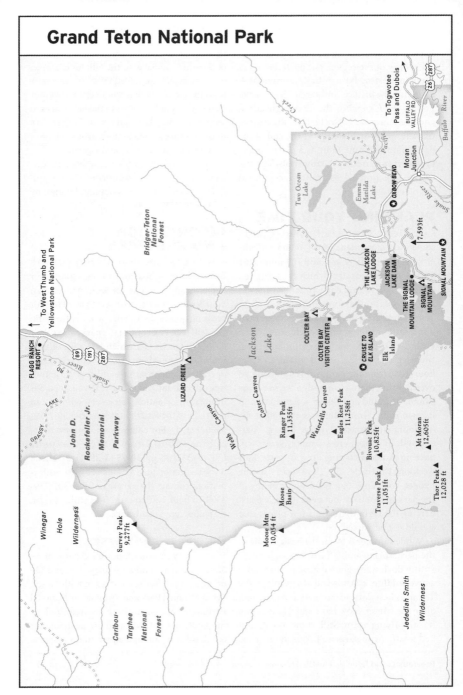

To Togwotee
Pass and Dubois

26 287

BUFFALO
VALLEY RD

Buffalo River

Pacific

Moran
Junction

Two Ocean
Lake

Emma
Matilda
Lake

Snake River

OXBOW BEND

Bridger-Teton
National
Forest

THE JACKSON
LAKE LODGE

JACKSON
LAKE DAM

THE SIGNAL
MOUNTAIN LODGE

7,593ft

SIGNAL
MOUNTAIN

SIGNAL MOUNTAIN

To West Thumb and
Yellowstone National Park

COLTER BAY

COLTER BAY
VISITOR CENTER

Jackson
Lake

CRUISE TO
ELK ISLAND

Elk
Island

FLAGG RANCH
RESORT

89 191

287

Snake River

LIZARD CREEK

John D.
Rockefeller Jr.
Memorial
Parkway

GRASSY
LAKE

RD

Colter Canyon

Webb Canyon

Colter Canyon

Ranger Peak
11,355ft

Waterfalls Canyon

Eagles Rest Peak
11,258ft

Bivouac Peak
10,825ft

Mt Moran
12,605ft

Winegar
Hole
Wilderness

Survey Peak
9,277ft

Moose
Basin

Moose Mtn
10,054 ft

Traverse Peak
11,051ft

Thor Peak
12,028 ft

Caribou-
Targhee
National
Forest

Jedediah Smith
Wilderness

© MOON.COM

GRAND TETON NATIONAL PARK

Avoid the Crowds

(OR, BETTER YET, MANAGE YOUR EXPECTATIONS AND VISIT RESPONSIBLY)

Between January and September 2021, Grand Teton Park recorded more than 3,493,937 visits, surpassing the park's busiest year, even with three months left to go. Of the first nine months of the year, six set records for visitation. And trail use was way up too—29 percent higher than in 2019. Between 2017 and 2021, trail use in the park increased by roughly 49 percent. Make no mistake: Grand Teton is nobody's secret. And it's likely to only get busier.

Park administrators are seeing changing patterns and behavior, including more visitation during what have traditionally been the shoulder seasons—March, April, and May—and increased traffic in the backcountry. They are analyzing the data to figure out ways to protect the visitor experience which, according to Park Superintendent Chip Jenkins, is a resource "just like moose or clean air, and it's something we are actively working to preserve and protect."

The bottom line is that crowds are becoming as much a part of the park as wildlife, and it's every visitor's responsibility to minimize their own impact for the benefit of the environment, the animals, and fellow visitors. Here are some ways you can visit the park responsibly and steer clear, hopefully, of the largest crowds.

- Plan ahead. Way ahead. All of the lodging in the park can be reserved through Grand Teton Lodge Company (307/543-3100 or 307/543-2811, www.gtlc.com) up to 366 days in advance. Don't wait and hope to luck out. Make your plans nine months to a year in advance. As of 2022, all of the campgrounds in the park are by reservation only. No more first-come, first-serve. You can book camping spots though www.recreation.gov up to six months in advance, and C. J. Adams, public affairs specialist for Grand Teton National Park, says "the earlier, the better."

- Get on animal time when you are in the park to see the best wildlife *and* avoid the biggest crowds. Before 9am and after 4pm are the best times to find parking spots and be on the trails without hordes of people. However, since this is when the animals are most active too, at dawn and dusk, be sure to have your bear spray and know how to use it.

- While the shoulder seasons are seeing more traffic each year, they are still called shoulder seasons for a reason. "They are busier," says Adams, "but not as busy as July and August." Indeed March, April, May, and September to November are some of the best times to find accommodations and fewer visitors on the roads and trails. It's also really wonderful to watch the dynamic change of seasons here—seeing the first wildflowers of the season, or the stunning yellow of aspen forests in the fall.

- Look for ranger-led activities, which are likely to be reservable ahead of time as of 2022. The excellent guided ranger walks program was put on hold throughout the pandemic, but Adams says the park is trying to find ways to bring it back. Guided ranger snowshoe hikes, for example, which can be reserved ahead of time, are likely to be available as of 2022. Keep watching the park website for updates and opportunities.

- Last but not least, remember to manage your expectations. The jaw-dropping photos you see on Instagram of one person with nothing but open country between her and the Tetons is not reality. You will have company in the park. You will have to wait for a parking spot. You will pass, and be passed by, other people on the trail. Everyone is there for the beauty and wonder of the natural world, and the good it does us, so be patient and polite.

the Moose Entrance Station. Annual passes are $80 (free for military and 4th graders, $20 for seniors).

With more than 200 miles (320 km) of maintained trails in the park, backpacking and backcountry camping provide a unique way to explore the area. Permits are required and can be obtained in advance online or in person ($35) on a first-come, first-served basis no more than one day before the start of a trip at the Craig Thomas Discovery and Visitor Center, Colter Bay Visitor Center, or Jenny Lake Ranger Station. Roughly one-third of **backcountry campsites** in heavily used areas can be reserved in advance online ($45) January 1-May 15 (307/739-3309, www.recreation.gov) and must be picked up in person. After May 15, all permits must be obtained in person. All campers are required to use bear-proof canisters below 10,000 feet (3,048 m) and at sites without bear boxes. Free canisters are provided when registering for a permit.

Visitor Centers

There are four main visitor centers in the park. The impressive **Craig Thomas Discovery and Visitor Center** (307/739-3399, 8am-5pm daily spring and late fall, extended hours in summer) is 12 miles (19 km) north of Jackson and 0.5 mile (0.8 km) west of Moose Junction. Exhibits include a relief map of the park, a fantastic 24-minute high-def movie, and natural history displays.

Housed in the historic Crandall Studio, which was once the workplace of photographer Harrison Crandall, **Jenny Lake Visitor Center** (307/739-3392, 9am-5pm daily mid-May-late Sept., extended summer hours) is 8 miles (13 km) north of Moose Junction on Teton Park Road. Visitor services include guided walks and talks, and exhibits focus on park geology. The nearby Jenny Lake Ranger Station offers backcountry permits.

Half a mile (0.8 km) west of Colter Bay Junction is the **Colter Bay Visitor Center** (307/739-3594, 8am-5pm daily spring and late fall, extended summer hours), which is home

to the David T. Vernon Indian artifacts collection. The exhibit celebrates Native artwork and highlights the long history of humans in and around Jackson Hole. There are daily ranger-led programs and a fantastic American Indian Guest Artist program.

Four miles (6.4 km) south of Moose on the Moose-Wilson Road (which is closed to RVs and trailers) is the **Laurance S. Rockefeller Preserve Center** (307/739-3654, 9am-5pm daily early June-late Sept.), which offers 8 miles (13 km) of hiking trails, fishing and swimming opportunities in Phelps Lake, and unique sensory exhibits. There are daily ranger programs including a hike to Phelps Lake. Opening and closing dates for all visitor centers can change annually and are listed online (www.nps.gov).

Entrance Stations

Grand Teton National Park has two official entrance stations but can be accessed from the south (Jackson), the east (Dubois), and the north (Yellowstone). Although you will be in Grand Teton National Park starting just 5 miles (8 km) north of Jackson, the southernmost **Moose Entrance Station** is about 20 miles (32 km) north of town. The eastern entrance at **Moran Junction** is 30 miles (48 km) north of Jackson and 55 miles (89 km) west of Dubois, Wyoming, over the Togwotee Pass, which is closed in winter. From the north, visitors enter Grand Teton National Park from Yellowstone; the $35 admission (for private passenger vehicles) is valid for seven days. Visitors coming in from Yellowstone can stop for information at **Flagg Ranch Information Station** or the **Colter Bay Visitor Center** 18 miles (29 km) south of Yellowstone.

Services

The main concessionaire in the park is the **Grand Teton Lodge Company** (307/543-3100 or 307/543-2811, www.gtlc.com), which operates lodging, restaurants, tours, and activities. Its website can also be a great aid in planning your visit. The Grand Teton Lodge

Company's mission is to preserve, protect, and inspire, and to do so in part by following sustainable business practices. It is responsible for the lodging, restaurants, tours, and activities at Jackson Lake Lodge, Jenny Lake Lodge, Colter Bay Village, Headwaters Lodge & Cabins at Flagg Ranch, and campgrounds throughout the park. The restaurants use free-range, naturally raised meat and dairy, organic coffee and produce, and support sustainable farming practices.

For **medical emergencies** within the park, dial 911. **St. John's Medical Center** (625 E. Broadway, Jackson, 307/733-3636) is open 24 hours a day, year-round, and the **Grand Teton Medical Clinic** (307/543-2514 during business hours or 307/733-8002 after hours, 9am-5pm daily mid-May-mid-Oct.) is located in the Jackson Lake Lodge.

TRANSPORTATION
Getting There
BY AIR

The only airport within a national park, **Jackson Hole Airport** (JAC, 1250 E. Airport Rd., Jackson, 307/733-7682, www. jacksonholeairport.com) is served by Alaska, American, Delta, United, and Frontier. The schedules change seasonally but include regular flights from Salt Lake City, Denver, Seattle, Chicago, Minneapolis, Dallas, Houston, Phoenix, San Francisco, and Los Angeles. Be aware that the airport will be closed entirely for runway reconstruction April 11-June 28, 2022.

The airport has on-site car rentals from **Alamo** (307/733-0671), **Enterprise** (307/733-7066), **Avis/Budget** (307/733-3422), and **National** (307/733-0671). **Dollar** (307/733-9224), **Thrifty** (307/734-8312), **Hertz** (307/733-2272), and **Leisure Sports** (307/733-3040) are available off-site with complimentary shuttles.

Somewhat amazingly for this part of the country, Jackson has 32 taxi companies serving the area, including **Broncs Car Service** (307/413-9863, www.jackson-hole-taxi.com), **Snake River Taxi** (307/413-9009, www.

snakerivertaxi.com), and **Teton Mountain Taxi** (307/699-7969, www.jacksonholecab. com). Transportation to Jackson from the airport runs roughly $45 for 1-2 people. A taxi to Teton Village averages $75. A complete list of taxi services can be found under the Transportation heading on the airport website.

BY CAR

Grand Teton National Park is 20 miles (32 km) from Jackson, 195 miles (315 km) from Bozeman through Yellowstone, 290 miles (465 km) from Salt Lake City, and 550 miles (890 km) from Denver. Grand Teton National Park is immediately south of Yellowstone and about 100 miles (161 km) southwest of Cody when the park roads are open and 323 miles (360 km) in the winter when park roads are closed. If you are driving from Yellowstone, take US 89 south, which will lead you directly into the park. If you are coming from Idaho Falls, from I-15 take US 26 east to Highway 31, continuing east to Highway 33, which will take you east through the scenic Teton Pass, where it becomes Highway 22. Continue until you reach US 89, taking it north into the park. An alternative route, flatter but slightly longer, is to take US 26 until it hits US 89 and head north.

BY BUS

Alltrans/Jackson Hole Express (307/733-3135 or 800/443-6133, www.jackson holealltrans.com) offers shuttles between Jackson Hole, eastern Idaho, and Salt Lake City. The nearest **Greyhound** stop is in Idaho Falls.

Getting Around
PRIVATE VEHICLES

If you are driving through the park, don't forget to keep an eye on your fuel gauge. The only gas station open year-round is at **Dornan's** (10 Moose Rd., gas pumps available 24 hours if paying with a credit card) in Moose. Other gas stations open May-October are at Signal Mountain, Jackson Lodge, and Colter Bay.

Bear #399 and the Grizzlies of Grand Teton

In July 1975, grizzly bears were listed as "threatened" under the Endangered Species Act. At that time, and for several years afterward, not a single grizzly was known to wander the wilds of Grand Teton National Park. Estimates put the number of grizzlies in Yellowstone around 136 at the time, but in Grand Teton, there wasn't even one.

The animal's listing and, thankfully, passionate involvement by good people have changed that. In early 2021, the number of grizzlies in the Greater Yellowstone Ecosystem—which includes Yellowstone and Grand Teton National Parks and their surrounds—hovered somewhere between 700 and 750.

Because it's true that we protect what we love, and love what we know, perhaps no bear has done as much for grizzly protection as #399. First captured and collared in 2001 when she was five years old, #399 has become the most famous grizzly in the world. She has had more than 20 cubs and grandcubs and been watched along roadsides by thousands upon thousands of park visitors over the years. "Along with her cubs, she made you want

grizzly bear

to protect her," said acclaimed photographer Tom Mangelsen, who, with writer Todd Wilkinson, put out a marvelous book on #399, *Grizzlies of Pilgrim Creek* (www.mangelsen.com).

Because she is so visible, Bear #399 has shown us the challenges bears face to simply survive. According to Wilkinson, nearly 75 percent of her descendants have died as a result of human encounters—struck by cars, killed illegally by big-game hunters, euthanized for preying on cattle or for coming too close to human development. She has lost other cubs to starvation or encounters with dominant males. In the fall of 2021, #399 was implicated in 10 conflicts south of the park when humans left food out for other wildlife or livestock. She and her cubs wiped out a bee colony too, and had to be hazed repeatedly with cracker shells, nonlethal projectiles, and other things. Experts are worried not only for #399, but for her cubs who are being taught how to access human and livestock food. In late fall of 2021, the U.S. Fish & Wildlife service was monitoring her almost around the clock in hopes that she would make it back to the park and her winter den safely.

Even with postcard bears like #399 and citizen advocates, the fight to protect bears is far from won. After the success of their recovery over the last 40 years, in the early part of 2016, the U.S. Fish and Wildlife Service proposed that grizzly bears be removed from the federal List of Endangered and Threatened Wildlife, which strips away various protective measures and eventually opens grizzlies up for hunting. In 2017, 56 grizzlies died from poachers, conflicts with hunters and ranchers, and car collisions. Even so, with all the threats, in the fall of 2018, plans for a sport hunt threatening as many as 22 grizzlies were only stopped by the court within hours of the opening day. As the status of grizzly bears is questioned—and tied up in court—their value in our wild world should not be.

While scientists call the grizzly an "umbrella" or "indicator" species—meaning that when the grizzlies thrive, so too do the other plants and animals that inhabit their world—naturalist and writer Doug Peacock, who has dedicated his life to making the world a safer place for grizzlies, goes further in asserting the importance of their survival. "Really, we are as much endangered as the grizzly bears. The fate of humans and grizzlies is a single, collective one," he said.

Twenty-five years old in 2021 when she emerged from hibernation with four yearling cubs, Bear #399 will probably not be around much longer. But let us hope—and fight—to make sure grizzly bears still are.

For up-to-date road information and closures in the park, call 307/739-3682, or 307/344-2117 for Yellowstone road reports. For Wyoming road information, contact the **Wyoming Department of Transportation** (888/996-7623, www.wyoroad.info), or the Wyoming 511 app.

TOURS

The **Grand Teton Lodge Company** (307/543-3100 or 307/543-2811, www.gtlc. com) offers tours throughout the park, including four-hour tours departing from Jackson Lake Lodge during summer.

A great educational opportunity is provided by the **Teton Science Schools** (307/734-3707, www.tetonscience.org), based in Jackson. The organization is committed to creating a deeper appreciation and understanding of the wilderness and natural ecosystems found in the Greater Yellowstone area. Its experts provide classes and programs to engage every type of learner from small children to adults. The courses focus on everything from ecology and geology to unique plant and animal life. Even if you only plan to be in the park for a day or two, visit the website to see what is being offered. Regular programs can include hikes, campfires, canoe tours, and wildlife-viewing. The school also offers renowned **Wildlife Expeditions** (877/404-6626). These can be 8-12 hours or multiple-day guided tours, with professional wildlife biologists who provide you with an up-close and unique opportunity to experience the natural wonders of the park.

Another tour company that focuses on getting visitors up close and personal with the park's wildlife in comfy four-wheel-drive vehicles is **EcoTour Adventures** (307/690-9533, www.jhecotouradventures.com). Guided half-day tours, often at sunrise or sunset, run roughly four hours and start at $155 per person. Full-day trips—which can include snowshoeing and wildlife adventures, geology explorations, birding, and more—last 8-12 hours and can take visitors into Grand Teton and Yellowstone. These tours include lunch at one of the park lodges and start at $270 per person.

PLANTS AND ANIMALS

Despite the fact that every square inch of Grand Teton National Park is at or above 6,400 feet (1,951 m) in elevation, there is a remarkable diversity of both plant and animal life in the three main growing zones and four distinct habitat regions. Throughout the short summer, the valleys are awash in colorful wildflowers. And although animals aren't quite as visible as they are in the vast open spaces or burned-out forests of Yellowstone, wildlife watchers will have terrific opportunities in the park.

All three of Grand Teton's growing zones—alpine, subalpine, and valley—fall between 6,400 feet (1,951 m) and 13,770 feet (4,197 m) in elevation, meaning harsh climates and a short growing season. Still, upward of 1,000 species of vascular plants grow in the park. Porous soil allows for an abundance of colorful wildflowers. And even in the high reaches of the mountains, delicate jewels like alpine forget-me-nots grow close to the ground in mats.

Because of the short growing season, the vast majority of trees in the park are conifers—as in Yellowstone, lodgepole pine is the most common tree—but aspens and cottonwoods have chlorophyll in the bark, allowing them to photosynthesize before putting out leaves. As a result, Grand Teton National Park is illuminated in the fall by changing leaves. Sagebrush is everywhere, lending an almost minty smell to the crisp air.

Along with Yellowstone, Grand Teton National Park is a critical part of the more than 11-million-acre Greater Yellowstone Ecosystem, considered one of the last nearly intact temperate ecosystems on earth. As such, it provides critical home habitat and migratory routes for a number of species.

The park's four main habitat types are alpine, sagebrush, forest, and aquatic. The alpine habitat, above 10,000 feet (3,048 m), is home to some of the park's hardiest creatures:

yellow-bellied marmots, pikas, and bighorn sheep. In the ubiquitous sagebrush areas, with more than 100 species of grasses and wildflowers, wildlife watchers can look for pronghorn, coyotes, bison, badgers, elk, and Uinta ground squirrels. While not as easy to explore, the park's forested regions are home to elk, mule deer, red squirrels, black bears, and snowshoe hares. And finally, in and around the plentiful lakes, rivers, and ponds of Grand Teton National Park are populations of moose, river otters, beavers, muskrat, coyotes, bison, and mule deer.

HISTORY

The history of this region dates back 11,000 years, when it was a seasonal hunting ground for such tribes as the Shoshone, Gros Ventre, Flathead, and Blackfeet. John Colter was likely the first non-Native American to explore the region; he is thought to have traveled through the area in 1808, guided by wildlife and Native American trails. By the 1820s the area was widely known for its abundance of beavers, and mountain men arrived with traps in hand. Trapper David E. Jackson spent the winter of 1829 along the shores of Jackson Lake; the valley, the lake, and the nearby town of Jackson bear his name. Many of the park's features were named by the Hayden Geological Survey in 1871.

The region was sparsely settled and farmed due to the climate and the soil, but it was used for cattle ranching in the late 1800s. The area was also well known among hunters and eventually became the setting for a handful of dude ranches.

In 1897, President Grover Cleveland established the Teton Forest Reserve, and the Teton National Forest was created in 1908. The park itself—96,000 acres in its first incarnation—was set aside by Congress in 1929 and included primarily the mountains and alpine lakes. There were some attempts through the 1930s to add to the park, none of which were successful. John D. Rockefeller Jr., however, was quietly purchasing land in the Teton Valley through his Snake River Land Company. Between 1926 and 1946, Rockefeller bought 35,000 acres adjacent to the park, and in 1949 he deeded all but 2,000 acres to the federal government, which had established the 210,000-acre Jackson Hole National Monument under President Franklin Roosevelt in 1943. In 1950, Congress agreed to merge the monument and the Rockefeller-donated land with the park, bringing it to its current boundaries.

Flagg Ranch and Colter Bay

Just south of the Yellowstone border, Flagg Ranch was at one time a U.S. Cavalry outpost. Converted to a guest ranch in 1910 and now known as Headwaters Lodge & Cabins at Flagg Ranch, it is ideally situated for visitors looking to explore both Yellowstone and Grand Teton National Parks from one location. In addition to full resort lodging and services, Flagg Ranch offers activities and services—a gas station, a grocery store, a deli and coffee shop—for those just passing through.

One of the busiest spots in the park, with a marina, lodging, a campground, a visitor center, and a museum on the shores of Jackson Lake. Colter Bay is a practical, if not exactly quiescent, place to stay, and it is a worthwhile region to explore.

SIGHTS

Colter Bay Visitor Center and the David T. Vernon Indian Artifacts Collection

The unassuming **Colter Bay Visitor Center** (307/739-3594, 8am-5pm daily spring and late fall, summer extended hours, free) offers the same useful information as all of the visitor centers in the park. And more. The David T. Vernon collection—which includes more than 1,000 objects ranging from dolls, shields, pipes, and weapons to photography—was donated by the Rockefeller family with the provision that it be displayed permanently in Grand Teton National Park. In 2012, almost the entire collection was sent to a conservation facility but is slowly coming back to the park, at both the Colter Bay and Craig Thomas Visitor Centers. As of 2016, more than 80 objects had been returned to the park, and digital images of many of the artifacts are available online through the **Google Cultural Institute** (www.google.com/culturalinstitute). It is a remarkable collection that could just as easily be on display at the Smithsonian were it not for the wishes of an extremely generous family. Meanwhile, Native American artisans practice their crafts in the center intermittently throughout summer with the **American Indian Guest Artist Program,** and prominent lecturers and educational events are scheduled on-site.

SPORTS AND RECREATION
Boating and Fishing
On the shores of **Jackson Lake,** by far the largest body of water in the park, Colter Bay and the **Colter Bay Village Marina**

(307/543-2811, ext. 1097, or 307/543-2811, www.gtlc.com) are excellent launching points for boating expeditions. From the marina, you can arrange cruises, canoe or kayak excursions, motorboat rentals, and guided fishing trips.

Guided fly-fishing tours can be arranged through the marina as well. Guided Jackson Lake **fishing** (307/543-2811) can be arranged from Colter Bay Marina starting at $115 per hour for 1-2 adults with a two-hour minimum and $25 per hour per additional person; day trips start at $525-625 for 1-2 people.

★ Cruise to Elk Island
Since nothing builds an appetite like time spent on an alpine lake, there are wonderful breakfast cruises and dinner cruises (307/543-2811, www.gtlc.com, $42-76 adults) departing from the marina that whisk guests across the lake to Elk Island, in the shadow of Mount Moran. Each cruise takes approximately three hours. The **breakfast cruise,** offered daily except Thursday (which can change from year to year), serves hearty fare with eggs and trout, pancakes, pastries, fresh fruit, and the all-important cowboy coffee. Typically, it departs at 7:15am from June to August and at 8am late August to early September.

Jackson Lake

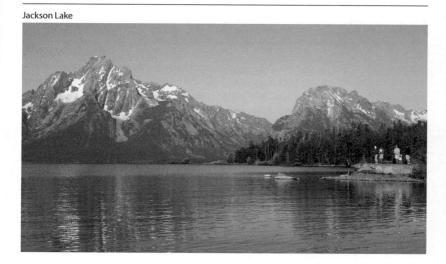

The lunch cruise includes a sack lunch and plenty of time to explore the island. It departs Monday, Wednesday, Friday, and Saturday at 12:15pm. The dinner cruise (5:15pm Fri.-Wed. June-Sept. 5) includes such delectable mountain fare as steak and trout, baked beans, corn on the cob, a salad bar, roasted potatoes, and mouthwatering fruit cobbler. Scenic lake cruises (10:15am, 1:15pm, and 3:15pm daily, $42 adults, $21 children 3-11) last about 90 minutes and are geared to different aspects of the park (with one cruise designed especially for kids). An extra tour departs at 6:15pm on Thursdays.

Hiking and Biking

There is a lot of marvelous terrain in every corner of the park for hiking and biking, and the northern section near Colter Bay is no exception. The hike to Hermitage Point is one of the most significant hikes (and long, at nearly 9 mi/14.5 km round-trip). The elevation gain is minimal (980 vertical ft/299 m), and the trail, which starts immediately across from the boat launch at the southern end of the parking lot, meanders through forest, meadow, and alongside ponds and streams. The easy Lakeshore Trail is only 2 miles (3.2 km) long round-trip and circumnavigates Colter Bay with stunning views in every direction.

North of Colter Bay, near the Flagg Ranch, is Grassy Lake Road, a 52-mile (84-km) dirt road—great for mountain biking—that follows an ancient Indian thoroughfare all the way to Ashton, Idaho. Along the way are hiking trails, streams, ponds, and splendid scenery.

FOOD

The main lodge at Headwaters Lodge & Cabins at Flagg Ranch is the center of all activity at the ranch. It has a gas station, a general store, and Sheffields Restaurant & Bar (800/443-2311, www.gtlc.com, 7am-10am, 11:30am-2pm, and 5pm-9:30pm daily June-late Sept., breakfast $7-14, lunch $10-17, dinner $13-32, dinner reservations required),

which serves a broad range of local cuisine—including bison burger, elk medallions, and grilled local trout—in a family-friendly setting. The Bistro & Saloon (7am-close, $8-12) is open all day and serves grab-and-go meals and snacks.

The Café Court Pizzeria (11am-10pm daily late May-late Sept., $9-28) in Colter Bay Village serves up specialty salads, toasted subs and pizza, both by the slice and whole pies. Also at Colter Bay is the Ranch House Restaurant (6:30am-10:30am, 11:30am-1:30pm, and 5:30pm-9pm daily late May-late Sept.). The restaurant offers family-style meals with an emphasis on barbecue. The breakfast buffet ($12-18 adults, $9-11 children) can include eggs, French toast, hot specials, and organic oatmeal, or if you want to order à la carte ($7-16), you can easily fill up on the New York steak and eggs, pan-fried oatmeal, or the breakfast burrito. Lunch ($11-17) consists of a good selection of salads, burgers, and sandwiches, while dinner ($16-32) offers hearty steaks, chops, and seafood dishes. The bar is open 11:30am-10:30pm daily and has a small food menu as well.

ACCOMMODATIONS AND CAMPING

The Headwaters Lodge & Cabins at Flagg Ranch (800/443-2311 or 307/543-3100, www.gtlc.com, June-Sept.) is touted as the oldest continuously operating resort in upper Jackson Hole. It is ideally situated to take advantage of both Yellowstone and Grand Teton National Parks. The options include standard, deluxe, or premium log cabins ($269-375). Log cabins have two queens or one king bed, coffeemakers, private baths, and patios furnished with rocking chairs. Note there is no cell service or Wi-Fi in the area.

Colter Bay Village (307/543-3100, www.gtlc.com, late May-early Oct.) on the northern shore of Jackson Lake offers some of the park's most affordable lodging, which isn't saying too much anymore. The village has rustic cabins ($232-320), an RV park (back-in sites $102.12, pull-through sites $112.11) with

102 full-hookup pull-through sites and 12 full-hookup back-in sites, and a tent village (late May-early Sept., $79 tent cabins). The original homestead cabins, purchased by the Rockefellers and moved to the area, have been refurbished but still offer a glimpse into the past. Each cabin displays a description of its own history. While most of the one-room cabins sleep 2, one can sleep up to 6 people, and the two-room cabin can sleep up to 10 with rollaways. Prices vary depending on the number of occupants in the room and the arrangement of double, twin, and rollaway beds. The **Colter Bay Campground** (www.recreation.gov, late May-late Sept.,

from $49.95/vehicle, $14.43 pp for hikers or bicyclists, $78.81 electric only sites) has 330 sites. All tent cabins, campsites, and RV sites are discounted up to 50 percent with the presentation of a Golden Access Pass. Note that all Grand Teton National Park campgrounds moved to a reservation-only system in 2022. Reservations can be booked six months in advance through www. recreation.gov. Walk-up sites are not available.

Located 30 miles (48 km) north of Moose between Flagg Ranch and Colter Bay Village, the **Lizard Creek Campground** (307/543-2831, early-June-early Sept., $41) has 60 individual sites with no hookups.

Jackson Lake Lodge and Signal Mountain

Its breathtaking setting, coupled with excellent amenities and access to hiking and sightseeing in the park's northeastern corner, makes Jackson Lake Lodge a vacation destination all its own. Though the lodge is not adjacent to Jackson Lake in the way that the Colter Bay Village is, the views over the lake to the Tetons are magnificent. Nearby, the rustic Signal Mountain Lodge is situated immediately on the water, offering unlimited opportunities for enjoying Jackson Lake and its proximity to hiking and adventuring.

SIGHTS

TOP EXPERIENCE

★ Oxbow Bend

Just southeast of Jackson Lake Lodge on the main road is Oxbow Bend, a picturesque river area created when the Snake River carved a more southerly route. One of the most photographed areas in the park, the slow-moving water perfectly reflects towering Mount Moran. The serenity of the area attracts an abundance of wildlife, including moose, beavers, and otters along

with a vast number of birds. White pelicans can occasionally be spotted passing through, as can sandhill cranes, majestic trumpeter swans, nesting great blue herons, and bald eagles. Avid boaters like to paddle the area in their canoes and kayaks. Don't forget your binoculars and your camera.

★ Signal Mountain

One mile (1.6 km) south of Signal Mountain Lodge is the turnoff to Signal Mountain Road and one of the greatest viewpoints in Grand Teton National Park. The winding 5-mile (8-km) road is completely **unsuitable for RVs and trailers.** Along the way, there are ample spots for wildlife-viewing—look for moose in the pond on the right as you start up the road; the pond lilies bloom in June. Two small parking lots are near the summit. The first offers the best view of the Tetons: Sunsets are sensational. From the second, a short walk takes you down to an overlook with a view of Oxbow Bend. Visitors in August might even have a chance to pick some succulent

1: Oxbow Bend **2:** view from Signal Mountain

huckleberries as they ripen in the late-summer sun.

The story of Signal Mountain's name is a rather tragic one. Around the turn of the 20th century, a local rancher named Roy Hamilton got lost when he was out hunting. Rescuers agreed to light a fire on the mountain as soon as anyone found Hamilton. After nine days, a fire was lit atop the mountain, signaling the end of rescue efforts. Tragically, Hamilton's body was found in the Snake River, and some speculated his business partner had suggested he cross the river in a particularly dangerous spot.

SPORTS AND RECREATION

Fishing

Anglers will be pleased with the varied offerings in this stretch of the park. From the lunkers in Jackson Lake, which can be fished on shore or by boat, to the healthy but discerning trout in the Snake River, guided trips can be arranged through **Grand Teton Lodge Company** (307/543-2811 and ask for the marina, www.gtlc.com), from $115/hour for 1-2 adults with a two-hour minimum and $25/hour per additional person; day trips are $525-625 per day for 1-2 anglers, $125 each additional person.

From **Signal Mountain Lodge** (307/543-2831, www.signalmountainlodge.com), anglers can go out with experienced guides (late May-mid-Sept.) in pursuit of Jackson Lake's cutthroat, brown, and lake trout for $149/hour for 1-2 people with a two-hour minimum and $43/hour per additional person; half-day trips are $429 for 1-2 people and $109 per additional person.

Half-day and multiple-day fishing trips on Jackson Lake can also be arranged through **Grand Teton Fly Fishing** (307/690-0910 or 307/690-4347, www.grandtetonflyfishing.com, all-day floats from $750, half-day floats from $650 for 2 people). Bruce has been guiding people in the park for more than 46 years, and he knows just where the fish are likely to hide.

A Wyoming fishing license is required for all fishing in the park and can be purchased at **Snake River Angler at Dornan's** (12170 Dornan Rd., 307/733-3699, www.snakeriverangler.com), **Signal Mountain Marina** (307/543-2831, www.signalmountainlodge.com), and **Colter Bay Marina** (307/543-3100, www.gtlc.com). Pick up a fishing brochure from any of the visitor centers to learn about all park regulations.

Boating

With so much beautiful water in the park, boating is a fantastic way to explore. Rafting on the **Snake River,** canoeing or kayaking on any number of lakes, or cruising across **Jackson Lake**—there are options for adrenaline junkies and die-hard landlubbers alike.

Scenic 10-mile (16-km) floats down the Snake can be arranged through **Signal Mountain Lodge** (307/543-2831, www.signalmountainlodge.com, from $85 adults, $56 children 6-12), **Grand Teton Lodge Company** (307/543-3100 or 307/543-2811, www.gtlc.com, half day $55-97 ages 6 and up), or **Solitude Float Trips** (307/733-2871, www.grand-teton-scenic-floats.com, $95 adults, $75 children 5-15, $1,080 for a private boat for up to 12 guests). Most floats on the Snake River inside the park last about two hours. Both Grand Teton Lodge Company and Solitude offer a wonderful sunrise float, perfect for spotting wildlife. Grand Teton Lodge Company also offers four-hour luncheon floats (Mon.-Sat. May-Labor Day, call for updated pricing and schedule) and dinner floats (call for updated pricing and schedule) with fun riverside cookouts.

Human-powered boats like kayaks and canoes are permitted on Emma Matilda Lake and Two Ocean Lake, east of Jackson Lake Lodge. Jackson Lake is open to motorboats, human-powered boats, sailboats, waterskiing, and windsurfers. Permits are required for motorized boats ($56) and nonmotorized crafts ($17), including stand-up paddleboards, and can be purchased at the visitor centers in Moose, Jenny Lake (cash only),

Finding a Guide

Setting off into the wilds of Grand Teton National Park can be slightly intimidating, making guided tours a good option. The Park Service maintains a list of licensed, permitted, and park-approved guides.

For any type of technical rock climbing, a guide is as necessary as a helmet and rope. Exum Mountain Guides (307/733-2297, www.exumguides.com) has been offering instruction and guided mountain climbing since 1931, making it the oldest guide service in North America and certainly one of the most prestigious. Exum offers numerous programs, from easy day climbing for families with kids to guided expeditions up the 13,770-foot (4,197-m) Grand Teton. They also offer guided backcountry skiing and snowboarding in the Tetons. Detailed information, including climbing routes and trail conditions, can be found at www.tetonclimbing.blogspot.com.

The Hole Hiking Experience (307/690-4453, www.holehike.com) offers a range of guided hikes and snowshoe or ski tours (half day from $520 for 1-3 people) in and around the park for all interests and ability levels, from sunrise or sunset discovery tours to all-day wildlife-watching hikes (4 hours from $520 for 1-3 people, 8 hours from $925 for 1-2 people). Kids will love the family day hikes with fun survival-like activities that include eating "lemon drop" ants and using butterfly nets. Winter cross-country ski and snowshoe tours are guided by naturalists and show off the best winter has to offer.

There are several options for guided horseback riding trips, May-September, from a number of lodges in the park, including Colter Bay Village, Flagg Ranch, and Jackson Lake Lodge. The Grand Teton Lodge Company (307/543-3100 or 307/543-2811, www.gtlc.com) can arrange everything from a 1-2-hour ($50-80) horseback ride to breakfast wagon rides (call for updated pricing and schedule) and dinner rides (call for updated pricing and schedule) to pony rides ($5). All riders in the park must be at least eight years old and under 225 pounds (102 kg).

With so many varied bodies of water, fishing outfitters can guide any type of trip you can dream up. A good place to start is the Grand Teton Lodge Company (307/543-3100 or 307/543-2811, www.gtlc.com), which can arrange trips from any of the accommodations inside the park. Fishing trips on the Snake River or Jackson Lake can also be arranged through the lakefront Signal Mountain Lodge (307/543-2831, www.signalmountainlodge.com) or Grand Teton Fly Fishing (307/690-0910, www.grandtetonflyfishing.com).

Rafting is popular in Grand Teton National Park, and there are 11 licensed outfitters to guide visitors down the Snake River. As with all activities, Grand Teton Lodge Company (307/543-3100 or 307/543-2811, www.gtlc.com) can make arrangements for the park's most popular 10-mile (16-km) scenic float. Other outfitters include Barker-Ewing (307/733-1800 or 800/448-4202, www.barker-ewing.com) and Solitude Float Trips (307/733-2871, www.grand-teton-scenic-floats.com).

Throughout the year, Park Service rangers offer excellent naturalist-guided tours. Late December-March, depending on conditions, daily guided snowshoe hikes depart from the Craig Thomas Discovery and Visitor Center (307/739-3399, reservations required, $5 donation suggested). During the summer months, the range of offerings is vast—from 30-minute map chats and campfire programs to three-hour hikes, evening astronomy programs, and tipi demos. For more information on ranger programs, pick up the park newspaper at any of the entrance stations, call 307/739-3300, or check out the visitor centers in Moose, Jenny Lake, Colter Bay, and the Laurance S. Rockefeller Preserve.

or Colter Bay. Boats can be rented through Signal Mountain Lodge (307/543-2831, www.signalmountainlodge.com), including pontoon boats ($119/hour, $535/day for up to 10 people), runabouts ($71/hour, $349/day for up to 5 people), fishing boats ($43/hour, $196/day for up to 5 people), and sea kayaks ($23/hour, $99/day single, or $29/hour, $119/day double). The Grand Teton Lodge Company (307/543-3100 or 307/543-2811, www.gtlc.

com) can also arrange various boat rentals (motorboats $48/hour, canoes $25/hour, single kayak $30/hour, double kayak $40/hour) throughout the park. Note that all the boat rentals have a two-hour minimum.

Hiking and Biking

Sandwiched between Jackson, Emma Matilda, and Two Ocean Lakes, the area around Jackson Lake Lodge offers some wonderful hiking. The **Christian Pond Loop** is a relatively flat and easy 4.3-mile (6.9-km) round-trip hike through prime waterfowl habitat. The trailhead is east of the parking lot adjacent to the Jackson Lake Lodge corrals. Nearby, **Two Ocean Lake** offers a moderate 6.4-mile (10.3-km) round-trip hike around the lake though forest and meadow. **Emma Matilda Lake** offers an even longer 9.1-mile (14.7-km) hike, with fabulous Teton views from the north shore ridge.

A nice area for visitors who travel with their bicycles is in the vicinity of **Two Ocean Road,** southeast of Jackson Lake Lodge and northeast of Signal Mountain Lodge. The road itself is just 3 miles (4.8 km) long, but the scenery is sublime for a short, sweet ride. **River Road** is 15 miles (24 km) of gravel running along the west side of the Snake River between Signal Mountain and Cottonwood Creek. Do remember that this is bear country and every precaution—including bear spray—should be taken.

Horseback Riding

The **Grand Teton Lodge Company** (307/543-3100 or 307/543-2811, www.gtlc. com) can arrange one-hour ($50) or two-hour ($80) horseback tours that depart from Jackson Lake Lodge and can include trips to Emma Matilda Lake and an overlook of Oxbow Bend. All riders must be at least eight years old and under 225 pounds (102 kg).

FOOD

It's worth pointing out again that the pandemic had a huge impact on restaurants in the park, and things are not yet back to normal. For the most part, hours are shortened. But it makes sense to check the website or call ahead.

There are a lot of options for dining at the **Jackson Lake Lodge** (307/543-3100, www. gtlc.com). The **Mural Room** (307/543-3463, 7am-9:30am, 11am-2:30pm, and 5:30pm-9pm daily mid-May-early Oct., breakfast buffets $12-21 adults $8-13 children, lunch $13-20, dinner $18-48) has unmatched ambience with

floating on the Snake River

its windowed wall looking out onto the lake, Mount Moran, and the Teton Range along with the colorful murals by famed artist Carl Routers depicting life out West. The food is upscale and innovative—also known as Rocky Mountain cuisine—and when coupled with the view, it makes this one of the most pleasurable dining experiences in the park. Breakfast includes classic eggs Benedict and huckleberry French toast. Lunch is a mix of sandwiches and salads as well as regional cuisine including Idaho rainbow trout and beef Bourguignon. Dinner is a hearty affair with delectable main entrée items including seared elk strip loin, Idaho ruby red trout, and wild mushroom saffron risotto. A delightful end to the meal is the flourless dark chocolate cake or the huckleberry pound cake. Kids' menus are available. Dinner reservations are required and can be secured on OpenTable.

Also in the lodge is the much more casual and less pricey **Pioneer Grill** (6am-10pm daily mid-May-early Oct., $10-26), a true-to-style 1950s diner; supposedly it has the largest soda fountain counter still in use. A fun place for a meal, the counter snakes 200 feet through the room and encourages guests to interact with other diners. The Pioneer Grill offers American cuisine with a slight gourmet twist (try the poutine) and has a takeout service if you decide you'd rather watch the sunset while munching on your burger. Its famous desserts keep customers returning, and you should not leave without ordering a huckleberry shake. And for breakfast, try the huckleberry pancakes.

The **Blue Heron Lounge** (307/543-2811, 11am-11pm daily late May-early Oct., food served until sunset, $13-31) is another casual dining experience in Jackson Lake Lodge. It has a bar menu with a good selection of appetizers and creative sandwiches and even offers sustainable draft beer from local breweries. Enjoy your meal on the deck with a huckleberry mojito and an incredible panoramic view of the mountains.

If you are at the pool or with your kids at the playground, you may want to fill up on the terrific Mexican food at the outdoor **Poolside Cantina** (food service 11am-4pm daily, beverage service 11am-8pm daily early June-late Aug. depending on weather, $7-14), which also serves salads, plus burgers and hot dogs for the kids. Don't forget the soft-serve ice cream!

There are three options for dining at the **Signal Mountain Lodge** (307/543-2831, www.signalmountainlodge.com). The **Trapper Grill** (7am-10pm daily early May-early Oct., $11-18) serves three meals a day. It mostly sticks to American fare with some Tex-Mex thrown in. The nachos are a favorite. The breakfast menu ($4.75-10) switched to grab-and-go options during the pandemic, with various breakfast sandwiches and burritos, and baked goods. The lunch and dinner menu is filled with specialty sandwiches, salads, and burgers, but the restaurant prides itself on its homemade desserts. You may want to share an entrée so that you'll have room for the Colter's Run chocolate pecan pie or the mountain cookie for two. **The Peaks Restaurant** (5:30pm-10pm daily early May-early Oct., $18-41) was closed during the pandemic but may serve again. Their menu shows a commitment to offering environmentally sustainable meals. Past specialties have included Snake River Farms Kurobuta pork shank, bison meatball, or grilled Colorado white bass. **Leek's Pizzeria** (11am-10pm daily late May-early Sept., $10-28) is at the marina on Jackson Lake. It serves specialty pizzas and calzones, sandwiches, salads, and microbrews in a fantastic outdoor setting. For a drink, snack, and a glimpse of television, you may want to stop at **Deadman's Bar** (noon-8pm daily), which serves the largest plate of fully loaded nachos you've ever seen. They pair perfectly with a blackberry margarita and a Wyoming sunset.

ACCOMMODATIONS

The **Jackson Lake Lodge** (307/543-3100, www.gtlc.com, mid-May-early Oct., $394-952 cottages and cottage suites, $394-502 lodge rooms) is one of the largest resorts in the park and commands an unparalleled view of Jackson Lake and the Teton Range from the lobby's panoramic 60-foot-high windows. There are 385 guest rooms in the main lodge and surrounding cottages, and the grounds also house a playground and swimming pool. The cottages are in clusters and come in a range of styles. The classic cottages ($394) have two queen beds and sleep a maximum of four. The mountain view cottages ($502) have a view of the Tetons, can sleep up to five people, and include a mini fridge and a patio or balcony. The Moran suite ($952) has a spectacular view of Willow Flats, where moose often meander, and the majestic range; it comes with a king bed and a comfortable sitting area. The lodge guest rooms ($394-502) are on the 3rd floor and also come in two price ranges, depending on the view. Unlike the cottages, these guest rooms do not accommodate rollaways.

The **Signal Mountain Lodge** (307/543-2831, www.signalmountainlodge.com, early May-mid-Oct.) is an independently owned resort on the banks of Jackson Lake with a gorgeous view of the Tetons. It has a variety of options for lodging, ranging from rustic log cabins (1-room cabin $241-266, 2-room $271-301) and premier Western rooms ($408) to one- or two-room bungalows ($293-450)

on the beach. The country rooms ($293) are motel-style accommodations, and the deluxe country rooms ($333) have one king bed and fireplaces. The two-room lakefront retreats ($408-450) are ideal for families; they overlook the lake with fantastic views of the mountains and have kitchenettes. There is one three-bedroom cabin aptly named Home Away from Home ($535); if you are lucky enough to get it, you'll have a bedroom, dining area, living room with a gas fireplace, kitchen, and small laundry room all to yourself; the only drawback is that there is no view.

CAMPING

The **Signal Mountain Campground** (800/672-6012, mid-May-mid-Oct., $49.95/vehicle standard site, $75.48 electric site) is nestled among spruce and fir trees with views of the mountains, lakes, and hillside. It is also wildly popular and, as of 2022, requires reservations through www.recreation.gov. There are 86 smallish sites, each with a picnic table and fire ring, and RVs up to 30 feet (9.1 m) in length are permitted. Restrooms with cold running water are available but no showers.

Jenny Lake and Vicinity

Carved some 12,000 years ago by the same glaciers that dug out Cascade Canyon, Jenny Lake is perhaps the most picturesque and popular spot in the park. The hiking—to places like Inspiration Point and the even more beautiful Leigh Lake—is sublime, and the water activities—scenic cruising, canoeing, kayaking, swimming, and fishing—are plentiful. The park's fanciest and most expensive lodging and dining can be found at the historic Jenny Lake Lodge.

In much the same way that Old Faithful embodies the Yellowstone experience for many visitors, so too does Jenny Lake conjure up all that is wonderful about Grand Teton.

A scenic drive from North Jenny Lake to South Jenny Lake skirts the water and affords breathtaking views of the Grand Teton, Teewinot, and Mount Owen. Those who are more interested in solitude would be well advised to get off the main drag here, away from the crowds and into the wilderness.

SIGHTS
★ **Jenny Lake**

In 1872 an English-born mountain man, known widely as "Beaver Dick" Leigh for his enormous front teeth and his penchant for the animal, guided Ferdinand Hayden around the Tetons. Hayden named the alpine lake for

Dick's wife, Jenny, a member of the Shoshone tribe. In the fall of 1876, pregnant Jenny took care of an ailing Native American woman, not knowing the woman had smallpox. Jenny and all four of her children became ill. Her baby was born just before Christmas and, along with Jenny and the other four children, died within a week. Beaver Dick buried his family in Jackson Hole.

Despite its tragic namesake, Jenny Lake is indeed one of the most beautiful and visited spots in the park. From cruising across the lake to hiking along its shores, there are an endless number of ways to enjoy this idyllic spot.

Set between two parking areas, and with easy walking access to the lake, trails, and campground, the Jenny Lake Visitor Center is 8 miles (13 km) north of Moose at South Jenny Lake.

★ Hidden Falls and Inspiration Point

One of the area's most popular hikes is the spectacular **Hidden Falls Trail**. From Jenny Lake's south shore, the hike follows a moderate 2.5-mile (4-km) trail (one way) with 550 feet (168 m) of elevation gain to the cascade. Visitors who want to put fewer miles on their feet can take the **Jenny Lake Shuttle** (307/734-9227, www.jennylakeboating.com, 10am-4pm mid-May-early June, 7am-7pm early June-early Sept., round-trip $18 adults 12-61, $15 seniors, $10 children 2-11 years, one-way $10 adults, $8 children), which runs every 10-15 minutes throughout the day, to shorten the hike to 1 mile (1.6 km) with 150 feet (46 m) of elevation gain. The hike to **Inspiration Point**, a breathtaking overlook 5.8 miles (9.3 km) round-trip with 700 feet (213 m) of elevation gain from the trailhead, or 2.2 miles (3.5 km) round-trip with 420 feet (128 m) of elevation gain from the boat shuttle, earns its name. In summer 2018, a horizontal crack in a rock buttress was measured at 100 feet long. The route remains accessible (after a brief closure); the park service continues to monitor the crack. Hikers can also get to Cascade Canyon via the horse trail along Jenny Lake.

Leigh Lake

Named for mountain man "Beaver Dick" Leigh, Leigh Lake is much quieter and perhaps even more beautiful than the more southerly Jenny Lake. The lake offers unrivaled views of Mount Moran, Mount Woodring, and Rockchuck Peak, and it is dotted with sandy beaches ideal for picnics. The 5.4-mile (8.7-km) round-trip (out-and-back) trail is flat and weaves in and out of the forest with a constant water view. The Leigh Lake Trailhead is at the northwest corner of the String Lake Picnic Area. The trail can be hiked as early as May or June, depending on snowmelt, and is typically passable well into September. Although popular, Leigh Lake does not attract the crowds that Jenny Lake does.

SPORTS AND RECREATION

Fishing

Fishing is permitted in Jenny, String, Leigh, Bradley, and Taggart Lakes. A Wyoming fishing license is required and can be purchased at **Snake River Angler at Dornan's** (12170 Dornan Rd., 307/733-3699, www.snakeriverangler.com), **Signal Mountain Marina** (307/543-2831, www.signalmountainlodge.com), and **Colter Bay Marina** (307/543-3100, www.gtlc.com). Pick up a fishing brochure from any of the visitor centers to learn about all park regulations.

Boating

Scenic one-hour **cruises** (noon and 2pm daily mid-May-early June and early Sept.-late Sept.; 11am, 2pm, and 5pm daily early June-early Sept., $25 adults, $20 seniors 62 and over, $15 children 2-11), **shuttles** to Cascade Canyon hiking trails (round-trip $18 adults, $10 children, departing every 10-15 minutes), and canoe or kayak **rentals** ($20/hour, $30/day) can be arranged through **Jenny Lake Boating** (307/734-9227, www.jennylakeboating.com).

Hiking and Biking

Jenny Lake is at the heart of the park's largest concentration of popular hiking trails. In addition to the **Hidden Falls, Inspiration Point,** and **Leigh Lake** trailheads, there are other excellent trails in the region. The mostly level **Jenny Lake Loop Trail** circumnavigates the lake with a 6.6-mile (10.6-km) round-trip hike. The **Lupine Meadows Trailhead** offers hikers a number of ways to get up into the Teton Range.

The multiuse pathway from South Jenny Lake to Taggart Lake Trailhead offers bikers (and all nonmotorized travelers) a round-trip of 16 miles (26 km) of smooth, level pavement. Bike racks are available at Taggart Lake Trailhead and in Moose. Bicycles can be rented from **Dornan's** (12170 Dornan Rd. in Moose, 307/733-2415, www.dornans. com, 9am-6am daily). In addition to a range of adult bikes (call for availability and current rates), Dornan's rents kids' bikes, Trail-a-Bikes, bike racks, and Burley carriers for toddlers.

FOOD

The **Jenny Lake Lodge Dining Room** (307/543-3100, www.gtlc.com, 7:30am-10am, 11:30am-1:30pm, and 6pm-9pm daily June-early Oct.) offers a fine-dining experience in an original log cabin. Reservations are required for dinner and recommended for breakfast and lunch. Men are required to wear dinner jackets. The food is incredibly creative and incorporates local flavors. Crabcake Benedict and a prime rib cowboy skillet appear on the breakfast menu ($12-18), and lunch ($15-25) consists mostly of upscale sandwiches and salads. The main event at the restaurant is the prix fixe five-course dinner ($100 pp, not including gratuity or alcohol). Options for each course rotate every night. Depending on the day, you may be dining on Lockhart beef tartare, whitetail venison

medallion, Colorado striped bass, or pan-seared pheasant—no matter what's on the menu, it is sure to be a memorable meal (and an expensive one!).

ACCOMMODATIONS

A former dude ranch for sophisticated Easterners, **Jenny Lake Lodge** (307/543-3100, www.gtlc.com, mid-May-early Oct., cabins starting at $636/night for 2 people) is the finest lodging in the park and the only four-diamond eco-resort. The cabins have log walls, renovated baths, and touches such as handmade bed quilts that add to the charm of each room. Situated among the three lakes, the lodge is comfortably secluded but offers beautiful vistas in all directions. The rooms are pricey, but guests get a lot for their dime. A gourmet breakfast, five-course dinner, horseback riding, and access to bicycles are all included in the rates. Each week, different activities are available and include options such as live raptor displays on the front patio, stargazing, interpretive programs, live musicians, and garden games like bocce ball and croquet. If you are looking for a romantic getaway, consider booking one of the suites, which come with wood-burning stoves.

A much more affordable, and truly rustic, option is the **Grand Teton Climbers Ranch** (307/733-7271 or 303/384-0110 off-season, www.americanalpineclub.org, early June-early Sept., $83-133 AAC members, $105-155 nonmembers), owned by the American Alpine Club and located just 3 miles (4.8 km) south of Jenny Lake. The ranch has small log cabins that serve as dormitories for 4-8 people. Guests must bring their own sleeping bags and pads, towels, cooking equipment, and food. Cooking and dishwashing facilities, toilets, and showers with hot water are available. No camping is allowed. A general store on the grounds allows you to stock up on groceries as well as hiking and camping supplies. The ranch often offers a work week in early June that allows volunteers to stay at the ranch for free.

1: old barn on Mormon Row **2:** the view from Inspiration Point **3:** shuttle boats on Jenny Lake **4:** view from Antelope Flats

CAMPING

The **Jenny Lake Campground** (307/543-3100 or 307/543-2811, early May-Sept., $29/vehicle, $12 hikers and bicyclists) is the smallest in the park with 61 sites, and like all the others, can be reserved up to six months in advance on www.recreation.gov. Most can accommodate one vehicle, two tents, and up to six campers ($36). Additional sites are set aside for hikers or bicyclists ($12). There are no large group sites, nor are trailers, campers, or generators allowed in the area. Because of its size and popularity, the maximum stay is seven days (at the other campgrounds it is 14 days). Flush toilets are available but no shower facilities.

Moran to Moose

The stretch of road between Moran Junction and the southernmost entrance to the park at Moose is scenic and full of interesting sights, both natural and human-made. From the historic crossing at **Menors Ferry** to the architecturally inspired **Craig Thomas Discovery and Visitor Center** and the wildlife-rich **Antelope Flats,** this part of the park is heavily traveled for a good reason: There is so much to see.

SIGHTS

Cunningham Cabin

A relic of hardscrabble ranching days before the turn of the 20th century—and the site of the murder of two alleged horse thieves—**Cunningham Cabin** is 6 miles (9.7 km) south of Moran Junction. The cabin reflects the common building materials and style of 1890, the year it was built. Known as a "dogtrot," it consists of two small structures connected by a breezeway and topped with a dirt roof.

Pierce Cunningham built a modest home for his family on Flat Creek in 1888. A neighbor introduced Cunningham to two strangers, George Spenser and Mike Burnett, asking if they could buy hay for their horses. Cunningham sold them 15 tons of hay and arranged for them to winter in his cabin near Spread Creek. The rumor among the locals was that the men were in fact horse thieves.

In April 1893, Spenser and Burnett were the target of a posse of vigilantes from Montana. Sixteen men on horseback rode up to the little cabin on Spread Creek under cover of darkness and waited in silence for dawn. Spenser and Burnett's dog barked in the early morning hours, perhaps warning the men of the ambush that awaited them. Spenser dressed, armed himself, and walked out the front door. When the posse called for him to hold his hands up, Spenser fired his revolver in the direction of the speaker and was immediately shot. He propped himself up on one elbow and continued to fire until he collapsed. Burnett came out next, armed with a revolver and a rifle. The men shot at him, but Burnett managed to shoot the hat off one of the posse members and "crease his scalp" with the bullet. Burnett was shot and killed moments later. The two men were buried in unmarked graves a few hundred yards southeast of the cabin on the south side of a draw. Some of their bones were eventually excavated by badgers.

Mormon Row and Antelope Flats

Interesting both for its wildlife and its human history, the area around **Mormon Row** is instantly recognizable from some of the region's most popular postcards, featuring a weathered barn leaning into the jagged mountains behind it. Listed on the National Register of Historic Places, Mormon Row is a collection of six fairly dilapidated homesteads that can be explored on a **self-guided tour** (brochures are available near the pink house). The area was settled around the turn of the 20th century by a handful of Mormon families who built homes, a church, a school, and a swimming hole. The settlement was abandoned and left to the elements when the Rockefellers bought up much of the land and transferred it to the National Park Service. In the 1990s the historical and cultural value of the site was recognized; the area was added to the National Register of Historic Places in 1997, and steps were taken to preserve the structures.

The **Antelope Flats** area—excellent for walking or biking on a flat, unpaved road—offers prime habitat for pronghorn, bison, moose, coyotes, ground squirrels, northern harriers, kestrels, and sage grouse. In the winter, the first mile (1.6 km) of Antelope Flats Road is plowed to a small parking area, giving visitors easy snowshoe or cross-country ski access to Moulton Ranch, one of the homesteads on Mormon Row. On the NPS website, visitors can access **audio tours** (www.nps.gov/grte/learn/photosmultimedia/audio-descriptions.htm) of Mormon Row and other historical spots and places of interest.

★ Craig Thomas Discovery and Visitor Center

Twelve miles (19 km) north of Jackson in Moose, the **Craig Thomas Discovery and Visitor Center** (307/739-3399, 8am-5pm daily, extended summer hours) is, among other things, an architectural masterpiece, mimicking the nearby natural masterpiece of the Teton Range. The $21.6 million structure has more than 22,000 square feet and is being used as a model for other national parks—in that more than half the funds used to build the center were donated by private individuals. The state-of-the-art facility, including video rivers that flow beneath your feet, places emphasis on the connection between humans and the natural world. Fantastic interpretive displays include a large relief model of the park that uses technology to show glacier movement and animal migration; there is also a photographic tribute to mountaineering in the region. Many of the excellent ranger-led

hikes and tours depart from the Craig Thomas Discovery and Visitor Center.

Menors Ferry Historic District

In 1894, William D. Menor came to Jackson Hole and built a homestead along the Snake River. He built a ferryboat on cables to carry settlers and hopeful miners across the river, which was otherwise impassable during spring runoff. Entire wagon teams crossed on the ferry, paying $0.50 per trip, while a horse and rider paid $0.25. In 1918, Menor sold the ferry operation to Maud Noble, who doubled the fares ($1 for automobiles with local plates, $2 for out-of-staters) in the hope of attracting more tourists to the region. When a bridge was built in 1927, the ferry became obsolete, and in 1929 Noble sold her land to the Snake River Land Company, the same year the park was created. She had already donated a portion of her land for the construction of the Chapel of the Transfiguration.

Today, a replica of the ferryboat and cables has been built on-site, and visitors can meander down the 0.5-mile (0.8-km) self-guided **Menors Ferry Trail** past Menor's cabin, which doubled as a country store. On the NPS website, there are **audio tours** (www.nps.gov/grte/learn/photosmultimedia/audio-descriptions.htm) of Menors Ferry, Mormon Row, and the Murie Ranch, along with other historical spots and places of interest.

Chapel of the Transfiguration

Built in 1925 to serve the ranchers and dudes in the Teton Valley, the **Chapel of the Transfiguration** (307/733-2603, services 8am and 10am Sun. Memorial Day-Sept.) is a humble log cabin structure with the most spectacular mountain view framed in the window behind the altar. An Episcopal church, operated by St. John's in Jackson, it was built on land donated by Maud Noble and is a favorite spot for summer weddings. A candlelight Christmas night service and sunrise Easter service are particularly wonderful ways to experience this historic place of worship.

★ Laurance S. Rockefeller Preserve

Four miles (6.4 km) south of Moose on the Moose-Wilson Road, the former JY Ranch and longtime summer home of the Rockefeller family, known as the **Laurance S. Rockefeller Preserve** (307/739-3654, 9am-4:30pm daily), offers 8 miles (12.9 km) of trails through forest, wetlands, and meadows on reclaimed property along Phelps Lake and Lake Creek. The preserve is 1,106 acres and was donated to the Park Service in 2007 by the Rockefeller family with the mission of giving people access to the natural world that Laurance Rockefeller found so inspiring and sustaining.

The Laurance S. Rockefeller Preserve Center is the first platinum-level LEED-certified building constructed in a national park and was constructed to give visitors a sensory experience of the natural elements found on the preserve. A poem by beloved writer Terry Tempest Williams features prominently, and visitors can learn about the preserve and Rockefeller's beliefs about land stewardship in a comfortable and environmentally sustainable building. Several ranger programs, including sunrise hikes and children's programs, are available from the center daily throughout summer. The preserve is accessible by car from May to October.

Murie Ranch

The onetime STS Ranch and former residence of wilderness champions Olaus and Mardy Murie, the **Murie Ranch** (1 Murie Ranch Rd., Moose, 307/732-7752, www.tetonscience. org/murie-center/home, 9am-5pm Mon.-Fri. mid-Mar.-mid-Oct.) is dedicated to connecting people and wilderness. It is where the Wilderness Act was authored in the 1950s and early 1960s. The ranch itself is a National Historic Landmark and the site of ongoing conservation seminars and educational workshops. On-site accommodations are available to participants, and the entire facility can be rented for conservation education programs. An excellent library and bookstore is on-site, and rangers host

The Chapel of the Transfiguration was built in 1925.

naturalist programs throughout the summer. Free tours (11:30am-12:30pm Mon.-Fri.) of the Murie home are given in summer. Call ahead or check with the Craig Thomas Discovery and Visitor Center for up-to-date tour information.

SPORTS AND RECREATION

As in most of Grand Teton National Park, there is an abundance of excellent hiking terrain to be discovered between Moran and Moose, and many easy strolls can combine with historic sites like the Cunningham Cabin, Menors Ferry, and Mormon Row.

For more substantial hikes, try the **Taggart Lake-Bradley Lake Loop** from a trailhead 2.3 miles (3.7 km) northwest of the Moose Entrance Station. The loop trail is 5.5 miles (0.0 km) total with 585 feet (178 m) of elevation gain. It leads first to Bradley Lake and then up to Taggart. To make the hike longer by 0.5 mi / 0.8 km, hikers can return to the trailhead via the Beaver Creek Trail. Three miles (4.8 km) south of Moose is the **Death Canyon Trailhead,** not nearly as ominous as the name would imply. The road is not suitable for trailers or RVs and very rough for vehicles in general. However, the hike to **Phelps Lake** is perfect for families, only 1.8 miles (2.9 km) round-trip with 420 feet (128 m) of elevation gain. Black bears, moose, and marmots frequent the area, so have your bear spray at the ready.

There are plenty of biking opportunities on the paved and unpaved roads in the region, including **Antelope Flats Road** all the way to Kelly, the **Shadow Mountain Road,** and the **Moose-Wilson Road** linking Moose and the Laurance S. Rockefeller Preserve. The **multiuse pathway** from Moose or the Taggart Lake Trailhead to South Jenny Lake is popular for good reason.

FOOD

You'll find most of your food options in this area at Dornan's ranch. ★ **Dornan's Moose Chuck Wagon** (12170 Dornans Rd.,

307/733-2415, ext. 300, serving breakfast, lunch, and dinner daily mid-June-Labor Day, weather dependent) serves up hearty "cowboy cuisine" during the summer. Dornan's uses beef from its own butcher shop and Dutch ovens heated over wood fires. Breakfast ($7-13) offers great sourdough pancakes, and dinner ($26-32 adults, $15-17 children 5-11) is an all-you-can-eat affair with prices based on your choice of barbecued beef or chicken, pork ribs, or trout. Lunch ($10-16) is served as well. The restaurant is used for private events on weekend evenings. And Monday night is the hootenanny starting at 6pm, an evening of acoustic delight. There's often live music Tuesday-Saturday between 5:30pm and 8:30pm. It's a good idea to call ahead for evening reservations and check that it's not privately booked for the evening.

Dornan's Pizza and Pasta Company (307/733-2415, ext. 204, 11:30am-9pm daily in season with reduced hours in spring and fall, $11-25) is located in the **Spur Bar** and offers a large variety of salads, hot sandwiches, gourmet pizzas, rich pasta dishes, and calzones. If you are looking to pick up something to eat on your hike, stop at **Dornan's Moose Trading Post & Deli** (307/733-2415, ext. 201, 8am-8pm daily) for everything from freeze-dried meals and cold drinks to gourmet groceries and any camping equipment you might need. The deli is open May-September; it's a good option for a quick meal or a sweet treat. If you have the time, don't miss a visit to **Dornan's Wine Shoppe** (307/733-2415, ext. 202, 10am-9pm daily in summer, reduced hours off-season). It is a find for wine connoisseurs and novices alike, with an award-winning selection of around 1,500 varieties of wines and 150 types of cheese. *Food & Wine* magazine named it one of the 50 most amazing wine experiences in the country, and *Wine Spectator* has bestowed its Wine Award on the shop several times.

ACCOMMODATIONS

★ **The Triangle X Ranch** (2 Triangle X Ranch Rd., 307/733-2183, www.trianglex.com, late May-mid-Oct. and Dec. 26-mid-Mar., $2,119-2,936 pp/week summer when paid with credit card, 3% discount for paying cash, off-season $294-329 pp/night, $165 pp/night winter) has been in operation since 1926. Twenty-six miles (42 km) north of Jackson and 32 miles (52 km) south of Yellowstone, it is the only authorized guest ranch concessionaire in the entire National Park System and sits right inside Grand Teton National Park. Not surprisingly, the setting is gorgeous, and you can see the entire mountain range from this secluded getaway.

The lodge, which is the center of activity and meals, is the original main house used by two generations of the Turner family. The 20 log cabins are also originals that once housed families in different parts of Jackson Hole. The cabins come with 1-3 bedrooms; all have modern amenities and are decorated with cozy Western charm.

The ranch is also the only concession in the park that is open during winter. During the peak season (early-June-late Aug.), the minimum stay is one week (Sun.-Sun.). During the spring and fall seasons, the ranch requires a minimum four-night stay but offers reduced rates, and during the winter season, visitors can book per night. All meals, served family-style in the main lodge, are included in the price, as are the endless horseback rides, cookouts, square dancing, and special programs for children. Winter activities include cross-country skiing, snowshoeing, and snowmobiling. Regardless of the season, there are always great opportunities for wildlife-viewing.

Dornan's Spur Ranch Cabins (12170 Dornan Rd., Moose, 307/733-2522, www. dornans.com, year-round) sits idyllically on the Snake River in the middle of a wildflower meadow and gives alpine views in all directions. This is a small, family-owned business that provides quality service with personal touches, and the location affords easy access to fly-fishing and floating adventures. There are eight one-bedroom cabins and four two-bedroom duplexes (call or check online for updated rates) on the premises. The cabins were built in the early 1990s and are bright, airy, and furnished with lodgepole pine furniture. They each have queen beds, kitchens, living-dining areas, and covered porches with a barbecue grill nearby. Also on these 10 acres of property are a grocery and camping store, two restaurants, and an award-winning wine shop. Visitors can rent mountain bikes, canoes, and kayaks during the summer and cross-country skis and snowshoes in the winter to make the most of the surrounding area.

CAMPING

Gros Ventre (307/543-2811 or 307/543-3100, www.gtlc.com, early May-early Oct., tent and dry RV sites $38, electric sites $60) is the closest park campground to Jackson and the largest campground in the park, situated at the southeast end, 11.5 miles (18.5 km) southeast of Moose. Booked through www. recreation.gov up to six months in advance, the 279 sites offer a fire pit and picnic table, and can accommodate two tents, two vehicles, and up to six people. The campground isn't far from the river, and there are sites to be had in the cottonwoods and open sage. Nearby bathrooms include flush toilets, but no shower facilities are available. A grocery store and service station are within 2 miles (3.2 km) of the campground.

Jackson Hole, Cody, and the Wind Rivers

Northwest Wyoming swings dramatically from stunning vistas and a sublime outdoor culture to the arts scene and high style of Jackson and Cody.

Some of the state's most exquisite lodgings and legendary ranches can be found in this corner of Wyoming. The area is jam-packed with obvious destinations such as world-class museums—Cody's Buffalo Bill Center of the West and Jackson's National Museum of Wildlife Art are among the best—as well as landmarks like Sinks Canyon near Lander, Hot Springs State Park near Thermopolis, the Wind River Range, and a string of scenic drives. The region provides a marvelous launching point into both Grand Teton and Yellowstone National Parks. Naturally, opportunities to explore the great outdoors are

Highlights

Look for ★ to find recommended sights, activities, dining, and lodging.

★ **Jackson Town Square:** Surrounded by archways constructed entirely out of elk antlers, this is the heart of the community for shoppers, art lovers, and diners (page 112).

★ **National Museum of Wildlife Art:** This collection is dedicated to all things wild, spanning George Catlin's bison to incredible works by Georgia O'Keeffe, Charlie Russell, and marvelous contemporary artists (page 114).

★ **National Elk Refuge:** Most magical in winter under a blanket of snow, this refuge is home to more than 5,000 elk. Tour the area by horse-drawn sleigh (page 114).

★ **Rafting on the Snake River:** The Snake winds through the valley, giving floaters unparalleled access to the area's most stunning views (page 118).

★ **Sinks Canyon State Park:** This natural wonder occurs where the Middle Fork of the Popo Agie River "sinks" into a cave and then emerges again in a great spring (page 138).

★ **Hot Springs State Park:** This park has fabulous limestone terraces as well as public baths in therapeutic waters (page 145).

★ **Wyoming Dinosaur Center and Dig Sites:** You can learn about dinosaurs, see their remains up close, and even dig for a day. There's a chance you'll find a fossil (page 146).

★ **Buffalo Bill Center of the West:** Five remarkable museums capture the art, natural

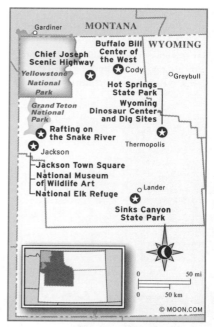

history, Native American cultures, and legends of the Old West. If you can visit only one museum in the West, this should be it (page 150).

★ **Chief Joseph Scenic Highway:** This scenic drive has high mountain plateaus speckled with wildflowers, cascading rivers, and narrow canyons teeming with wildlife (page 154).

Jackson Hole, Cody, and the Wind Rivers

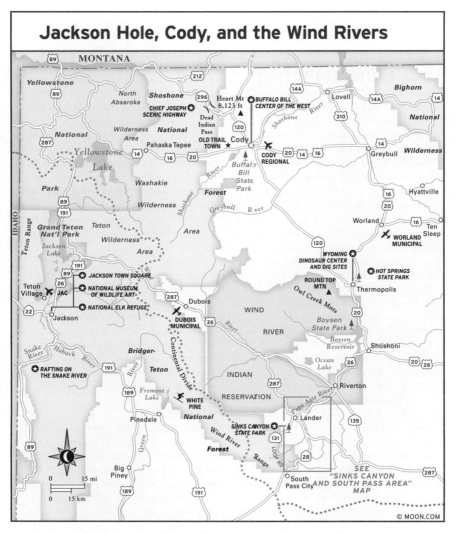

abundant and include rafting, fishing, skiing, and hiking.

While bigger towns like Jackson and Cody are natural attractions in themselves, other towns in the region, such as Pinedale, Thermopolis, and tiny Ten Sleep, offer an authentic Wyoming experience with great

museums, hot springs, historical monuments, and hole-in-the-wall cafés. Though towns like Lander and Powell lack the glitz and pomp of Jackson and Cody, they possess so much of what defines the state—rugged beauty, open space, rich history, and unrivaled wilderness access. In Wyoming, the journey from one

---

Previous: performers at Eastern Shoshone Indian Days Pow wow and Rodeo on the Wind River Reservation; fountain in Thermopolis; the National Elk Refuge is a great backdrop for photos.

town to the next is often the destination itself, and by far the best way to appreciate this sparsely populated state.

PLANNING YOUR TIME

Jackson Hole and Cody are obvious destinations, with easy (but pricey) air access; each could easily occupy visitors for 2-3 full days, and both are excellent launching pads for day trips into Yellowstone and Grand Teton National Parks. Both have their own distinctive cultures that include art and entertainment, the great outdoors, and elegant accommodations and eateries. The dude ranches outside both Jackson and Cody offer tremendous opportunities to experience the state's vast open spaces in close proximity to the hustle and bustle of town. For many people, this is the ideal way to spend a week enjoying the best of Wyoming's offerings.

The charm of Jackson is that it is pretty much anything you want it to be. Boutique shopping? Check. Gallery strolls? Check. Kitschy bars with saddle-topped stools? Check. Gourmet dining? Hard-core outdoor pursuits? Quiet afternoons in the museum? Check. Check. Check. Jackson is a great destination because it is geared to visitors who want to be entertained, pampered, challenged, and wined and dined. A few hours in the **National Museum of Wildlife Art** is time well spent. And you will want to allow an afternoon to stroll around town, browsing the shops and galleries—but don't let Jackson's shopping sirens lure you away from the majestic wilderness in every direction. In winter, try skiing at Jackson's original ski hill, **Snow King,** right in town, or at **Jackson Hole Mountain Resort** in nearby Teton Village. In summer you'll find trails to hike and dirt roads to bike, and two of the world's most incredible national parks are just up the road. Make sure to book a raft trip on the Snake River, and consider a wagon or sleigh ride on the sprawling **National Elk Refuge.**

Decidedly less glitzy than Jackson and more for the working cowboy than the urban variety (except during Rendezvous Royale),

Cody is a rugged Western town with a rich history and just enough refinement to appeal to sophisticated travelers. The **Buffalo Bill Center of the West** is far and away the heart of Cody and should not be missed. A quick tour at a breakneck pace could probably be accomplished in two hours, but history buffs and Western art lovers could spend several days in the museum and not see the same exhibit twice. Cody's **nightly rodeos** in summer are a treat for the entire family, and a trip to Buffalo Bill's town would not be complete without a visit to the beautiful old hotel he built and named for his daughter, the **Irma Hotel.** The restaurant and saloon are open to nonguests, and if you go in the evening, watch the old **Cody Gunfighters** hash it out right outside the hotel Monday-Saturday at 6pm.

While disparate in philosophy, perhaps, the energy boomtown of Pinedale and the outdoor mecca of Lander both offer excellent access to the spectacular Wind River Mountains. The region is absolutely worth exploring as a destination for outdoor and nature lovers and as a beautiful setting for travelers en route from one place to the next.

HISTORY

Wyoming had long been home to the Sioux, Crow, Cheyenne, Arapaho, Shoshone, Gros Ventre, Bannock, and Ute before a party of Frenchmen, traveling and trapping in the northwestern corner of the state as early as 1743, arrived and are thought to be the first Europeans in the area. Perhaps the most influential visitor in encouraging other trappers and mountain men to visit the region was John Colter, a member of the Lewis and Clark expedition who plied his skills as a trapper in the vicinity of what is now Jackson Hole in 1807-1808. His exploits and subsequent stories opened the area to an influx of mountain men, trappers, and traders, and by 1825 folks like Jedediah Smith, David Jackson, and Bill Sublette had made names for themselves as fearless explorers and shrewd businesspeople.

Chief Washakie and the Shoshone Tribe

Born around the turn of the 19th century to a Flathead (Salish) father and a Shoshone (Lemhi) mother, Washakie lived through the most tumultuous century for Native Americans. When his father was killed during a Blackfeet raid, the young boy and his mother left to live with the Lemhi people in Idaho. During his adolescence, Washakie joined a nomadic band of Bannocks, and eventually settled with the Shoshone tribe in southwest Wyoming's Green River Basin. During the early 1820s Washakie befriended Jim Bridger, who would become a celebrated explorer and mountain man. Together they hunted, trapped, and traded. Their friendship was so great that one of Washakie's daughters became Bridger's third wife. Although trading and trapping ingratiated him with the settlers and explorers, Washakie also earned the respect of his fellow Native Americans as a skilled warrior.

Chief Washakie of the Shoshone tribe

By the mid-1800s, Washakie was already an influential leader, having forged an alliance between the Shoshone tribe and the Europeans. The skills Washakie acquired through his friendship with Bridger and other traders and trappers served him well as a leader. He was able to negotiate for the best interests of his people, getting them much-needed supplies. When younger warriors questioned his leadership after his alliances with settlers, Washakie left camp, only to return a week later with seven Sioux scalps, challenging anyone who questioned him to match the feat.

Washakie was also considered forward-thinking. When Shoshone tribal land was threatened in the early 1850s by the influx of settlers, Washakie suggested to leaders, including Brigham Young, that land be set aside for the tribe. By the end of the decade, he was negotiating directly with the U.S. government. In 1863 the Treaty of Fort Bridger designated land for the tribe.

On the reservation, Washakie continued to lead, maintaining a balance between the new reservation life and their traditions. Living in a log cabin rather than a tipi, Washakie sent his children to the agency schools and even farmed a small piece of land. But he also made sure his children joined him on buffalo hunts. He defended Native American practices and led his fellow Shoshone warriors in the U.S. Army battles against the Sioux and Cheyenne. In 1900, Chief Washakie was buried with full military honors. A warrior and peacemaker, a diplomat and an advocate for change, Chief Washakie is considered the last of the great Shoshone leaders. Wyoming has paid tribute by naming various public places in his honor.

By 1840, the demand for beaver pelts had bottomed out, leaving little incentive for mountain men in the region. The population temporarily swelled with pioneers headed west on the Oregon Trail. Conflicts with Native Americans were inevitable as settlers encroached on traditional hunting grounds and, more importantly, nearly wiped out the bison altogether. There were great battles that always ended tragically, most often for the Native Americans, and a series of treaties that

reduced the size of their lands until there was virtually none left. Today Wyoming is home to two recognized tribes—the Shoshone and Arapaho—once enemies and now neighbors sharing the Wind River Reservation.

By the 1880s, cattle ranching had taken hold, and sheep ranchers moved in just over a decade later. Both Jackson and Cody were settled much later, closer to the turn of the 20th century, because of the harsh snowy winters in Jackson and the desertlike conditions around Cody. What irrigation did for Cody by increasing the population, the creation of Grand Teton National Park did for Jackson in 1929 by attracting tourists and jump-starting dude ranching in the area.

Wyoming's biggest boom, however, came in the form of energy—oil, gas, and coal, the production of which still dominates the state's economy despite plummeting prices and subsequent layoffs. Oil was discovered outside Cody in 1904. The largest coal deposits in the country are being mined in the Powder River Basin, and much of the western portion of the state produces natural gas.

Wyoming's motto—"Equal Rights"—attests to the fact that Wyoming was the first territory to grant voting rights to women, in 1869, more than 20 years before its statehood was established. It was also the first state to elect a woman as governor, Nellie Tayloe Ross, who served 1923-1925. A darker time in Wyoming's history includes the creation of the Heart Mountain Relocation Camp, between Powell and Cody, where more than 10,000 Japanese Americans were held during World War II.

Jackson Hole

Visitors love Jackson (pop. 10,760, elev. 5,672 ft/1,729 m) because it encompasses the best of the West in a charming town with a spectacular setting. Western indeed, Jackson boasts a classic boardwalk around town, saloons with swinging doors and saddles for bar stools, and architecture built on elk antlers. At the same time, Jackson is clearly mountain chic, with high-end boutiques and art galleries, a phenomenal performing arts center, gourmet dining, and ritzy accommodations.

The valley itself, known as Jackson Hole because it is entirely surrounded by mountains, is 48 miles (77 km) long and up to 8 miles (13 km) wide in places. With the Tetons as the most significant landmark, the region gives rise to the headwaters of the Snake River, fed abundantly by numerous mountain streams. Because of its remarkable setting, Jackson Hole is a natural playground with offerings for just about anyone. In winter, outdoors enthusiasts can ski downhill at two well-known ski areas, Snow King and Jackson Hole Mountain Resort, or go the cross-country route just about anywhere, including nearby Grand Teton National Park. For those less interested in working up a sweat, a sleigh ride in the National Elk Refuge is a memorable experience. When the snow melts, there is no end to the adventurous options this valley offers, with fly-fishing and wildlife-watching among the less exhausting. From hiking and mountain biking to rafting and rock climbing, Jacksonians do it all.

SIGHTS
★ Town Square
Almost European in its layout with a central square, Jackson's **Town Square** is uniquely distinguished by four dramatic archways constructed in 1932 entirely from naturally shed and sun-bleached elk antlers. It is the focal point of town and a good meeting spot, with shady trees and the occasional musician. In the summer, late May-early September, Town Square is the site of the free **Jackson Hole Shootout** (6pm-6:30pm Mon.-Sat. Memorial Day-Labor Day), a spirited reenactment of frontier justice. In winter, the arches are illuminated by strings of lights, creating a magical setting.

Within easy walking distance of the square are more than 70 eateries—from mouthwatering pizza joints with ski-bum prices to the very tony—and fine art galleries and shops that sell everything from high-end furs to T-shirts and knickknacks. There are

Downtown Jackson

To
⊗ **NATIONAL MUSEUM OF WILDLIFE ART,**
Grand Teton and Yellowstone National Parks

JACKSON HOLE AND
■ GREATER YELLOWSTONE
VISITOR CENTER

⊗ **NATIONAL
ELK REFUGE**

■ WYOMING GAME AND
FISH DEPARTMENT

PERRY ST

ROSECRANZ DR

■ BRIDGER-TETON
NATIONAL FOREST
OFFICE

MERCILL AVE

● INN ON
THE CREEK

■ JACKSON
RECREATION
CENTER

JACKSON HOLE
HISTORICAL
SOCIETY AND
MUSEUM ★

P

THE
ANVIL MOTEL ●

PUBLIC
■ RESTROOMS

GILL AVE

● THE RUSTY PARROT
▼ LODGE & SPA

WILD
SAGE

*Miller
Park*

THE BLUE LION
▼

TETON
■ MOUNTAINEERING

THE MERRY
PIGLETS ▼

■ ALTAMIRA
■ FINE ART

JACKSON HOLE
THE TOY STORE
BUNNERY

THE KITCHEN ▼

MADE
SKINNY ■
SKIS ■

PUBLIC
RESTROOMS
■

DELONEY

P

LEGACY ■
GALLERY

THE
WORT HOTEL ●

MILLION ▼
DOLLAR
COWBOY BAR

JACKSON
TOWN SQUARE
⊗

CAFÉ PERSEPHONE
GENEVIEVE BAKERY
▼

To
Cache Creek
Canyon Loop

W BROADWAY

(26)(89)(191)

JD HIGH
E BROADWAY

←
To
Teton Village,
Hoback Sports,
and Pica's

BIN 22 ▼

THE ROSE ▼ ▼

PIZZERIA
CALDERA

BELLA ■
COSE

■ COUNTRY
OUTFITTERS

■ TRAILSIDE
GALLERIES

▼ TERRA OF
■ JACKSON HOLE

▼
THE
SNAKE RIVER
GRILL

■ WRJ
DESIGN

VALLEY
■ BOOKSTORE

■ TAYLOE PIGGOT
GALLERY

PEARL

■
POST
OFFICE

★
JACKSON HOLE
CENTER FOR
THE ARTS

ST

0   100 yds

0   100 m

SIMPSON AVE

SIMPSON AVE

To
↓ Jackson Rodeo Grounds

© MOON.COM

also plentiful espresso and ice-cream shops for those in need of instant energy.

Jackson Hole Historical Society and Museum

Just down Cache Street from Town Square, the **Jackson Hole Historical Society and Museum** (225 N. Cache St., 307/733-2414, www.jacksonholehistory.org, 10am-5pm Tues.-Sat., $10 adults, $6 seniors over 60, military, and students, free for active military and children 6 and under) is dedicated to the connection of people and place, with emphasis on the history of homesteading and dude ranches in the area, and Indian history of the Tetons. The collections include historical photos of the region, Indian artifacts, fur trade-era tools, and firearms. The society also operates the hands-on Mercill Archaeology Center, which is open on a program basis only. In summer, the historical society offers hour-long **walking tours** (Tues.-Fri. Memorial Day-last full week in Sept., $10 adults, $6 seniors over 60, military, and students, free for active military and children 6 and under, combo passes for museum and tour $15 adults, $9 seniors over 60, military, and students, free for active military and children 6 and under) that explore landmarks and historic buildings, and include stories of unforgettable local characters. Tours depart from the museum. For a historical perspective on the town and valley, this is the best place to begin.

★ National Museum of Wildlife Art

Just 3 miles (4.8 km) north of Town Square overlooking the National Elk Refuge, the **National Museum of Wildlife Art** (2820 Rungius Rd., 307/733-5771, www.wildlifeart. org, 9am-5pm daily May-Oct., 9am-5pm Tues.-Sat. Nov.-Apr., $15 adults, $13 seniors 60 and over, $8 for one child 5-18, $4 each additional child, free for children under 5) is an absolute find. In existence in various forms since 1984, the museum's 14 galleries represent the lifetime study and collection of wildlife art by Bill and Joffa Kerr. More than 5,000

objects reside in the permanent collection, primarily paintings and sculptures by artists that range from early Native American artists to masters both past and present, including Pablo Picasso, Carl Rungius, John James Audubon, Robert Bateman, and Kent Ullberg. A 0.8-mile (1.3-km) sculpture trail, which is free and open to the public, was added in 2012. The trail combines marvelous art with the stunning landscape around Jackson, and often plays host to live music, theater, yoga, and other programs. Audio guides to the museum are included with paid admission, and coupons for discounts on admission are offered on the museum's website.

The museum itself is a work of art: Inspired by the ruins of a Scottish castle, the red Arizona sandstone building emerges from the hillside like a natural outcropping of rock and often reminds visitors of Ancestral Puebloan ruins.

★ National Elk Refuge

During the winter months, more than 5,000 elk—often as many as 8,000—descend from their mountain habitat to the nearly 25,000-acre **National Elk Refuge** (532 N. Cache St., 307/733-9212, www.fws.gov, free) in Jackson Hole. The large number of elk make the refuge a popular wintertime attraction (in the summer, birds and other wildlife populate the range). Forty-seven different mammal species and nearly 175 species of birds have been observed on the refuge. The elk are accustomed to the vehicles, allowing visitors to travel easily through the herds on the **Refuge Road** scenic drive. In winter, only 3.5 miles (5.6 km) of the scenic drive is accessible by car. Horse-drawn sleigh rides through the refuge are offered mid-December through the first Saturday in April. Reservations (307/733-0277 or 800/772-5386, www.nersleighrides.com) are strongly suggested. Tickets for the roughly 90-minute tour can be purchased from the **Jackson Hole and Greater Yellowstone**

1: Jackson's Town Square is magical in winter.
2: National Elk Refuge

The Elk Conundrum

Established in 1912, the National Elk Refuge was the first Wyoming state-run feeding ground for elk. In the 1930s and 1940s, more feeding grounds were created to help the animals survive the harsh winters, and in part to keep them from entering areas reserved for cattle grazing. The thriving herd in Jackson ultimately was used to replenish other herds of elk and aid the reintroduction of elk throughout the country. However, as a result of the large number of elk concentrated in these feeding grounds, the animals are much more susceptible to contagious diseases including brucellosis and, as of December 2020, chronic wasting disease. Wyoming lost its federal brucellosis-free status in 2004 when cattle acquired the disease after coming into contact with elk from the refuge.

In 2005 the U.S. Department of Agriculture's Animal Plant Health Inspection Service reported that there was a 50-80 percent rate of brucellosis infection among elk on feedlots, and though that number has dropped to 30 percent in more recent reports, it is still substantially higher than the 1-3 percent infection rate in wild free-ranging elk. Before the National Elk Refuge was created, the elk from southern Yellowstone would migrate and spread past the area of the refuge into southwestern Wyoming. As the winter came to a close, they moved back to their summer habitat. Today it's believed that the 11,000 elk in the Jackson herd alone migrate to and from the refuge at the risk of spreading both brucellosis and chronic wasting disease. As of 2021, the National Elk Refuge is one of 22 feeding grounds for some 20,000 elk in the western part of the state. A study published in 2016 showed that four of the five strains of brucellosis are found on Wyoming feeding grounds, a discovery that pinned the blame for the spread of brucellosis outside Yellowstone on the elk, as opposed to the bison that have long been treated as the culprits.

The question now is, what can be done? The argument has been made that the elk should return to their historical migration routes and original winter ranges rather than being concentrated in the feedlots. Today, however, many of those routes and ranges have been developed for housing, ranches, or other businesses. Furthermore, the idea of elk and cattle competing for food on the open range is worrisome to many Wyoming ranchers. So, although the scientific consensus is that it would be best for the elk to return to their natural migration patterns, the challenge is finding places in the wild that can sustain them throughout the year.

Visitor Center (532 N. Cache St., 307/733-3316, $30 adults, $15 children 5-12, free for children under 5), and a free shuttle will take visitors 3 miles (4.8 km) north of Jackson to the departure point. Tours run 10am-4pm daily and last about an hour. Dress warmly as the wind can be quite biting during the tour and visitors are on the sleigh for 45-60 minutes of the tour.

Jackson Hole and Greater Yellowstone Visitor Center

A terrific place to start any type of exploration of the area, including the National Elk Refuge, which operates out of the same building, the **Jackson Hole and Greater Yellowstone Visitor Center** (532 N. Cache St., 307/733-3316, www.fws.gov, 8am-7pm daily Memorial Day-Sept., 9am-5pm daily Oct.-Memorial Day) is a phenomenal resource with seven agencies represented, including the local chamber of commerce, the National Park Service, and the Bridger-Teton National Forest. Visitors can obtain annual park passes and hunting and fishing licenses as well as get trip-planning assistance, directions, and maps aplenty. Talk about convenient one-stop shopping. The wildlife exhibits inside are matched by sweeping wildlife observation decks outside that overlook the National Elk Refuge. The real treasure here, though, is the staff, all of whom are friendly, knowledgeable, and more than willing to roll up their sleeves for whatever help you need. Short interpretive talks are offered throughout the season, and naturalists are often on hand at the upper viewing deck with spotting scopes, binoculars, and field guides.

Teton Village

Twelve miles (19 km) northwest of Jackson is **Teton Village,** an Alps-like enclave nestled around the state's largest and most popular ski hill. The area pulses with energy and activity as soon as the snow flies, and although it quiets down in the shoulder seasons, it is an enormously popular destination in summer as well. Even so, these days it's quite a bit quieter than the center of Jackson. In addition to the abundant lodging, shopping, and dining options, the area is a hub for outdoor activities such as hot-air ballooning, paragliding, horseback riding, and, of course, a myriad of mountain-oriented sports. Plenty of concerts and special events are also held year-round.

National Bighorn Sheep Interpretive Center

Set in Dubois, 85 miles (137 km) east of Jackson on US 287/26, the **National Bighorn Sheep Interpretive Center** (10 Bighorn Ln., 307/455-3429 or 888/209-2795, www.bighorn. org, 9am-6pm daily summer, 10am-4pm Tues.-Sat. Labor Day-Memorial Day, $6 adults, $3 children 8-17, seniors, and military, free for children under 8) is dedicated to educating the public about these majestic creatures and their habitats. Visitors are welcomed by a stunning bronze of a ram and led inside to several hands-on exhibits that will delight little ones and fascinate animal lovers. There are 16 mounts of wild sheep from around the world and a great little gift shop with everything from T-shirts to children's toys and wares by local artists. November-March, the center offers tours to the winter range of the **Whiskey Mountain Habitat Area,** providing an excellent opportunity to see the bighorn sheep in their natural, windswept environment. Reservations for the tours (3-4 hours, $100 pp 2 or more, $200 for 1 person)

should be made at least 48 hours in advance by calling the center.

SPORTS AND RECREATION
Fishing

Surrounded by abundant rivers and streams, including the Snake River and its myriad mountain tributaries, plus Grand Teton and Yellowstone National Parks, Jackson has become something of a fly-fishing mecca.

The best-known trout stream in the region is the Snake River, which winds more than 60 miles (97 km) on lazy flats and then blasts through the Snake River Canyon, which offers more white-knuckle rafting than graceful casting. The Upper Snake, much of which is in Grand Teton National Park, is characterized by braided channels with cutbanks and logjams, and the water holds native cutthroats. Drift boating is popular as a way to maximize the water covered (and scenery enjoyed), but there are ample opportunities to get out and wade-fish. The section of the river that goes through the canyon is almost exclusively fished by boat (self-bailers come in handy in the Class II-III rapids), and despite the action of the waves, the fish are more plentiful in the canyon, though not always easy to catch.

Jackson has no shortage of fly-fishing guides or fly shops. Among the best is a small outfit, **Teton Fly Fishing** (420 S. Jackson St., 307/413-1215, www.tetonflyfishing.com), run by Nate Bennett, who loves teaching his clients about the art of fishing as much as he loves hooking a fish. He books only one trip daily so that the pace can be less breakneck and far more enjoyable. Bennett gets his clients on a variety of types of water and, like a good fish whisperer, somehow gets the fish to bite. An artist by training, Bennett ties all his own flies and loves to share. His trips ($500 half day, $650 full day for up to 2 anglers) on the Snake, Salt, and Green Rivers include all equipment, flies, transportation, streamside lunch, and full access to his unlimited knowledge and expertise. He also offers half-day wade-fishing trips ($450 for up to 2 anglers) on the Snake River in winter and overnight fishing trips ($900-1,800 for up to 2 anglers) all year long.

Another great resource for fishing would be the friendly folks at **JD High Country Outfitters** (50 E. Broadway, 307/733-3270, www.jdhcoutfitters.com, 9am-8pm daily summer, 10am-6pm daily fall-spring). The staff are experts on waters all over the region, and in addition to guiding services on the Snake and Green Rivers (from $475/half day, $575/full day), the shop has a great selection of flies, equipment, and clothing. They even teach casting lessons for novices.

★ Rafting on the Snake River

One of the greatest attractions for summertime visitors to Jackson is rafting the Snake River. There are close to two dozen rafting companies to choose from in the area, and most are open mid-May through September. Here are a few options for those who are interested in experiencing the river, whether it be a tranquil day float through Grand Teton National Park or white-water adventure a little farther south in the canyon.

Most adult fares average $95-110 for an 8-mile (13-km) trip. Increasingly popular are combination trips, which include a scenic float or white-water raft trip with other activities ranging from wildlife tours to horseback rides to gourmet Dutch-oven meals.

Barker-Ewing (307/733-1000 or 800/448-4202, www.barker-ewing.com, $85-110 adults, $75-110 children) is a family-operated business that has been running small trips for more than 50 years. They offer both scenic and white-water trips.

Dave Hansen Whitewater (800/732-6295, www.davehansenwhitewater.com, $100-110 adults, $85-110 children) has been in the business since the late 1960s. Dave actually named two of the largest waves on the river, the Lunch Box and the Big Kahuna.

Another option with a variety of trips down the Snake River is **Mad River Boat Trips** (800/458-7328, www.mad-river.com, from $92-115).

For experienced floaters who want to tackle the Snake unguided, **Rent-a-Raft** (10925 US 89, Hoback Jct., 13 mi/21 km south of Jackson, 307/733-2728, www.rentaraft.net) offers 12-foot ($140), 13-foot ($160), 14-foot ($180), and 16-foot rafts ($200), as well as sit-on-top kayaks, one- and two-person duck

rafting on the Snake River

kayaks ($50-75), and shuttle service from its headquarters.

Skiing and Mountain Sports

Jackson's reputation among the West's premier ski towns is not hard to explain. There are three developed downhill ski resorts, the closest one being right in town.

Snow King Mountain (400 E. Snow King Ave., 307/201-5464, www.snowkingmountain. com, full day $75 adults, $60 seniors 65 and over, $50 juniors 6-14, free for children 5 and under, half day $60 adults, $40 seniors 65 and over and juniors 6-14; night skiing 4pm-7pm $30 adults and seniors, $20 juniors 6-14, discounts available for multiday passes) soars skyward just six blocks from Town Square, so Jackson is a ski town in the most literal sense. The mountain was developed for skiing in 1939, making it the first in the Jackson area and one of the first in the country. The area boasts 1,571 feet (479 m) of vertical drop over 400 acres with two double chairlifts, one triple lift, a surface tow, and the ever-popular **Snow Tubing Park** ($25/hour all ages, $50 coaster and 1 hour tubing) and **Cowboy Coaster** ($20 drivers single ride, $10 for additional rides, $10 passengers single ride, $5 for additional rides). The area is open for day and night skiing. Discounts are available for lodging guests. Visitors who want to try every activity on the hill can get a $125-149 day pass. Nonskiers can pay to ride the lift ($30 all ages) just to enjoy the breathtaking views of town and the valley from the summit. In the summer, the trails and lifts are open for hiking, mountain biking, and paragliding, plus a cowboy rollercoaster, an alpine slide, a maze, a bungee trampoline, mini-golf, bouldering, and a treetop ropes course.

In nearby Teton Village, the ski area at **Jackson Hole Mountain Resort** (3395 Cody Ln., Teton Village, 307/733-2292 or 888/333-7766, www.jacksonhole.com, $107-179 adults, free for children 5 and under, prices rise as the season progresses, especially around the holidays, discounts available online) is in fact two mountains, Apres Vous and Rendezvous, which together offer skiers 2,500 skiable acres, a vertical drop of 4,139 feet (1,262 m), and open access to more than 3,000 acres of backcountry terrain. COVID restrictions make reservations and advance purchase strongly recommended, and parking availability is posted on the website. There are 131 trails, of which a whopping 50 percent are geared to experts, 40 percent for intermediate skiers, and 10 percent for beginners. The ski hill has averaged 526 inches (1,336 cm) of snow annually the last five years! In Jackson, this is the mountain to ski and be seen.

The **aerial tram** (3275 West Village Dr., Teton Village, 307/733-2292, late May-early Sept., call for updated prices and schedules), known as Big Red or the Red Heli, takes hikers, bikers, paragliders, backcountry skiers, and lookie-loos up to the summit of Rendezvous Peak (4,139 ft/1,262 m) in 12 minutes. At the top, **Corbet's Cabin** (307/739-2688, 9am-4:30pm daily in season), a fabulous little waffle hut, makes you wish you had hiked the whole way.

Although you need to go through Idaho to get there, **Grand Targhee Resort** (3300 Ski Hill Rd., 307/353-2300, www.grandtarghee. com, full day $93-115 adults, $72-93 seniors 65 and over, $42-53 juniors 6-12, free for children under 6) in Alta, Wyoming, is a destination in itself. The skiing in winter is out of this world, with huge dumps of powder and expansive terrain. The resort also offers Nordic skiing, tubing, guided snowcat tours, sleigh-ride dinners, snowmobile tours, and ice climbing. In summer, the mountain stays awake for hiking, mountain biking, horseback riding, and a couple of renowned musical events, including **Targhee Fest** and the **Grand Targhee Bluegrass Festival.** Since parking at most ski hills is at a premium, you can sign up online for push notifications about current availability.

For avid Nordic skiers, the blanket of snow transforms many favorite local hiking trails into first-rate ski trails. From hitting the groomers at local golf courses to hoofing into the backcountry in Grand Teton National Park, there is terrain for everyone, including at **Teton Pines Nordic Center** (3450 N. Clubhouse Dr., Wilson, 307/733-1733 or 800/238-2223, www.tetonpines.com, $20 adults, $17 seniors 65 and up, $10 children 6-12, rentals available for $25 cross-country ski package adults, $15 cross-country ski package kids, $35 skate ski package adults, $20 kids skate ski package, $30 backcountry touring package, high rates for off-site ski rentals). The **Jackson Hole Nordic Center** (3395 Village Dr., 307/739-2629, www.jhnordic.com) at Teton Village offers 11 miles (18 km) of groomed trails for classic and skate skiers, plus fat biking and snowshoeing. Rentals are available on-site.

In town, alpine, cross-country, skate, or snowshoeing gear can be purchased or rented from **Skinny Skis** (65 W. Deloney Ave., 307/733-6094, 9am-6pm Mon.-Sat., 10am-5pm Sun., www.skinnyskis.com, general touring package from $25/full day adult and $15 youth, skate skiing package $30-40/full day, snowshoes from $20/full day, telemark skis from $50/full day, with discounts for multiday rentals) or **Teton Mountaineering** (170 N. Cache St., 307/733-3595, www.tetonmtn.com), which rents alpine and telemark ski packages, along with cross-country ski packages.

Hiking and Mountain Biking

Although plenty of hikers choose to hit the trails in Grand Teton and Yellowstone National Parks, with so many mountains in every direction around Jackson, there is no shortage of amazing hikes outside the parks. Many of the trails outside the parks are open to mountain bikers as well.

One trail with immediate proximity to town that skirts the Gros Ventre Wilderness Area is the **Cache Creek Canyon Loop,** which is part of the Greater Snow King Trail Network. It is a popular trail for hikers, mountain bikers, and cross-country skiers. To get to the trailhead, drive east on Broadway to Redmond Street, across from the hospital;

turn right and go 0.4 mile (0.6 km) to Cache Creek Road. Turn left and continue just over 1 mile (1.6 km) to the parking lot at road's end. Hikers can amble along both sides of the creek on this 4-mile (6.4-km) loop, gaining only 350 vertical feet (107 m). Connecting trails lead to Game Creek and Granite Falls, or back to Snow King in Jackson.

Ten miles (16 km) west of town near Teton Pass is **Phillips Pass,** an incredible and somewhat strenuous day hike at the edge of the Tetons and the Jedediah Smith Wilderness Area. The trail is open to hikers and mountain bikers. To get to the trailhead, head west to Teton Pass on Highway 22. Two miles (3.2 km) east of the summit is Phillips Canyon Road (Forest Rd. 30972). There is no parking at the trailhead, which is 0.5 mile (0.8 km) down this road, so park safely across the highway in a small pullout or on Phillips Canyon Road close to the highway. The 8-mile (12.9 km) out-and-back trail starts at 8,000 feet (2,438 m) in elevation and is spectacularly beautiful, particularly in late summer, as it winds through flower-drenched meadows and forest to the alpine country above the tree line. As always in this part of the country, be prepared for significant weather changes and encounters with wild animals.

For excellent guided hiking in the Tetons and around the valley, contact **The Hole Hiking Experience** (307/690-4453 or 866/733-4453, www.holehike.com, private half day from $455 for up to 3 hikers, mixed half-day tour from $99 pp adults, private 3/4 day from $630 for up to 3 hikers, private full day from $805 for up to 3 hikers), which offers a wide variety of trips from half-day naturalist-guided trips geared to families to strenuous all-day hikes and even yoga-hiking combinations. They offer hiking and fly-fishing combos, hiking and hot springs, and many others. In winter they offer guided snowshoe (half-day mixed tours from $140 pp adults and $105 children, private half-day tours from $520 for up to 3 people) and cross-country skiing treks that can be combined with wildlife tours, sleigh rides, and more.

For guided mountain bike trips for the whole family (including kids on Trail-a-Bikes and in trailers) or more extreme riders, contact **Teton Mountain Bike Tours** (545 N. Cache St., 307/733-0712, www.tetonmtbike.com) for half-day (from $90 pp), full-day (from $135-185 pp plus $15 box lunch), multiple-day, and specialty trip offerings. In winter, they offer fat bike rentals and guided tours. Bikes and accessories can be rented year-round.

Hoback Sports (520 W. Broadway Ave., 307/733-5335, www.hobacksports.com, 10am-6pm daily) has all kinds of rental bikes for adults and kids, from road bikes ($59 for 3 hours, $69 full day) and e-bikes ($85 for 3 hours, $95 full day) to full-suspension mountain bikes ($69 for 3 hours, $79 full day), and can point bikers in the direction of any kind of ride they seek. They also rent car racks.

Horseback Riding

Another popular way to experience the great outdoors in Jackson is on horseback. Several options, including hourly rentals, half-day trail rides, or overnight pack trips, are available from the many local outfitters in and around town.

Located 35 miles (56 km) south of Jackson, **Jackson Hole Outfitters** (307/699-3541, www.jacksonholetrailrides.com, early June-early Sept.) starts its private trail rides in the secluded Greys River camp and follows trails through the Bridger-Teton National Forest. It offers half-day rides ($195 pp), full-day rides ($265 pp), 5.5-hour extreme rides ($295), and overnight stays ($115) in comfortable canvas tents and real beds with dinner and breakfast included.

Spring Creek Ranch (1600 N. East Butte Rd., 307/733-8833 or 800/443-6139, www.springcreekranch.com, mid-May-mid-Oct.) offers one-hour rides ($60) and two-hour rides ($80). They also offer wagon rides to a chuck wagon dinner (call for updated prices and schedule). Age restrictions vary for the different rides.

Mill Iron Ranch (3495 Horse Creek Rd., 307/773-6390 or 888/808-6390, www.

millironranch.net, mid-May-late Sept.), 10.5 miles (16.9 km) south of Jackson on US 89/191, offers two-hour ($90-110 pp), four-hour ($180-200 pp), or full-day trips ($350-370) that can be combined with breakfast, lunch, fishing, or a steak dinner for an additional charge.

Golf

Golf is becoming increasingly popular in Jackson Hole (maybe because the ball seems to fly so much farther at altitude), and there are a couple of world-class public courses. The **Jackson Hole Golf & Tennis Club** (5000 Spring Gulch Rd., 307/733-3111, www.jhgtc.com, $150-250 with twilight discounts after 3pm) offers an award-winning 18-hole course designed by Bob Baldock and renovated twice by Robert Trent Jones II, most recently in 2004. TaylorMade rental clubs are available ($90 pp). Local conservation hero Laurance Rockefeller once owned the course, which says a lot about its natural beauty. The 18-hole course at **Teton Pines Country Club** (3450 Clubhouse Dr., 307/733-1005 or 800/238-2223, www.tetonpines.com, $75-195 depending on season and time of day) in Teton Village was designed by Arnold Palmer and has been highly ranked by *Condé Nast Traveler, Audubon International,* and *Golf Digest,* among others.

ENTERTAINMENT AND EVENTS
The Arts

Among the most impressive facilities in the state is the **Jackson Hole Center for the Arts** (240 S. Glenwood St., 307/734-8956 or box office 307/733-4900, www.jhcenterforthearts.org), a truly inspired art campus in the heart of downtown that offers educational programs and facilities along with professional theater, dance, and music as well as a remarkable space for major community events. Check out the schedule online—there is always something happening. Of particular note at the Center for the Arts is the **Off Square Theatre Company** (240 S. Glenwood St., 307/733-3021, www.offsquare.

org), which produces excellent and wildly diverse shows ranging from family-favorite American musicals (*A Chorus Line*) and dramatic masterpieces (*Macbeth*) to side-splitting improv by Laff Staff. Regardless of the offerings, a night at the theater in Jackson is a night well spent.

ART GALLERIES

The art scene in Jackson is both rarefied and approachable, and an increasingly important part of both the community and the local economy. There are more than 30 galleries in town. Among the favorites are **Trailside Galleries** (130 E. Broadway, 307/733-3186, www.trailsidegalleries.com, 10am-5pm Mon.-Sat., noon-5pm Sun. June-Oct., 10am-5pm Mon.-Sat. Nov.-May) and **Legacy Gallery** (75 N. Cache St., 307/733-2353, www.legacygallery.com, 10am-6pm Mon.-Sat., 11am-5pm Sun.), both with classic examples of Western art in its traditional and contemporary forms. **Altamira Fine Art** (172 Center St., 307/739-4700, www.altamiraart.com, 10am-5pm Mon.-Sat. or by appointment) has a more loftlike urban feel and represents groundbreaking contemporary artists, including Rocky Hawkins, Duke Beardsley, Ed Mell, Mary Roberson, and John Nieto. The **Tayloe Piggot Gallery** (62 S. Glenwood St., 307/733-0555, www.jhmusegallery.com, 10am-6pm Mon.-Sat.) is cutting-edge cool with both emerging and mid-career artists in a variety of media. For more information on all the galleries in Jackson, visit the **Jackson Hole Gallery Association** (www.jacksonholegalleryassociation.com).

Festivals and Events

Weekly events in Jackson during the summer season (Memorial Day-Labor Day) include the **Jackson Rodeo** (447 W. Snow King Ave., 307/733-7927, www.jhrodeo.com, 8pm Wed. and Fri.-Sat., call for current ticket prices), a fun family event with bull riding, team roping, barrel racing, bareback broncs, and plenty of other action. Food and refreshments are sold at the chuck wagon.

For one of Jackson's favorite regular events, check out the **Town Square Shootout** (6pm Mon.-Sat.) on the Town Square. It's free and a lot of fun for visitors.

An annual event built around the well-known Boy Scout Elk Antler Auction, where the scouts sell the shed antlers they collect from the National Elk Refuge, **Elk Fest** (307/733-5935 or 307/733-3316, www.elkfest.org) takes place the weekend before Memorial Day and includes plenty of food, community concerts, children's activities, and many opportunities to learn about elk.

Happening over 10 days in late May all around town is Jackson's long-running **Old West Days** (307/733-3316, www.jacksonholechamber.com), which features a horse-drawn parade, old-town entertainment, a rodeo, a mountain man rendezvous, and a host of other events that celebrate Jackson's rough-and-tumble origins.

Happening late July-early August, the nearly weeklong **Teton County Fair** (Teton County Fairgrounds, 305 West Snow King Ave., 307/733-5289, www.tetoncountyfair.com, call for ticket prices) includes family-friendly events like pig wrestling, rodeo, demolition derby, concerts, a carnival, and plenty of agricultural and animal exhibits.

The equivalent of Cody's Rendezvous Royale, Jackson's **Fall Arts Festival** (307/733-3316, www.jacksonholechamber.com) is a 10-day event in mid-September that unites the community and attracts a crowd of art lovers with a phenomenal range of art-related events, including the prestigious **Jackson Hole Art Auction** (www.jacksonholeartauction.com) and **Western Design Conference** (www.westerndesignconference.com), gallery walks, open-air art fairs, historic ranch tours, and culinary coups.

The **Grand Teton Music Festival** (McCollister Dr., Teton Village, 307/733-1128, www.gtmf.org, call for ticket prices) takes place annually July-August. It is held in the all-wooden Walk Festival Hall, which underwent a $4.85 million renovation in 2007 to improve the intimate setting and provide top-notch acoustics. Known as one of the top classical music festivals in the country, running annually since 1962, it showcases an impressive list of musicians and singers. Past performers include Sarah Chang, Itzhak Perlman, the New York Philharmonic, and the Mormon Tabernacle Choir. In addition to the summer festival, the organization hosts concerts during the winter. Family concerts are free and open rehearsals (Friday mornings at 10am) can be attended for reduced prices.

One of the most renowned bluegrass festivals in the country takes place on the western slopes of the Grand Tetons in at the Grand Targhee Resort during mid-August. The **Grand Targhee Bluegrass Festival** (3300 Ski Hill Rd., 307/353-2300, www. grandtarghee.com, pricing announced each March) draws a large number of the best bluegrass musicians in the country, including Brother Mule, Danny Barnes, and Sarah Jarosz, along with a large number of fans. At the Grand Targhee Resort (800/827-4433), tent and RV camping is allowed in the national forest during the festival weekend. In addition to performances all day long, the festival features plenty of food, arts, and crafts.

Also taking place at Grand Targhee Resort, in mid-July, the **Targhee Fest** (www. grandtarghee.com, pricing announced each March) is a lively three-day music festival held since 2005 with an eclectic mix of artists such as Los Lobos and John Hiatt. Camping is also allowed in the national forest during this event.

The **Jackson Wild** (307/200-3286, www. jacksonwild.org), formerly the Jackson Hole Wildlife Film Festival, is an annual event dedicated to inspiring deeper connections to the natural world, held in late September or early October. The six-day festival attracts leaders in science, conservation, and media as numerous films are screened and related social events and activities are organized throughout the week. The festival has traditionally been held at the Jackson Lake Lodge. Winners in 2020 included *My Octopus Teacher*.

Winter Fest (www.jhfoodandwine.com/ winter-fest) gives residents and visitors alike one more reason to celebrate the snow. Happening in Teton Village over a weekend in March, the celebration includes events that showcase Jackson Hole's status as a food and wine destination.

Another winter event everyone looks forward to is the **Pedigree Stage Stop Dog Race** (307/734-1163, www.wyomingstagestop. org). It takes place from the last weekend in January through the first week of February. Begun in 1996, it is the largest U.S. dog-sled race outside Alaska. The race begins in Jackson and runs 500 miles (805 km) to Park City, Utah. It is unusual in that the participants stop for the night in towns along the way, including Lander, Pinedale, Big Piney-Marbleton, Alpine, Kemmerer, Lyman, Evanston, and Uinta County. Each town along the route celebrates with different festivities as they greet and cheer on the racers. The purse was $165,000 in 2022.

SHOPPING

For those with time and money, shopping can practically be an athletic pursuit in Jackson, particularly in the streets and alleyways around **Town Square.** In the early 1990s, Jackson was populated with a number of outlet stores, but today all of those have been pushed out by more sophisticated boutiques. There are lots of fascinating little shops to pop into, from gorgeous high-end art galleries to the few remaining tacky but fun T-shirt and tchotchke shops.

For an independent bookstore, **Valley Bookstore** (140 E. Broadway St., 307/733-4533, www.valleybookstore.com, 9am-9pm daily June-Aug., 10am-5pm Sun. Sept.-May) is pretty great and has been providing local readers with fabulous books and stellar recommendations since 1949. The owners grew up in Jackson and have a superb local and regional section. For an excellent selection of gifts, cards, stationery, candles, jewelry, clothing, and more, visit **MADE** (Gaslight Alley, 125 N. Cache St., 307/690-7957, www. madejacksonhole.com, 10am-6pm daily), which features work made by local and regional artists.

For top-of-the-line women's and children's clothes in a spacious, almost Zen-like setting, visit **Terra of Jackson Hole** (160 E. Broadway, 307/734-0067, www.terrajh.com, 11am-6pm Mon.-Sat., noon-4pm Sun.), which would not be out of place in Manhattan or San Francisco. Another glorious place filled with beautiful things is **Bella Cose** (48 E. Broadway, 307/733-2640, www.bellacose.com, 10am-6pm Mon.-Sat., noon-5pm Sun.), which offers elegant home decor as well as kitchen and dining items; it clearly caters to the second-home crowd. For a chance to actually play with some cool toys, visit the **Jackson Hole Toy Store** (165 Center St., 307/734-2663, www.jacksonholetoystore.com, 10am-8pm daily high season, 10am-6pm daily off-season). There's an animatronic Wild West shooting gallery ($5), and the owner can tell you anything about any of the creative toys they stock from all over the world.

One of the most exquisite design studios anywhere, **WRJ Design** (30 S. King St., 307/200-4881, www.wrjdesign.com, 10am-6pm Mon.-Fri., weekends by appointment) has a Jackson showroom filled with furnishings, unique objects, fine art, and curated lines from around the world. Owned by renowned designers Klaus Baer and Rush Jenkins, WRJ's style is elegant, earthy, and contemporary.

FOOD

For every opportunity this region provides to exert energy by skiing, hiking, biking, or other pursuits, Jackson offers many more ways to replenish your supply. The number of outstanding restaurants in this town puts just about every other town in Wyoming—and many Western states—to shame.

As a rule, every day in Jackson should start with a trip to **The Bunnery** (130 N. Cache Dr., 307/733-5474, www.bunnery.com, 7am-3pm daily summer, 7:30am-2pm daily winter, $10-17). The food is entirely made from scratch and utterly scrumptious. The baked goods—including its trademark OSM bread (oats, sunflower, millet) and homemade granola—are beyond compare, and the enormous and diverse menu offers plenty of healthy options as well as a few decadent ones. The "Get Your Buns in Here" bumper stickers are also good for a laugh. Be prepared to wait, however; The Bunnery is beloved by visitors and locals alike.

Just as the best days in Jackson should start at The Bunnery, so too should they finish at the **Million Dollar Cowboy Bar** (25 N. Cache Dr., 307/733-2207, www.milliondollarcowboybar.com, 11am-2am daily summer, 4pm-1am daily Thurs.-Sat. winter, bar food $8-18), right on Town Square. The bar has been a centerpiece of Jackson since 1937 when the first liquor license was issued in the state. The saddle bar stools should absolutely be sat upon, and visitors are encouraged to check out the impressive collection of Western memorabilia adorning the bar. There is live music regularly, and patrons who don't want to go too far can enjoy a hearty meal downstairs in the **Million Dollar Cowboy Steakhouse** (307/733-4790, www.milliondollarcowboybar.com, check for days, hours, and prices), featuring specialties like beer and bone marrow fondue, short rib nachos, grilled halibut, and any kind of steak you can imagine. The restaurant was closed during COVID, renovated in the fall of 2021, and scheduled to reopen in 2022. Reservations are recommended.

Inspired by New York's Eataly, but every bit Jackson Hole, **Bin 22** (200 W. Broadway, 307/739-9463, www.bin22jackson.com, wine bar 11am-10pm Mon.-Sat., 3pm-10pm Sun., retail shop 10am-10pm daily, $10-21) is a great spot for a light bite or to pick up a bottle of wine to go. It has all sorts of salamis and cheeses, plus appetizers, tapas-style plates including pork belly sliders, paella, lamb chops, and—you're in Wyoming after all—steak.

1: downtown Jackson 2: Jackson's Million Dollar Cowboy Bar 3: Jackson Hole Historical Society and Museum 4: the aerial tram

Just off the square, and often with a line out front, **Persephone Bakery** (145 E. Broadway, 307/200-6708, www.persephonebakery. com, 7am-3pm daily, pastry case and beverages 7am-6pm Mon.-Sat. and 7am-5pm Sun. summer, call for winter hours, $10-15) is an artisanal bakery and café, known for French-style rustic, elegant breads and pastries, and excellent salads and sandwiches for lunch. It also offers afternoon tea service (reservations required) and a nice wine list and cocktail menu. How's that for a Jackson Hole bakery?

Started by the same genius couple who own Persephone's Bakery, **Coelette** (85 S. King St., 307/201-5026, www.coelette.com, 5pm-9pm Weds.-Sun., $25-51) is housed in the old Coe Cabin serves dishes that are an exploration of snow-line cuisines from around the world. They use seasonal local ingredients—from whitetail venison and sunchokes to gold oyster mushrooms and elk—in Old World recipes invented at high elevations. The restaurant creates its Asian flair with Wyoming ingredients.

One of the most interesting places for craft cocktails, excellent wine, and a gourmet meal is **The Rose** (50 W. Broadway, 307/733-1500, www.therosejh.com, 5pm-midnight Sun.-Thurs. and 5pm-1:30am Fri.-Sat. summer, closed Mon.-Tues. winter, $22-29), founded by the same team who created the insanely hip Death & Co. in New York City. Everything here is artisanal and local, from the food and cocktails to the dinner plates and art. Adjacent to the bar and restaurant is the **Pink Garter Theatre,** an excellent venue for a diverse range of live music and special events.

Because every great tequila bar should be open for three meals a day, **Hatch Taquería & Tequilas** (120 W. Broadway, 307/203-2780, www.hatchjh.com, 8am-9pm daily, breakfast $12-14, family style lunch and dinner serving 4-6 people $36-59) fires up the grill at 8am with platos fuertes including the classic huevos rancheros, breakfast sandwiches, omelets, and burritos. Lunch and dinner are served family style, serving 4-6 people, and include such delights as seared yellowfin

wrap platters, elk quesadillas, enchiladas suizas, 10 different varieties of tacos, and more. Everything is as fresh as it is beautiful. And the drinks are legendary. They serve 25 different varieties of tequila and are known around town as having the best margaritas.

Set in a 1910 log cabin, one of the oldest residential structures in town, **Café Genevieve** (135 E. Broadway, 307/732-1910, www.genevievejh.com, 8am-3pm daily, $14-20) serves inspired home cooking for brunch and lunch daily. They serve a killer breakfast until 3pm with specialties like grits and eggs, sweet and spicy candied bacon (known as pig candy), corned beef hash, Cajun eggs Benedict, and fried chicken and waffles. And for lunch their burgers, sandwiches, and salads are sure to satisfy. Fido will appreciate the pet-friendly deck.

A fresh and delicious arrival on Jackson's culinary scene is **Pica's Mexican Taqueria** (1160 Alpine Ln., 307/734-4457, www. picastaqueria.com, 11am-9pm daily, $10-17.50), which offers the freshest take on tacos, burritos, great salads, and authentic Mexican dishes including mole, *chilaquiles,* wet burritos, and *conchinita pibil,* the Yucatan's most famous dish. Their margaritas are outstanding. Another terrific Mexican restaurant right in town is **The Merry Piglets** (160 N. Cache St., 307/733-2966, www.merrypiglets.com, 11:30am-9pm daily, $14-28), which serves classic Tex-Mex taco, burrito, chimichanga, and enchilada plates with fresh salsas, sauces, and tortilla chips, all made in-house daily. The fish is wild, the meat is pasture-raised, and no partially hydrogenated oils are used. The portions are big, and the flavors are very satisfying.

Known for its rack of lamb, but accomplished at everything on the menu, **The Blue Lion** (160 N. Millward St., 307/733-3912, www.bluelionrestaurant.com, 5:30pm-9:30pm daily, $23-44) has been a staple of the Jackson food scene since 1976, with menu items ranging from grilled wasabi elk filet, buffalo tenderloin, and Idaho trout to rack of lamb and huckleberry scallops. There's also a children's menu. Reservations are recommended.

Every ski town worth its salt needs a good hometown pizza joint. **Pizzeria Caldera** (20 W. Broadway, 307/201-1472, www. pizzeriacaldera.com, 11am-9:30pm Mon.-Thurs., 11am-11pm Fri.-Sat., closed Sun., $11-19) serves up thin-crust Napoletana-style pizza baked over stone-hearth fires. Options range from classic Italian margherita to pure Jackson Hole, like the Bisonte, with bison sausage and fresh sage. There is also a great beer and wine list, plus yummy salads, pastas, and tapas. Folks who can't get enough thrill to find out that the restaurant ships pizza nationwide.

Although it is every inch a Four Seasons, this is still Wyoming, and there is a casualness that puts visitors at ease. The hotel has some exquisite restaurants, **Westbank Grill** (serving breakfast, lunch, and dinner) among them, but a great little spot is the **Ascent Lounge** (7680 Granite Loop Rd., Teton Village, 307/732-5000, www.fourseasons. com/jacksonhole, 2pm-11pm daily, $18-30), which feels like an oversize living room and serves casual but still elegant light fare with pan-Asian flair, including Thai chicken lettuce cups, tuna poke bowl, and salmon-hamachi avocado roll. It's smaller than the resort's other restaurants, with seating for 38. As it's quite popular with the locals, the overflow spills out onto the gorgeous mountainside patio that is heated in winter.

Also in Teton Village, a longtime favorite is the **Mangy Moose Restaurant and Saloon** (3295 Village Dr., 307/733-4913, www. mangymoose.com, 7am-9pm daily, saloon 11:30am-late daily summer and ski season). The breakfast menu has a lot of Mexican specialties ($9-16), and for lunch ($8-16) there is more Mexican and pizza. The dinner menu ($18-54) is packed with upscale pub fare including a bison burger with truffle fries, prime rib, baby back ribs, and elk stroganoff. The restaurant commits up front to adding 20 percent gratuity to all food and beverage tabs, which goes directly to the waitstaff "who are

living in one of the most expensive housing markets in the world."

Right on the Town Square is one of Jackson's most celebrated eating establishments, the **Snake River Grill** (84 E. Broadway, 307/733-0557, www.snakerivergrill. com, 5:30pm-9:30pm daily summer, from 6pm daily winter, closed late Oct.-early Dec., $26-56). A visual feast in addition to being a gastronomical delight, the Snake River Grill has largely defined Jackson Hole cuisine with offerings like steak tartare pizza, bison New York steak, venison rib eye, Colorado striped bass and duck breast with a sarsaparilla glaze. The menu is diverse, constantly changing, and completely mouthwatering. It's worth noting that although children are welcome in the restaurant, no high chairs or children's menus are available.

Another elegant option for an unforgettable meal is at the Rusty Parrot's **Wild Sage** (175 N. Jackson St., 307/733-2000, www. rustyparrot.com, 5:30pm-9:30pm daily, $31-57), which sadly burned in 2019 and is scheduled to reopen by the end of 2022. With only eight tables, the service is as notable as the food. From Wagyu beef sirloin to veal osso buco, Wild Sage has made quite a name for itself in the Intermountain West culinary scene. Reservations are strongly recommended when the restaurant reopens. Equally delicious is **The Kitchen** (155 Glenwood St., 307/734-1633, www.thekitchenjacksonhole.com, 5:30pm-9:30pm Tues.-Sat., $22-56), a modern eatery that embraces an Asian influence and serves the freshest fish, meats, and seasonal vegetables. It's an interesting space architecturally, with the curvature of a modern diner, and the outside patio in summer is a wonderful place to eat an uncomplicated and delicious meal.

ACCOMMODATIONS

While there are plenty of places to hang your hat in Jackson, during the prime seasons those places will not come cheap. The best time to get a good deal on a great room is April or

November, when the ski hill is closed but the days aren't summery yet. Keep in mind though, many hotels in the area shut down during the shoulder seasons. In summer, there really is no such thing as a good deal. Just off Town Square, the **Anvil Motel** (215 N. Cache St., 307/733-3668, www.anvilmotel.com, $117-589), might be as close as you can get, and only in the off-season. The rooms are mountain-rustic with thoughtful details and custom furnishings, and some have air-conditioning.

Almost as close to Town Square but quite a bit higher on the luxury scale is **The Wort Hotel** (50 N. Glenwood St., 307/733-2190 or 800/322-2727, www.worthotel.com, $227-893), built in 1941 and a landmark in town, complete with the legendary Silver Dollar Bar & Grill, which has more than 2,000 inlaid silver dollars as time capsule-type decorations. The 55 rooms (some of which are pet-friendly, for dogs under 40 pounds, for a $45 nightly fee) and five suites are plush, and the location is great. Just down the street, the **Rusty Parrot Lodge & Spa** (175 N. Jackson St., 307/733-2000 or 888/739-1749, www.rustyparrot.com, check for rates when the hotel reopens) is in the process of being rebuilt after a 2019 fire. The scheduled reopening is late 2022. The Rusty Parrot is like a little oasis at the edge of town. From the on-site spa to the world-class dining at Wild Sage Restaurant, every little detail is well considered.

Just four blocks from Town Square, **Rustic Inn Creekside Resort & Spa** (475 N. Cache, 800/323-9279 or 307/733-2357, www.rusticinnatjh.com, rooms and cabins from $169) is an oasis of calm. The creekside cabins are farther from the road and quieter, but the whole property is lovely on 12 acres of beautiful landscaping. The log cabins are cozy and elegantly appointed. The spa is excellent, as are on-site dining options.

Although independent hotels and inns tend to reflect more of Jackson's charm, there are plenty of nice chain hotels, some of which can offer good deals, particularly in the off-season. Among them are **Hampton Inn** (350 S. Hwy. 89, 307/733-0033, www.hamptoninn3. hilton.com, from $127); **Jackson Hole Super 8** (750 S. Hwy. 89, 307/733-6833, www.jacksonholesuper8.com, from $85), which is steps away from the free bus service in town; and **Motel 6** (600 S. Hwy. 89, 307/733-1620, www.motel6.com, from $76).

A comfortable bed-and-breakfast with easy access to both town and country is **Inn on the Creek** (295 N. Millward, 307/739-1565, www.innonthecreek.com, $179-399), which offers balconies, fireplaces, king beds, and private Jacuzzis in some of its rooms. Another very peaceful place to stay with a babbling creek to help lull you to sleep is the seven-bedroom **Wildflower Lodge at Jackson Hole** (3725 Shooting Star Ln., Wilson, 307/222-4400, www.jhwildflowerlodge.com, call for rates), which boasts cozy handcrafted log beds, fluffy comforters, and delicious chef-made breakfasts. There are even two kids' bunk rooms for families traveling together. There are minimum stays for the various accommodations. And for larger groups, the whole house can be rented starting at $3,324/night.

For unparalleled luxury in the heart of this mountain village, Jackson has plenty of options. **Amangani** (1535 NE Butte Rd., 307/734-7333, www.amanresorts.com, from $1,350) is perched on the edge of a butte with stunning views from every window of meadows and mountains. In addition to deluxe suites and first-class service, Amangani rents spectacular homes. In Teton Village at the base of the ski hill, the five-star **Four Seasons Resort** (7680 Granite Loop Rd., 307/732-5000, www.fourseasons.com, from $850) offers ski-in/ski-out access from their suites and resort residences with exquisite amenities including fine dining, a spa, and flawless service.

Away from the hustle and bustle of town, perched on a ridge overlooking the entire valley is the **Spring Creek Ranch** (1800 Spirit Dance Rd., 307/733-8833 or 800/443-6139, www.springcreekranch.com, call for rates and availability), which boasts a variety of accommodations, including hotel rooms, cabins, condos, and exclusive mountain villas. The property is entirely self-contained with two restaurants on-site, a spa, and a slew of activities. The views from here beat just about everything else in the region, and the quiet gives Spring Creek Ranch tremendous appeal.

At Teton Village, **Hotel Terra** (3335 W. Village Dr., 307/201-6065 or 800/318-8707, www.hotelterrajacksonhole.com, from $369) is a hip choice, at once luxurious and sustainable. The ecofriendly rooms have clean lines, retro-funky appointments, and lots of gadgets for techies, including iPod docking stations, flat-screen high-definition TVs, and Bose surround sound. The 132 guest rooms and suites range in size and style from urban studios and Terra guest rooms to one- to three-bedroom suites. There are two restaurants on-site, a lively bar, a rooftop swimming pool and hot tub, a day spa, and a fitness center.

GUEST RANCHES

For many visitors, the best way to enjoy Jackson Hole is to while away the days at a scenery-soaked dude ranch somewhere in the valley. After all, it was the dude ranches that jump-started Jackson's economy in the 1920s and 1930s. A multitude of wonderful choices are available, ranging from the historic and rustic, like the **Flat Creek Ranch** (15 bumpy mi/24 km from Jackson in isolated splendor, 307/733-0603 or 866/522-3344, www.flatcreekranch.com, $625 pp for up to 2 people, $450/night additional guests, minimum stays apply), to the extravagant, like **Lost Creek Ranch & Spa** (17820 Old Ranch Rd., Moose, 30 minutes north of Jackson, 307/733-3435, www.lostcreek.com, cabins from $12,900/week per cabin for up to 4 people), to the family-oriented, like the **Heart Six Guest Ranch** (Moran, 35 mi/56 km north of Jackson, 307/543-2477, www.heartsix.com, rooms from $99/night).

There are options for every preference: proximity to town, emphasis on riding, this century or last, weekend or weeklong stays,

and more. For a comprehensive listing of the dude ranches in the vicinity of Jackson Hole, contact the **Dude Ranchers' Association** (866/399-2339 or 307/587-2339, www.duderanch.org).

CAMPING

Camping is by far the most economical way to stay in and around Jackson, and there are 14 campgrounds within a 15-mile (24-km) radius of downtown. Among the closest to town is the **Curtis Canyon Campground** (Flat Creek Rd., 8 mi/13 km northeast of Jackson, 307/739-5400, www.fs.usda.gov/btnf, mid-May-early Sept., $15/night for 1 vehicle, $7 for 2nd vehicle), which offers phenomenal views of the Tetons from its 12 sites, immediate access to the National Elk Refuge, and terrific mountain hiking trails. Vault toilets and drinking water are available.

For more information on specific public campgrounds, contact the **Bridger-Teton National Forest** (340 N. Cache Dr., Jackson, 307/739-5500, www.fs.usda.gov).

For RV parks in Jackson, try the large and conveniently located **Virginian Lodge** (750 W. Broadway, 307/733-2792 or 800/262-4999, May 1-Oct. 15, www.virginianlodge.com), which has both motel rooms ($159-479) and 103 RV sites (from $119/night) in addition to all the amenities you could want, including laundry, a pool, a hot tub, a salon, a restaurant, and a saloon.

INFORMATION AND SERVICES

The most comprehensive spot to get information on the area is the **Jackson Hole and Greater Yellowstone Visitor Center** (532 N. Cache St., 307/733-3316, www.fws.gov, 8am-7pm daily Memorial Day-Sept., 9am-5pm daily Oct.-Memorial Day), which houses representatives from the Jackson Hole Chamber of Commerce (307/733-3316), the National Park Service, the Bridger-Teton National Forest, and four other agencies all under the same sod roof.

TRANSPORTATION
Getting There

The only airport within a national park, **Jackson Hole Airport** (JAC, 1250 E. Airport Rd., Jackson, 307/733-7682, www. jacksonholeairport.com) is served by American, Delta, United, and Frontier. The schedules change seasonally but include regular flights from Salt Lake City, Denver, Seattle, Chicago, Minneapolis, Dallas, Houston, Phoenix, San Francisco, and Los Angeles. Make note that the airport will be entirely closed for runway reconstruction April 11-June 28, 2022.

The major routes into Jackson Hole—including US 89/191/287 from Yellowstone and Grand Teton National Parks, US 26/287 from the east, Highway 22 from the west over Teton Pass, and US 189/191/89 from the south—can all experience weather closures in the winter, particularly over Teton Pass. There is no car traffic in the southern portion of Yellowstone during the winter. For Wyoming **road reports,** call 800/996-7623 (www. wyoroad.info).

Jackson is roughly 240 miles (385 km) south of Bozeman, 177 miles (280 km) southwest of Cody through Yellowstone National Park, and 275 miles (445 km) northeast of Salt Lake City. Keep in mind that while distances through the national parks may be shorter in actual mileage, the time is often extended by lower speed limits, traffic congestion, and animal jams. In addition, most of the park roads are closed in winter, and car travel is not possible between Bozeman and Jackson or between Cody and Jackson. Driving distances around the parks increase significantly.

Getting Around

The airport has on-site car rentals from **Alamo, National, Enterprise,** and **Avis/ Budget. Dollar, Thrifty, Hertz,** and **Leisure Sports** (307/733-3040) are available off-site.

In town, **Alltrans** (307/733-3135 or 800/443-6133, www.jacksonholealltrans. com) provides airport shuttles and a variety of tours. They can offer service to and from Salt Lake City. Shuttles can also be arranged through **Jackson Hole Shuttle** (307/200-1400, www.jhshuttle.com).

Somewhat amazingly for this part of the country, Jackson has more than 30 taxi companies serving the area, including **Broncs Car Service** (307/413-9863, www. jackson-hole-taxi.com), **Snake River Taxi** (307/413-9009, www.snakerivertaxi.com), and **Teton Mountain Taxi** (307/699-7969, www.jacksonholecab.com). Transportation to Jackson from the airport runs roughly $45 for 1-2 people. A taxi to Teton Village averages $80 for two people. A complete list of taxi services can be found under the Transportation heading on the airport website.

Pinedale

Like so many small communities that dot the West, Pinedale (pop. 1,867, elev. 7,201 ft/2,195 m) started as a ranch that doubled as a post office. Organized in 1904 and incorporated in 1912, the small community has an interesting mix of people and, thanks to the state's energy boom and extraction of natural gas nearby, some unavoidable boom-and-bust growing pains.

Nestled between the western flank of the Wind River Mountains and the 11-mile-long (18-km) Fremont Lake, Pinedale is a natural playground for hiking, climbing, sailing, and fishing. The other great pastime in these parts is history, and the town has done an excellent job of preserving it with the Museum of the Mountain Man and annual events like the Green River Rendezvous in July.

Not necessarily a well-known destination, Pinedale, which is the county seat for Sublette County, is a natural stopping point between Jackson (78 mi/126 km north) and Rock Springs (100 mi/161 km south), with great access to some of Wyoming's most extraordinary mountains and lakes.

SIGHTS
Museum of the Mountain Man

The **Museum of the Mountain Man** (700 E. Hennick St., 307/367-4101 or 877/686-6266, www.museumofthemountainman.com, 9am-5pm daily May-Oct., $10 ages 13 and over, $8 seniors 60 and over, free for children 12 and under) is dedicated to preserving the history of the fur trapping and trading era. Its exhibits are full of interesting artifacts and interpretive materials related to the Western fur trade and the life of Native Americans in the region during this period. Visitors can view Jim Bridger's rifle, learn about beaver trapping and the processing of fur, and see a full-size buffalo hide tipi (there are not many of these remaining in the United States) that has been extensively and authentically furnished. The museum also houses exhibits related to local history, including the settling of Sublette County and the development of Pinedale over the last 100 years.

Granite Hot Springs

En route from Jackson to Pinedale, some 12 miles (19 km) south of Hoback Junction on US 189/191, is the turnoff for **Granite Hot Springs** (307/690-6323, 10am-7pm daily late May-Labor Day, 10am-6pm daily Labor Day-Oct., 10am-4pm Dec.-mid-Feb., 10am-5pm mid-Feb.-early Apr., closed November and early April-late May, $8 adults, $5 children). The 10-mile-long (16-km) scenic drive is on a gravel road that ends at the parking lot for the hot springs. Camping is allowed along the road but not within the last 1.5 miles (2.4 km) before the springs. In the winter the road is groomed to allow access on skis, snowshoes, snowmobiles, fat bikes, or dogsleds. The

concrete pool is situated below the Gros Ventre mountain range and was built by the Civilian Conservation Corps in 1933. The water is usually about 93°F (34°C) in the summer and 112°F (44°C) in winter. There is a nice deck for lounging, and one family changing room is available. Soaking is limited to one hour. **Granite Creek Campground** is a nearby 51-site campground (mid-May-late Sept., $15), run by the same people who manage the hot springs. There is no cell coverage in the area.

If you are visiting during the winter, a popular way to access the hot springs is by dogsled. **Jackson Hole Iditarod Sled Dog Tours** (307/733-7388 or 800/554-7388, www.jhsleddog.com), run by eight-time veteran of the Iditarod Frank Teasley, offers full-day trips to the hot springs ($400 pp) that cover 20 miles (32 km) of trail and can include a hearty lunch prepared on-site while you are enjoying a dip in the springs. Other options include snowmobiling, cross-country skiing, and fat-tire biking.

SPORTS AND RECREATION
Fremont Lake

The second-largest natural lake in the state, **Fremont Lake** (3.2 mi/5.2 km north of Pinedale, www.pinedale.com) was formed glacially and is more than 600 feet deep in places. The lake was named for John C. Fremont, who mapped the area in 1842 in advance of the Oregon Trail. The lake is a natural recreation site with opportunities for boating, sailing, waterskiing, fishing, and camping. Though there are no designated hiking trails around the lake, most of the shoreline is undeveloped and can be walked on. The 54 RV and tent campsites at **Fremont Lake Campground** ($15-50), operated by the U.S. Forest Service at the lower end of the lake, are generally open late May to early September (early May and late September non-electric only) and can be reserved through www.recreation.gov (877/444-6777). Also at the lower end of the lake, the **Sandy Beach** picnic area is for day use only.

For an incredibly scenic drive or bike ride, **Skyline Drive** is a 16-mile (26-km) paved road along the lake's eastern shore that leads to a campground and hiking trails at the edge of the Bridger Wilderness.

The only commercial facility at Fremont Lake is the idyllic **Lakeside Lodge Resort & Marina** (99 Forest Service Rd. 111, 307/367-2221 or 877/755-5253, www.lakesidelodge.com, year-round), which offers 12 beautiful cabins ($65-279), a full-service restaurant (307/367-3555, lunch and dinner daily summer, dinner Thurs.-Sat. winter), and pontoon boat rentals ($450 full day), fishing boats ($180 full day), deck boats ($500 day), plus stand-up paddleboards, kayaks, and canoes (all $15/hour). When snow covers the ground, the lodge rents snowmobiles ($200-1,925).

Fishing and Boating

There are literally hundreds of lakes in the vicinity of Pinedale that contain several species of trout and a few Montana grayling, as well as an assortment of freestone waterways that include the world-class Green, Hoback, and New Fork Rivers. Wild trout abound in smaller streams too, including Faler Creek, Fish Creek, and North Cottonwood Creek in the Wyoming Range, some of which are private-lease streams.

The best place to start any fishing expedition is at **Two Rivers Emporium** (232 W. Pine St., 307/367-4131, www.tworiversfishing.com, 8am-6pm daily high season, reduced hours off-season), which can outfit you from rod to leader to fly and offers a range of guided trips (float fishing from $550/half day, $650/full day for 1-2 people), including wading on private waters, backcountry trips, and llama treks. Trips can include lodging and gourmet meals.

With so many lakes in the region, canoeing is a wonderful and quiet way to navigate the myriad waterways. Lake-use canoe and kayak rentals ($35/day) and stand-up paddleboards

($45/day) are available in town from the **Great Outdoor Shop** (332 W. Pine St., 307/367-2440, www.greatoutdoorshop.com, 8am-6pm daily). It also offers an amazing range of services, including guided fishing trips and gear rental, shuttles to the best trailheads and the airport in Jackson, backpacking, and gear rentals for rock- or ice-climbing. Their online fishing and trail reports are excellent.

Motorized and nonmotorized boats are available for rent on Fremont Lake at **Lakeside Lodge Resort & Marina** (99 FS Rd. 111, 877/755-5253, www.lakesidelodge.com, $15/hour-$500/day).

Hiking and Rock Climbing

The Wind River and Wyoming Ranges, which include the Jim Bridger and Gros Ventre Wilderness Areas, offer some of the best hiking and climbing in the state. Hundreds of miles of trails crisscross the area and give hikers and backpackers access to hundreds of thousands of acres of gorgeous alpine and subalpine terrain. Many of the trailheads are at 9,000 feet (2,743 m) and higher, so be prepared for significant and immediate changes in the weather. Prime hiking season this high is short—mid-July to mid-September—and it can snow any day of the year. Average daytime summer temperatures peak in the 70s and 80s Fahrenheit (approximately 22-31°C), with nighttime lows dropping into the 30s Fahrenheit (approximately 0-4°C). Afternoons often bring rainstorms with lightning, so be prepared to get lower in a hurry. Always be aware that this is black bear and grizzly bear country, so plan ahead and bring pepper spray.

Among the favorites in the area is the easily accessible **Elkhart Park Trail,** the only one accessed by a paved road, just 15 miles (24 km) northeast of Pinedale. The heavily hiked trail departs from the **Trails End Campground** at 9,100 feet (2,774 m) in elevation. Great day hikes will lead you into the Wind River Mountains and places like **Photographer's Point** and **Miller Lake.** A staffed Forest

Service visitor center at the Elkhart Park trailhead can provide information about trails and trail conditions.

Another excellent series of trails is in the Green River Lakes, 52 miles (84 km) north of Pinedale (31 paved mi/50 km and 21 mi/34 km of good gravel). The Hiline Trail, among others, starts at a 39-site campground at 8,000 feet (2,438 m) in elevation and runs almost the length of the Winds, 80 miles (129 km) south over jaw-droppingly beautiful terrain. There are several fishable lakes in the area and an abundance of ways to enjoy a day hike.

For more information on specific trails, conditions, and maps, contact the Bridger-Teton National Forest office (29 E. Fremont Lake Rd., Pinedale, 307/367-4326, www.fs.usda.gov).

Mountain Biking

The 2,700-mile (4,345-km) Great Divide Mountain Bike Route from Banff, Alberta, to the U.S.-Mexican border, along the spine of the Rockies, passes directly through Pinedale. There is plenty of rugged terrain to be explored by mountain bike. Due to the weather, however, most trails are only good for biking 3-5 months of the year. Sweeny Creek and Grouse Mountain Trails have some good short rides, or for the more adventurous (and fit), try the ride up Half Mountain. From the top you can bike almost the entire length of the ridge and take in some spectacular views. Other favorite local spots for mountain biking include Kelly Park, Fortification Mountain, and The Old Skyline Drive.

During the summer, White Pine Ski Resort (74 White Pine Rd., 10 mi/16 km northeast of Pinedale, 307/367-6606) is open to mountain bikers who aren't afraid of a good climb or fast downhill ride. Special biking trails for all levels of experience have been groomed for the ride downhill. For a more tranquil and scenic ride, opt for one of the flatter cross-country trails. There are also plenty of trails in the vicinity, including some that lead to Kelly Park.

For more trail ideas in the Pinedale area, visit www.singletracks.com.

Skiing

The state's oldest ski area, White Pine Ski Resort (74 White Pine Rd., 10 mi/16 km northeast of Pinedale, 307/367-6606, www.whitepineski.com, all-day $50 adults 19-69, $37 youth and seniors, $6 children 5 and under, discounts for half day) is tucked in the Bridger-Teton National Forest above Fremont Lake. Though relatively small when compared to others in the Jackson area, the resort is a wonderful family-oriented ski hill with lodging, two restaurants, rentals, and free access to 35 kilometers (22 mi) of groomed cross-country ski trails in winter. There's also a tubing hill ($20 pp unlimited rides, $60 family pack for up to 4 people) that's open on Saturdays and Sundays, with more openings around holidays.

In summer, the mountain is open for mountain biking, hiking, horseback riding, and, because of its proximity to the lake, fishing.

Horseback Riding

The Bridger-Teton National Forest is a wonderful experience on horseback. The White Pine Ski Resort (74 White Pine Rd., 10 mi/16 km northeast of Pinedale, 307/367-6606, www.whitepineski.com) offers multi- and single-night pack trips. One amazing option is the overnight pack trip to Sweeney Lake (call for rates), during which anglers can fish for prized golden trout. An excellent outfitter with a stellar reputation for everything from horseback riding and snowmobiling trips to hunting and fishing is Green River & Bridger-Teton Outfitters (138-2 Forty Rod Rd., 307/733-1044, www.grbto.com). Among the offerings are two-hour rides (from $165 pp) through meadows and thick timber, half-day-plus (from $225 pp) rides through mountain meadows and along a stream to a historic log cabin for lunch, and all-day rides (from $350 pp) through alpine terrain. Those who

1

2

3

want to book an exclusive trip (without other guests) have that option for increased rates (2-hour rides from $300 pp with 4-person minimum, half day from $500 pp with 4-person minimum, and full day from $650 pp with 4-person minimum.)

Golf

At the west end of town, **Rendezvous Meadows Golf Course** (55 Club House Rd., 307/367-4252, www.golfpinedale.com, $20 for 9 holes, $35 for 18 holes, carts $15 pp for 9 holes and $20 pp for 18 holes) is a nice nine-hole public course.

ENTERTAINMENT AND EVENTS

The **Green River Rendezvous** (307/367-2242, www.meetmeonthegreen.com) is a huge community event that takes place the second full weekend of July. The city prides itself on the fact that 6 of the 15 Rocky Mountain Rendezvous were held here in the Green River Valley at Horse Creek. The rendezvous became an annual event in the 1830s. For about three weeks trappers, traders, and Native Americans would come together to trade and resupply their outfits, exchange stories, catch up with old friends, get incredibly drunk, and participate in all sorts of boisterous behavior.

Today the Green River Rendezvous is more family-friendly while still bringing the era of the mountain man to life. There are plenty of games, crafts, living history demonstrations, guest speakers, a mountain man encampment, programs for children, and a rodeo. The pageant, which is usually held on Sunday, should not be missed. It is an entertaining reenactment of an 1830s rendezvous. The participants, in original costumes, are lively characters who barter, trade, and duel.

A newer addition to the summer lineup is

the **Wind River Mountain Festival** (www. windrivermtfest.com) held in late July. In addition to concerts, you'll find music, yoga, hiking, camping, gear demos and workshops, a craft beer fest, and other adventures. The events are held in Pinedale at the American Legion Park. On the Sunday of the festival, adventurers can compete in the three-person-team Surly Pika Adventure Race—a biking, hiking, boating extravaganza to various checkpoints—in either a 6-hour or 12-hour division.

FOOD

For authentic Mexican and big, juicy burgers, **Los Cabos** (120 W. Pine St., 307/367-6781, 11am-9pm Mon.-Sat., 11am-8pm Sun., $9-18) is the spot. Tuesday nights are burger specials that bring a lot of locals out.

For a fun evening with excellent beer, try the **Wind River Brewing Company** (402 W. Pine St., 307/367-2337, www. windriverbrewingco.com, 11:30am-9pm Wed.-Sun., $12-18) for great salads, appetizers, sandwiches, burgers, and steaks. Its award-winning handcrafted ales are the icing on the cake. They also host the **Windriver Brew Fest** in mid-September, which features plenty of beer and live music.

A good place for a filling meal for the whole family is **Old Stones Smokehouse & Country Pizza** (4 Country Club Ln., 307/367-6760, www.windriverpizza.com, 11am-9pm Mon.-Sat., 11am-8pm Sun., $7-14), which serves barbecue and gourmet stone-hearth pizza, plus calzones, pasta, salads, and all variety of bar-type appetizers. There's also a salad, soup, and pizza buffet and lunch specials.

A unique dinner option that reflects the people and culture of Pinedale is the family-run ★ **Pitchfork Fondue** (9888 US 191, 307/367-3607 or 307/360-8969, www.pitchforkfondue.com, 5pm-8:30pm Thurs.-Sat., late May into Sept., $35 adult steak or chicken, $18 buffet only, $10 kids 12 and under), an ingenious Western outdoor cookout at the fairgrounds south of town.

1: hiking in the Green River Lakes area
2: performers at Eastern Shoshone Indian Days Powwow and Rodeo 3: a kayak on Green River Lakes

Tender steaks are seared in large cast-iron cauldrons of oil (yes, on pitchforks) and served with fondue sauces, hot homemade potato chips, fruit salad, green salad, beverages, and homemade brownies. There are options for vegetarians too, and hot dog meals for kids. The picnic tables can accommodate 240 people, but call ahead for reservations and current pricing.

ACCOMMODATIONS

Because of a population boom driven by the energy industry, there are quite a few accommodations in and around Pinedale, particularly given the size of the town. **The Log Cabin Motel** (49 E. Magnolia St., 307/367-4579, www.thelogcabinmotel.com, from $79) is as charming as it is conveniently located. Built in 1929, the motel lives up to its name by remaining true to Pinedale's architectural style. The cabins vary in size, but most are quite spacious with partial or full kitchens, covered porches, satellite TV, and Wi-Fi. Pets are welcome in certain rooms with advance reservations. A comfortable and more modern option is the pet-friendly **Sundance Motel** (148 E. Pine St., 307/367-4789, $75-135), which offers singles, doubles, triples, and even a bunk room. The doubles and triples have kitchenettes.

The **Chambers House Bed & Breakfast** (111 W. Magnolia St., 307/231-7100 www.chambershouse.com, $119-239) is a charming inn, the oldest in the state, and run by a historian. There are seven cozy rooms and great breakfasts. Pets are welcome for a fee. Larger, modern chain hotels in town include **Best Western Pinedale Inn** (864 W. Pine St., 307/367-6869, www.bestwestern.com, $79-299) **Hampton Inn & Suites** (55 Bloomfield Ave., 307/367-6700, www.hilton.com, $94-173), and **Quality Inn & Suites** (1054 W. Pine St., 307/367-8800, from $73), all of which are clean and comfortable with standard amenities.

A great lakeside resort 3.5 miles (5.6 km) out of town is the **Lakeside Lodge Resort & Marina** (99 Forest Service Rd. 111, 307/367-2221 or 877/755-5253, www.lakesidelodge.com, year-round), which offers 12 beautiful cabins ($65-189), all with immediate waterfront access and splendid views, and a full-service restaurant (307/367-3555, lunch and dinner daily summer, dinner daily winter).

CAMPING

Sublette County is 80 percent public land, making camping in the region a viable option. The closest (and happily, the most scenic) RV and tent campsites can be found at **Fremont Lake Campground** (5 mi/8 km northeast of Pinedale, www.recreation.gov, late May-early Sept., $15-50) and the **Half Moon Lake Campground** (10 mi/16 km northeast of Pinedale, late May-early Sept., 877/444-6777, www.recreation.gov, $12). There is no potable water at Half Moon Lake, and 11 of its spots can be reserved. Just two blocks south of Pine Street is **South Jackson Tent Camping** (204 S. Jackson Ave., 307/231-1558, June 15-Sept. 15, call for rates), which has 50 sites, a portable toilet, and access to drinking water.

For more information on U.S. Forest Service campgrounds and backcountry camping, contact the **Bridger-Teton National Forest office** (29 E. Fremont Lake Rd., Pinedale, 307/367-4326, www.fs.usda.gov).

INFORMATION AND SERVICES

The **Sublette County Visitor Center** (19 E. Pine St., 888/285-7282, www.visitpinedale.org, 10am-5pm daily summer, 10am-5pm Mon.-Fri. winter) can provide information about the local area and the region for everything from hiking trails to fishing guides and up-to-date event calendars.

Two comprehensive websites for activities and businesses in the area are www.pinedaleonline.com and www.visitpinedale.org.

The **Sublette County Library** (155 S. Tyler Ave., 307/367-4114, www.sublettecountylibrary.org, 10am-8pm Mon.-Thurs., 10am-6pm Fri., 10am-5pm Sat.) offers plenty of interesting events in addition to its sizable collection. Free Wi-Fi is provided, and public computers with free Internet access are available for 30 minutes at a time.

Though the nearest hospital is still 78 miles (126 km) north in Jackson, Pinedale is served by the **Pinedale Medical Clinic** (625 E. Hennick St., 307/367-4133, 8am-5pm Mon.-Fri.).

TRANSPORTATION
Getting There
The nearest commercial airports are in Jackson (78 mi/126 km), Rock Springs (100 mi/161 km), Idaho Falls, Idaho (190 mi/305 km), and Salt Lake City (250 mi/405 km). Private jets can be accommodated at **Pinedale Wenz Field** (307/367-4136 or 307/367-6425).

Rental cars are available in Jackson and Rock Springs. The closest Greyhound bus service is also in Rock Springs.

Getting Around
For shuttle service in Pinedale, the **Great Outdoor Transportation Company** (1308 Wilson St., www.gotcoshuttle.com, 307/360-3660) offers taxi service, gear drops, fishing shuttles, and shuttles from the airports in Jackson and Rock Springs.

Lander

Tucked in the foothills of the Wind River Mountains on the banks of the Popo Agie (po-PO-zhuh) River and adjacent to the Wind River Indian Reservation, Lander (pop. 7,364, elev. 5,357 ft/1,633 m) is an outdoors lover's town and a vibrant, growing community. The area was first visited by fur trappers as early as 1811, and oil was discovered in 1824 but not developed until the mid-1880s. The area was the home ground of Chief Washakie and his Shoshone. In 1869 a small military post was established here to protect the Shoshone from enemies that included the Sioux and Arapaho. The valley, once known by Native Americans as Pushroot for its fertile soil, was farmed early on to great success thanks to the relatively mild winters and little wind.

Not a large town by any stretch, Lander is a welcoming place with friendly people, a decidedly outdoor-oriented culture, and immediate access to some of the most rugged wilderness in the country.

SIGHTS
Wind River Reservation
The **Wind River Reservation** sits on 2.2 million acres and is home to more than 9,800 Northern Arapaho (www.northernarapaho.

com) and 4,400 Eastern Shoshone (www.easternshoshone.org) tribal members. It surrounds the city of Riverton, with the towns of Lander, Shoshoni, and Thermopolis close to its borders. There is not a lot of intermingling between the Indigenous and non-Indigenous communities, or between the Arapaho and Shoshone themselves, for that matter; the arrangement to leave both tribes on the same reservation was decided by the U.S. government without their consent. The western part of the reservation, including the towns of Fort Washakie, Burris, and Crowheart, is occupied by the Shoshone, and the eastern part, including the towns of Ethete and Arapaho, is occupied by the Arapaho. Although the reservation struggles with problems of poverty and unemployment, it is also home to an incredibly rich history, important traditions, and pristine wilderness.

A drive through the reservation affords visitors magnificent views of Wyoming's undeveloped natural beauty and the majestic Wind River Mountains. The reservation is easily accessible by car, and its roads are open to visitors. If you'd like to hike, fish, camp, or boat, however, access is restricted to certain parts of the reservation, and a recreation fee or fishing permit is required. Hunting by non-Native Americans is not allowed. The chambers of commerce in Lander, Riverton, and Dubois can provide more information about fees and permits. Fort Washakie is also the location of the **Shoshone Tribal Cultural Center** (90 Ethete Rd., 307/332-3177, 9am-4pm Mon.-Fri., call for admission prices) and the gravesites of the two most prominent Shoshone, Chief Washakie (it was his hometown) and Lewis and Clark's fearless guide Sacagawea. Be sure to call ahead since the cultural center is located in the school library and closes when school is not in session.

The biggest draw to the reservation is the powwows held throughout the summer season. These large cultural celebrations usually take place over a three-day weekend and include dancing, singing, parades, and traditional games. Competitors come from across the country, and both tribes host their own powwows. The largest Shoshone powwow is the **Eastern Shoshone Indian Days Powwow and Rodeo** (800/645-6233, www.windriver.org), an all-Indian rodeo usually held the fourth weekend in June. The event hosts more than 700 dancers and 15 professional drumming groups. The largest Arapaho powwow is the **Ethete Celebration** (307/223-6430 or 307/438-3707) in late July. For additional information about the powwows and weekly events, contact the **Wind River Heritage Center** (1075 S. Federal Blvd., Riverton, 307/856-0706, www.windriverheritagecenter.com) or the **Wind River Visitors Council** (800/645-6233 or 307/332-5546, www.windriver.org).

WIND RIVER WILD HORSE SANCTUARY

Since 2016, the Oldham family has offered free-roaming refuge for up to 250 un-adoptable mustangs on their 900-acre working cattle ranch. The **Wind River Wild Horse Sanctuary** (8616 Highway 287, Lander, 307/438-3838, www.windriverwildhorses.com, 9am-5pm Mon.-Fri. and 9am-4pm Sat.

in summer, open by appointment only in winter, ATV tours $40 adults, $15 for kids 13-17, free for 12 and under) is one of only four public off-range pastures for the country's wild horse population, and the only one located on an Indian Reservation. There's an interpretive center (free admission) with displays describing Native American horse culture, and a small gift shop, but the highlight will be climbing aboard the Oldham's ATV and cruising around the ranch to see the mustangs. This is an extraordinary family doing important work in an outrageously beautiful setting.

★ Sinks Canyon State Park

A place that is as beautiful as it is fascinating, **Sinks Canyon State Park** (3079 Sinks Canyon Rd., 6 mi/10 km south of Lander, 307/332-6333 or 307/332-3077, www.sinkscanyonstatepark.org, sunrise-10pm daily, visitor center 9am-6pm daily Memorial Day-Labor Day, free) is filled with recreational opportunities and one of the state's geological wonders. Here in the canyon is where the Middle Fork of the Popo Agie River plunges into a cave, only to emerge 0.5 mile (0.8 km) away in an area known as **The Rise.** What makes it so interesting is that geologists have determined that it takes more than two hours for the water to make the journey. In addition, there is plenty of water emerging at the Rise that did not enter at the Sinks. Adding yet another layer of mystery is that the water is a couple of degrees warmer when it emerges than when it disappeared.

Aside from its geological and scenic attributes, Sinks Canyon is a fantastic place for hiking, rock climbing, fishing (but not in the trout-laden waters at the Rise, where vending machines dole out food for these lunkers), and wildlife-watching. Keep your eyes peeled for transplanted bighorn sheep, moose, and any number of bird species.

Loop Road

Among the most scenic drives in the region, and perhaps the state, is a roughly 70-mile

Peaceful Coexistence:
The Shoshone and the Arapaho Tribes

The Treaty of Fort Bridger, signed in 1863, designated 44 million acres as "Shoshone Country." This large parcel of land not only included territory in Wyoming but also crossed into Colorado, Utah, and Idaho. However, there was no formal demarcation, and settlers and migrants continued to settle the land in the south, up into the Green River Valley, forcing the Shoshone tribe into Arapaho tribal territory in order to hunt. Furthermore, gold was discovered near South Pass, and coal near Rock Springs, and both mining towns and farms were popping up along the Wind River drainage.

In 1868, another treaty was signed, establishing the much smaller 2.2-million-acre Wind River Reservation. For a variety of reasons, land continued to be ceded to the government, including the Popo Agie Valley and the present-day towns of Shoshoni and Thermopolis. Shoshone Chief Washakie bartered determinedly to improve life on the reservation for his people. He asked for specific physical improvements, goods, and protection from their Indian enemies. (Fort Brown, renamed Fort Washakie in 1878, resulted from this bargaining.) Today the reservation stretches 70 miles (113 km) west-east and 55 miles (89 km) north-south and is home to about 4,400 Eastern Shoshone and 9,800 Northern Arapaho.

Understanding why two tribes, historically great enemies, would share the same reservation requires a history lesson and some imagination. By 1877, most Native Americans had been re-located to reservations, yet the Northern Arapaho tribe remained landless. With winter rapidly approaching, the U.S. government turned to Chief Washakie, requesting that the Shoshone tribe share their reservation with the Arapaho tribe just for the winter. Washakie conceded, but made it clear that by spring the visitors must be relocated. Spring came and went with Washakie repeat-edly demanding that the Arapaho tribe be removed from the reservation. His pleas fell on deaf ears, and the former archenemies were forced to make the best of the situation.

They each established their own governments and mostly occupied separate parts of the reservation. The Arapaho tribe settled the eastern part of the land, with the towns of Ethete and Arapaho as their hubs; the Shoshone tribe developed the western portion, which includes the towns of Fort Washakie, Burris, and Crowheart. Although there have been few major conflicts, the two cultures tend to keep to their own with little interest in intermixing.

Today the reservation has some incredibly beautiful vistas of the Wind River Valley and its craggy mountains. Standing in the middle of its pristine wilderness, it's not evident that oil and gas fields are the primary source of revenue for the reservation. Although plagued by unemploy-ment and poverty, the two tribes possess great cultural pride, explicitly expressed each May-September through a series of powwows and other cultural celebrations.

For more information on the Wind River Reservation, or to plan a visit, contact the **Wind River Heritage Center** (1075 S. Federal Blvd., Riverton, 307/856-0706, www.windriverheritagecenter. com, 10am-4pm Mon.-Sat.).

(113-km) seasonal route known locally as the **Loop Road.** From Lander, follow the signs to Sinks Canyon State Park via Highway 131. Just beyond Bruce's Camp parking area, the 32-mile (52-km) Loop Road climbs past Frye Lake, Fiddler's Lake, and Louis Lake to a junction that leads south to South Pass City Historic Site or north to Atlantic City and Highway 28, which brings travelers 35 miles (56 km) back to Lander. Along the way, the Wind River Range unfolds in all its majesty,

and hikers will have no shortage of trailheads to amble down. Because of its extreme alti-tude, the road is often not open until July due to snow, and it closes as early as September again because of snow.

South Pass City Historic Site

One of the region's few gold mines, **South Pass City Historic Site** (125 S. Pass Main St., 35 mi/56 km south of Lander, 2 mi/3.2 km off Hwy. 28, 307/332-3684, www.southpasscity.

com, mid-May-Sept., $8 nonresidents, $4 residents) is a beautifully restored site with 20 original log, frame, and stone structures including the jail, a livery, a stable, a school, saloons, and homes. The city was founded in 1867 and, in addition to its mining legacy, is well remembered for its pivotal role in women's suffrage. A territorial representative from South Pass City, William Bright, introduced the bill that made Wyoming the first territory to grant women the right to vote in 1869; South Pass City's justice of the peace, Esther Hobart Morris, was the first woman to hold political office in the United States.

The South Pass Hotel has been refurbished to give visitors a sense of 1880s Wyoming. The Smith-Sherlock General Store is open for shopping, and the Miner's Exchange Saloon offers visitors a chance to shoot pool on an 1840s billiards table.

Every year in mid-July, **Gold Rush Days** celebrates the town's heritage with a vintage baseball tournament, food, entertainment, and interpretive programs. The town's **Carissa Mine** was purchased by the state, overhauled significantly for safety, and can now be toured. There's also a nice 1.6-mile (2.6-km) trail, the **Flood & Hindle Mining Trail,** which winds along the creek through willows and pine forest. Guided walks are offered on Saturdays in July and August (call for updated schedule). Reservations are strongly suggested and can be made online.

SPORTS AND RECREATION
Hiking and Rock Climbing
Known as the roof of Wyoming and the spine of the Rockies, the Wind River Range offers phenomenal hiking and climbing from Lander. Among the trails accessible from the Loop Road between Sinks Canyon State Park and South Pass City are the easy 7-mile (11.3-km) **Christina Lake Trail,** the easy-to-moderate 6.5-mile (10.5-km) **Louis Lake Trail,** and the difficult 17-mile (27-km) multiuse **Shoshone Lake Trail.**

For a good opportunity to stretch your legs, visit the **Popo Agie Falls Trail,** 3 miles (4.8 km) northwest of Moose. The out-and-back trail is 3.3 miles (5.3 km) round-trip with 682 feet (208 m) of elevation gain. The well-marked and heavily traveled trail follows the Middle Fork of the Popo Agie River to the

Sinks Canyon and South Pass Area

To the Wind River Reservation, Fort Washakie, and Dubois

7899

287

To Hudson and Riverton

Lander

131

Popo Agie River

SINKS CANYON STATE PARK

SAWMILL

Popo Agie Falls Trail

VISITOR CENTER

POPO AGIE SINKS CANYON

SWITCHBACK OVERLOOK

Table Mountain

SITE OF FIRST OIL WELL IN WYOMING

7899

287

Frye Lake

To Jeffrey City

Shoshone

Little Popo Agie River

Red Canyon

Fiddler's Lake

National

FIDDLER'S LAKE

LITTLE POPO AGIE CREEK

Forest

28

Louis Lake

LOUIS LAKE

LOOP RD

Lander Cutoff

ABANDONED STEEL MINE

BIG ATLANTIC GULCH

MINER'S DELIGHT

Continental

ATLANTIC CITY

Atlantic City

CARISSA MINE

Lewiston

SOUTH PASS CITY HISTORIC SITE

Divide

Oregon Trail

28

To Farson

Oregon Buttes

0   4 mi

0   4 km

© MOON.COM

Outdoor Student Programs in the Wind River Range

In 1965, one year after the Wilderness Act had passed, an Outward Bound instructor named Paul Petzoldt founded the National Outdoor Leadership School (NOLS) in Sinks Canyon. Having spent much of his youth in the Tetons and the Wind River Range, much of which was not even mapped, Petzoldt created a school specifically to train outdoor leaders, educators, and conservationists. That year, a small group of male NOLS students spent a full month in the Wind River Range.

Within a year, female students were admitted to NOLS for the 30-day outdoor leadership training in the Winds, and in 1970, more than 750 students enrolled in summer courses. NOLS started branching out in the 1970s with programs (and eventually bases) in Alaska, East Africa, Mexico, Idaho, and Washington's Northern Cascades. Still, the school never lost touch with Wyoming and the Winds, and in 2002 an impressive world headquarters (284 Lincoln St., Lander, 307/332-5300 or 800/710-6657, www.nols.edu) was completed in Lander.

So what are these mountains that gave rise to one of the world's most esteemed wilderness education programs?

The Wind River Range cuts through Wyoming with 100 miles (161 km) of jagged peaks, crystalline lakes, boulder-strewn meadows, two national forests, and three pristine wilderness areas. The range has 48 summits topping 12,000 feet (3,658 m), 8 summits above 13,500 feet (4,115 m), and 7 of the largest glaciers in the Lower 48. At 13,804 feet (4,207 m), Gannett Peak is the crown of this magnificent range and the highest peak in the state. The Cirque of the Towers, 10 miles (16 km) into the Bridger Wilderness at the southern end of the range, offers some of the most scenic hiking in the Lower 48, and plenty of technical rock climbing. The Winds are bisected by the Continental Divide to form three major drainages for the Columbia River, the Colorado River, and the Missouri River.

The area has long been a favorite backpacking destination for the adventurous, and access is possible from both the east and west sides. In addition to the Continental Divide Trail, which traverses the range from South Pass to Union Pass on its way between Canada and Mexico, there are hundreds of miles of hiking trails crisscrossing the Winds. Among the more popular trailheads are Big Sandy, Boulder Creek, Elkhart Park, and Green River Lakes. For more solitude, try some of the low-use trailheads like Burnt Lake, Half Moon Lake, and Meadow Lake.

For information on trails and backcountry regulations, contact the Bridger-Teton National Forest office (29 E. Fremont Lake Rd., Pinedale, 307/367-4326, www.fs.usda.gov).

stunning Popo Agie Falls. Dogs are welcome, as are horses. There can be an occasional rattlesnake in the area so stay alert.

For hiking that is somewhat closer to Lander, with scenery no less dramatic, Sinks Canyon State Park (www.sinkscanyonstatepark.org) offers 6 miles (9.7 km) of easy-to-moderate trails in a figure-eight layout.

For expert guidance and equipment related to rock climbing, the best resource in town is Wild Iris Mountain Sports (166 Main St., 307/332-4541, www.wildirisclimbing.com, 10am-6pm Mon.-Sat., 10am-4pm Sun.),

named for one of the region's best-known climbing areas. Another renowned spot for climbers is Sinks Canyon State Park.

For more information on trails and conditions, contact the Shoshone National Forest's Washakie Ranger Office (333 Hwy. 789 S., 307/332-5460, www.fs.usda.gov, 8am-4:30pm Mon.-Fri.).

Fishing

With the Wind River Range as an impressive backdrop to Lander, the fishing in this part of the state varies from crystalline alpine lakes to small but productive rivers, including the **Wind River, Bull Lake Creek,** the **Sweetwater River,** and various forks of the **Popo Agie River.** Unlike most of the state, around Lander the fishing is exclusively wade fishing.

Daily guided fishing trips can be arranged through **Sweetwater Fishing Expeditions** (2939 Sinks Canyon Rd., 307/332-3986, www.sweetwaterfishing.com), whose adventures include day trips ($515 for 1 angler, $550 for 2), 5- to 10-day expeditions ($2,160-3,040 pp), and horseback trips (additional $1,000-1,500 pp). Shorter trips can be arranged.

Golf

The **Lander Golf Club** (1 Golf Course Dr., 307/332-4653, from $16 for 9 holes, from $33 for 18) is an 18-hole, par-71 course.

ENTERTAINMENT AND EVENTS

The most popular event in Lander is its **Pioneer Days** festival (www.lotra.org). It takes place around the Fourth of July and includes a parade, Indian dancing, a buffalo barbecue, fireworks, and a nightly rodeo ($10 adults, $5 children 6-12, presale discounts) with bull riding and saddle broncs, among other events. The rodeo celebrates 130 years in 2024, making it the oldest paid rodeo in the world.

A much younger but also entertaining event is the **Lander Brew Fest** (307/332-3892 or 800/433-0662, www.landerbrewfest.com), which takes place in mid-June. More than 25 breweries from the Rocky Mountain region participate, allowing visitors to sample more than 80 different types of beer while enjoying family-friendly music, food, and games.

The **International Climber's Festival** (307/349-1561, www.climbersfestival.org) is held each July and attracts outdoors enthusiasts from around the world. The festival features lectures, activities, social events, and a trade show. Visit the website to check which events require tickets.

Lander is also a stop on the **Pedigree**

Stage Stop Dog Race (307/734-1163, www.wyomingstagestop.org), which takes place late January-early February.

Stop by the **Lander Area Chamber of Commerce** (100 N. 1st St., 307/332-3892 or 800/433-0662, http://landerchamber.org, 8am-5pm Mon.-Fri., 10am-4pm Sat.-Sun. summer, 8am-5pm Mon.-Fri. fall-spring) to get more information or to buy tickets for any of the events in town.

FOOD

With so many ways to burn energy, it's surprising that there aren't more eateries to refuel. Still, you won't starve in Lander. The **Breadboard** (1350 W. Main St., 307/332-6090, 11am-7pm Mon.-Fri., 11am-4pm Sat.-Sun., closed Sun. in winter, $4-12) has been serving up soup and subs for more than 35 years. Don't miss the green chili! A hub of the community in more ways than one, The Breadboard donates proceeds from refills ($0.25) to local charities.

Foodies in Lander need look no farther than four wonderful establishments, owned by the same folks and sharing one historic block downtown. ★ **Cowfish** (148 Main St., 307/332-8227, www.cowfishlander.com, 8am-2pm and 5pm-9pm daily summer, 5pm-9pm daily winter, $19-39) offers an assortment of fresh seafood, salads, steaks, pasta, and homemade desserts impressive enough to make you forget you are a long way from any big city; it's impossible to leave hungry. Right next door, the **Gannett Grill/Lander Bar** (126 Main St., 307/332-8228, www.landerbar.com, 11am-9pm daily, $10-24) is a local favorite with hand-tossed pizzas, juicy burgers made from local beef, gorgeous salads from the on-site organic garden, and locally brewed beer. The outdoor dining option is insanely popular when the weather is good. **Scream Shack** (11am-10pm daily summer) at the Gannett Grill operates in the summer, serving delicious ice cream and thick shakes. The chokecherry shake is delicious. For drinks, **The Coalter Loft** (www.landerbar.

com, 11am-9pm daily) is an elegant bar with a second-story deck overlooking Main Street; its trivia night (call or check the website for current schedule) is good fun.

ACCOMMODATIONS

Since it's a great launching point into the Winds, Lander's number of accommodations is growing. Chain hotels include the newer and extremely comfortable **Holiday Inn Express & Suites** (1002 11th St., 307/332-4005 or 800/465-4329, www.ihg.com, $122-183), plus the **Inn at Lander** (260 Grand View Dr., 307/332-2847 or 866/452-6337, www.book.bestwestern.com, $72-140), which has 101 guest rooms as well as an on-site restaurant, guest laundry, and a year-round hot tub. The **Rodeway Inn Pronghorn Lodge** (150 E. Main St., 307/332-3940 or 800/424-6423, www.choicehotels.com, $88-108) is another good bet in town. For gamblers, nothing beats the 60 rooms at the **Shoshone Rose Casino & Hotel** (5690 US 287, 307/206-7001, www.shoshonerose.com, from $120), 5 miles (8 km) north of Lander. The hotel boasts an indoor pool, outdoor fire pits, and more than 400 slot machines.

For a more historical and completely unique option, the **Miner's Delight Inn Bed & Breakfast** (290 S. Pass Rd., Atlantic City, 307/332-0248, www.minersdelightinn.wordpress.com, 2-night minimum in summer, $120-160) offers both rooms and 1930s cabins, which share a bathroom in the inn. The setting beside Little Beaver Creek is second-to-none, and the handmade quilts and cast-iron wood stoves give the place a historical and welcoming atmosphere.

CAMPING

As evidence of the community's commitment to the outdoor experience, free overnight camping is permitted for up to three nights in Lander's **City Park** (405 Fremont St.). RVs are invited to park in the parking lot.

The best public camping is found in Sinks

Canyon State Park (3079 Sinks Canyon Rd., 6 mi/10 km south of Lander, 307/332-6333 or 307/332-3077, www.sinkscanyonstatepark.org, $17 residents, $30 nonresidents), which has two primitive state park campgrounds: **Sawmill** and **Popo Agie**. Three camping yurts (up to $60/night plus the camping fee), with a bunk bed, futon, dining table and two chairs, electric lighting, and grill, can be reserved year-round at www.wyo-park.com. There is an oversized premier yurt ($200/night) and a premier cabin ($200) available for rent as well. There is also one campground in the national forest, **Sinks Canyon Campground** ($15/night). Several national forest campgrounds are located along the Loop Road, including sites at **Louis Lake** ($10/night), **Fiddlers Lake** ($15/night), and **Worthen Meadow** ($15/night). No advance reservations are available. **Showers** are available in town at the community swimming pool (450 S. 9th St.) and the NOLS campus (284 Lincoln St.).

Sleeping Bear RV Park and Campground (715 E. Main St., 307/332-5159 or 888/757-2327, www.sleepingbearrvpark.com) offers 4 tent sites ($25), 40 full RV hookup sites ($50), 6 water and electric hookup sites $32-39), cabins with shared bath ($50), and cabins with private bath ($65). Amenities include Wi-Fi, picnic tables, and fire rings, plus access to clean bathrooms with showers.

INFORMATION AND SERVICES

The **Lander Area Chamber of Commerce** (100 N. 1st St., 307/332-3892 or 800/433-0662, http://landerchamber.org, 8am-5pm Mon.-Fri., 10am-4pm Sat.-Sun. summer, 8am-5pm Mon.-Fri. fall-spring) acts as a visitor center.

For information and maps related to backcountry hiking and camping, contact the Shoshone National Forest's **Washakie Ranger Office** (333 Hwy. 789 S., 307/332-5460, www.fs.usda.gov, 8am-4:30pm Mon.-Fri.).

The **Fremont County Library** (307/332-5194, 10am-7pm Tues.-Thurs., 10am-5pm Fri.) is at 200 Amoretti Street.

The largest medical facility in the area is the **SageWest Health Care** (1320 Bishop Randall Dr., 307/332-4420, www.sagewesthealthcare.com), which has a 24-hour emergency department. The **Lander Medical Clinic Urgent Care** (307/332-2941, www.landermedicalclinic.com, 7am-5pm Mon.-Fri.) is at 745 Buena Vista Drive.

TRANSPORTATION
Getting There
The closest commercial airport to Lander is 26 miles (42 km) away, the **Riverton Regional Airport** (RIW, 4830 Airport Rd., Riverton, 307/856-7063, www.flyriverton.com). **United Express** (800/864-8331, www.united.com) operates daily flights to and from Denver. Private air travel is available at **Hunt Field Airport-Lander** (KLND, 307/332-2870).

Shuttles to and from nearby airports can be arranged through **Share-a-Ride Wyoming** (307/696-6116, www.sharearidewyoming.com) in Riverton ($83 for first passenger one-way to Lander), Jackson ($342 for first passenger one-way), and Casper ($195 first passenger one-way). Reductions apply for more than one passenger, and additional fees apply for late-night arrivals. Rides can also be arranged through **Elite Taxi Service** (307/253-9221) and **Gator Creek Taxi Service** (307/851-3619, www.gatorcreek.com), which serves the entire state of Wyoming 24/7.

By road, Lander is 163 miles (265 km) south of Cody, 160 miles (260 km) southeast of Jackson, 157 miles (250 km) southeast of Yellowstone National Park, 136 miles (219 km) east of Pinedale, and 79 miles (127 km) southwest of Thermopolis.

Getting Around
The **Wind River Transportation Authority** (307/856-7118, www.wrtabuslines.com) offers fixed-route bus service around town.

Thermopolis

At the south end of the Bighorn Basin, Thermopolis (pop. 2,725, elev. 4,504 ft/1,373 m) is a notably sunny town with 235 sunny days on average each year; it also has natural hot water forming the world's largest mineral hot spring.

The town was originally called Old Town Thermopolis, one of two Wyoming settlements built around mineral hot springs; the other is Saratoga. Around the turn of the 20th century, when an analysis of the water suggested potential health benefits, the town's name was shortened to Thermopolis in a calculated marketing move. Local mineral deposits—including coal, copper, and oil—plus the arrival of the railroad bolstered the Thermopolis economy, but for the most part tourism was and continues to be the major economic force. Teddy Roosevelt and Butch Cassidy and his gang were among the most famous frequent visitors to Thermopolis.

A surprising number of fantastic attractions can be found in this small, friendly town surrounded by the Owl Creek Mountains. At **Hot Springs State Park,** mineral terraces create a stunning background for herds of grazing bison. The **Wyoming Dinosaur Center** is among the best paleontology sites in the state. And the **Legend Rock Petroglyph Site** (which can only be opened in the off-season with a key from the Hot Springs County Museum, State Bath House, or the Thermopolis-Hot Springs Chamber of Commerce!) has some of the most compelling examples of prehistoric rock art in the state. From fishing and rafting on the Bighorn to horseback riding in the Owl Creek Mountains, there are various ways to enjoy the natural beauty surrounding town. This is small-town Wyoming in its truest and best form.

SIGHTS
★ Hot Springs State Park

Hot Springs State Park (538 N. Park St., 307/864-2176, http://wyoparks.state.wy.us, 6am-10pm daily) is a natural phenomenon featuring terrain with brilliant hues, unique rock formations, and, of course, hot springs. The mineral deposits and various life-forms paint the park different shades of red, orange, green, brown, and yellow. In summer the park explodes with vibrant flower gardens. Because the two national parks in the state's northwest corner draw the large crowds, if you make it to this park, you're guaranteed a more leisurely, chaos-free visit.

Originally part of the Wind River Reservation, the hot springs were believed by the Shoshone to be a gift from the Great Spirit. The U.S. government bought Big Springs and the surrounding territory from the Arapaho and Shoshone in 1896. Chief Washakie, who signed the agreement, had one stipulation: The waters should be freely available to all so that anyone could receive the great health and healing benefits. As a result, Wyoming's first state park was created along with the State Bath House, which is free and open to the public to this day. Although one might argue that the 20 minutes that come free with entry to the pool is not exactly what Chief Washakie had in mind, it's still a great place that reflects his deep respect for these medicinal waters.

Big Spring, considered the largest hot spring in the world, is the main attraction in the park. The water's temperature is 128°F (53°C), and more than 8,000 gallons per day trickle and gush freely over large mineral-painted terraces into the Bighorn River. Boardwalks allow visitors to walk along the terraces, springs, and cooling pools; they lead to a long suspension bridge that crosses the Bighorn and provides great views of the area.

The State Bath House (168 Tepee St., 307/864-3765, http://wyoparks.state.wy.us, 8am-4pm daily, hours can change seasonally so call ahead) has the only free thermal pools in the park, for 20 minutes every two hours if you like. Those who stay more than 20 minutes will pay a fee. The bath house has an indoor and outdoor soaking pool (although the outdoor pool is closed in the winter), along with smaller private tubs in the locker rooms. The water from the hot springs is piped to these mineral pools and is kept at

Hot Springs State Park

104°F (40°C). Open year-round, the pools are small but clean and well maintained. Lockers, towels, and even swimsuits (if you dare) can be rented for a nominal charge.

If you are looking for more elaborate swimming facilities (including slides, steam rooms, and hot tubs), there are several commercial facilities inside the park, including **Hellie's Tepee Spa** (144 Tepee St., 307/864-9250, www.tepeepools.com, 9am-9pm Wed.-Mon., 9am-8:30pm Tues., $15.50 ages 5-62, $12.50 military and seniors 63 and over, $7 children aged 3-4, free for children 2 and under) and **Star Plunge** (115 Big Springs Dr., 307/864-3771, www.starplunge.com, 11am-5pm Mon.-Fri., 11am-6pm Sat.-Sun. Memorial Day-Labor Day, 9am-9pm daily winter, $15.50 ages 5-64, $12.50 seniors 65 and over, $7 children 4 and under), the latter having indoor and outdoor pools and slides. Part of being in this community is feeling like you have stepped back into the 1980s. You'll rock out to Journey and Whitesnake while you soak, but if you go with it, you will love this place. Most of the pools do not take credit cards, so come prepared with cash or a checkbook, and bring coins for the lockers, too.

Hot Springs County Museum and Cultural Center

This small town has done an impressive job of collecting and displaying artifacts from its lively past. **Hot Springs County Museum and Cultural Center** (700 Broadway St., 307/864-5183, www.hschistory.org, 9am-5pm Mon.-Sat. May-Sept., 9am-4pm Tues.-Sat. Oct.-Apr., $6 adults, $4 seniors 60 and over and children 17 and under, free kids 5 and under) consists of the two-story main museum building and five additional structures in the vicinity. The museum building was, in various incarnations, a Ford garage, a Coke bottling plant, and a technical college before opening as the county museum in 1980.

One of the museum's more interesting exhibits is dedicated to the outlaws of Wyoming. Thermopolis was frequented by outlaws such as Butch Cassidy and the Sundance Kid. The museum has the cherrywood bar from the Hole in the Wall Saloon and the stained-glass windows from Hack Hollywood's Saloon, two of their favorite watering holes in town. There are also exhibits highlighting the town's varied sources of revenue, including coal mining, oil drilling, and petroleum extraction. The 1st floor of the main museum re-creates businesses from an early 1900s Main Street, including a dentist's office, a post office, a general store, and a jail. They have been designed mostly using artifacts from the time period and even from the original stores. The cultural center has rotating exhibits by local artists.

★ Wyoming Dinosaur Center and Dig Sites

Located at the Warm Springs Ranch, where dinosaur fossils from the Jurassic period have been unearthed, the **Wyoming Dinosaur Center** (110 Carter Ranch Rd., 307/864-2997 or 800/455-3466, www.wyomingdinosaurcenter.org, 8am-6pm daily mid-May-mid-Sept., 10am-5pm daily mid-Sept.-mid-May, closed on holidays) is a 16,000-square-foot complex that houses more than 200 displays. In addition to 20-some full-size dinosaur skeletons and casts from the local site and from around the world, there is also a preparation lab on-site. Visitors can watch technicians cleaning recently discovered fossils. One of the special features of the museum is its proximity to the **Warm Springs Dig Site.** Excavations still take place here each summer.

During the summer, visitors can take a tour of the site or participate in the **Dig for a Day Program** (307/864-2997 for reservations, $150 adults, $125 children with paying adult), which allows you to work at the actual dig site, learning about the process and the science involved. Advanced registration is required, and digs happen daily late spring-early fall. Specific days throughout the summer also are set aside for the **Kids' Dig Program** ($100) for kids ages 7-12, which caters to budding archaeologists.

Admission to the museum is $12 adults 13-64, and $10 children 4-12, seniors 60 and over, and veterans. The dig site tour is $14.50 adults and $12.50 children, seniors, and veterans. The best option is to purchase the combination package, which includes entrance to the museum and the tour, for $20.50 adults, $16.50 children, seniors and veterans. Families of four can pay a flat rate of $68 for two adults and two children, which includes both the museum and the tour.

Legend Rock Petroglyph Site

Although it may seem like a small adventure just to find the prehistoric drawings at **Legend Rock Petroglyph Site** (2861 W. Cottonwood Rd., Thermopolis, 307/864-2176), 29 miles (47 km) northwest of Thermopolis, the sheer number and variety make it a worthwhile visit. The easiest way to visit the petroglyphs is first to stop at the **Hot Springs State Park office** (at the corner of Park St. and Hwy. 789, 307/864-2176, http://wyoparks.state.wy.us), where you can pick up a map to the site (the unmarked route can be difficult to locate) and a gate key in non-summer months. Once at the parking lot for Legend Rock, you can choose to hike the 0.5 mile (0.8 km) to the petroglyphs or drive down the hill (in non-summer months when there is no host at the site, you will need the key to unlock the gate). A host is on-site 8am-6pm daily in summer and there is a visitor center. Etched along the sandstone cliffs are numerous animal and human figures that have been linked to different time periods throughout history, some dating back 2,000 years. There are more than 92 prehistoric petroglyph panels and upward of 300 petroglyph figures. Unfortunately, not all visitors to the site have treated the paintings respectfully, and it's important not to touch or try to remove the petroglyphs.

SPORTS AND RECREATION

Hiking

Although there is no national forest in immediate proximity to Thermopolis, the locals like to hike around their landmark **Round Top Mountain.** In Hot Springs State Park, there are 6.2 miles (10 km) of accessible walking and hiking trails, the most popular being **Spirit Trail,** which meanders through the park.

Boating and Fishing

Both white-water and scenic river trips are offered on the Wind and Bighorn Rivers and can be arranged exclusively through the Indian-owned **Wind River Canyon Whitewater and Fly Fishing** (210 Hwy. 20 S., Ste. 5, 307/864-9343 or 888/246-9343, www.windrivercanyon.com). Roughly two-hour white-water trips on the dramatic upper or lower canyon sections start at $79 per person ($69 kids 12 and under), and all-day trips covering the whole canyon are $125 per person ($115 kids 12 and under). Scenic 80-minute trips are $59 per person ($49 kids 12 and under). Trips run Memorial Day-Labor Day. As the only outfitter on the Wind River, the company also offers a variety of guided fishing trips. All-day float-fishing trips on the upper or lower canyon are $795 for 1-2 people with lunch included. Full-day trips on the Bighorn are $695 for up to two anglers.

Golf

There is a nine-hole public course at **Thermopolis Golf Course** (143 Airport Rd., 307/864-5294, $17 for 9 holes and carts $12 pp, $26 for 18 holes and carts $20 pp).

ENTERTAINMENT AND EVENTS

The **Gift of the Waters Pageant** is held during the first weekend in August and re-creates the selling of the hot springs by the Shoshone and Arapaho to the U.S. government, based on a play written in 1925.

The pageant suggests it was a fair transaction between equal partners, which wasn't exactly the case. However, Native Americans from the Wind River Reservation do participate in the event, which is followed by a powwow. The event is a one-hour performance on both Friday and Saturday nights, starting at 6pm. Contact the **Thermopolis-Hot Springs Chamber of Commerce** (220 Park St., 307/864-3192 or 877/864-3192, www.thermompolischamber.com) for more information.

The **Thermopolis Cowboy Rendezvous** (www.thermopoliscowboyrendezvous.com) is a PRCA rodeo held the weekend after Father's Day and includes a pancake breakfast, street dance, parade, and more, in addition to riding events. This is real rodeo with events including bull riding, bareback riding, saddle bronc, steer wrestling, and team roping.

FOOD

Widely considered the best restaurant in town, **One Eyed Buffalo Brewing Company** (528 Broadway St., 307/864-3555, www.oneeyedbuffalobrewing.com, 11am-9pm Mon.-Sat., 11am-8pm Sun., $11-29) offers everything from loaded nachos and salads to burgers, steaks, pasta, prime rib and pork Jäger-schnitzel.

Another place for a satisfying meal is the **Black Bear Café** (111 N. 5th St., 307/864-3221, 6:30am-2pm Tues.-Sun., $5-18). It serves up the biggest cinnamon rolls you can imagine, plus a delicious buffalo breakfast plate, homemade chili, and milk shakes you'll dream about. Another favorite spot in town for breakfast or lunch is **Kirby Creek Mercantile** (535 Broadway St., 307/864-3533, www.kirbycreekmercantile.com, $7-12), which serves outstanding crepes, omelets, paninis, sandwiches, and salads, plus their own incredible baked goods. Do not pass up the caramel pecan roll.

A hit with locals, **Nature's Corner Featuring the Crow Bar** (530 Broadway St., 307/864-3218, 8:30am-5:30pm Mon.-Sat.,

$5-10) is an excellent place for a quick healthy bite. Their wraps and smoothies come highly recommended. A health food store with a deli/coffee/smoothie bar, Nature's Corner carries plenty of organic and gluten-free groceries.

No matter where you fill your belly in Thermopolis, always save room for an ice-cold treat from **Dairyland & Hot City Coffee** (510 Park St., 307/864-2757, 11am-10pm Mon.-Sat., 1pm-10pm Sun. Apr.-Sept., 6am-2pm off-season, $5-10), which serves delicious frozen yogurt and ice cream the old-fashioned way. It offers burgers and fries too, but it is the ice cream that brings people back.

ACCOMMODATIONS

With its history of attracting visitors to its medicinal waters, Thermopolis has quite a large, if not necessarily diverse, number of accommodations.

The snazziest hotel by far is the pet-friendly ★ **Best Western Plaza Hotel** (116 E. Park St., 307/864-2939, www.bestwesternwyoming. com, $78-180), a historic hotel in Hot Springs State Park.

Right across the street in this beautiful parklike setting is the also pet-friendly **Hot Springs Hotel & Spa** (115 E. Park St., 307/864-3131, www.thermopolisdaysinn.com, $89-143). Hunters will flip for the vast number and types of taxidermied mounts throughout the property and the hunting photos that line the walls. Vegetarians, however, may want to reconsider a meal at the hotel's **Safari Club Restaurant & Lounge**. The hotel is slightly run-down (perhaps just the pet-friendly rooms), but the location is ideal.

Some of the more budget-friendly options in town include the **Paintbrush Inn** (605 S. 6th St., 307/864-3155 or 877/621-7811, www.paintbrushinn.com, from $72), which features basic air-conditioned ground-floor rooms with Wi-Fi and kitchenettes, and the very comfortable and homey **Elk Antler Inn** (501 S. 6th St., 307/864-2325, www.elkantlerinn. com, from $60), with two- and three-bed suites and two-bedroom suites. There is also a nice **Quality Inn** (166 S. Hwy. 20 S., 307/463-4206, www.choicehotels.com, from $73) in town.

CAMPING

While there is no camping permitted in the most desirable of spots—Hot Springs State Park—there are a few RV parks in Thermopolis that allow tent camping as well. The **Fountain of Youth RV Park** (250 US 20 N., 307/864-3265) is open year-round and offers both RV sites ($45-50) and tent sites ($35 for up to 2 campers). Amenities include a large hot springs pool on-site, laundry facilities, and free Wi-Fi.

The **Eagle RV Park** (204 US 20 S., 307/864-5262 or 888/865-5707, www.eaglervpark.com) features a shady campground with RV sites (from $43), tent sites (from $23.19), and air-conditioned camping cabins ($54-90 for 2 people). Amenities include free Wi-Fi, a game room and playground, and laundry facilities. The **Wyoming Gardens RV Park and Cabins** (720 Shoshoni St., 307/864-2778, www.wyominggardensrvpark.com) has 15 RV spaces including full-hookup sites ($39-45 for 2 people), water and 30 amp sites ($35 for 2 people), and RV cabins ($75-85 for 2 people) in a shady, graveled park.

The nearest public campgrounds to Thermopolis are 17 miles (27 km) south of town in **Boysen State Park** (15 Ash St., Shoshoni, 307/876-2796, http://wyoparks.state.wy.us, $17 for residents, $30 for nonresidents, additional $10 for electrical sites, 3 standard cabins from $60) in the Wind River Canyon. Though barren by

every definition, the reservoir is beautiful and offers great swimming and colorful rockhounding.

INFORMATION AND SERVICES

The **Thermopolis-Hot Springs Chamber of Commerce** (220 Park St., 307/864-3192 or 877/864-3192, www.thermopolis.com, 8am-5pm Mon.-Fri. summer, 9am-5pm Mon.-Fri. winter) is the very best place to get interesting and accurate information on the area. You will walk away with 100 ideas of cool things to do.

The **Hot Springs County Library** (307/864-3104, 9am-6pm Mon.-Fri., 10am-2pm Sat., closed holidays) is at 344 Arapahoe Street. They have an active Facebook page and regularly post fun activities.

There is a 24-hour emergency room at **Hot Springs County Memorial Hospital** (150 E. Arapahoe St., 307/864-3121, www.hotspringshealth.com).

TRANSPORTATION

The closest commercial airport to Thermopolis is 65 miles (105 km) away in Riverton: **Riverton Regional Airport** (RIW, 4830 Airport Rd., Riverton, 307/856-7063, www.flyriverton.com). **United Express** (800/864-8331, www.united.com) operates daily flights to and from Denver. No bus service is available to or from Thermopolis.

By road, Thermopolis is 82 miles (132 km) southeast of Cody, 150 miles (242 km) southeast of the east entrance to Yellowstone National Park, and 190 miles (305 km) south of Billings.

Cody

It seems somehow fitting that this Western town was the brainchild of one of the West's most colorful and dynamic entertainers. Indeed, Cody (pop. 10,028, elev. 5,088 ft/1,551 m), named for Buffalo Bill Cody, is a small town that packs a lot of punch. Set as it is in the arid Bighorn Basin, you might expect Cody to be all dust and tumbleweeds. But that couldn't be further from reality, although there are plenty of both when the Wyoming wind kicks up. Cody is high style with shiny boots and fringe on almost everything. Cody is Molesworth furniture, a little gaudy sometimes, but an absolute classic. Cody is a nightly rodeo and old-time gunslingers. In many ways, Cody is the Old West, the *cinematic* West, that visitors want to see and experience.

An obvious destination in and of itself, Cody is home to what is arguably the best Western art and history museum in the world. The Buffalo Bill Center of the West is beyond compare. Visitors could spend a week in the complex's five separate museums and never see the same exhibit twice. The compact downtown is scenic and historic, with world-class art galleries, fun tourist shops, and great eateries. There are plenty of Western entertainment options as well across the valley.

Just outside town, the landscape shifts into the lush South Fork and then into the high country the closer one gets to Yellowstone National Park. There are a hundred reasons to go to Cody, including its proximity to Yellowstone.

SIGHTS

★ Buffalo Bill Center of the West

The West's version of the Smithsonian, the **Buffalo Bill Center of the West** (BBCW, 720 Sheridan Ave., 307/587-4771, www.centerofthewest.org, 10am-5pm Thurs.-Sun. Dec.-Feb., 10am-5pm daily Mar.-Apr. and Nov., 8am-6pm daily May-Sept. 15, 8am-5pm daily Sept.16-Oct., online tickets $21 adults, $20 seniors 65 and over, $19 students over 18 with ID, $14 children 6-17, free for children under 6, admission good for 2 consecutive days) is a collection of five extraordinary museums plus a research library. The **Buffalo Bill Museum** celebrates the private and public life of town father W. F. "Buffalo Bill" Cody. The **Whitney Gallery of Western Art** reflects the diverse history of art of the American West from the early 19th century to today with original paintings, sculpture, and prints by some of the best-known deceased masters and contemporary geniuses. The **Plains Indian Museum** examines the culture and history of the Arapaho, Crow, Cheyenne, Blackfeet, Sioux, Shoshone, and others through an impressive collection of Native American art and artifacts. The **Cody Firearms Museum** is home to more than 10,000 artifacts, the world's largest assemblage of American arms, including some European arms dating back to the 1500s. The **Draper Museum of Natural History** offers exhibits that interpret the Greater Yellowstone Ecosystem from human and natural science perspectives. Finally, the **Harold McCracken Research Library** is an extraordinary resource for studies of the American West.

This complex is indeed the grande dame of Western history and art. In addition to its own unrivaled permanent collections, the museums feature a constantly shifting assortment of compelling traveling exhibits and special events. Check the website for events before you arrive. If you only see one museum on your journey out West, this one is it.

The BBCW also has two restaurants, the Eatery and the Coffee Bar, for quick bites—including sandwiches, burgers, bison brats, salad, and more—and caffeine fixes. And with

Cody and Vicinity

© MOON.COM

The Legend of Buffalo Bill

When it comes to Buffalo Bill Cody, born William F. Cody, it can be difficult to discern fact from fiction. The man was legendary in every sense of the word, and for the most part he earned the reputation that still follows his name. Born in Iowa in 1846, Cody made his way out west in 1857 with his father. Cody's father died en route, leaving the boy to fend for himself, finding work as a cowboy and Pony Express rider. He became an army scout at the end of the Civil War and even earned the Congressional Medal of Honor in 1872 for valor in action during the Indian Wars. He reportedly earned his nickname after the Civil War when he shot 4,280 bison in the span of 18 months on behalf of the Kansas Pacific Railroad. Although we see that kind of cruel carnage very differently today, in his time, it was considered a feat.

Cody was a natural hunter and frequently asked by the army to guide visiting dignitaries. The hunts were greatly publicized, and an eager public greedily consumed tales of Cody's adventuresome pursuits. In 1873, with a string of dime-store novels glorifying him, Cody agreed to perform a melodramatic stage show highlighting his exploits alongside other legendary figures Wild Bill Hickok and Texas Jack Omohundro. In July 1876, just weeks after Custer's defeat at the Little Bighorn, Cody and the Fifth Regiment for whom he was scouting at the time met a band of Cheyenne warriors. Cody murdered and scalped a warrior named Yellow Hair, an attempt to avenge Custer's death and secure his place among the country's military heroes of the day. Again, we see this today through a very different lens.

In 1883, Cody produced his well-known Wild West Show, which would travel the world for more than three decades, earning him both fame and fortune. Cody became a shrewd businessman, investing in an Arizona mine, hotels in Sheridan and his namesake Cody, ranching, coal and oil development, filmmaking, publishing, and tourism. He used his wealth and reputation to espouse such causes as women's suffrage and, eventually, in a stark turnaround, the just treatment of Native Americans.

As a symbol of the burgeoning West, Cody's expertise was relied on by every U.S. president from Ulysses S. Grant to Woodrow Wilson. He mingled with world-famous artists and dined with kings. Indeed, Buffalo Bill lived a life quite worthy of the legends that continue to define the man.

advance reservations (307/899-2027), visitors can enjoy **Cowboy Rich's Chuckwagon Dinners** (cooking demonstrations at 6pm, dinner at 6:30pm Tues. and Sat. June-Sept., $40 adults, $15 kids 10 and under), which feature traditional Dutch oven cooking methods that result in a delicious steak dinner with beans, sourdough biscuits, and fresh cobbler.

Cody Trolley Tours

Early June to late September, one of the best ways to get an overview of Cody, its founding father, and the natural environment that rolls out in every direction is the **Cody Trolley Tours** (307/527-7043, www.codytrolleytours. com, $28 adults, $26 seniors 65 and over, $16 children 6-17, free for children under 6, dogs are welcome with advance notice, call for tour schedules), which offer hour-long narrated tours and cover 100 years of history in 22 miles (35 km). Highlights include stories about Buffalo Bill, Annie Oakley, the Crow Indians, and a 1904 bank robbery in Cody by the Hole-in-the-Wall gang. The tour includes a *Best of Cody* souvenir guide. Reservations can be made and tickets purchased on the front porch of the Irma Hotel (1192 Sheridan Ave.), which is also where the tours depart. In addition to tours, visitors can reserve chairs ($3 pp) for the nightly Cody Gunfight Show (6pm Mon.-Sat. June-mid-Sept.) outside the Irma.

Old Trail Town

On the site of the original Cody City (about 2 mi/3.2 km west of Cody), **Old Trail Town** (1831 Demaris Dr., 307/587-5302, www.oldtrailtown.org, 8am-6pm daily mid-May-Sept., $10 adults, $9 seniors over 65, $5 children 6-12, free for children under 6, tickets available online) is a fascinating collection of historic buildings from the Wyoming frontier. The re-created town is the result of local historian and archaeologist Bob Edgar's hard work and dedication, with more than 26 buildings dating 1879-1901 and at least 100 wagons, maintained in nearly original condition, helping create an authentic feel of the bygone pioneer era. Among the highlights is the old Rivers Saloon, its walls still marked by bullet holes (it was a favorite meeting place of Butch Cassidy and the Sundance Kid) and a cabin from Hole-in-the-Wall country. A graveyard in the Old Trail Town complex has the reinterred bodies of many infamous characters of the Old West, including that of John "Liver Eating" Johnston (frequently spelled Johnson). The reburial of his body in Old Trail Town was attended by more than 2,000 people including the actor Robert Redford, who played the famous mountain man in the 1972 movie *Jeremiah Johnson*.

Irma Hotel

Naming it after his beloved youngest daughter and calling it "just the sweetest hotel that ever was," Buffalo Bill built the stately **Irma Hotel** (1192 Sheridan Ave., 307/587-4221 or 800/745-4762, www.irmahotel.com, $80-225) in 1902 with the idea that tourists from around the world could stay here en route to Yellowstone National Park. The hotel was designed by a well-known church architect from Nebraska, and some exterior walls are made of local river rock. The cherrywood bar, one of the most photographed features in town, was built in 1902 as well. Additions were added in 1929 and 1976-1977. Still the heart of downtown, the Irma is starting to show her age a little bit. The rooms are basic but still charming, and it's fun to stay in Buffalo Bill's original suite or imagine the royalty that stayed in many of the other rooms. You don't need to spend a night, though, to get a real sense of the history. Visitors can enjoy a drink at the bar or a full meal at **The Irma restaurant**,

which serves breakfast, lunch, and dinner and is known for prime rib and delicious steaks. The atmosphere alone is worth the price of the meal.

Heart Mountain

Heart Mountain lies halfway between Cody and Powell and takes its name from the twin summits atop the mountain range that resemble a heart. Driving east on US 14A, the mountains become clearly visible. The range is a puzzle for many geologists and has inspired heated debate. It seems to be part of rock formations found in Yellowstone National Park, 60 miles (97 km) away, but how they ended up in their present location is unclear. Furthermore, it is an "upside down" mountain, with strata of limestone appearing at the top with younger strata below.

Heart Mountain was the site of a Japanese American internment camp during World War II. Between 1942 and 1945, more than 14,000 people of Japanese descent (at least two-thirds of whom were American citizens) were relocated to this isolated terrain. Confined by barbed-wire fences and armed prison guards, they did their best to create a sense of community and normalcy under desperate living conditions. Of the 120,000 people detained in the 10 internment camps across the country, not one was ever found guilty of espionage or conspiring with the enemy. The camps were a result of heightened wartime hysteria, the fearmongering of politicians, and acute racism.

Opened in 2011, the **Heart Mountain Interpretive Center** (1539 Road 19, Powell, 307/754-8000, www.heartmountain.org, 10am-5pm daily May 15-Oct. 1, 10am-5pm Wed.-Sat. Oct. 2-May 14, $9 adults, $7 seniors/students, free for children under 12) is dedicated to preserving the memory of this dark period in American history and telling the stories of those it affected.

Today, in addition to the interpretive center and a short, paved walking trail, there are three buildings in various stages of decay and different plaques noting the memories of the

Heart Mountain Relocation Center

Situated between the towns of Cody and Powell, in the midst of some overgrown barley fields, stand a few dilapidated buildings. Utterly abandoned, they are remnants of a dark period in U.S. history.

With the bombing of Pearl Harbor in December 1941, war hysteria and anti-Japanese fervor peaked in the United States. There had been anti-Asian sentiment along the West Coast for decades, primarily directed at hardworking Chinese laborers. When the government stopped Chinese immigration, Japanese immigrants quickly became the targets of racism. The attack on Pearl Harbor somehow cemented the racism. President Roosevelt signed Executive Order 9066 in February 1942, authorizing the roundup and removal of all people of Japanese ancestry, regardless of their U.S. citizenship status.

By the early spring, Japanese immigrants and Japanese Americans were given 10 days to gather their families, packing only what they could carry, and report to makeshift assembly centers where they would be deported to camps. Heart Mountain was one such camp.

The camp covered more than 4,600 acres and housed 468 barracks. These poorly assembled, tar-papered buildings provided little relief from Wyoming's searing summers and frigid winters. Also constructed on the site were mess halls, communal bathrooms, laundry rooms, a hospital, a sewage plant, two places of worship, and a high school. The camp at Heart Mountain became Wyoming's third-largest city.

More than 14,000 internees entered the camp from 1942 to 1945. Despite dire conditions and human rights violations, life at Heart Mountain proved to be a testament to the human spirit. The internees demonstrated a deep resilience and determination to create and maintain a community within its ragged confines. There were general stores, two movie theaters, barber shops, high school athletic teams, a weekly newspaper, and a democratically elected camp government. They also made the most of their barren surroundings, extending the irrigation system, planting 27 different types of fruits and vegetables, and raising profitable hog and poultry farms. During the three years the camp was open, 552 births and 185 deaths were registered.

Internees were allowed to leave beginning January 1945. Each internee was granted $25 and a bus ticket to his or her destination, though many internees no longer had any other place to call home. The last internees left the camp on November 10, 1945. In 1990, all survivors of Heart Mountain were issued a check for $20,000 and a signed apology from President George H. W. Bush.

victims, including one honoring the more than 600 internees who left the camp to fight in the U.S. Army during the war.

Also in this region is the **Heart Mountain Ranch Preserve** (307/754-8446, www.nature.org), a 13,000-acre plot of land managed by The Nature Conservancy. It has a large number of rare plants, numerous species of birds, and large mammals such as elk and mule deer. A 7-mile (11.3-km) easy-to-moderate hiking trail takes hikers to the mountain's summit. Dogs are not permitted and the trail is occasionally closed due to wildlife. An **interpretive cabin** (8am-5pm Thurs.-Sun. June-Sept.) offers information about the geology, cultural significance, and ecology of Heart Mountain and the

surrounding land. In order to bring predictability for users and reduce impacts on wildlife, the preserve is closed to unscheduled visits from March 1 to the first Sunday in June, and again from October 1 to December 30.

TOP EXPERIENCE

★ Chief Joseph Scenic Highway

Linking Cody with the northeast entrance to Yellowstone National Park is the seasonally open 47-mile (76-km) **Chief Joseph Scenic**

1: The Heart Mountain Interpretive Center tells the story of a Japanese internment camp. 2: view from Chief Joseph Scenic Highway

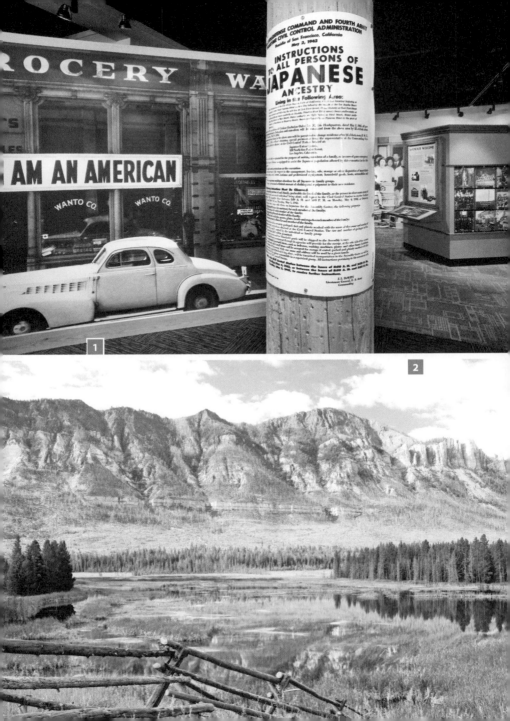

Highway. It is a winding and at times hair-raising drive that cuts through mountainous country, providing views of spectacular waterfalls and mountain vistas of the Absarokas, Cathedral Cliffs, and the mouth of Sunlight Basin and occasionally a glimpse of wildlife. Interpretive signs along the way tell the story of the Nez Perce's 1877 flight from the U.S. Army under the leadership of Chief Joseph, for whom the highway is named. For adventurers, the highway gives unparalleled access to some incredible hiking trails.

From Cody, drive north 17 miles (27 km) on Highway 120, turning left (west) onto Highway 296, known as the Chief Joseph Scenic Highway. The road climbs over Dead Indian Summit, above 8,000 feet (2,438 m), and then drops into the magnificent Clarks Fork Valley. The road ends at Crandall, Wyoming, the only place on the highway to buy provisions or find lodging. Ten miles (16 km) west of Crandall on the Beartooth All American Road (known locally as the Beartooth Highway) is Cooke City and the northeast entrance to Yellowstone National Park. Plan on spending at least two hours to drive the full 74 miles (119 km) or so from Cody to Cooke City.

Buffalo Bill Scenic Byway

The shorter of two routes to Yellowstone, this one to the east entrance, the 52-mile (84-km) **Buffalo Bill Scenic Byway** winds through the rugged North Fork Canyon along the Shoshone River. President Theodore Roosevelt was among its admirers, calling the road the most beautiful 50 miles (80 km) in the United States.

From Cody, head west on US 20/14/16. The road ends at the east entrance to Yellowstone.

SPORTS AND RECREATION
Hiking

Even though Cody itself is in something of a desertlike bowl, there is abundant hiking in the beautiful forests and mountains to the north, south, and west of town. There are

several districts of the Shoshone National Forest within relatively close proximity to town. Trails worth pursuing include the **Bald Ridge Trail** (County Rd. 7RP, off Hwy. 120, 18 mi/29 km north of Cody). The 5-mile (8-km) trail climbs nearly 4,000 vertical feet (1,219 m) through Bureau of Land Management territory to the summit of Bald Ridge. The views, naturally, are breathtaking. The area is closed December-April to protect critical winter habitat for elk and mule deer. And remember, this is grizzly bear territory, so you should take all necessary precautions.

For more information on trails and conditions, contact the **Shoshone National Forest** (808 Meadow Lane Ave., 307/527-6241, www.fs.usda.gov) or the **Bureau of Land Management** (1002 Blackburn Ave., 307/578-5900, www.blm.gov, 7:45am-4:30pm Mon.-Fri.).

For less vigorous hiking, visit the **Cody Country Chamber of Commerce** (836 Sheridan Ave., 307/587-2777 or 800/393-2639, www.codychamber.org, 8am-7pm daily summer, 8am-5pm Mon.-Fri. fall-spring) and pick up the *Cody Pathways* brochure and map of nonmotorized trails in the region.

Fishing and Rafting

The Shoshone River runs right through the heart of Cody, offering both white-water rafting opportunities and plenty of excellent fishing. Among the rafting companies in town that offer everything from two-hour white-water floats and half-day scenic tours to weeklong trips are **River Runners** (1491 Sheridan Ave., 307/527-7238 or 800/535-7238, www.riverrunnersofwyoming.com, $45 adults, $41 children 12 and under for 2 hours, $99 adults, $89 children half day, reservations required), **Wyoming River Trips** (233 Yellowstone Ave., 307/587-6661 or 800/586-6661, www.wyomingrivertrips.com, $45 adults, $40 children 4-13 for 2 hours, from $72 half day, from $125 full day, full canyon kayak from $85, Red Rock Canyon kayak from $60), and **Red Canyon River Trips** (1119 12th St., 307/587-6988 or 800/293-0148, www.

codywyomingadventures.com, $40 adults, $38 children for 2 hours, discounts for families, $75-80 half day, $129 adult full day white water, $99 all ages full-day scenic float).

To rent your own kayak (1 hour from $10, 8 hours from $50), ducky (1 hour from $10, 4 hours from $30), or paddleboard (1 hour from $10, 4 hours from $30), visit **Cody Wyoming Adventures** (1119 12th St., 307/587-6988, www.codywyomingrentals.com).

There is an abundance of prime fishing waters within an easy drive from Cody, including the Shoshone River, the Clarks Fork of the Yellowstone River, and hundreds of lakes. For fishing gear or advice on local hatches and water conditions, head to **Tim Wade's North Fork Anglers** (1107 Sheridan Ave., 307/527-7274, www.northforkanglers.com, 8am-8pm daily June-mid-Oct., 9am-6pm Mon.-Sat. and 9am-2pm Sun. mid-Oct.-Mar., 8am-6pm daily Apr.-May). In addition to all the gear, the shop offers guided wading trips (from $350 half day and $450 full day) or float trips (from $400 half day, $520-525 full day). Hours can change according to the weather, so call first.

Mountain Biking

If you are looking to do some exploring on bikes, **Joyvagen** (901 12th St., 307/527-0640, 10am-6pm Mon.-Sat.) offers bike rentals, guided bike tours, repair, and expert advice on bike trails and "all things bike" around the area. E-bike rentals and tours are available through **Cody Wyoming Adventures** (1119 12th St., 307/587-6988, www.codywyomingrentals.com, 2 hours from $50, 5-12 hours from $80, all ages).

Horseback Riding

Head out 1 mile (1.6 km) past the rodeo grounds on the left to **Cedar Mountain Trail Rides** (12 Spirit Mountain Rd., 307/527-4966 or 307/899-1909, call for current prices), where you will be attended by knowledgeable and friendly guides who are especially good with beginners. The trails wind up Cedar Mountain and provide great views of the town below. If you are interested in a full-day

ride, guides take the horses and riders by trailer 35 minutes north to Elk's Fork; lunch is provided. **Boulder Basin Outfitters** (3348 North Fork Hwy., 307/250-0076, www.wycmingsummerpacktrips.com) offers two-hour rides, half-day rides, and all-day rides June-August. For additional riding opportunities through various local outfitters, contact **Cody Country Outfitters and Guide Association** (307/587-6054).

Golf

Golfers can hit the links at the 18-hole semi-private **Olive Glenn Golf & Country Club** (802 Meadow Lane Ave., 307/587-8105, www.oliveglengolfclub.com, $59 for 18 holes, $39 for 9 holes, golf carts $10 for 9 holes and $20 for 18 holes) or at the **Powell Golf Club** (600 Hwy. 14, 7 mi/11.3 km east of Powell, 307/754-7259, www.powellgolfclub.org, $39-65 for 18 holes, $35-39 for 9 holes).

There is also a great miniature course for the whole family at **Cody Miniature Golf** (Cody's City Park, 902 Sheridan Ave., 307/587-0400, 11am-10pm daily June-Aug., limited hours May and Sept., $5 adults 16 and over, $3 kids ages 1-15).

ENTERTAINMENT AND EVENTS

Nightlife

Although drinking while driving was only outlawed in Wyoming in 2002, drive-through liquor stores are still a surprise to many visitors. People often take their parties to go. For traditionalists who like to have a drink in a more stationary location, Cody offers plenty of great bars. Among them, in the historic Irma Hotel is the **Silver Saddle Saloon** (1192 Sheridan Ave., 307/587-4221 or 800/745-4762, 11am-2am daily), and, down the street, the **Silver Dollar Bar** (1313 Sheridan Ave., 307/527-7666, kitchen 11am-9pm daily, 11am-2am Mon.-Sat., 11am-midnight Sun., if there are customers), which often has live country music and serves good bar food.

For family-oriented nightlife, try **Dan Miller's Cowboy Music Revue** (1131 12th

St., 307/899-2799, www.cowboymusicrevue. com, 4pm-5:15pm Mon.-Sat. May, 6:30pm-7:45pm Mon.-Sat. June-Sept., $20 pp for music only, $41 pp includes buffet dinner at 5:30pm prior to 6:30pm show, $59.50 combo ticket includes buffet dinner, musical revue, and admission to the Buffalo Bill Center of the West), which features a night of music, comedy, and poetry. The event takes place in the Dining Pavilion of the Buffalo Bill Center of the West.

Festivals and Events

Making this Western town one of the best places in the state to see rodeo, the **Cody Nite Rodeo** (421 W. Yellowstone Ave., 307/587-5155, www.codystampederodeo.com, June-Aug., $23 adults, $11.50 kids 7-12, free for kids 6 and under) is held nightly in summer at the rodeo grounds except July 1-5 during the Cody Stampede. Running every summer since 1938, the rodeo is two hours filled with daring cowboys and cowgirls looking to make a name for themselves on the circuit. Kids are invited to join in on the calf scramble. Gates open at 7pm, and the action begins at 8pm.

The town's rodeo fever hits its high over the Fourth of July during the annual **Cody Stampede Rodeo** (519 Yellowstone Ave., 307/587-5155, www.codystampederodeo.com, June 30-July 4, $30 adults, discounts for children). The Stampede has been running for 100 years, as of 2019, and was inspired by Buffalo Bill's own Wild West Show. This is one of the biggies for pro rodeo cowboys and cowgirls, with the bull-ride purse alone bringing the winner $50,000. For world-class rodeo action, it's hard to beat.

One of the few towns to stage nightly gunfights in summer (Jackson is another), Cody enchants visitors with Old West characters that stage a hilarious, silly, and at times gripping street performance and gunfight known as the **Cody Gunfighters** (6pm Mon.-Sat. June-mid-Sept.). The shows are free and performed adjacent to the Irma Hotel (1192 Sheridan Ave.). Chairs ($3 pp) for watching the gunfights can be reserved

through the Cody Trolley Tours (307/527-7043, www.codytrolleytours.com).

By far the biggest arts-related event of the year in Cody is the **Rendezvous Royale** (307/587-5002 or 888/598-8119, www. rendezvousroyale.com), which happens in mid-September and ushers in the last hurrah of Cody's almost manic summer season. The week is packed with events that include **Cody High Style,** which celebrates Western design in its myriad forms, and the **Buffalo Bill Art Show and Sale,** which boasts its own impressive line of events, with a quick draw in the park and studio tours. The town is full of style icons, design gurus, and blissed-out art collectors, and the energy pulses nearly around the clock. Several galleries and shops host concurrent events. Some of the best shows by contemporary Western masters open at **Simpson Gallagher Gallery** (1161 Sheridan Ave., 307/587-4022, www. simpsongallaghergallery.com).

SHOPPING

Cody is a great town for shopping, particularly if fine art or Western fashion is your thing. A stroll up and down **Sheridan Avenue** can be very productive, and expensive.

Start at **Wayne's Boot Shop** (1250 Sheridan Ave., 307/587-5234, www. waynesbootshop.com, 9am-8pm Mon.-Sat. summer, 9am-5:30pm Mon.-Fri., 9am-5pm Sat. fall-spring) for the right pair of kicks. Wayne's has been selling the best-quality cowboy, hiking, and hunting boots since 1955. Now owned by Wayne's son, the store also sells casual and comfort shoes, as well as hats.

For outdoor gear and casual wear at great prices, visit **Sierra Trading Post** (1402 8th St., 307/578-5802, www.sierratradingpost. com, 9am-8pm Mon.-Sat., 10am-6pm Sun., extended holiday hours), which sells everything from clothing and footwear to outdoor gear, luggage, and home goods at deep discounts. Quilters will delight in an afternoon at **Friends and Co. Quilt Shop** (402 E. Warren, 307/527-7217, www. friendsandco.net, 10am-5pm Mon.-Fri.,

10am-4pm Sat.), which offers classes, private lessons, and more fabric than you can imagine. Book lovers will want more time at **Legends Bookstore** (1350 Sheridan Ave., 307/586-2320, www.legendsbooks.com, 9:30am-9pm Mon.-Sat. and 10am-8pm Sun. in summer, 10am-6pm Mon.-Sat. and noon-4pm Sun. fall-spring), an outstanding independent bookstore with plenty of events featuring local and regional authors, plus gifts, cards, and great toys.

Cody has an impressive number of fine art galleries, and you should wander Sheridan Avenue to see many of them. But be sure not to miss **Simpson Gallagher Gallery** (1161 Sheridan Ave., 307/587-4022, www.simpsongallaghergallery.com, 10am-5:30pm Mon.-Sat.), which carries the work of contemporary Western masters including Clyde Aspevig, Carol Guzman, T. D. Kelsey, T. Allen Lawson, William Matthews, Julie Oriet, and Kathy Wipfler. The gallery has marvelous rotating shows and features both painting and sculpture.

If shopping wears you out, fuel up on made-in-Wyoming smoked elk and bison jerky or summer sausage, barbecue sauces, jams, spices, and other local specialties at **Wyoming Buffalo Company** (1270 Sheridan Ave., 307/587-8708, www.wyobuffalo.com, 9am-8pm daily summer, 10am-6pm Mon.-Sat. fall-spring). Or appease your sweet tooth at **Cowtown Candy Company** (1323 Sheridan Ave., 307/587-8212, www.cowtowncandy.com, 10am-9pm Mon.-Sat. summer, 10am-6pm Mon.-Sat. fall-spring), which specializes in turtles, fresh cream and butter truffles, and homemade fudge.

FOOD

Although much of the state can be classified as meat and potatoes only, Cody leans toward slightly more variety. For a great cup of coffee and a light breakfast of homemade pastries and bagels (admittedly the homemade cinnamon rolls may not count as light), stop into the **Beta Coffeehouse** (1450 Sheridan Ave., 307/587-7707, 7am-2pm Tues.-Fri.,

8am-1pm Sat., 8am-noon Sun., $3-7.50). A favorite community gathering spot, the Beta often hosts live music and open-mic nights. In the winter, the homemade soups are beyond compare. **Peter's Café & Bakery** (1219 Sheridan Ave., 307/527-5040, 7am-7pm Mon.-Sat. summer, 7am-5pm Mon.-Sat. winter, $4-12) is another great place for a quick bite, whether breakfast, buffalo burgers, espresso, or ice cream. Daily soups, specials, and desserts should not be missed. You can find them on Facebook. Another solid breakfast choice in Cody is **Our Place** (148 Yellowstone Ave , 307/527-4420, 6am-2pm daily summer, 6am-1:30pm Wed.-Sun. winter, $4-12, cash only), which dishes up veggie egg white omelets, hash browns, pancakes, and all the classics. They have great lunch specials too. Try the chili. But bring cash because they don't take credit cards.

For Mexican food, nothing beats **Zapata's** (1362 Sheridan Ave., 307/527-7181, www.zapatascody.com, 11am-9pm Mon.-Sat., noon-8pm Sun. summer, 11am-2pm and 5pm-9pm Wed.-Fri., 11am-9pm Sat., noon-8pm Sun. winter, $9-20), which serves outstanding New Mexico-style Mexican food including fish tacos, snow crab enchiladas, and homemade salsas and sauces you can buy and take home.

Open only in summer, **The Cody Cattle Company** (1910 Demaris St., 307/272-5770, www.thecodycattlecompany.com, doors open at 5:15pm daily late May-mid-Sept., dinner and show $38 adults, $19 children 7-12) serves up a bountiful all-you-can-eat chuck wagon dinner—including brisket, steak, potato, beans, and more—and a live country music show starting nightly at 6:30pm. You can pair your dinner and a show with tickets to the nightly rodeo, which is within walking distance, for the cowboy trifecta (from $60).

Cody's best-kept culinary secret is likely ★ **The Local** (1124 13th Ave., 307/586-4262, 8:30am-2pm and 5pm-9pm Tues.-Sat., closed in shoulder seasons, $12-38), an American bistro with inventive creations relying on ingredients sourced from local producers. This is farm-to-table cuisine in its best Wyoming iteration. The salads are phenomenal, as are the whitefish curry, the Ishawooa Mesa beef burgers, and the yam chips.

Serving mouthwatering Texas barbecue, **Fat Racks BBQ** (1491 Sheridan Ave., 940/453-8840, 11am-7pm Mon.-Fri., www.fatracksbbq.com, $6.25-28) was a wildly popular food truck and now offers inside and outdoor seating. The pulled pork nachos are worth a postcard home.

An absolute must for at least one meal (if you are not staying at the hotel) is **The Irma** (1192 Sheridan Ave., 307/587-4221, www.irmahotel.com, 7am-9pm daily year-round, à la carte breakfast $8-11, lunch $10-18, dinner $12-32). The prime rib dinner buffet (5pm-8:30pm daily May-June 15, 5pm-9pm daily mid-June-Aug., 5:30pm-8pm Fri.-Sat. Sept.-Apr., $28.50 adults, $10 kids 7-10, free for kids 6 and under) is famous, but it's really the history and ambience of the place that make it a must. The Irma also serves a breakfast buffet (7am-11am daily June-Sept., 7am-11am Sat.-Sun. Oct.-May, $13 adults, $7 children 7-10, free for children under 6) and lunch buffet (11:30am-2pm Mon.-Sat. summer, $13 adults, $7 children 7-10, free for children 6 and under, 11:30am-2pm Sun. year-round, $18 adults, $16 seniors, $7 children 7-10, free for children 6 and under).

It doesn't get more local or more traditional than **Cassie's Supper Club** (214 Yellowstone Ave., 307/527-5500, www.cassies.com, noon-11pm Mon.-Fri., 11am-1am Fri.-Sat., Sun. brunch 11am-2pm, $12-50), named for its original proprietor, Cody's most beloved madam. When the city asked her to close her brothel in the early 1930s, Cassie complied, sort of: She opened her supper club at the west end of town, where it stands today. The atmosphere is dark, the mood light, the food hearty, and the history rich. It is Cody's hot spot for two-stepping and has three bars to help lubricate dancers. It should be stated that Cassie's brothel business died with her in 1952.

ACCOMMODATIONS

Geared as it is toward the flocks of visitors headed to Yellowstone, Cody has an abundance of accommodations, many of them newer. Among the best deals in town is the basic but appealing and independently owned **A Wyoming Inn** (720 Yellowstone Ave., 307/587-4208, www.hotelcody.com, May-Oct., from $125). Among the chain hotels in town are **AmericInn** (508 Yellowstone Ave., 307/587-7716, www.wyndhamhotels.com, $109-359), **Comfort Inn** (1601 Sheridan Ave., 307/587-5556, www.comfortinn.com, $96-260), **Holiday Inn** (1701 Sheridan Ave., 307/587-5555, www.ihg.com, $117-316), and the very upscale **Best Western Premier Ivy Inn & Suites** (1800 8th St., 307/587-2572, www.bestwesternwyoming.com, $115-325), which offers fine dining in an excellent American bistro, 8th Street at the Ivy.

For significantly more charm, the ★ **Chamberlin Inn** (1032 12th St., 307/587-0202 or 888/587-0202, www.chamberlininn.com, $149-699) is a stately complex built in 1904 and beautifully restored in 2007. There are 21 individual rooms, including several suites, a cottage, and a house, all of which are unique. Ernest Hemingway spent the night in one of them in 1932—his signature is still in the guest register.

Buffalo Bill's beloved **Irma Hotel** (1192 Sheridan Ave., 307/587-4221 or 800/745-4762, www.irmahotel.com, $80-225) is another classic in Cody. Showing a few more signs of wear than the Chamberlin, but with its own marvelous history and central location, the Irma is an important landmark and central to this community.

Just outside Yellowstone's east entrance, **Pahaska Tepee** (183 North Fork Hwy., 307/527-7701 or 800/628-7791, www.pahaska.com, $140-1,450) is another of Buffalo Bill's historic lodges. The complex is vast, with the old 1904 lodge, newer housekeeping cabins, deluxe modern condos, and a seven-bedroom family reunion lodge, but so are the recreational opportunities. From horseback riding to cross-country skiing, Pahaska Tepee is like a giant playground with immediate proximity to Yellowstone. Also on the way from Cody to Yellowstone, the **Wapiti Lodge** (3149 North Fork Hwy., 307/587-2420, www. wapitilodge.com, 18 miles (29 km) west of Cody and 29 miles (47 km) east of the East Entrance to Yellowstone, $190-375) is another historic property—open since 1904—that offers six guest suites, all with private bath and kitchenette, a two-bedroom river house, and two cabins.

GUEST RANCHES

Since Cody is cowboy country, after all, it's fitting that there are a number of guest ranches in the area. Most are geared heavily toward horseback riding and provide lodging in individual and often charmingly rustic cabins. Other activities such as fishing and hiking are regularly available. Things like cell phone coverage, satellite TV, and Wi-Fi are simply not on the menu. These ranches provide true opportunities to get away from life as you know it in some of the most spectacular country on the planet.

Forty miles (64 km) west of Cody, the **Absaroka Mountain Lodge** (1231 North Fork Hwy., 307/587-3963, www. absarokamtlodge.com, mid-May-Sept., $135-235 off-season cabins May and late Sept., $155-255 prime season Memorial Day-mid-Sept.) dates back to 1917 and is one of the largest and best known. Unlike many guest ranches in the area, the Absaroka Mountain Lodge is not all-inclusive; guests select and pay for activities, including fishing and horseback riding, and eat meals in a restaurant. Wi-Fi is available in the main lodge.

Founded by the grandson of Buffalo Bill, the **Bill Cody Ranch** (2604 North Fork Hwy., 26 mi/42 km west of Cody, 307/587-2097 or 800/615-2934, www.billcodyranch.com, $130-270 cabins) is exactly halfway between Cody and Yellowstone in the magnificent North Fork Valley. Meals and activities are paid for separately for standard cabins. Packages are also available and include breakfast, dinner,

a four-hour horseback ride with lunch, and overnight accommodations (call for current rates).

The **7D Ranch** (774 Sunlight Rd., 307/587-9885 or 888/587-9885, www.7dranch.com, from $2,388 pp/week for 2 adults in a cabin, discounted rates for children 6-12) is a small, remote ranch in the Sunlight Basin, 50 miles (80 km) northwest of Cody, offering cozy, rustic accommodations, horseback riding and fishing, pack trips, and hunting trips. Packages include six nights of accommodations; they also offer adult-only weeks.

For more guest ranches in the Cody area, contact the **Wyoming Dude Ranchers' Association** (1122 12th St., Cody, 307/587-2339, www.wyomingdra.com).

CAMPING

Buffalo Bill State Park (4192 North Fork Hwy., 307/587-9227, http://wyoparks.state. wy.us, May-Sept., $17/night residents, $30/ night nonresidents, $10 extra/day for electric site), 11 miles (18 km) west of Cody, offers the closest public campgrounds. Situated below the Absaroka Mountains, the park has two campgrounds: North Shore Bay Campground has 37 sites, and North Fork Campground has 62 sites.

A good, fully equipped private facility in town is the **Ponderosa Campground** (1815 8th St., 307/587-9203, www.codyponderosa. com, mid-Apr.-mid-Oct., $40 tents, $40-55 RVs, $40 tipis, $80 camping cabins for 2 people, discounts for Good Sam, AAA, and military). There is a cowboy cappuccino bar, a convenience store, a playground, clean restrooms and showers, and many other amenities in this large complex. **Absaroka Bay RV Park** (2001 Hwy. 14/16/120, 2002 Mountain View Dr., 307/527-7440, www. cody-wy.com, from $42 full hookup) has 81 full-hookup sites, each offering water, sewer, and a picnic table. The roads are paved and Wi-Fi is available throughout the campground. Amenities include clean showers and a laundromat.

INFORMATION AND SERVICES

The **Cody Country Chamber of Commerce** (836 Sheridan Ave., 307/587-2777 or 800/393-2639, www.codychamber.org, 8am-7pm daily summer, 8am-5pm Mon.-Fri. fall-spring) acts as a visitor center and a ticket outlet for events around town, and avid walkers can pick up a map of trails. Excellent planning tools are also available online at www.codyyellowstone.org.

For information on recreational trails and public camping in the region, contact the **Shoshone National Forest** (808 Meadow Lane Ave., 307/527-6241, www.fs.usda.gov) or the **Bureau of Land Management** (1002 Blackburn St., 307/578-5900, www.blm.gov, 7:45am-4:30pm Mon.-Fri.).

The main **post office** (307/527-7161, 8am-4:30pm Mon.-Fri., 9am-noon Sat.) is located at 1301 Stampede Avenue.

The airy and bright **Park County Library** (307/527-1880, www.parkcountylibrary.org, 9am-6pm Mon.-Thurs., 9am-5pm Fri.-Sat.) is at 1500 Heart Mountain Street.

Cody's **West Park Hospital** (707 Sheridan Ave., 307/527-7501 or 800/654-9447, www.codyregionalhealth.org) has a 24-hour emergency room. The hospital also runs the **Cody Regional Health Walk-In Clinic** (424 Yellowstone Ave., Suite 110, 307/578-2903, 8am-6:30pm Mon.-Fri., 9am-5:30pm Sat., 9am-3:30pm Sun.) for illnesses and injuries that do not require hospital care.

Visitors can do laundry at **Cody's Laundromat** (1728 Beck Ave., 307/587-8500, www.thecodylaundromat.weebly.com, 24 hours daily).

TRANSPORTATION

Getting There

The Cody area is served commercially by the **Yellowstone Regional Airport** (COD, 2101 Roger Sedam Dr., 307/587-5096, www.flyyra.com), just a two-minute drive from downtown, which has daily flights on **Delta** and **United Express**. The airport is 52 miles (84 km) from the east entrance to Yellowstone National Park. Air and shuttle services are also available from Billings (107 mi/172 km). Long-term and short-term outdoor vehicle parking at the airport is free.

By road, Cody is 177 miles (280 km) northeast of Jackson, 163 miles (265 km) north of Lander, 84 miles (135 km) northwest of Thermopolis, and 52 miles (84 km) east of Yellowstone National Park.

Getting Around

Car-rental companies operating at the Yellowstone Regional Airport include **Avis, Budget, Dollar, Hertz,** and **Thrifty.**

For travel between Cody and Billings, local taxi service in town, and tours to Yellowstone, contact **Cody Shuttle/Yellowstone Tours** (307/527-6789 or 866/527-6789, www.codyshuttle.com).

For regular taxi service, contact **Cody Cab** (307/272-8364) or **Town Taxi** (307/250-3939, www.town-taxi-service.business.site). Tours of Yellowstone and Grand Teton National Parks can also be arranged.

Sheridan and Northeast Wyoming

Northeast Wyoming encompasses rocky peaks, meadows full of wildflowers, river-carved canyons, and wide-open spaces, as well as the classic Western town of Sheridan and the Powder River Basin towns of Gillette and Buffalo.

Long a prime buffalo hunting territory for Native Americans, the area has seen great conflict between Indians and encroaching settlers. Today that relationship is dynamic and evident throughout much of the region, even at Devils Tower, where climbers are making strides toward working in cooperation with the Native Americans for whom the feature is sacred.

The economy is based almost entirely on natural resources: coal and coal-bed methane, livestock production, and tourism in these

Highlights

Look for ★ to find recommended sights, activities, dining, and lodging.

© MOON.COM

★ **King's Saddlery:** Part museum, part Western tack store, this is the hub of Sheridan (page 169).

★ **Medicine Wheel National Historic Landmark:** High in the Big Horns on a narrow ridge is this mysterious, Stonehenge-esque feature thought to be 500-800 years old (page 169).

★ **Eatons' Ranch:** The oldest dude ranch in the world is certainly one of the most traditional (page 177).

★ **Big Horn:** This tiny little town is full of character, with a gem of an art museum, plenty of polo, and wonderful Western celebrations (page 179).

★ **Occidental Hotel:** Catch a glimpse of what the good life looked like in the Old West (page 181).

★ **Cloud Peak Skyway Scenic Byway:** This stunning road climbs over and cuts through the Big Horn Mountains, passing by beautiful spots and providing access to historic sites (page 184).

★ **Hiking and Climbing at Devils Tower:** An iconic sentinel rising above the Belle Fourche River, the nation's first national monument is a magnet for hikers and climbers (page 195).

Sheridan and Northeast Wyoming

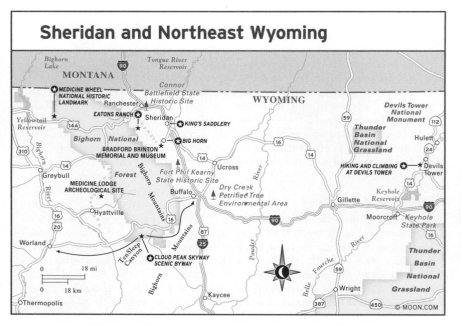

vast and beautiful places. There are tiny museums in towns like Sheridan and Big Horn, among many others, that celebrate a way of life that seems in no danger of disappearing here, with the relative vastness and remote feel of the region. Although towns like Gillette are growing as quickly as trains can haul coal—then shrinking just as fast when production slows—plenty of places exist where time stands still in northeast Wyoming. From horseback riding and fishing to hiking and rock climbing, the region has no shortage of recreational opportunities.

PLANNING YOUR TIME

Travelers heading east or west on I-90 will have easy access to much of the region. **Sheridan** is a wonderful town to visit and a terrific hub for many of Wyoming's **dude ranches.** Although most ranches are busiest in summer, a few open in May, and some stay open into fall for hunters. Just down the road from Sheridan, the tiny town of **Big**

Horn is home to **The Brinton Museum,** on a gentleman's ranch where you could easily while away an afternoon. Nearby **Buffalo,** the starting point for the 47-mile (76-km) **Cloud Peak Skyway Scenic Byway,** has a historic downtown with a great little museum and easy access to sites that feature prominently in Wyoming history, including **Fort Phil Kearny** and the infamous **Hole-in-the-Wall** region where Butch Cassidy and the Sundance Kid were known to hide out. Though not exactly a touristy destination, **Gillette** offers nice parks and a terrific public pool with water slides. Summer, late spring, and early fall are the best times to hit this corner of the state because of the blue skies and easy opportunities to be outdoors. They're still here in the winter, of course, but one gets the feeling that everyone is hunkered down, waiting for spring.

Though **Devils Tower National Monument** is not exactly on the way to anywhere, it is for many the highlight of a trip to

Previous: Devils Tower National Monument; charming downtown Buffalo; horses at Eatons' Ranch.

Wyoming as an obvious recreation spot for climbers, hikers, and campers. The trip can be made fairly easily in a day from just about anywhere in northeast Wyoming. It's wise to plan your visit to Devils Tower sometime other than June, when the voluntary ban on hiking and climbing is in place; or the first and second weeks in August, when bikers headed to or from the huge Sturgis Motorcycle Rally in South Dakota's Black Hills can descend on the tower in crowds of hundreds and even thousands.

HISTORY

Stretching from the eastern flank of the Big Horn Mountains east to the Black Hills and bordered on the south by the North Platte River, the Powder River Basin was prime hunting territory for a number of different Native American groups. In order to bypass inevitable conflict, most miners traveling through the region to Montana's goldfields steered south of the Powder River Basin on the Oregon Trail. In 1864, however, as mining towns were booming overnight in Montana, John Jacobs and John Bozeman built the first trail through the area. The Bozeman Trail became known as the "Bloody Bozeman."

The area was essentially a war zone as early as 1854, during the first of three Sioux wars. Only after the 1876-1877 Great Sioux War, which included Crazy Horse's surrender, and the Ghost Dance War, which ended with the Massacre at Wounded Knee in 1890, did the Sioux commit to living on the reservation. The Fort Laramie Treaty of 1868, signed by both the Sioux tribes and the U.S. government, recognized the Black Hills as part of the Sioux Nation, and determined that food and clothing annuities would be provided to the Native Americans, and that the Bozeman Trail, and all the military forts along it, would be closed. But the treaty did not bring peace, and in the end it was not honored. During those decades numerous battles flared between significant leaders on both sides, including Sioux chief Red Cloud,

Dull Knife, and Col. H. B. Carrington. The 1876 "Dull Knife Fight" robbed the Cheyenne of all their winter supplies, including winter food storage. Part military tactic, part revenge for the recent death of Custer and his men at the Battle of the Little Bighorn in June of that year, the U.S. Army destroyed everything the Cheyenne had gathered for winter, and the surviving Indians, women and children included, fled on foot in temperatures that fell below -30°F (-34.4°C). The Cheyenne surrendered a few weeks later.

The reservation included the Black Hills, much of which was thought to be gold-rich and so was seized by the government from the Sioux in 1876. Although the Indian Peace Commission had originally offered $6 million, and the Sioux, understanding the value the settlers saw in the soil, had asked for $70 million, in the end the government reclaimed the land without paying the tribe a penny. The case was still being argued in 1980 when the U.S. Supreme Court ruled that the government owed the Sioux $102 million for the land they had stolen. The money was placed in trust and today is worth nearly $2 billion. The tribes have not accepted the payment because they say the land was never for sale. They want the Black Hills, an area they consider the spiritual center of the Sioux nation, rather than the money.

With the Indian Wars winding down, a new type of conflict arose between the moneyed cattle ranchers and the hardscrabble homesteaders across the Powder River Basin. Texas cattle had come into the region between 1875 and 1884. They were grazed on the open range until homesteaders started fencing off pastureland and watering holes. The cattle herds continued to increase while the open rangeland decreased. With drought followed by freezing temperatures, more than 500,000 cattle died over the winter of 1886-1887, later referred to as the "Great Die-up." Ranchers became even more resolved to make their outfits profitable.

While the ranchers were trying to rid themselves of pesky rustlers and homesteaders, a hired group called the Regulators pursued a "dead list" of ambitious and outspoken homesteaders and people believed to be rustlers. This was known as the Johnson County War, and there were major conflicts between ranchers and townspeople who supported the outspoken homesteaders.

The last Indian battle in Wyoming took place on October 31, 1903, southwest of Newcastle, when Sioux returning to their reservation from Montana ran into lawmen from Newcastle. At stake was the issue of whether or not the Sioux were violating game laws by hunting off the reservation. Three lawmen were killed, and the Sioux eventually surrendered, were put on trial, and were ultimately acquitted.

Throughout the 20th century, the story of this corner of Wyoming centered on cattle and sheep production and, more recently (and far more lucratively), coal and coal-bed methane production. With wide-open ranch country and the Devils Tower as the country's first national monument, it's not a stretch to see why tourism, too, continues to play an important role in the region.

Sheridan and Vicinity

Although Sheridan (pop. 18,154, elev. 3,753 ft/1,144 m) continuously touts itself as the midpoint between Yellowstone National Park and the Black Hills, it sells itself short. It's true that it is conveniently located, but this authentic Western town has much more to offer than proximity to other places.

Rich with history, Sheridan is the town where Martha Jane Canary transformed herself into Calamity Jane. The iconic Sheridan Inn was opened in 1893; Buffalo Bill operated it for two years, using the inn as a place to audition acts for his Wild West Show.

One of the most charming towns in the state, Sheridan has the feel of the Old West, although that is slowly beginning to change as traditional Main Street businesses are gradually replaced by high-end art galleries and gourmet eateries. Still, Wyoming's best-known saddlery is here and in no danger of leaving, as are some classic watering holes like the Mint Bar, along with numerous historic sites.

The tiny (and unincorporated) town of Big Horn (pop. 483, elev. 4,081 ft/1,244 m) is on the eastern slopes of the Big Horn Mountains, with Little Goose Creek running through. The town was settled in the late 1880s by such well-known sheep and cattle ranchers as the Moncreiffe brothers, the Wallop family, the Gallatin family, and Bradford Brinton, whose home is a gem of a museum and one of the best reasons to visit Big Horn. The other reason to visit is to check out a polo match, a favorite pastime of the town.

SIGHTS

Trail End State Historic Site

The **Trail End State Historic Site** (400 Clarendon Ave., 307/674-4589, www.trailend. org, 1pm-4pm daily Apr.-May, 9am-6pm daily June-Aug., 1pm-4pm daily Sept.-mid-Dec., 10am-5pm Memorial Day and Labor Day weekends, closed mid-Dec.-Mar., $8 nonresidents, $4 residents, children 17 and under free if accompanied by an adult) is situated high on a bluff overlooking town. The 4-acre grounds are impeccably manicured and have retained much of their original landscaping, designed nearly a century ago. The museum is the former home of John B. Kendrick, one of Wyoming's most famous sons. Kendrick was orphaned early in life and got his start at age 15 as a ranch hand. Originally from Texas, he followed cattle into Wyoming and, taken with its beauty, decided to stay. He went on to become a successful rancher and businessman, accumulating more than 200,000 acres of land. Kendrick would become Wyoming's first governor and later a

U.S. senator. Kendrick referred to the house, begun in 1908 and completed in 1913, as the "end-of-the-trail mansion," and it's where he would spend the last 20 years of his life when he wasn't in Washington DC.

The house is built in the Flemish revival style, with rich mahogany walls, exposed-beam ceilings, and 18 beautifully decorated rooms. What is unique to this historic house is that almost everything on display (furniture, rugs, magazines, books, and photographs) is the original property of the Kendrick family. In early December, the mansion is spectacularly decorated with lights, greenery, and decorations. Open houses (check website for schedules) include live music and a visit from old Santa Claus himself. Self-guided tours are available; for groups larger than eight, reservations for guided tours can be made two weeks in advance.

Sheridan Inn

When the **Sheridan Inn** (856 Broadway, 307/655-7861, www.sheridaninn.com) opened in 1893, it was considered the finest hotel between Chicago and San Francisco. Designed after a Scottish inn and with a bar imported from England, the inn was the only hotel in Sheridan to have electric lights (200 of them, to be exact). The porch runs the full 130-foot length of the hotel, and there are 62 dormer windows.

Buffalo Bill Cody helped inaugurate the hotel—chilled champagne was served—and went on to become a co-owner. He would hold auditions for his Wild West Show on the hotel's veranda, and the Sheridan Inn quickly became the social center for Sheridan's affluent residents. Today, the 22 refurbished rooms reflect Buffalo Bill and 21 other key characters in his life, including Sitting Bull, Annie Oakley, and Queen Victoria.

The hotel has hosted famous guests, including presidents Theodore Roosevelt, Howard Taft, and Herbert Hoover. Its longest resident, however, is said to still reside in the hotel: Catherine B. Arnold worked and lived at the inn for 64 years, from her arrival in 1901 until she left, only when the hotel closed, in 1965. She had worked as a desk clerk, seamstress, housekeeper, and hostess, and her dying request was to be buried in the hotel. When she died three years later, her ashes were placed in the wall of the 3rd-floor room she often occupied. According to local lore, the presence of "Miss Kate" is still felt. From the sound of footsteps and lights turning on and off to doors being opened and shut, the rumor is that she still likes to manage the inn.

The hotel reopened in 1967 and continued to operate for another 20 years before closing its doors again. In 1991 a restaurant opened in the inn and tours of the building were available, but it no longer functioned as a hotel. In

Downtown Sheridan

To Sheridan County Fairgrounds

WYOMING'S RIB & CHOP HOUSE

SHERIDAN INN

To U.S. Forest Service and Comfort Inn

5TH ST
4TH ST
3RD ST
2ND ST
1ST ST

VAL VISTA
Big Goose Creek

BEST WESTERN SHERIDAN CIRCLE

0   200 yds
0   200 m

To Koltiska Distillery

LUMINOUS BREWHOUSE

LEWIS ST
To Trail End State Historic Site, The Carriage House Theater

DOW ST
MANDEL ST
ALGER ST
GRINNELL AVE

MAIN ST
GOULD ST
BROADWAY
Little Goose Creek

CUSTOM COWBOY SHOP

BLACKTOOTH BREWING COMPANY

LIBRARY
SHABBY SHACK
BROOKS ST

Whitney Park

THE SPORT SHOP
THE SUGAR BOOT
KING'S SADDLERY

RED BISON STUDIO
WESTERN GRACE
GRINNELL PLAZA

OVER THE MOON BOUTIQUE
SMITH ST

MINT BAR
SCOTT ST

LITTLE WILLOW TRADERS
COWBOY CAFE
FRACKLETON'S

To Birch

BRUNDAGE ST

To
EATONS RANCH

WYO THEATRE

To Mill Inn, Canyon Ranch, Wyoming Culinary Institute, and Sheridan County Airport

POST OFFICE

© MOON.COM
LOUCKS ST

the fall of 2012, the property was completely shuttered until Bob and Dana Townsend of Oklahoma purchased it, continued the restoration, and reopened the hotel in 2015. Today the hotel is, once again, at the center of the Sheridan community.

★ King's Saddlery

In a town full of Western stores, **King's Saddlery** (184 N. Main St., 307/672-2702 or 800/443-8919, www.kingssaddlery.com, 8am-5pm Mon.-Sat.) is indeed aptly named. A legendary tack store established by the King family in the late 1940s, its founder Don King is a local hero and was a renowned saddle maker. Many of his saddles are on display in the store's **Don King Museum** (8am-5pm Mon.-Sat., donation requested) as well as at the National Cowboy Hall of Fame and the PRCA Rodeo Hall of Fame. For six years, Don handcrafted the PRCA World Championship saddles.

In addition to the store's dizzying selection of rope, hats, and Western tack, the museum houses hundreds of saddles, wagons, coaches, Native American artifacts, cowboy memorabilia from around the world, and original art. Don't leave without a King Ropes baseball cap, which promotes the saddlery's most famous product; it will connect you with other cowboy aficionados the world over.

Ucross Foundation

Twenty-seven miles (43 km) east of Sheridan, nestled in the midst of a 20,000-acre working cattle ranch (half of the land is protected by The Nature Conservancy), is the artists' haven known as **Ucross** (30 Big Red Ln., 307/737-2291, www.ucrossfoundation.org). About 80 artists from around the globe are invited to take up residence at the foundation each year, since 1981, for 2-6 weeks at a time. The foundation's mission is simply to provide a workplace where writers, composers, painters, and other artists can live and work uninterrupted for an extended period of time. There are usually 8-9 residents on the grounds at the same time. Pulitzer Prize-winning author Annie Proulx has been a significant supporter of Ucross, and Elizabeth Gilbert wrote part of her novel *Eat, Pray, Love* while in residence.

Big Red was the main house of the original ranch and now serves as an important part of the complex. It is decorated with antique furniture and houses a gallery (10am-4pm Mon.-Fri.) that hosts four annual exhibitions, which are open to the public. The gallery is closed between exhibitions, so call ahead or check online before you go.

Bighorn Scenic Byway

One stretch of stunning road between Yellowstone to the west and Mount Rushmore and the Black Hills to the east is the **Bighorn Scenic Byway,** a 58-mile (93-km) stretch of road that starts at Shell, Wyoming, in the dramatic Shell Canyon. Winding up through the Bighorn National Forest past Shell Falls, the byway slips through narrow canyons past red chimney rocks and towering cliffs. The highest point on the drive is Granite Pass, just above the Antelope Butte Ski Area. North of the pass, the byway intersects with US 14A, known as the Medicine Wheel Passage for its access to Medicine Wheel National Historic Landmark. In addition to a diversity of landscapes—rangeland, forest, subalpine, and alpine—there is an abundance of wildlife in the region; travelers can watch for elk, moose, and deer. The access to public campgrounds and hiking trails is better on this byway than just about anywhere in the Bighorn National Forest. The byway's eastern end (although US 14 continues on) is just west of Ranchester in Dayton.

★ Medicine Wheel National Historic Landmark

High atop a bluff in the Big Horn Mountains, some 70 miles (113 km) or about a 90-minute drive west of Sheridan on US 14A, **Medicine Wheel National Historic Landmark** is an 82-foot-wide (25-m) stone circle with 28 interior spokes connecting the exterior with an interior circular mound. Made of limestone slabs and boulders, the Medicine Wheel is a

mysterious landmark that has spiritual but unexplained significance to many Native American groups. It was first seen by Eastern explorers in the late 1800s, and thoughts on its origins are vast and varied: Some link it back to the worship of the Aztecs; others attribute it to early French or Russian explorers. The most common viewpoint, however, is that it was built by one of the tribes in the region: Crow, Arapaho, Shoshone, Sheep Eater, or Cheyenne. The star alignments suggest the medicine wheel could have been constructed as early as the 13th century, and the solstice alignments are accurate even today. The only carbon dating from the site, done on a piece of wood, suggests a minimum age of 1760. There are tipi rings around the site and worn travois trails to it, suggesting heavy usage. Stone markers in the shape of arrows point to nearby medicine wheels, including those in Meeteetse and Steamboat Mountain in southwest Wyoming near Rock Springs.

Although the site was designated a National Historic Landmark in 1970, little was done to protect the artifacts from the elements, livestock, and, rather unfortunately, disrespectful visitors. Today the **U.S. Forest Service** (2013 Eastside 2nd St., Sheridan, 307/674-2600, www.fs.usda.gov) is responsible for protecting and preserving the area, and Native American guides have been hired to interpret the site for visitors. Driving to the site itself is restricted, so plan to park at the ranger station and walk about 1.5 miles (2.4 km) on a gravel road.

SPORTS AND RECREATION

Hiking

With the Big Horn Mountains looming so close to town, there is plenty of country to get lost in within an easy drive from Sheridan. To plan a good hike or backpacking trip, visit the **U.S. Forest Service** (2013 Eastside 2nd St., Sheridan, 307/674-2600, www.fs.usda.gov/bighorn) for maps and advice. Right

---

1: the western store King's Saddlery **2:** Medicine Wheel National Historic Landmark

downtown, **The Sport Shop** (208 N. Main St., 307/672-5356, 9am-5:30pm Mon.-Fri., 9am-5pm Sat. summer, 10am-5pm Mon.-Sat. fall-spring) can outfit hikers and backpackers or just offer friendly advice.

For adventurous types keen to head out, there are hundreds of trails in the **Bighorn National Forest,** many of which can be accessed from the Bighorn Scenic Byway on US 14. One such trail is the **Tongue River,** an 18.2-mile (29.3-km) out-and-back hike that leaves from a trailhead roughly 9 miles (14.5 km) west of Ranchester on County Road 92 in the Tongue River Canyon. Though the trail climbs more than 3,000 vertical feet (914 m) over 9 miles (14.5 km), hikers looking for a shorter route will be delighted with the 2-mile (3.2-km) round-trip hike along the gushing river and up a set of switchbacks to a rather large limestone cave that can be explored if you have the right equipment (headlamps are essential). Be on the lookout, however, for livestock, poison ivy, and rattlesnakes; even with them, this is a beautiful spot.

An interactive map of the trails and campgrounds in the area is available online (www.sheridanwyoming.org).

Fishing

There is no shortage of fantastic fishing spots around Sheridan. Anglers have long flocked to the region to wet a line on the **Tongue River, Little Goose Creek,** and **Big Goose Creek,** as well as any of the dozens of pristine alpine lakes in the region, including **Sibley Lake** and **Lake DeSmet.**

For up-to-date information and all the gear you could possibly need, stop into **Fly Shop of the Bighorns** (201 N. Main St., 307/672-5866, www.anglingdestinations.com, 7am-7pm Mon.-Sat., 7am-3pm Sun., shortened hours off-season). It offers guided walks and wades as well as float trips to blue-ribbon trout waters on both public and private lands as **Rock Creek Anglers.** Half-day wade-fishing trips start at $400 for one angler and $500 for two. All-day wade-fishing trips are $500 for one angler and $600 for two. All-day float trips are $600 for one angler and $650 for two. Casting lessons ($100) are available and private water leases can add fees of $100-150 per rod to the cost. Gear is available for rent as well.

Horseback Riding

While Sheridan is surrounded by some of the best guest ranches in the country that focus on riding, there aren't many options for visitors to town who are looking for a riding opportunity without the full-on ranch experience. About 20 minutes from Sheridan is **Rangeland Enterprises** (394 Beaver Creek Rd., 307/672-6717, www.rangelandhuntingadventures.com, $40/hour, minimum age 6, reservations required). Day trips, overnight adventures, and hunting expeditions are also offered. Outside of Buffalo on US 16 West, **South Fork Mountain Lodge & Outfitters** (307/267-2609 or 307/351-4606, www.lodgesofthebighorns.com/south-fork-mountain-outfitters-wyoming.php) offers a range of activities and amenities, included horseback riding options ($125/pp 2-hour ride, $300/pp 4-hour ride, including lunch), June-early September. The remote and lovely **Spear-O-Wigwam Ranch** (Red Grade Road, Buffalo, 307/200-9655, www.spearowigwam.com, mid-June-late Sept.) in Buffalo offers two-hour rides ($75 pp) at 9am, noon, and 2pm; half-day rides ($125 pp) that start at 10am and include lunch; full-day rides ($200 pp); and overnights ($300 pp) that get riders out into the wilderness.

Golf

One semiprivate and one public golf course are in the vicinity of Sheridan. The **Hidden Bridge Golf Club** (550 Mydland Rd., 307/752-6625, www.hiddenbridgegolf.com, $27-32 for 9 holes including cart, $40-45 for 18 holes including cart) is close to downtown. The municipal **Kendrick Golf Course** (65 Golf Course Rd., 307/674-8148, www.golfkendrick.com, $40 pp for 9 holes with cart, $58 pp for 18 holes with cart) offers 18 holes with discounts for families and twilight play. There is a very limited number of "member for a day" opportunities at **The Powder Horn Golf Community** (23 Country Club Ln., 307/672-5323, www.thepowderhorn.com, call for availability and rates), a private club and residential community centered around a 27-hole championship course, with three distinct nines that pay homage to the Old Course at St. Andrews and the alpine landscape in Wyoming.

ENTERTAINMENT AND EVENTS
Nightlife

Whether you are cruising in a beat-up pickup truck or on foot, you don't have to leave Main Street for a taste of Sheridan's nightlife. The most famous of all the watering holes, and for good reason, is the **Mint Bar** (151 N. Main St., 307/674-9696, www.mintbarwyo.com, noon-2am Mon.-Fri., 10am-2am Sat.), which boasts hundreds of artifacts and mounts, furniture made in the tradition of Thomas Molesworth, 9,000 Wyoming cattle brands on the wall, and ambience that cannot be beat. During Prohibition, the bar was known as the Mint Cigar Company and Soda Shop, but loyal customers knew about the speakeasy in back. Don't leave without a pair of satin underpants that touts the Mint as a place "where good friends meet."

The craft brew scene is gaining steam in Sheridan with two excellent brewpubs and a distillery. **Blacktooth Brewing Company** (312 Broadway, 307/675-2337, www.blacktoothbrewingcompany.com, noon-10pm Mon.-Thurs., noon-11pm Fri.-Sat., noon-7pm Sun.) pours brown ales, amber ales, wheat beers, IPAs, and seasonal offerings in a very cool space. Just down the street, **Luminous Brewhouse** (504 Broadway, 307/655-5658, www.luminousbrewhouse.com, 2pm-10pm Mon.-Thurs., noon-midnight Fri.-Sat., 2pm-6pm Sun.) brews beers including red ale, coffee ale, IPA, session ale, a roasted pueblo chile ale, and a handful of seasonal brews. They also offer live local music every Wednesday 5pm-7pm, bluegrass jams on Tuesday nights

The Mustangs of the Pryor Mountains

One of the most unforgettable experiences you can have in the West is to witness the wild mustangs of the Pryor Mountains that straddle Montana and Wyoming. The majority of these horses share the hereditary line of those brought by Spanish explorers to the Americas more than five centuries ago. The mustangs are small horses with narrow but deep chests and strong, short backs. They are often distinguished by a solid stripe running down their backs or the unique "zebra" stripes across their legs.

wild mustangs of the Pryor Mountains

Although initially wary of the animals that the conquistadores rode, Native Americans quickly learned to prize them. Through the years they were traded and often stolen in raids. Horses used by the Indians or settlers were known to stray, and by the mid-1800s enough free stallions and mares had mated that there were more than 2 million wild horses living west of the Mississippi. At the same time, however, homesteaders were staking out their land and settling in the area. The mustangs' land was needed for houses, farms, and cattle grazing. Seen as an impediment to progress, the wild horses quickly began to disappear, hunted for sport or captured alive, where they were sent to slaughter and used by pet food companies. By the 1950s only a handful of herds were left.

In response to the work of grassroots organizations and public outcry, the U.S. government sanctioned the **Wild Horse Range** in 1968. Some 31,000 acres were set aside to protect these majestic animals in the Pryor Mountains. Three years later, the Wild Free Roaming Horse and Burro Act stipulated that these horses were "an integral part of the natural system of the public land" and were to be protected from future harassment.

Today 90-120 mustangs live on a now 39,650-acre range, which is maintained by the Bureau of Land Management (BLM). The mustangs live in small social units known as harems, which consist of a dominant stallion, a head mare, other mares, and colts. There are currently estimated to be about 30 harems, which produce 20-30 foals each year. In order to balance the well-being of the horses with the well-being of the public land, the BLM has overseen a wild horse adoption program since 1973.

The best place to launch a visit to the Pryor Range is the **Pryor Mountain Wild Mustang Center** (US 14A, Lovell, Wyoming, 307/548-9453, www.pryormustangs.org, 9am-5pm Mon.-Sat. summer, 10am-3pm Mon.-Fri. winter, hours can vary and there are seasonal closures so call ahead), where staff can tell you about current sightings and locations.

If you drive north along Highway 37 from US 14A east of Lovell into the Bighorn Canyon Recreation Area, you may get lucky and see some mustangs. Sightings are more frequent on East Pryor Mountain, but travel is much more difficult and requires four-wheel drive. There are outfitters willing to take you into the backcountry for a better chance of seeing these wild and beautiful creatures. It is critical that your presence does not impact or change their behavior in any way. The standard distance to keep from the mustangs is 33 yards/meters.

---

at 7pm, and an open-mic night Thursdays at 7:30pm. There is root beer made on premises for the kids, and non-beer drinkers can order cold press coffee, kombucha, and soft drinks. Formerly Kolts Fine Spirits, and now called

Koltiska Distillery (644 Crook St., 307/673-7307, www.koltiska.com, 3pm-10pm Wed.-Sat., noon-5pm Sun. summer, reduced hours in winter), this family-run operation produces Koltiska Original Liqueur, KO 90 Liqueur, vodka, and a winter-mint liqueur and gives visitors tours of the production facility.

The Arts

Sheridan is home to two wonderful old theaters. The **Carriage House Theater** (419 Delphi Ave., 307/672-9886) was formerly the carriage house for the Flemish-style Trail End mansion and converted to a theater in 1979. The 1923 **WYO Theater** (42 N. Main St., 307/672-9084, www.wyotheater.com) was built as the Lotus, a vaudeville theater. It entertained the residents of Sheridan for nearly 60 years until it was shuttered in 1982. The community rallied to save the building and return it to its glory. The WYO has been hosting live performances, educational experiences, and much more since its reopening as an architectural centerpiece in 1989.

Festivals and Events

Sheridan is a strong community of locals and regular yearly visitors that supports a multitude of weekly events, including the Thursday **Sheridan Farmers Market** (307/672-8881, www.downtownsheridan.org, 5pm-7pm Thurs. mid-June-mid-Sept.) at Grinnell Plaza Park (W. Algers St. and N. Brooks St.) and Tuesday evening **Concerts in the Park**

(www.sheridanwyoming.org) at 7:30pm in Kendrick Park (late June-mid-Aug.). The third Thursday of each month (June-Sept.) is the **Third Thursday Street Festival** (www.downtownsheridan.org), with music and food vendors in the heart of downtown. The annual **WYO Film Festival** (www.wyofilmfestival.org) is a three-day festival, held in late September or early October, showcasing indie and short films from around the world.

Since 1930, the **Sheridan WYO Rodeo** (www.sheridanwyorodeo.com) has been one of the most celebrated events in the state, and its renowned posters hang as graphic art all across the West. The mid-July event entails four nights of PRCA rodeo, multiple concerts, a traditional Indian Relay with a $50,000 payout, a parade, and a footrace. The **First Peoples' Pow Wow and Dance** (www.sheridanwyoming.org) is a celebration with traditional dancers and drum teams held on the lawn at the Sheridan Inn over several days during the Sheridan WYO Rodeo.

Held annually the first week of August, the **Sheridan County Fair** (1650 W. 5th St., Sheridan, 307/672-2079, www.sherfair.com, free) offers games, contests, and events to entertain the whole family, including a pancake breakfast, horse and livestock shows,

the Mint Bar

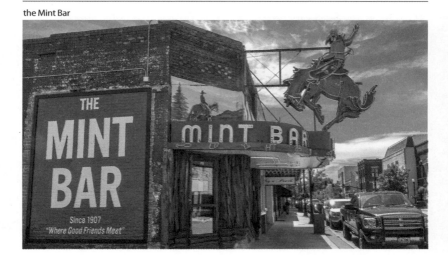

community exhibits, inflatable games and slides, and the usual 4-H and FFA events.

Later in the summer, typically in early to mid-August, the **Sheridan County Rodeo** (307/672-2079, www.sherfair.com) is held at the local fairgrounds. Less flashy than the Sheridan WYO Rodeo, this old-school small-town rodeo showcases the abundant local talent the region is known for. Events are open to adults and kids in more than two dozen events, including roping, racing, pole bending, goat tying, and steer wrestling.

SHOPPING

After a requisite stop at **King's Saddlery** (184 N. Main St., 307/672-2702 or 800/443-8919, www.kingssaddlery.com, 8am-5pm Mon.-Sat.), shoppers can stroll up and down historic **Main Street** with its abundance of art galleries, boutiques, and classic Western stores.

For appropriate cowboy and cowgirl duds, stop into the **Custom Cowboy Shop** (1286 Sheridan Ave., 800/487-2692, www. customcowboyshop.com, 9am-6pm Mon.-Fri., 10am-5pm Sat., noon-4pm Sun. Oct.-May, 9am-8pm Mon.-Sat., 10am-7pm Sun. June-Sept.), which was founded by cattle rancher and saddle maker Don Butler in 1976 as a way to make ends meet. Today this store, as well as another location in Cody, carries everything from saddles and tack to hats, buckles, scarves, clothing, jewelry, and housewares. Another decidedly Western shop is **Tom Balding Bits & Spurs** (655 Riverside, 307/672-8459, www.tombalding.com, 8am-4:30pm Mon.-Fri.), which sells the obvious, plus a unique selection of jewelry, rowels, reins, head straps, apparel, and other equine necessities.

A few great Main Street shops worth visiting are **Little Willow Traders** (166 N. Main St., 307/672-0200, www.littlewillowtraders. com, 10am-5pm Mon.-Sat.), which sells rustic home furnishings, gifts, clothing, and more, and **Over the Moon Boutique** (176 N. Main St., 307/673-4821, www.shopoverthemoon. com, 10am-5pm Mon.-Fri., 10am-4pm Sat.), which sells women's clothing, jewelry, bath and body products, handmade jewelry, baby clothing, and gifts. For high-end Western duds that could be in the pages of Vogue, **Western Grace** (225 N. Main St., 614/507-5859, www.westerngrace.com, call ahead for hours) is the brainchild of a local fashion designer who wanted classic and elegant, timeless and versatile Western pieces.

The Sugar Boot (200 N. Main St., 307/675-1825, 10am-7pm Mon.-Sat. May-mid-Sept.) is an old-timey candy shop with hand-dipped ice cream and retro toys, too.

For outdoor apparel, gear, and Wyoming gifts and clothing, try **Sheridan Sport Shop** (208 N. Main St., 307/672-5356, 10am-5pm Mon.-Sat.). **Red Bison Studio** (227 N. Main St., 307/655-8696, www.redbisonstudio.com, 10am-6pm Mon.-Fri., 10am-4pm Sat.) produces beautiful modern American ceramics inspired by the West. They also offer classes (check website or call for current schedule) for those who want to make their own memento in the form of a bowl or mug or vase.

FOOD

Unlike much of rural Wyoming, Sheridan is quite cosmopolitan when it comes to dining options. There is plenty of variety—think Chinese, Korean, and Mexican—plus some sophisticated gourmet eateries. Even so, it's never hard to find a juicy burger or steak in this cattle country.

A high-end restaurant in the Sheridan community since 2013 is **Frackelton's** (55 N. Main St., 307/675-6055, www.frackeltons. com, 11am-9pm Mon.-Thurs., 11am-10pm Fri.-Sat., 10am-2pm Sun., lunch $9-16, dinner $14-38), with the comfort-gourmet cuisine. The restaurant serves American bistro cuisine featuring familiar, mouthwatering burgers, salads, pastas, and juicy steaks. Among the local favorites are penne pasta with gorgonzola sauce, pan-roasted beef tenderloin, and the Original Bar & Grill Burger. Dinner reservations are a good idea.

Birch (342 Whitney Ln., 307/655-5551, 5pm-9pm Tues.-Sat., $17-38) is Wyoming at its fancy foodie best. Everything about the restaurant is elegant and creative, from the lamb meatballs and shishitos, to the braised ox cheeks and spiced hanger steak with burrata whipped potatoes. Even the cocktails look like a postcard. Owned by a young couple with two young children and boundless energy (transplants from the culinary scene in San Francisco) this little gem of a restaurant is a standout in every way.

A tried-and-true favorite in town (and across Montana and Wyoming) is **Wyoming's Rib & Chop House** (847 N. Main St., 307/673-4700, www.ribandchophouse.com, 11am-10pm daily, $14-80), which is known for its steaks, seafood, and baby back ribs. The $80 Cote de Boeuf is 36 ounces of French-cut rib eye served on a sizzling platter.

For classic Western fare all day long, look no further than the **Cowboy Cafe** (138 N. Main St., 307/672-2391, www.cowboycafewyo.com, 7am-9pm daily summer, 7am-8pm daily winter, breakfast $6-15, lunch $10-16, dinner $14-27). Some of their specialties include soft tacos, corned beef hash, burgers, the Reuben sandwich, and the Cowboy Cuban sandwich. They also serve specialty cocktails, wine, and beer. Another great place for a quick, delicious lunch or weekend brunch is **Shabby Shack** (1 E. Alger St., 307/763-4133, www.uptownshabbyshack.com, 11am-2pm Wed.-Fri., 9am-2pm Sat.-Sun., $10-15). You can't go wrong with the uptown brisket grilled cheese or Meemaw's double-decker BLT. It's comfort food with a twist. Donut burger anyone?

For another gourmet and rather unexpected treat for a weekday lunch, try the **Wyoming Culinary Institute** (1841 S. Sheridan Ave., 307/675-0320, www.sheridan.edu, 11:30am-2pm, call ahead for days and seasons, $8-14) at Sheridan College. Specialties include risotto croquettes, starburst grapefruit salad, shrimp sliders, and lobster thermidor penne. There's even a kids' menu.

ACCOMMODATIONS

Sheridan has a broad assortment of roadside hotels and motels. One of the most interesting is the ★ **Mill Inn** (2161 Coffeen Ave., 307/672-6401 or 888/357-6455, www.sheridanmillinn.com, from $77 in winter, from $95 in summer), cleverly built in an 1890s flour mill and listed on the National Register of Historic Places. The modern rooms are standard and comfortable. For historic charm, though, nothing beats the **Sheridan Inn** (856 Broadway, 307/674-2178, www.sheridaninn.com, $139-269). Built in 1893 and reopened as a hotel in 2015, the hotel has long been a hub of the community. Buffalo Bill even auditioned performers for his Wild West Show on the rambling front porch. The 22 rooms and suites are named for important people in Buffalo Bill's storied life.

Surprisingly budget friendly, the **Comfort Inn** (1950 E. 5th St., 307/675-1101, www.choicehotels.com, from $56) is geared to business travelers and has spacious oversize rooms with nice amenities, including a complimentary continental breakfast buffet, a fitness room, free Wi-Fi, a pool, and a self-service business center. Every room offers a view of either the Big Horn Mountains or the prairie. Located on a hilltop east of I-90, the Comfort Inn is quiet with easy access to town.

Among the other chain hotels in town are **Baymont by Wyndham** (911 Sibley Cir., 307/673-9500, www.wyndhamhotels.com, $64-139); **Days Inn** (1104 E. Brundage Ln., 307/672-2888, www.wyndhamhotels.com, $50-134), the pet-friendly **Best Western Sheridan Center** (612 N. Main St., 307/674-7421, www.bestwestern.com, $90-190), which has a great restaurant on-site, Bistro 307; and **Holiday Inn Sheridan— Convention Center** (1809 Sugarland Dr., 307/672-8931 or 800/315-2621, www.ing.com, from $95).

For a unique experience just 15 miles (24 km) south of Sheridan (take Hwy. 335 to County Rd. 77 to Canyon Ranch Rd.), the 3,000-acre **Canyon Ranch** (59 Canyon Ranch Rd., Big Horn, 307/751-6785 or 307/751-3580, www.canyonranchbighorn.com) has been run by the Wallop family for more than a century and offers ranch-type accommodations and vacation rentals as well as activities like fly-fishing, polo, and wildflower viewing. From the Foreman's House ($1,800/week) and the Hay Meadow House ($2,600/week), upgraded with all the modern amenities—flat-screen TVs, Wi-Fi, modern kitchens, and laundry rooms—to the Canyon Ranch Lodge ($2,800/week), this is ranch living at its most beautiful.

GUEST RANCHES

One beloved dude ranch in the area, operating for more than a century, is the **HF Bar** (1301 Rock Creek Rd., 307/684-2487, www.hfbar.com, $395/day ages 13 and over, $250/day children 5-12, all-inclusive, 7-day minimum June-Sept.), about 35 miles (56 km) from Sheridan or 20 miles (32 km) northwest of Buffalo. The cabins are at once rustic and comfortable, and activities include horseback riding, fishing, hiking, and sporting clays, among others.

Another option is the **Wyoming High Country Lodge** (Forest Rd. 13, 307/529-0914, www.wyhighcountry.com, $90-150 pp/night Oct.-Apr., $100-175 pp/night June-Sept., children 5-10 are half price, children 4 and under are free), which is about 30 miles (48 km) outside of Lovell in the Bighorn National Forest. This year-round ranch offers rustic rooms or cute cabins and any number of activities (except horseback riding!) including fishing, hiking, mountain biking, ATV trips, hunting, snow-kiting, cross-country skiing, and snowmobiling.

For a comprehensive list of dude ranches across the region, contact the **Dude Ranchers' Association** (866/399-2339 or 307/587-2339, www.duderanch.org), which represents more than 100 of the West's most respected ranches. Another excellent resource for finding the ideal dude ranch vacation is **Gene Kilgore's Ranchweb** (www.ranchweb.com).

★ Eatons' Ranch

A half-hour's drive from Sheridan, nestled along Wolf Creek in the Big Horn Mountains, is **Eatons' Ranch** (270 Eaton Ranch Rd., 307/655-9285, www.eatonsranch.com, $300-365/day pp early June-mid-Aug., $280-325/day pp mid-Aug.-Sept., all-inclusive, discounts for kids ages 6-17), the oldest dude ranch in the world and the cream of the crop. The cabins are old and charming, and the wonder of Eatons is that it rarely changes through the decades. The founding family is still running the ranch, which can accommodate up to 125 guests, and many of the dudes' families have been coming for generations as well. The riding is excellent, and Eatons is among the only ranches where riders can take to the mountains or prairies without a wrangler (although one is always available). The setting is magnificent and diverse—with mountains, canyons, and prairies to ride—and the traditions are time-tested. In the winter, bed-and-breakfast packages are available for single night or longer stays.

CAMPING

There are numerous public campgrounds in the Bighorn National Forest, many of which are easily accessed from the Bighorn Scenic Byway. For information about specific sites and, in some cases, to make reservations, contact the **U.S. Forest Service** (2013 Eastside 2nd St., Sheridan, 307/674-2600, www.fs.usda.gov/bighorn). Reservations can be booked at some sites through www.recreation.gov.

A handful of RV parks are scattered around town. The **Sheridan KOA** (63 Decker Rd., 307/674-8766 or 800/652-7621, www.koa.com) offers tent (from $31) and RV sites (from $45), one- to two-room cabins ($66-130), bike rentals, fishing, miniature golf, a swimming pool, and free Wi-Fi.

INFORMATION AND SERVICES

The office of **Sheridan Travel and Tourism** (1517 E. 5th St., 307/673-7120, www.sheridanwyoming.org, 8am-5pm daily summer, 8am-5pm Mon.-Sat. fall-spring) is conveniently located at the **State of Wyoming**

The Nation's First Dude Ranch

horses near Eatons' Ranch in Wolf

In 1868, the first of three brothers left Pittsburgh in pursuit of more adventure than their father's dry goods store promised. Howard Eaton settled in the Badlands of North Dakota; his brothers Alden and Willis joined him a few years later, and together the trio established a small ranch near what would become the town of Medora, North Dakota. On the Custer Trail Ranch, the brothers made their living by supplying wild game to railroad workers and hay to the nearby U.S. Army fort, all while establishing their own herds of horses and cattle.

Information Center (just east of I-90 at exit 23) and can offer very helpful advice in person or over the phone.

For information on hiking, camping, and other recreation in the Bighorn National Forest, contact the **U.S. Forest Service** (2013 Eastside 2nd St., Sheridan, 307/674-2600, www.fs.usda.gov/bighorn). Information on fishing and hunting is available through the **Wyoming Game and Fish Department** (700 Valley View Dr., 307/672-7418, http://wgfd.wyo.gov).

The **main post office** (307/672-0714, 7:30am-5:30pm Mon.-Fri., 8am-noon Sat.) in Sheridan is at 101 East Loucks Street.

The **Sheridan County Fulmer Public Library** (335 W. Alger St., 307/674-8585, www.sheridanwyolibrary.org, 9am-7pm Mon.-Thurs., 9am-5pm Fri.-Sat.) has both Internet-connected computers and free Wi-Fi available.

Sheridan Memorial Hospital (1401 W. 5th St., 307/672-1000, www.sheridanhospital.org) has a 24-hour emergency room. There are also two urgent care facilities in town: **Cedars Health Sheridan Clinic** (813 Highland Ave., 307/673-5501, 9am-5pm Mon.-Fri.) and **Sugarland Walk-in Clinic** (1005 Sugarland Dr., 307/675-7777, 8:30am-5:30pm Mon.-Fri., 10am-3pm Sat.-Sun.).

Do laundry at **Wash Yer Wooleys Laundry** (2220 Coffeen Ave., Unit D, 307/752-0389, 24 hours daily).

TRANSPORTATION
Getting There
The tiny **Sheridan County Airport** (SHR, 908 W. Brundage Ln., 307/674-4222) offers

Stories of their adventures trickled east, and before long the much-loved brothers hosted an endless string of friends. In 1882, realizing the financial strain he and others were placing on the hospitable Eatons, Bert Rumsey insisted on paying for the privilege of staying on the ranch. In so doing, Rumsey became the world's first "dude," a term coined by Howard Eaton. Modest as it was—guests slept several to a bed or on the floor, paying $25 per month for the right to do chores—the dude ranching industry was born.

The brutal winter of 1886-1887 changed dude ranching from a practicality to a necessity: The Eatons lost all but 150 of their 1,500 cattle to the cold and snow. The paying guests kept the Eatons afloat.

In 1904, the Eaton brothers bought 7,000 acres of land on the northeastern slope of the Big Horn Mountains. They announced to their friends that they'd be taking a year off to build structures on the ranch: cabins, barns, and a dining hall. Some 70 dudes showed up anyway and for about $100 apiece built many of the cabins that stand today. Although Howard and Willis remained lifelong bachelors, Alden married and set into motion the family that would run the ranch for more than a century. His great-great-grandson, Jeff Way, is the ranch general manager today, and like those before him, he and his own family welcome guests every summer.

Not much has changed since 1904. Days start early with the thunder of horses being brought down from night pasture. The clanging of an old locomotive wheel signals the start of hearty meals served family-style in the old dining hall. There are still Saturday-night cookouts and Western dances, picnics, softball games, rodeos, and more riding than the horsiest Easterner could ever dream of.

The dude season at **Eatons' Ranch** (307/655-9285, www.eatonsranch.com) runs early June-September, and the ranch can accommodate 125 guests in 47 cabins and three suites in the main ranch house. Depending on the dates and cabin selected, adult nightly rates for a six-night stay range $280-365, children 6-17 are $250-270 per night, and children under 6 are not charged. Rates include transportation to and from Sheridan, accommodations, all meals, and riding.

daily flights to and from Denver on **United Express** (800/864-8331, www.united.com). The nearest larger airports are about 135 miles (217 km) away (2 hours by car) in Billings (BIL) and Casper (CPR).

Bus service in the region is provided by **Jefferson Bus Lines** (307/674-6188 or 800/451-5333, www.jeffersonlines.com). The non-ticketing bus stop in Sheridan is at Maverick Adventure's First Stop (1242 E. Brundage Ln., 800/451-5333). The nearest ticketing stop is in Buffalo, Wyoming.

By car, Sheridan is 103 miles (166 km) northwest of Gillette, 147 miles (237 km) east of Cody, 199 miles (320 km) east of Yellowstone National Park, and 324 miles (525 km) northeast of Jackson.

Getting Around

Rental cars are available from **Avis** and **Budget.** Local taxi service is available by calling **Sheridan Taxi Service** (307/674-6814) and **WYO Rides** (307/675-8294).

★ BIG HORN

On the eastern flank of the Big Horns, the tiny town of **Big Horn** (pop. 483, elev. 4,081 ft/1,244 m) packs a lot of punch. The town was initially settled by upper-class ranchers and European aristocrats; among them was the Moncreiffe family, who raised prize sheep in the region. Although the town never officially incorporated, at one time the population purportedly passed 1,000 but rapidly dwindled in 1893 when the railroad came to Sheridan, 9 miles (14.5 km) northeast. Still, with its heritage of gentleman ranchers and a significant population boom since 2000, Big Horn has an assortment of fascinating sites and a unique culture that make a stop in town worthwhile.

Sights

For starters, **The Brinton Museum** (239 Brinton Rd., 307/672-3173, www.thebrintonmuseum.org, 9:30am-5pm Thurs.-Mon., admission in 2020-2021 was free thanks to a donation by First Interstate Bank, but call or check online for rates in 2022 and after) is an exquisite museum housed on the grounds of a genteel 1920s and '30s working ranch. Bradford Brinton was a wealthy businessman from Chicago when he bought the ranch in 1923. He turned it into an elaborate estate to showcase his ever-growing collection of art, which he left to his sister when he died. She meticulously maintained the home and collection and left both to the Northern Trust Company of Chicago. Tours through the 20-room Brinton home are available June-Labor Day. And inside the 24,000-square-foot eco-conscious rammed-earth museum is one of the most important collections of Native American and Western art in the Rocky Mountains. It showcases the largest collection of works by Hans Kleiber in the world, in addition to a surprising number of works by Charlie Russell and Frederic Remington. In addition to four galleries on three floors, the museum has a gift store and farm-to-table bistro (11am-2pm Thurs.-Fri., 10am-2pm Sat.-Sun., brunch $10-14, lunch $9-16), which utilizes fresh produce grown on-site and, in good weather, opens onto a lovely patio with views to the mountains.

Another surprising museum in this tiny little town is the **Bozeman Trail Museum** (335 Johnson St., 307/674-6363 or 307/674-8050, 11am-4pm Sat.-Sun. Memorial Day-Labor Day, free). Built in what was a log blacksmith shop to serve travelers along the trail, the museum includes Native American artifacts, photos, pioneer clothing, books, tools, and other artifacts.

Sports and Recreation

Big Horn is also the **polo** hotbed of Wyoming, with practice games on Wednesday and Friday (1pm and 3pm) and tournament games on Sunday (2pm in June, 1pm and 3pm in July and Aug.) at the noteworthy **Big Horn Equestrian Center** (932 Bird Farm Rd., 307/673-0454, www.thebhec.org). Admission to the announced matches is free, and concessions are available. Every year on Labor Day Sunday-Monday, the center closes out the season with **Don King Days,** a classic Western celebration with polo, championship steer roping, bronco riding, and wild-cow milking. The center is also one of the local favorite places to spend the **Fourth of July,** with a phenomenal fireworks display.

Buffalo and Vicinity

A neat little Western town with a lot of history and a surprising Basque influence, Buffalo (pop. 4,593, elev. 4,645 ft/1,416 m) was settled in 1879. Historically it is among Wyoming's biggest sheep towns, which was true as recently as the 1980s, until a late-spring storm after shearing in 1984 caused major losses and reminded locals of the Great Die-up of 1886-1887. Political and environmental conditions never allowed ranchers to recover. Instead, Buffalo makes the most of its beautiful location in the foothills of the Big Horn Mountains, its easy access to scenic drives and outdoor adventures, and its historic buildings and museums.

SIGHTS

Jim Gatchell Memorial Museum

The origins of the **Jim Gatchell Memorial Museum** (100 Fort St., 307/684-9331, www.jimgatchell.com, 9am-5pm Mon.-Sat.,

The Bozeman Trail

Although the Bozeman Trail was not given a name until John Jacobs and John Bozeman plowed through the region to give optimistic miners and settlers access to the quickest route through the Powder River Basin, the trail was an ancient migratory route long used by animals and Paleo-Indians. Today this modern transportation corridor is rich with evidence from the past: pictographs, petroglyphs, and ledger art. There are oral histories of trappers and traders in the area that date back to the mid-1700s; written records from Lewis and Clark, who zigzagged across the trail; and evidence that mountain men, missionaries, and the U.S. military all used the trail that, until the first gold rush in southwest Montana in 1862, probably resembled a well-used, age-old game trail.

Enter Jacobs and Bozeman in 1863. Leading a wagon train toward the goldfields in Montana, the men were just 140 miles (225 km) beyond Deer Creek when they met a large party of Northern Cheyenne and Sioux warriors. Although the bulk of the wagon train turned back toward the Oregon Trail crossing southern and central Wyoming, Bozeman and a few of the men continued on horseback through the region. The following year, Bozeman again led a wagon train through the region, this time with help from Allen Hurlbut and mountain man Jim Bridger. Although non-Indigenous traffic through the area was illegal under the Fort Laramie Treaty of 1851, military support for the Bozeman Trail was evident in various campaigns throughout the region. The treaties signed at Fort Sully in 1865 gave the military unchecked authority to build roads and forts along the Bozeman Trail, and in 1866 alone, more than 2,000 people traveled on it to Montana, with Fort Reno and Fort Phil Kearny established to protect civilians. On December 21, with tensions high between Native Americans and the military, an entire command of 81 men, under Capt. William J. Fetterman, was demolished by Sioux warriors.

In 1868, after several more battles, the Bozeman Trail and the forts along it were abandoned as indefensible by the U.S. Army. Still, the trail saw traffic from expeditions sent to scout the Yellowstone area and the Black Hills. When the Cheyenne were ultimately defeated by General Crook in November 1876 and forced to live on a reservation, the Bozeman Trail once again opened the region to significant settler traffic. Gradually, it became the preferred route for telegraph lines, stagecoaches, and eventually, an interstate highway.

noon-5pm Sun. Memorial Day-Labor Day, 9am-4pm Mon.-Fri. Labor Day-Memorial Day, $7 adults, $5 seniors, $5 children 12-18, $3 children 6-11, free for children under 6) can be traced back to the opening of the Buffalo Pharmacy in 1900, the first of its kind in town. People from all walks of life—cattle barons, outlaws, and homesteaders—frequented Jim Gatchell's drugstore, and many would give him small mementos, which he kept. Over time, they began entrusting him with pieces of Johnson County history. He also befriended the local Indians, and they too would bestow on him different cultural and personal artifacts.

After Gatchell passed away in 1954, his family donated his collection to Johnson County with the condition it would be shared with the public. The museum was established three years later. Its focus is on Johnson County's frontier-era history, and more than 15,000 pieces are on display. There is a large array of Native American artifacts and many pieces that can be traced back to the U.S. Cavalry, plus wagons, historical photos, a model of Fort Phil Kearny, artifacts from the fateful Fetterman Fight, and many interpretative materials related to the Bozeman Trail.

★ Occidental Hotel

Entering the **Occidental Hotel** (10 N. Main St., 307/684-0451, www.occidentalwyoming. com, $80-285), many visitors feel as if they've stepped back in time. The hotel has been painstakingly restored to its original 1880s splendor, which includes many of its original furnishings such as light fixtures, the back bar, tin ceilings, a piano, and stained glass.

1

2

3

4

FORT PHIL
KEARNY
1866 · 1868

Even the bullet holes throughout the bar are mementos of rowdier days. The place is said to be part museum, part hotel, part bar and restaurant. Visitors can follow a brochure for a self-guided tour or take a free 15-minute guided tour. Hotel guests have a variety of individual suites to choose from, each uniquely decorated with different antiques and features to match the original era. On Thursday nights, the saloon hosts a jam session featuring high-caliber bluegrass, Western, and folk musicians.

Dry Creek Petrified Tree Environmental Education Area

To find the unusual **Dry Creek Petrified Forest** (307/684-1100, www.blm.gov), drive east from Buffalo 7 miles (11.3 km) on I-90, take the Red Hills Road exit (exit 65), and drive north on Tipperary Road for 5 miles (8 km) to the Petrified Tree Area access road. In the midst of this sagebrush country, you can follow a 0.8-mile (1.3-km) loop that winds through the remnants of petrified trees that date back 60 million years to when the area was swampland covered by metasequoia trees. Some of the stumps are larger than 4 feet in diameter, and the numerous rings can be identified. The loop that takes visitors through the area is also an eight-station ecological trail with information about the process of petrifaction and the unique history of the land.

Fort Phil Kearny State Historic Site

Between Sheridan and Buffalo off I-90, the **Fort Phil Kearny State Historic Site** (528 Wagon Box Rd., Banner, 307/684-7629, www. fortphilkearny.com, grounds dawn-dusk daily, $8 nonresidents, $4 residents, free for children under 18) commemorates the fort that stood on the site 1866-1868.

The fort was commissioned at the height of the Indian Wars when the Sioux stood by their vow to fight for their traditional hunting grounds against anyone who dared cross into the Powder River Basin. Although Col. H. B. Carrington attempted to get permission for the fort's construction from Sioux chief Red Cloud, it was never given. The soldiers lived with nearly constant attacks by the Sioux. In the first six months, some 154 people were killed by Indians, and 700 horses, mules, and cattle were stolen.

At 17 acres, the fort was a complete settlement, with a stockade, living quarters, social club, guardhouse, hospital, even a laundress row. But the structures alone were little help in keeping the soldiers safe. The battles that took place close to the fort include the Fetterman Fight and the Wagon Box Fight. By 1868 the railroad had made the Bozeman Trail obsolete, and the military abandoned the fort as indefensible. It was burned to the ground, likely by the Cheyenne, in 1868.

At the site of the fort today, the **Fort Phil Kearny Interpretive Center** (8am-6pm daily May-Sept., noon-4pm Wed.-Sun. Oct., by appointment Nov.-Apr.) provides information for self-guided tours of the grounds and outlying sites. A cabin built by the Civilian Conservation Corps was crafted to resemble officers quarters. Several of the battlefields are accessible within 5 miles (8 km) of the fort.

Medicine Lodge Archeological Site

Managed as a state park, **Medicine Lodge Archeological Site** (4800 Co Rd 52, Hyattville, 307/469-2234, www.wyoparks. wyo.gov, grounds 6am-10pm daily, park headquarters 7:30am-4pm Mon.-Fri., visitor center closed Oct. 31-Apr. 30, day use is free for residents and non-residents, camping is $11 residents and $19.80 non-residents) is on the western slope of the Big Horn Mountains, northeast of Hyattville along Medicine Lodge Creek.

The area has been continuously occupied for more than 10,000 years and has a sandstone cliff with hundreds of Indigenous petroglyphs and pictographs that date back 2,000 years. The area was homesteaded in 1881 and

---

1: the Cloud Peak Skyway Scenic Byway **2:** the Occidental Hotel **3:** public art in Gillette **4:** Fort Phil Kearny State Historic Site

The Fetterman Fight of 1866

During the 1860s onslaught of eager gold seekers looking for a quick route to riches in Montana, John Bozeman led many travelers along the trail that would eventually bear his name, taking them from southeast Wyoming across the Powder River Basin into Montana. The Sioux who inhabited the region had fought and removed the Crow and were determined to prevent settlers from moving in as well. Travelers were warned not to venture past the Northern Platte River, and the military felt that in order to protect the Bozeman Trail, new forts would need to be established.

In June 1866 the military met with the Sioux chief Red Cloud to attain permission to build forts in the area. Though he refused, and despite a warning by the Sioux, the commander of the area, Col. H. B. Carrington, gave orders to build a fort at the fork of Big Piney and Little Piney Creeks. The fort was named after Civil War general Phil Kearny. Both the Cheyenne and Jim Bridger had warned Carrington that it was a death wish to build the fort in the middle of the Sioux's hunting ground. But the warnings went unheeded.

True to their word, the Sioux made numerous attacks on the fort. Within the first five months, there were many civilian and military losses as well as the theft of horses, mules, and cattle. The fort's construction required timber and logs to be shipped in from the nearby Big Horn Mountains, and the trains were easy targets for the Sioux.

In mid-December 1866, Capt. William J. Fetterman and his 18th Cavalry were stationed at the fort. Fetterman did not think highly of the Sioux's fighting skills and was convinced that if given the opportunity, his 80 men "could ride through the whole Sioux nation." In response, Jim Bridger reminded Fetterman and his men that although they had fought in the South during the Civil War, "they don't know anything about fighting Indians."

On December 21, 1866, the Sioux attacked a lumber train heading toward the fort. Fetterman and his men responded to the cries for help, intending to ward off the attackers. The 18th Cavalry pursued the attackers, chasing the Indians who dared to taunt them, and rode right into a well-designed ambush about 5 miles (8 km) from the fort. The 81 men were dead within 30 minutes. No one would see such an obliteration of U.S. troops until Custer's last stand at the Battle of the Little Bighorn 10 years later.

For this brief period, the Sioux had successfully defended their territory. The Bozeman Trail was no longer used, and by 1868 Fort Kearny was abandoned.

Today the site of the fight, which is 2 miles (3.2 km) from the fort along Old Highway 87, is marked by a stone monument. The site of **Fort Phil Kearny** (528 Wagon Box Rd., Banner, 307/684-7629, www.fortphilkearny.com, grounds dawn-dusk daily, $8 nonresidents, $4 residents, free for children under 18) has been designated a National Historic Landmark. Although the original fort was burned to the ground, most likely by Indians, it was partially reconstructed in 2000. There is also a small **interpretive center** (8am-6pm daily May-Sept., noon-4pm Wed.-Sun. Oct., by appointment Nov.-Apr.).

made a cattle ranch. The state bought the ranch in 1972 and created the Medicine Lodge Wildlife Habitat Area. A portion was set aside as the archeological site to preserve the cultural history and ensure recreational access. There is access to fishing, camping, and hundreds of miles of hiking, biking, and horseback trails. One of the things that makes this peaceful spot so unique is that there are five distinct vegetative zones within a 12-mile radius. Visitors can look for fossilized dinosaur tracks, disappearing streams, tipi rings, rock arches, and abundant wildlife.

TOP EXPERIENCE

★ Cloud Peak Skyway Scenic Byway

Traveling from Buffalo on US 16 over the southern portion of the Big Horn Mountains toward Ten Sleep and Worland, the 47-mile (76-km) paved Cloud Peak Skyway Scenic

Byway offers breathtaking scenery of the Cloud Peak Wilderness and the only view of Cloud Peak itself, the highest mountain in the Big Horns. This remarkable stretch of road is the southernmost route across the Big Horns. The summit is at 9,666 feet (2,946 m), and the road also winds through the spectacular Tensleep Canyon. Multiple turnouts are along the way for travelers to stretch their legs and enjoy the view; the road also passes **Fort McKinney** and runs just 20 miles (32 km) south of **Medicine Lodge State Archeological Site,** known for its ancient petroglyphs, pictographs, and idyllic campgrounds. There is also ample access to hiking trails in the Bighorn National Forest.

SPORTS AND RECREATION

Hiking

In addition to the wealth of trails in the nearby **Bighorn National Forest** (www. fs.usda.gov), Buffalo has an excellent 12-mile (19.3-km) trail system in town. Known as the **Clear Creek Trail System,** the well-marked trails can be accessed around town at various spots, including the historic shopping district on Main Street, the motel circle near the intersection of I-25 and US 16, the city park, and the Mosier Gulch picnic area. Mountain bikes are welcome on the trail, and maps are available through the **Buffalo Chamber of Commerce** (55 N. Main St., 307/684-5544 or 800/227-5122, www.buffalowyo.com, 9am-4pm Mon.-Fri. winter, extended hours in summer). There's a comprehensive list of trails in the Bighorn National Forest and Cloud Peak Wilderness at www.buffalowyoming. org; click on Recreation Guide.

Swimming

Buffalo has a wonderful free public outdoor swimming pool, the largest in the state, attracting locals and visitors alike on warm summer days. The enormous pool at **Washington Memorial Park** (S. Burritt Ave. and W. Angus St., free) is surrounded by trees, walking trails, and prime picnic spots.

There is also a water park for kids and a snack shack. The pool is open midmorning-sunset June-August.

Fishing

For fishing gear and current conditions on such varied water as **Clear Creek, Rock Creek,** the **Powder River,** and a variety of mountain and prairie lakes, stop in at **The Sports Lure** (66 S. Main St., 307/684-7682, www.sportslure.com, 8am-6pm Mon.-Sat., 10am-4pm Sun.).

Buffalo offers an excellent way to pair two of the state's favorite pastimes. For guided fishing trips on horseback to any of 200 mountain lakes and streams in the Big Horns, contact **South Fork Mountain Lodge & Outfitters** (US 16 W., 16 mi/26 km west of Buffalo, 307/267-2609, www. lodgesofthebighorns.com, from $500 pp full day). Its guides know how to find the rainbows, brookies, native cutthroats, browns, and golden trout.

To leave the horse behind and just focus on the fish, **Rock Creek Anglers** (1301 Rock Creek Rd., Saddlestring, 888/945-3876, www. rockcreekanglers.com, half-day wading trip for 1 angler $400, all-day wading trip for 1 angler $500, all-day drift boat trip for 1 angler $600) can get you onto any number of rivers, plus private waters, for a chance at hauling in some trout. They can also arrange accommodations.

Horseback Riding

Outside of Buffalo on US 16 West, the **South Fork Mountain Lodge & Outfitters** (307/267-2609, www.lodgesofthebighorns. com) offers the full range of activities and amenities, including two-hour rides (from $125), four-hour rides with lunch (from $300), and full-day wilderness rides including lunch ($500), June-September. It also offers pack trips, drop camps, fishing and hunting trips, plus overnight accommodations in streamside log cabins.

Golf

Golfers can hit the links at the 18-hole **Buffalo Golf Course** (500 W. Hart St., 307/684-5266, www.buffalowygolf.com, $37-40 for 9 holes with cart, $57-59 for 18 holes with cart). The course is regularly voted to be among the best municipal golf clubs in Wyoming.

ENTERTAINMENT AND EVENTS

The biggest event in Buffalo is the week-long annual **Johnson County Fair and Rodeo** (307/684-7357, www.johnsoncountyfairgrounds.com), held at the Johnson County Fairgrounds during the end of July and first week of August; it culminates with a three-day rodeo. There are also two rodeos weekly in the region: The **Johnson County Cowgirl Rodeo** (www.johnsoncountyfairgrounds.com), featuring women, girls, and boys under 16, is held each Tuesday night at the Johnson County Fairgrounds June-August, and the **Kaycee Lions Club Rodeo** (7pm-10pm, $5 admission) is held every Friday night at Harold Jarrard Park in nearby Kaycee; call the **Buffalo Chamber of Commerce** (307/684-5544, www.buffalowyo.com) or **Kaycee Chamber of Commerce** (307/738-2444, www.kayceewyoming.org), respectively, for more information. Also in the area, the tiny town of Ten Sleep has been hosting regular rodeos since 1908, when audience members circled their covered wagons to form a makeshift arena. The **Beauty and the Beast Rodeo** (307/366-2311, www.wtschamber.org) is held over Memorial Day, and the **Ten Sleep Fourth of July Rodeo** (307/366-2311, www.wtschamber.org) happens over two days.

Since 2012, **Longmire Days** (307/684-5544, www.longmiredays.com) has become the biggest event of Buffalo's summer season. A celebration of all things Longmire—the books by local author Craig Johnson and popular TV adaptation on Netflix—this event includes a 5K race, autograph sessions with the author and actors, an arts and crafts show, food vendors, and plenty of other entertainment. It's like an Old West version of Comic-Con, if such a thing is possible. In 2021, the proceeds of the event were donated to the National Indigenous Women's Resource Center in Lame Deer, Montana, an organization that featured prominently in Johnson's novel, *Daughter of the Morning Star*.

FOOD

Known for its hearty breakfasts and great burgers, **Tom's Main Street Diner** (41 N. Main St., 307/684-5627, 7am-1pm Tues.-Fri. winter, 7am-1pm Tues.-Fri., 7am-noon Sat., 8am-noon Sun. summer, $6-12, cash only) has a full menu and a homey small-town feel. **The Southside Grill** (94 S. Main St., 307/278-0221, 6am-9pm Sun.-Fri., 6am-11pm Sat.) serves up hearty Southern American food, from waffles and burritos, blintzes and omelets at breakfast ($7-11), to slow roasted barbecue—chicken, pork, brisket, ribs—for lunch and dinner ($14-25). This is a new favorite in Buffalo. They even have menus for smaller appetites.

Opened in 2019, ★ **4th on Main** (4 S. Main St., www.4thonmainwy.com, 11am-9pm Fri.-Tues., lunch $12-16, dinner $19-32) has fast become a local favorite and regional draw for their creative and artisanal fare. Try the whiskey maple burger or the hanger steak with red wine demi glace and horseradish mashed potatoes. Or try any of the steaks. You simply can't go wrong with their locally sourced ingredients and simply prepared dishes. **Pie Zanos** (17 N. Main St., 307/278-0161, www.piezanoswy.com, lunch $13-18, dinner $17-27) serves up made-from-scratch Italian food, including chicken saltimbocca roulade, pizzaiola, smoked Italian beef brisket, and various pastas. Their cappuccinos are outstanding. And don't forget dessert; the beignets are excellent.

For family dining and three square meals a day, the Western states chain restaurant **Bozeman Trail Steakhouse** (675 E. Hart St., 307/684-5555 or 888/351-6732, www.thebozemantrailsteakhouse.com, 11am-9pm daily, $11-40) is a safe bet for everyone. Little ones will love the kids' menu, and adults will appreciate the variety from steaks and game to Mexican specialties, huge salads, and good old-fashioned favorites like chicken-fried steak.

By far the most upscale dining experience in town is **The Virginian** (10 N. Main St., 307/684-0451, www.occidentalwyoming. com, from 5pm Tues.-Sat., $22-55), named for Owen Wister's iconic novel and housed in the historic Occidental Hotel. The ambience is 1890s chic, and the food is globally gourmet, with offerings including bison rib eye, elk tenderloin, and filet mignon Occidental. The beer and wine list is good too. For an unforgettable meal in a one-of-a-kind setting, this is a marvelous place for dinner. Also in the Occidental, a wonderful spot for breakfast, lunch, dinner, or an ice-cream treat anytime is the **Busy Bee Café** (7am-8pm daily summer, 7am-2pm off-season, hours may be shorter depending on patronage, $8-14), which serves hearty Western fare including biscuits and gravy, bison burgers, and world-class root beer floats.

ACCOMMODATIONS

For such a small town, Buffalo has a surprising number of chain hotels and motels, which indicates its popularity with travelers. A great mom-and-pop option with the best rates in town is the dog-friendly **Big Horn Motel** (209 N. Main St., 307/684-7822, www. bighorn-motel.com, $86-132). Rooms are clean and comfortable. There's a little art gallery on-site, and the personal touches—including baked goods made with eggs from the owners' chickens—make this a wonderful place to stay. Chain hotels include the **Holiday Inn Express Hotel & Suites** (106 US 16 E., 307/684-9900, www.ihg.com, $87-121) and the budget-friendly **Super 8 by Wyndham** (655 E. Hart St., 307/684-2531, www.wyndhamhotels.com, $47-76).

The ★ **Occidental Hotel** (10 N. Main St., 307/684-0451, www.occidentalwyoming. com, $80-285) is an upscale historic gem that is worth every penny. From its historical ties to such figures as Owen Wister and Teddy Roosevelt, among others, to its fantastic restaurant, this is a uniquely Wyoming getaway. Some of the rooms are pet-friendly, and all are charming and unique.

GUEST RANCHES

For an authentic cowboy and cowgirl experience at a working ranch, try the **TA Guest Ranch** (28623 Old Hwy. 87, 307/684-5833, www.taranch.com), south of Buffalo off I-25 on Crazy Woman Creek. Established as a working ranch in 1883, this 8,000-acre working cattle ranch offers beautifully restored Victorian accommodations, gourmet meals, riding twice daily, fly-fishing, and a variety of other dude ranch activities. The ranch focuses on local history and takes guests to tipi rings and Bozeman Trail sites on the property as well as important battlefields nearby. Since guests get to work, ride, and even share meals with the ranch crew, there is a real sense of camaraderie. The TA Ranch is one of the few in the area that do not require a weeklong stay, so visitors can enjoy the ranch's activities and amenities for as little as one night. Meals in the restaurant can be added to any stay and schedule, and activities can be selected and paid for à la carte. Rooms in the bunkhouse start at $120 per night May 15- Sept. 15, and at $100 per night Sept. 16-May 14. The Milk Barn, a cozy cabin on the creek, starts at $160 per night from May 15-Sept. 15, and from $140 per night in the off-season. Rooms in the historic and beautifully restored Ranch House start at $175 in high season and $155 in the off-season.

Another wonderful family-oriented ranch in the area is the **HF Bar Ranch** (1301 Rock Creek Rd., Saddlestring, 307/684-2487, www.hfbar.com, $395/day ages 13 and over, $250/day children 5-12, all-inclusive, 7-day minimum June-Sept.), which offers wonderful riding and an assortment of fun activities for kids. The HF Bar is the second-oldest dude ranch in the country after Eatons' Ranch in Wolf.

CAMPING

Thirty-two inexpensive public campgrounds ($16-18, www.fs.usda.gov/activity/bighorn/recreation/camping-cabins) can be found nearby in the **Bighorn National Forest** (877/444-6777, www.recreation.gov), and many of the sites can be reserved up to six months in advance. **West Tensleep Lake Campground** is set on the lake and provides easy access to the Cloud Peak Wilderness. The **Middle Fork Campground** is 13 miles (21 km) west of Buffalo adjacent to the Cloud Peak Skyway. Right in town, the **Indian Campground & RV Park** (660 E. Hart St., 307/684-9601 or 866/808-9601, www.indiancampground.com, mid-Apr.-mid-Oct., $33 tents, $50-60 RVs, $56-61 camping cabins) offers shaded sites and a stream running through. There's a large swimming pool, a 24-hour coin laundry, clean hot showers, Wi-Fi and, dear to any reader's heart, a trade-a-book exchange program.

INFORMATION AND SERVICES

The **Buffalo Chamber of Commerce** (307/684-5544 or 800/227-5122, www.buffalowyo.com, 8am-6pm Mon.-Fri., 10am-4pm Sat.-Sun. Memorial Day-Labor Day, 9am-4pm Mon.-Fri. Labor Day-Memorial Day) is at 55 North Main Street. The **Summer Info Center** (187 US 16 E., 307/425-1025, 9am-6pm daily June-Oct.) is a great source for local information.

For information on hiking, camping, and other recreation in the Bighorn National Forest, contact the **U.S. Forest Service** (2013 Eastside 2nd St., Sheridan, 307/674-2600, www.fs.usda.gov/bighorn).

The **Johnson County Library** (307/684-5546, www.jclwyo.org, 10am-6pm Mon., Wed., and Fri., 11am-7pm Tues. and Thurs.) is at 171 North Adams Avenue.

The **Johnson County Healthcare Center** (497 W. Lott St., 307/684-5521, www.jchealthcare.com) has a 24-hour emergency room.

TRANSPORTATION

Although Buffalo does have a small airport, the nearest commercial and charter air service is available in Sheridan (33 mi/53 km north) and Gillette (72 mi/116 km east).

Bus service throughout the region is provided by **Jefferson Bus Lines** (307/674-6188 or 800/451-5333, www.jeffersonlines.com).

By car, Buffalo is 123 miles (198 km) northeast of Thermopolis, 182 miles (290 km) east of Cody, 234 miles (380 km) east of Yellowstone National Park, and 341 miles (545 km) northeast of Jackson.

Gillette

Founded as a livestock center and transformed into a minerals hub with one of the largest and most easily accessible coal seams in the world, Gillette (pop. 31,978, elev. 4,550 ft/1,387 m) was organized in 1869 and named for a railroad engineer, Edward Gillette. After a significant oil boom in the late 1960s, coal extraction in the area was boosted by the 1970 Clean Air Act, which mandated cleaner-burning low-sulfur coal. But like so many other communities in the West, only more so, Gillette has experienced intense booms and busts related to energy production.

This is a working town with all sorts of growing pains related to coal, oil, and gas extraction. While it certainly has the infrastructure for people traveling through, Gillette is not typically on the top of the vacation radar. Still, it does make an excellent launching point to some of northeast Wyoming's wide-open spaces, and with its enormous tax base, it has managed to develop some phenomenal recreational facilities, many of which are free. The Avenue of Arts on 4J Road, for example, is a walking path lined with ever-changing sculptures. Visitors learn quickly that community means everything here—and Gillette residents are quick to point out that people came for the job, stayed for the money, then never left because of the community.

SIGHTS

Campbell County Rockpile Museum

The exhibits at the **Rockpile Museum** (900 W. 2nd St., 307/682-5723, www.rockpilemuseum.pastperfectonline.com, 8am-5pm Mon.-Sat., $10 adults, $8/person for groups of 5 or more, $8 seniors, $5 students) are focused on the local history of Campbell County. The museum has accrued a wide array of artifacts and displays them creatively. Visitors can see the inside of a general store, the tools and trade of an early medical clinic, and a large rifle collection. An actual homestead cabin and tiny one-room schoolhouse have been moved to the grounds, and there is an impressive collection of wagons, carriages, and even an old horse-drawn hearse. Hands-on activities for children are available, including a fun dress-up area with old-time garb. Since this is the heart of coal country, watch the short film about coal excavation and distribution; the large-scale explosions are sure to catch any viewer's attention.

CCSD Science Center

The **Campbell County School District's Science Center** (525 W. Lakeway Rd., 307/686-3821, www.sites.google.com/ccsd1schools.net/adventurarium, 9:30am-3:30pm Tues.-Thurs., 9:30am-noon Fri. summer, 9:30am-3pm Wed. fall-spring, closed late May-mid-June, free) is open to the public. Housed in the Lakeway Learning Center, the science center occupies over 10,000 square feet and offers young visitors numerous opportunities to discover, inquire, experiment, and learn. There are live animal displays (children can visit with an African pygmy hedgehog, an African bullfrog, ferrets, exotic birds, and even a python) and more than 50 interactive exhibits. Since hours can change without notice, it's best to call ahead.

Wright Centennial Museum

Thirty-five miles (56 km) south of Gillette in the small town of Wright, the **Wright Centennial Museum** (104 Ranch Court, 307/464-1222, www.wrightcentennialmuseum.org, 10am-4pm Tues.-Fri., 10am-2pm Sat. mid-May-early Oct., free) houses a small collection of artifacts from the surrounding area. The museum's collection has been largely amassed from the donations of residents. On display are vintage clothes, kitchen and bathroom furnishings from old homesteads, tools, saddles, and even a prostitute's "dresser box" with her personal items (including a gun). The town was established by the Atlantic Richfield mining company, and so there are many exhibits and interpretive materials dedicated to the mining industry.

SPORTS AND RECREATION

Swimming

With a soaring tax base in the 2000s, it's no surprise Gillette built up a wealth of terrific public facilities, including the outdoor **Gillette City Pool** (909 S. Gillette Ave., 307/682-1962, www.gillettewy.gov, 10am-8pm Mon.-Fri., 10am-4:30pm Sat., 1pm-4:30pm Sun. June-early Sept., weather-dependent, free). Admission is free to the massive outdoor pool and all of its facilities, which include a deep-diving well, zero-depth entry for toddlers, water slides, a bathhouse, a concession area, a sand playground, climbing structures, and a sunbathing area. The **Campbell County Recreation Center** (250 W. Shoshone Ave., 307/682-8527, www.ccgov.net, 5am-10pm Mon.-Fri., 8am-6pm Sat., 11am-6pm Sun., $6 adults, $4 junior and senior high school students, $3.50 children, $13 family) is a phenomenal facility that has a

Gillette

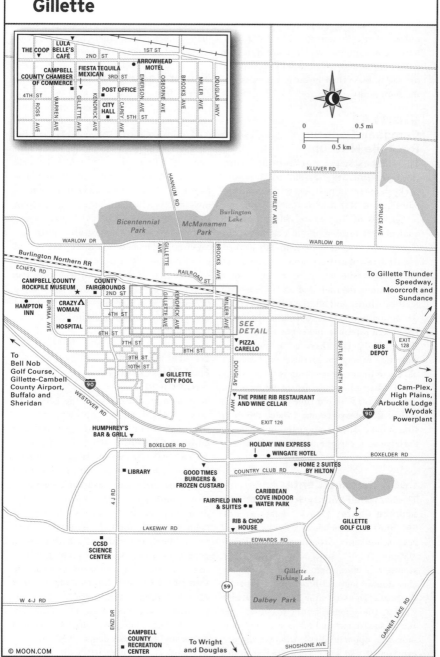

THE COOP

LULA BELLE'S CAFÉ

2ND ST

1ST ST

CAMPBELL COUNTY CHAMBER OF COMMERCE

FIESTA TEQUILA MEXICAN

3RD ST

ARROWHEAD MOTEL

POST OFFICE

4TH ST

WARREN AVE

ROSS AVE

GILLETTE AVE

KENDRICK AVE

CITY HALL

CAREY AVE

5TH ST

EMERSON AVE

OSBORNE AVE

BROOKS AVE

MILLER AVE

DOUGLAS HWY

0   0.5 mi

0   0.5 km

KLUVER RD

HANNUM RD

GURLEY AVE

SPRUCE AVE

Bicentennial Park

McManamen Park

Burlington Lake

WARLOW DR

GILLETTE AVE

BROOKS AVE

WARLOW DR

Burlington Northern RR

ECHETA RD

RAILROAD ST

To Gillette Thunder Speedway, Moorcroft and Sundance

CAMPBELL COUNTY ROCKPILE MUSEUM

COUNTY FAIRGROUNDS

2ND ST

GILLETTE AVE

KENDRICK AVE

MILLER AVE

HAMPTON INN

BURMA AVE

CRAZY WOMAN

4TH ST

HOSPITAL

6TH ST

SEE DETAIL

EXIT 128

BUS DEPOT

BUTLER SPAETH RD

7TH ST

9TH ST

10TH ST

8TH ST

PIZZA CARELLO

To Bell Nob Golf Course, Gillette-Cambell County Airport, Buffalo and Sheridan

90

WESTOVER RD

GILLETTE CITY POOL

DOUGLAS HWY

To Cam-Plex, High Plains, Arbuckle Lodge Wyodak Powerplant

THE PRIME RIB RESTAURANT AND WINE CELLAR

EXIT 126

90

HUMPHREY'S BAR & GRILL

BOXELDER RD

HOLIDAY INN EXPRESS

WINGATE HOTEL

BOXELDER RD

LIBRARY

GOOD TIMES BURGERS & FROZEN CUSTARD

COUNTRY CLUB RD

HOME 2 SUITES BY HILTON

4 J RD

CARIBBEAN COVE INDOOR WATER PARK

FAIRFIELD INN & SUITES

GILLETTE GOLF CLUB

LAKEWAY RD

RIB & CHOP HOUSE

EDWARDS RD

CCSD SCIENCE CENTER

Gillette Fishing Lake

ENZI DR

59

W 4-J RD

Dalbey Park

GARNER LAKE RD

CAMPBELL COUNTY RECREATION CENTER

To Wright and Douglas

SHOSHONE AVE

© MOON.COM

climbing wall, a kids' zone, an aerobics room, a gymnasium, a lap pool, a leisure pool, and a sports complex. Call for swim session hours, which include open swim and lap swim.

Kids will be deliriously happy at the **Caribbean Cove Indoor Water Park** (2577 S. Douglas Hwy., 307/682-1717, 4pm-10pm Mon.-Thurs., 4pm-10pm Fri., 8am-11pm Sat.-Sun., free for hotel guests, closed to nonguests during COVID so call ahead to check for openings and rates for nonguests), an 11,000-square-foot indoor water park with a lazy river, water slides galore, a kiddie pool, and an activity pool. The water park is inside the Fairfield Inn & Suites.

Golf

Golfers do not lack options in Gillette. The nine-hole **Gillette Golf Club** (1800 Country Club Rd., 307/682-4774, $45 for 9 holes with cart, $60 for 18 holes with cart) and the 18-hole **Bell Nob Golf Club** (4600 Overdale Dr., 307/686-7069, $60 for 18 holes with cart, $45 for 9 holes with cart), which underwent a vast remodel in 2013 with added putting greens and a clubhouse, are both open to the public. The Bell Nob course also has a par 3 nine-hole course ($8 adults, $2 children, $1 children with an adult).

ENTERTAINMENT AND EVENTS

Most of Gillette's large-scale events take place in the massive facility known as **Cam-Plex** (1635 Reata Dr., 307/682-0552, www.cam-plex.com), which hosts concerts, theater productions, conventions, expos, sporting events, public ice-skating, and good ol' Wyoming rodeos. Visit the website to see what events are scheduled when you're in town.

Rodeos are held almost every weekend during the summer at Cam-Plex. The **PRCA New Year's Eve Buck & Ball Rodeo**, which takes place on New Year's Eve, has a $60,000 payout, and the **National High School Rodeo Finals** in July are a huge draw.

Head out to the **Gillette Thunder Speedway** (13002 Hwy. 51, 307/660-8866,

www.gillettespeedway.com) for stock-car races almost every Saturday night during the summer; check the website for the current schedule.

In the winter, the **Powder River Symphony Orchestra** (307/660-9800, www.prsymphony.org) performs concerts at Cam-Plex, including family-friendly events.

FOOD

A great but tiny spot for breakfast, lunch, and sensational homemade pies, among other specialties, is **Lula Belle's Café** (101 N. Gillette Ave., 307/682-9798, 5am-2:30pm Sun.-Fri., 6am-2pm Sat., breakfast $4-14, lunch $8-13). A popular spot for lunch and dinner is **Humphrey's Bar & Grill** (408 W. Juniper Ln., 307/682-0100, www.humphard.net, 11am-10pm Mon.-Sat., 11am-9pm Sun., $9-31), which has an enormous menu of American and Cajun dishes, and more than 50 beers on tap.

After a significant expansion, **The Prime Rib Restaurant and Wine Cellar** (1205 S. Douglas Hwy., 307/682-2944, www.primeribgillette.com, 11am-10pm Mon.-Thurs., 11am-10:30pm Fri., 4pm-10:30pm Sat., 4pm-9:30pm Sun., $12-60) is a nice place for lunch or dinner, and a perfect choice for wine lovers. The menu is vast with appetizers of every variety, seafood, steaks, pasta, salads, sandwiches, and more. They also have a senior menu. For a hearty and sure-to-please meal, try the **Rib & Chop House** (2721 S. Douglas Hwy., 307/686-9400, www.ribandchophouse.com, 11am-10pm daily winter, $14-45), which has locations throughout Montana and Wyoming. The restaurant has several large-screen TVs and an impressive variety of craft beers on tap. A custom broiler cooks the Montana-founded chain's renowned steaks at 1,800°F (982°C), but the menu is hefty, offering everything from seafood pasta and cedar plank salmon to ahi, pulled pork, and pot roast. A patio with five outdoor fire pits is open when weather permits.

For artisan pizza cooked in a wood-fired brick oven, try **Pizza Carrello**

(601 S. Douglas Hwy., 307/363-1743, www. pizzacarrello.com, 11am-9pm Mon.-Sat., 10am-9pm Sun., $9-24, coupons online), which also serves plenty of appetizers, salads, stuffed pita wraps, rice bowls, and wood-fired pastas. Visitors with a hankering for Mexican food will not be disappointed at **Fiesta Tequila Mexican Restaurant and Tequila Bar** (311 S. Gillette Ave., 307/686-8010, 10:30am-9pm Mon.-Thurs., 10:30am-10pm Fri.-Sat., 10:30am-9:30pm Sun., $7-14), which offers standard Mexican fare at good prices.

The best chicken joint in town is **The Coop** (208 W. 2nd St., 307/257-7460, www. thecoopwy.com, 11am-8pm Mon.-Sat., $9-24), which serves everything from spicy chicken strips and rotisserie meals to chicken-based Mexican specialties. Little ones will love the kids' menu. For old-school deliciousness, nothing beats the burgers and frozen custard at **Good Times Burgers & Frozen Custard** (610 E. Boxelder Rd., 6am-10pm Mon.-Thurs., 6am-11pm Fri.-Sat., 7am-10pm Sun., www. goodtimesburgers.com, $6-16). They specialize in all-natural burgers, chicken sandwiches, wild fries, onion rings, and creamy frozen custard. Bring Fido along for this meal because they have all sorts of treats for dogs. The Pawbender is vanilla custard, doggie biscuits, and peanut butter.

ACCOMMODATIONS

Because of the influx of workers in the mining industry, Gillette has an abundance of accommodations, most of which are chain hotels. One notable exception is the friendly **Arrowhead Motel** (202 S. Emerson Ave., 307/686-0909, from $47), which offers clean, basic rooms with microwaves, refrigerators, and a daily continental breakfast. For more upscale accommodations, the **Arbuckle Lodge** (1400 S. Garner Lake Rd., 307/685-6363, www.arbucklelodge.com, $89-269) has a variety of rooms and suites, some with whirlpools and fireplaces, others with up to two sets of bunk beds.

Among the most popular upscale chain hotels, appealing to business travelers and families alike, are the **Holiday Inn Express** (1908 Cliff Davis Dr., 307/686-9576, www.ihg. com, from $95), **Hampton Inn** (211 Decker Court, 307/686-2000, www.hamptoninn3. hilton.com, $93-265), the **Wingate Hotel** (1801 Cliff Davis Dr., 307/685-2700, www. wyndhamhotels.com, from $89), and **Home 2 Suites by Hilton** (1120 E. Boxelder Rd., 307/257-7040, www.hilton.com, from $92), all of which offer a multitude of plush amenities for road-weary travelers. The **Fairfield Inn & Suites Gillette** (2577 S. Douglas Hwy., 307/682-1717, www.marriott.com, from $107) is the perfect place to stay if you want to spend time in the indoor water park.

CAMPING

If you are attending an event at Cam-Plex, campgrounds are available on-site. Otherwise, the interestingly named **Green Tree's Crazy Woman Campground** (1001 W. 2nd St., 307/682-3665, www. crazywomancampground.com, year-round, $22-56), has 85 RV sites, tent sites, clean restrooms, and, especially important in the summer, shaded sites. The campground doesn't accept credit cards. Other campgrounds in the area include **High Plains RV Resort and Campground** (1600 S. Garner Lake Rd., 307/687-7339, www.highplainscampground. com, call for rates), which has 65 lots across from the Cam-Plex but no shade, and **All Seasons RV Park** (1000 McIntosh Ln., Rozet, 307/686-2552, from $41), which offers 20 year-round sites 15 miles (24 km) east of Gillette.

INFORMATION AND SERVICES

The **Campbell County Convention & Visitors Bureau** (314 S. Gillette Ave., 307/686-0040 or 800/544-6136, www. visitgillettewright.com) is an excellent virtual resource for the region with an outstanding website.

Another source for business and relocation information for the Gillette area is the **Campbell County Chamber of**

Commerce (314 S. Gillette Ave., 307/682-3673, www.gillettechamber.com, 8am-5pm Mon.-Fri.).

The main branch of the **post office** (307/682-3727, 7am-5:30pm Mon.-Fri., 9am-1pm Sat.) in Gillette is at 311 South Kendrick Avenue.

The wonderful **Campbell County Public Library** (307/682-3223, www.ccgov.net, 9am-9pm Mon.-Thurs., 9am-5pm Fri.-Sat.) is at 2101 South 4J Road.

Campbell County Memorial Hospital (501 S. Burma Ave., 307/688-1000, www.cchwyo.org) has a 24-hour emergency room. There is also a walk-in clinic on hospital grounds (307/688-9255, 8am-5:30pm daily). You can "save your place in line" online at www.clockwisemd.com/groups/186. Last patients are taken 30 minutes before closing.

Wash clothes at **Eastside Laundry** (1080 E. US 14/16, 307/685-2722, 7am-9pm daily). Another laundry with free Wi-Fi is **Surf'n Suds** (203 S. Richards Ave., 307/686-9266, 8am-8pm daily).

TRANSPORTATION
Getting There
The **Northeast Wyoming Regional**

Airport (GCC, 2000 Airport Rd., 307/686-1042, www.iflygillette.com) offers daily flights to and from Denver on United Airlines (800/864-8331, www.united.com).

Bus service in the region is provided by **Powder River Transportation** (307/685-9326, www.coachusa.com), **Trailways** (307/682-1888, www.trailways.com), and **Greyhound** (800/451-5333, www.greyhound.com).

By car, Gillette is 70 miles (113 km) east of Buffalo, 136 miles (219 km) north of Casper, 250 miles (405 km) east of Cody, 301 miles (485 km) east of Yellowstone National Park, and 411 miles (660 km) northeast of Jackson.

Getting Around
Car rentals are available in town from **Enterprise** (603 E. 2nd St., 307/686-5655, www.enterprise.com), **Avis** (2000 Airport Rd., 307/682-8588, www.avis.com), and **Hertz** (307/686-0550, www.hertz.com).

Taxis are available through **DC Cab** (307/299-8294); **Need A Ride Taxi Cab** (307/632-3666); and **City Cab & Couriers** (307/685-1000), but note that only cash is accepted.

Devils Tower National Monument

Rising 1,267 feet (386 m) above the Belle Fourche River, Devils Tower is an iconic rocky sentinel that was formed some 50-60 million years ago and has fascinated people for generations. The tower was instantly recognizable in the 1977 film *Close Encounters of the Third Kind,* where it bridged human and alien life-forms. Composed of phonolite porphyry, which is a volcanic rock created by magma and similar to granite without the quartz, the massive columnar feature looks like an otherworldly cat-scratching post. Scientists refer to it as a laccolith, or igneous intrusion, meaning that magma welled up into a pocket of sedimentary rock, where it

cooled and hardened. Over millions of years, the sedimentary rock was eroded away by natural forces, leaving the phenomenal tower.

The country's first national monument, Devils Tower is both a sacred site to many Native Americans and a climbing mecca for rockhounds from around the globe. The two groups have managed a hard-won, if somewhat delicate, respect for each other through a voluntary climbing closure in June every year, the month traditionally known for the greatest number of Native American ceremonies. Climbers are strongly encouraged to refrain from climbing or hiking around the tower during the closure.

Still, Devils Tower is a recreational hot spot with several climbing routes for beginners and experts alike, plus some 8 miles (12.9 km) of hiking trails that circle the tower and wind through the nearby forests and meadows. Although it's not exactly conveniently located, being 33 miles (53 km) north of I-90, Devils Tower is the type of destination—like Mount Rushmore—that visitors are happy to go out of their way to see. Especially for those with an interest in hiking or climbing, it's easy to make a day of Devils Tower.

HISTORY

According to the National Park Service, more than 20 Native American tribes have historically attached cultural and spiritual significance to Devils Tower. Many of the tribes have sacred stories related to the tower, which often determined their name for the feature. The Arapaho people, for example, called the tower Bear's Tipi. Similarly, the Cheyenne Nation referred to it as Bear's Lodge, Bear's House, and Bear Peak. The Crow tribe is known to refer to it as Bear's Lair, and the Lakota Nation, who often had winter camps at the tower, called it a variety of names that include Bear Lodge, Grizzly Bear's Lodge, Ghost Mountain, and Penis Mountain. The Kiowa Tribe called the feature Tree Rock or Aloft on a Rock, and their origin story for the rock is among the best known. The story goes that the tribe was camped along the river, and seven sisters and their brother were playing when the brother turned into a bear, forcing the sisters to flee in search of safety. They climbed onto a rock and prayed for divine intervention. The rock began to grow skyward as the bear clawed at it to get to the sisters. Eventually, the girls were so high that they became the stars in the Big Dipper, and the tower still bears the scars of the bear's ferocious claws.

Many tribes conducted their most sacred events—including sun dances, sweat lodges, vision quests, and funerals—in the shadow of the tower, and they still do. In 2014 and 2015, formal requests were made by both the Lakota and Oglala Sioux nations to officially change the name of the monument from Devils Tower to Bear Lodge, the name that was on most maps between 1874 and 1901. Politicians in Wyoming have repeatedly rejected the request. A March 2018 resolution to make the name "Devils Tower" permanent was put before the House of Representatives by Wyoming congresswoman Liz Cheney. The measure failed but the issue was raised again in 2021 in a bill by Wyoming senator Cynthia Lummis, who wanted the name "Devils Tower" to be made permanent for both the geological feature and the populated place. A decision may be made as early as January 2023.

First studied in 1875 by scientists H. Newton and Walter P. Jenney, who were commissioned to complete a geological survey of the area, the land surrounding the tower was pulled from homestead acreage in 1892, and the government created Devils Tower Reserve the following year. President Theodore Roosevelt dedicated Devils Tower as the country's first national monument in 1906.

Although it is constantly overrun by people, the area around and on top of the tower is ecologically significant. A colony of threatened black-tailed prairie dogs, who today occupy only 2 percent of their former habitat, make their home in the soft soils around the tower. Prairie falcons are known to nest in the cracks of the tower, requiring temporary closures to protect their young. Even on the grassy top of the tower, which is about the size of a football field, many wildlife species have been recorded, including chipmunks, mice, packrats, and snakes.

Playing into the "because it's there" mentality, adventurers have long looked at ways to climb the soaring monolith. The first recorded ascent involved an oak peg ladder on July 4, 1893, by local ranchers Bill Rogers and W. A. Ripley, much to the delight of local revelers. Rogers's wife, Linnie, was the first woman to climb it (using the ladder), two years later on July 4, 1895. Both spectacles included crazy patriotic costumes, some 2,000 spectators, and live music. Although the ladder was no longer used after 1927, portions of it are still visible on the southwest side of the tower.

Technical rock climbers made the first ascent in 1937 in just 4 hours and 46 minutes, opening the tower to scores of climbers and dozens of firsts, including George Hopkins, who parachuted onto the summit in 1941 without an exit plan. Hopkins was stranded on the summit for six days before he was rescued. Since then, numerous routes have been established up the rock, and the fastest free climb of Devils Tower was in the 1980s by Todd Skinner, who made the climb without ropes or protection in an astonishing 18 minutes. Today's average climb for two people requires 4-6 hours up and 2 hours for the rappel down.

SPORTS AND RECREATION
★ Hiking and Climbing

Nonclimbers interested in hiking will delight in the 1.5-mile (2.4-km) **Joyner Ridge Trail,** which offers beautiful views of the tower, particularly at sunset. An additional 7 miles (11.3 km) of trails meander through the nearby forest and meadows. Trail maps are available at the visitor center (307/467-5283, www.nps.gov/deto). The 2.8-mile (4.5-km) **Red Beds** trail winds through meadows and ponderosa pines, with a significant elevation gain, to Joyner Ridge Trail. Plan on two hours for the Red Beds hike.

Each year the tower is climbed by some 5,000 people who come to slip their fingers and toes into the hundreds of parallel cracks that divide the hexagonal columns of Devils Tower. Although the entire tower offers more than 200 routes with technical difficulties ranging 5.7-5.13, the **Durrance Route,** first pioneered in 1938, is the most common. A few bolted face climbs were established in the 1980s and 1990s, but new bolts and fixed pitons are prohibited. Only a handful of fatalities have occurred over the years, most of which happened on the descent.

All climbers must register at the **climber registration office** next to the visitor center; registration is free.

Climbing is strongly discouraged during the **June voluntary climbing closure,** advocated by the National Park Service out

Devils Tower was the first national monument in the United States.

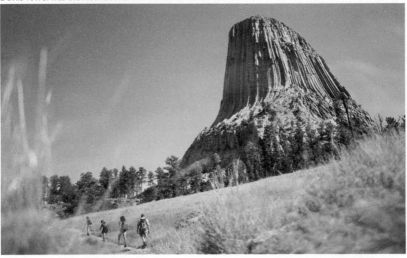

of respect for the many Native American cultures that recognize the tower as a sacred place.

CLIMBING GUIDES

For inexperienced climbers, hiring a licensed guide is the best way to approach the monolith. About seven companies are licensed to guide climbers on Devils Tower, a list that can change from year to year. Among them is **Devils Tower Climbing** (307/467-5267 or 888/314-5267, www.devilstowerlodge.com, $500 for 1 climber to summit, $425 pp for 2 climbers, discounts for additional climbers), headed by legendary climber Frank Sanders. Devils Tower Climbing offers excellent instruction and guiding through play days ($400 pp), introduction to rock climbing days ($150 pp for 5 hours), and two-day experience packages with summit ($800 pp for 1 climber, $650 pp for 2 climbers). Combination specials that include lodging are available.

Other guiding companies licensed to work in the monument include **Above Ouray Ice and Tower Rock Climbing Guides** (307/756-3516 or 888/345-9061, www.towerguides.com, $350 for 1 climber, discounts for additional climbers, no credit cards), which has been guiding climbers on Devils Tower for more than 37 years and requires a paid training day ($210 pp for up to 4 climbers) before summiting; and **Sylvan Rocks Climbing School and Guide Service** (605/484-7585, www.sylvanrocks.com), which requires two-day courses ($925 for 1 climber, $700 pp for up to 6 climbers) and offers two- and three-day experiences with summit attempts. All of the outfits can provide you with the right climbing gear.

ENTERTAINMENT AND EVENTS

A tradition since the early 1880s, when settlers would descend on the area for a few days at a time to camp, picnic, and enjoy one another's company, the **Old Settlers'** Picnic was formalized as an annual event in 1932 on Father's Day weekend. The tradition continues today, after a 40-year lapse starting in the 1960s, with a large gathering of locals and visitors who come to enjoy food, Western music, cowboy poetry, kids' activities, and nondenominational church.

The annual **Cultural Program Series** changes from year to year but consistently offers fascinating lectures, entertainment, and living history displays over the course of the summer season (June-Aug.). For information on current happenings, contact the visitor center at the base of the tower (307/467-5283) or look online at the *Park News* newsletter (www.nps.gov/deto).

The National Park Service hosts a fantastic spectrum of ranger-guided programs throughout the summer season. Offerings include a 1.3-mile (2.1-km) guided **Tower Walk,** a variety of 20-minute **Interpretive Talks,** hour-long **Evening Programs,** and fantastic 90-minute **Full Moon Walks** that leave from the Joyner Ridge Trail parking lot. For information on any of the regularly scheduled events, contact the visitor center at the base of the tower (307/467-5283, www.nps.gov/deto).

FOOD

No food is sold inside the monument, so you will have to bring your own supplies or eat before you arrive at Devils Tower. Restaurants and grocery/convenience stores are in Moorcroft (33 mi/53 km), Sundance (28 mi/45 km), and Hulett (9 mi/14.5 km).

ACCOMMODATIONS

Other than the Belle Fourche Campground, there are no accommodations inside the monument. The **Devils Tower Lodge Bed & Breakfast** (just north of the monument, 307/467-5267 or 888/314-5267, www.devilstowerlodge.com, $110-275) is owned by climbing guide Frank Sanders and offers comfortable rooms with unparalleled access to the tower.

CAMPING

The only campground in the monument proper is the 46-site **Belle Fourche Campground** (307/467-5283, ext. 635, $20), open in the summer season for tent campers and RVs on a first-come, first-served basis. Running water is available, but no RV hookups.

Just outside the monument, the **Devils Tower KOA** (60 Hwy. 110, 307/467-5395 or 800/562-5785, www.devilstowerkoa.com) has RV hookups ($58-89), cabins (from $89), tipi (from $79) and tent sites ($38-48), plus an on-site heated swimming pool, snack bar, nightly hayrides, and free Wi-Fi. With the tower looming in the background, the nightly outdoor showing of *Close Encounters of the Third Kind*, filmed largely at the campground, is an unforgettable experience.

About a 35-minute drive (21 mi/33 km) from Devils Tower is **Keyhole State Park** (22 Marina Rd., 307/756-3596, www.wyoparks.wyo.gov, $7 daily use or $17/night residents, $12 daily use or $30/night nonresidents, electric sites $10 extra) at the western edge of the Black Hills between Sundance and Moorcroft. Campers can swim, hike, boat, and fish. There are 10 campgrounds within the park, and all are by reservation only (www.reserveamerica.com). There are four cabins (from $60/night) and one premier treehouse (from $200/night) available for rent.

INFORMATION AND SERVICES

Vehicular **entrance fees** for seven days are $25. Motorcyclists can enter for seven days for $20, pedestrians and bicyclists for $15. Passes can be purchased online in advance (saving you time in the entrance line) at www.recreation.gov.

The National Park Service operates a great **visitor center** (Hwy. 110, Bldg. 170, 307/467-5283, www.nps.gov/deto, 9am-4pm Wed.-Sun. summer) in the parking lot beneath the tower. Housed in a classic 1938 Park Service log cabin constructed by the Civilian Conservation Corps, the visitor center is staffed and has interesting geological, natural, and cultural history exhibits.

While the number of visitors to the monument continues to grow, it is generally not overcrowded. That changes in August; be prepared to wait in long entrance lines in the weeks surrounding the Sturgis Motorcycle Rally in nearby Sturgis, South Dakota, each summer. If you don't like crowds, this is not the time to go to Devils Tower. To check on dates for the rally, visit www.sturgismotorcyclerally.com.

The nearest health-care facilities are the **Hulett Medical Clinic** (122 Main St., Hulett, 307/467-5281, www.ccmsd.org, 8am-5pm Mon.-Fri.), 7 miles (11.3 km) north of Devils Tower, and the **Moorcroft Clinic** (208 N. Bighorn Ave., Moorcroft, 307/756-3414, www.ccmsd.org, 8am-5pm Mon.-Fri.), 33 miles (53 km) south of Devils Tower. The nearest hospital to treat trauma is **Campbell County Memorial Hospital** (501 S. Burma Ave., Gillette, 307/688-1000, www.cchwyo.org), 61 miles (98 km) away in Gillette.

The speed limit in the monument is 25 mph (40 kph). Each year, dozens of wild animals are hit and killed by cars. Reduced speed can positively impact the number of fatalities.

Do not feed the wildlife. Prairie dogs are especially sensitive and can die from eating any human food.

TRANSPORTATION

By car, **Devils Tower National Monument** is 33 miles (53 km) northeast of the I-90 exit at Moorcroft and 27 miles (43 km) northwest of Sundance. The monument is 61 miles (98 km) northeast of Gillette, 131 miles (211 km) northeast of Buffalo, 309 miles (500 km) east of Cody, and 363 miles (590 km) east of Yellowstone National Park.

The nearest commercial airports are in Gillette (61 mi/98 km southwest) and Rapid City, South Dakota (120 mi/193 km east).

Southern Wyoming

An enormous expanse of diverse terrain that includes everything from vast prairie and rugged mountain peaks to red desert and windblown dunes, southern Wyoming in many ways defines the state.

It has celebrated events, an important intellectual culture, and a wealth of historic sites. This region is also at the heart and soul of Wyoming's agricultural tradition, both past and present. But interestingly, the lower half of the state is less traveled *to* and more often traveled *through*.

With I-80 in the far south and a series of smaller roads bisecting the landscape east-west and north-south, it seems this section of Wyoming is thick with travelers on their way someplace else, which has been

Highlights

Look for ★ to find recommended sights, activities, dining, and lodging.

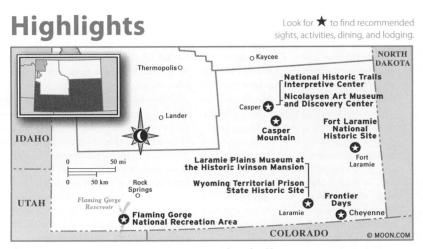

Thermopolis○

○Kaycee

NORTH DAKOTA

National Historic Trails Interpretive Center

Casper ⊗

Nicolaysen Art Museum and Discovery Center

○ Lander

⊗ **Casper Mountain**

Fort Laramie National Historic Site

IDAHO

○ Fort Laramie

Laramie Plains Museum at the Historic Ivinson Mansion

0   50 mi

0   50 km

Rock Springs ○

Wyoming Territorial Prison State Historic Site

UTAH

Flaming Gorge Reservoir

Laramie ⊗

Frontier Days

⊗ Cheyenne

⊗ **Flaming Gorge National Recreation Area**

COLORADO

© MOON.COM

★ **Nicolaysen Art Museum and Discovery Center:** With an impressive collection of more than 6,000 works by contemporary artists, The Nic is a phenomenal tribute to the current art scene in the West (page 204).

★ **National Historic Trails Interpretive Center:** Among the best museums in the state, this place gives visitors a sense of pioneer life on many of the historic trails that crisscross the state (page 205).

★ **Casper Mountain:** The skiing, hiking, camping, and fascinating local folklore give this area its own magical identity (page 205).

★ **Laramie Plains Museum at the Historic Ivinson Mansion:** This museum is a labor of love for the people who operate it and a gift to visitors (page 217).

★ **Wyoming Territorial Prison State Historic Site:** Part agriculture exhibit, part broom factory, and part Old West town, this is also the best old prison in the West (page 218).

★ **Fort Laramie National Historic Site:** This was a fur trading fort, a military outpost, and an important witness to the dramatic conflicts and sweeping change of the 19th century in the American West (page 230).

★ **Frontier Days:** The big daddy of Wyoming rodeos draws thousands of eager spectators to its big-name country music concerts, carnival, parades, and world-class professional rodeo (page 231).

★ **Flaming Gorge National Recreation Area:** Fed by the Green River, this natural playground composed of cliffs and Technicolor desert rock formations surrounds a 91-mile-long (147-km) reservoir (page 241).

true for more than a century. Most of the West's great travel routes—the Oregon Trail, the Overland Trail, the Bozeman Trail, and eventually the Northern Pacific Railway—cut through this dramatically shifting landscape, exposing travelers, if only briefly, to the diversity of terrain.

In the southeast corner around Cheyenne—the state's capital, known for its festive, even rowdy, rodeo, called Frontier Days—the landscape shifts, greens, and begins to look more like Colorado. Just north and west of Cheyenne, Laramie presents an interesting blend of university counterculture and age-old Western tradition in a literary-meets-cowboy dance. Beyond town, three impressive mountain ranges offer prime climbing opportunities, then give way to the plains and prairies where sheep and cattle rather than trees dot the horizon. Farther north on I-25, the frontier town of Casper is experiencing a renaissance as a fishing and outdoor-loving town.

Heading west on I-80, the landscape is loaded with minerals, and the entire area is rich with mining history, dinosaur fossils, and the stark beauty of the Flaming Gorge National Recreation Area. There are wildlife refuges, endless spots to wet a line, and little ranching communities and outposts that give southern Wyoming its flavor.

PLANNING YOUR TIME

Cheyenne, Casper, and Laramie are all sizable cities for Wyoming and could occupy visitors for at least a full day each. In Cheyenne, a number of museums are worth seeing, including the **Wyoming State Museum** and the **Cheyenne Frontier Days Old West Museum,** among others. In this part of the state, summer is the most popular time to travel thanks to sunny, warm days and easy road conditions. Bear in mind, however, that Cheyenne's population explodes during **Frontier Days,** the second half of July, and accommodations can be tough to find.

In Laramie, there are more museums including the outstanding **Wyoming Territorial Prison,** plenty of opportunities to get out and experience some of Wyoming's most beautiful landscapes, and a fascinating university culture that brings with it abundant entertainment and a lively downtown with some darn good eateries. Laramie can be a bit windy and bleak, even frigid, in winter, but the university culture keeps things lively with concerts, lectures, sporting events, and other happenings. In Casper, the state's second-largest city after Cheyenne, anglers stalk the region's trout on the **North Platte River,** and plenty of year-round recreational opportunities can be found in the nearby **Laramie Mountains, Medicine Bow-Routt National Forests,** and on **Casper Mountain.**

Southwest Wyoming, by contrast, is a series of small towns experiencing the boom-and-bust of energy extraction and a vast swath of starkly beautiful land primed for recreation. There are indeed a number of museums in the areas of Green River and Rock Springs, but the vast majority of people who come to spend time in this region do so for the outdoors, which can be pleasant mid-spring to late fall. Summer can be hot, but the **Flaming Gorge National Recreation Area** is a gateway to the dramatic Green River country and offers plenty of places and ways to cool down.

HISTORY

Southern Wyoming is a land of corridors, home to the Oregon, Mormon, California, Cherokee, and Overland Trails. The Pony Express crossed through here, as did the nation's first transcontinental railroad and the first transcontinental automobile route. It makes sense that early Wyoming was defined not by settlers so much as by travelers.

What initially attracted Native Americans to this region also attracted traders, trappers, and immigrants. The North Platte

---

Previous: buttes in Sweetwater County; hikers in Medicine Bow-Routt National Forests; summer carnival in Laramie.

Southern Wyoming

© MOON.COM

and Sweetwater Rivers created natural passageways across the land. They provided water and food for both humans and livestock and kept the grasslands well irrigated. Buffalo grazed across the grassy plains with Indians always in close pursuit. The Shoshone, Arapaho, Cheyenne, and Sioux all hunted in the region.

The movement into Wyoming really picked up after 1843, when a large wagon train left Missouri and arrived in Washington six months later. Hundreds of thousands of immigrants passed through Wyoming over the Oregon Trail. Today Wyoming is home to the longest unchanged portion of the Oregon Trail.

Initially, the Indians did little to prevent the travelers from crossing the land they used. Realizing that the wagons were just moving through with no intention of staying, they did not view the migrants as a threat. But soon it became evident that the migration was taking a toll. The grass that sustained the buffalo was being consumed by livestock. The buffalo were being killed to make way for cattle grazing land

and railroad tracks. The Indians were not ready to give up their traditional way of life; confrontations ensued, and by the 1860s military stations were established along the trails. By the time the transcontinental railroad entered Wyoming, it was evident that the land no longer belonged to the Indians.

In the early 1860s, stagecoaches, freight, and mail wagons ran along the Overland Trail, which loosely followed the Cherokee Trail of 1848. When the railroad arrived in Wyoming in 1867, Wyoming began to attract settlers. Tent cities sprang up overnight wherever railroad crews laid tracks. These small "hell on wheels" towns consisted of ramshackle houses, brothels, saloons, and gambling tents. Cheyenne, Laramie, Carbon, and Rock Springs were all initially settled in this manner. As the tracks moved west, the makeshift towns would often close up and follow suit. However, the more innovative entrepreneurs found other ways to prosper. The southern part of the state housed the first five original counties of the Wyoming Territory, which extended all the way from Colorado to Montana.

Casper

A sprawling town near the center of the state, Casper (pop. 58,763, elev. 5,123 ft/1,561 m) has long been a hub for people traveling the region, first the Native Americans and later the settlers making use of the multiple pioneer trails in the region. Casper's booms and busts came with the trails, the railroad, and eventually oil and gas exploration. Its reputation as a rough-and-tumble town is well earned, and one can't help but chuckle to think of Butte, Montana's minor league baseball team, the Copper Kings, ditching one of the roughest towns in the West to become the Casper Ghosts. (The team left Casper in 2011 for Colorado, where members now play as the Grand Junction Rockies, an affiliate of the Denver Rockies.)

Although Casper is indeed industrial, rather large, and perhaps overly spread across the landscape, the town is experiencing something of a renaissance. In addition to a world-class contemporary art museum, the beautiful North Platte River, once hopelessly polluted, has been cleaned up and has earned a reputation as one of the best fisheries in the West. The river boasts more than 4,000 fish per mile on most stretches, including the renowned 5.5-mile (8.9-km) "Miracle Mile" and the blue-ribbon tailwaters of the "Grey Reef." There is a wealth of incredible outdoor opportunities just outside town at the city's unofficial year-round playground, Casper Mountain. In the heart of town, the Platte River Trails offer 11 miles (18 km) of walking

Casper

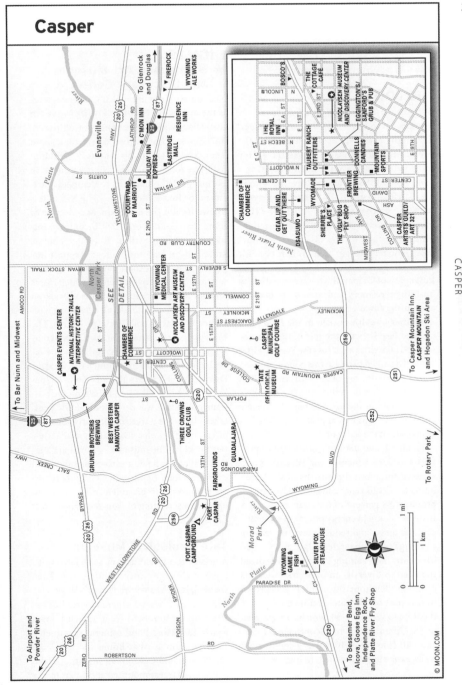

© MOON.COM

and biking trails alongside the river, connecting 10 city parks and offering an ideal spot to stretch your legs or take your pooch for a stroll and a dip. Casper is indeed worth a visit; you may well be surprised by all that is here.

HISTORY

A mixture of railroad and natural resources led to the establishment of Casper. Originally it was set up as a station for the Fremont, Elkhorn and Missouri Valley Railroad, with its first residents creating a town site in 1888. After a relatively common and lawless beginning, Casper prospered with the discovery of oil. When the first oil well was drilled in 1887, an onslaught of land speculators and other investors arrived, looking to get rich. When the Salt Creek Oil Field was established 40 miles (64 km) north of Casper, the town responded by building a refinery and went on to become a booming town.

Casper's wealth peaked in the 1920s and crashed heavily with the rest of the country in 1929. Like cities all across the West, Casper seemed destined to repeat this boom-and-bust cycle through the rest of the 20th century. The 21st century has brought another natural resource boom in the form of rehabbed rivers and hungry trout that appeal to avid anglers and lovers of the outdoors.

Coal, oil, and natural gas are still important sources of income for Wyoming and account for about three-fifths of the state's budget. A 2016 report show that Wyoming produces 88 percent of the country's coal. A two-year slump in energy prices led to significant job losses and reduced revenue, leaving a gaping hole in the state budget. But Casper, like many of Wyoming's towns, has realized the need to diversify in order to protect its economy. The tourism industry has grown in this part of the state, and if you can take the time to veer off I-80, which runs parallel to the Union Pacific transcontinental route, you will find yourself crossing century-old trails, exploring abandoned trading posts, and

experiencing traditions that bring southern Wyoming's unique history to life.

SIGHTS

★ Nicolaysen Art Museum and Discovery Center

The museum around which Casper revolves is the impressive **Nicolaysen Art Museum and Discovery Center** (400 E. Collins Dr., 307/235-5247, www.thenic.org, 10am-5pm Tues.-Sat., $5 adults, $4 seniors, $3 children 3-17, free for military and children under 3). Focusing solely on work by contemporary artists in the Rocky Mountains, The Nic, as it is known locally, has a permanent collection of more than 6,000 works that includes paintings, sculpture, textiles, drawings, photos, and prints; it features the region's most important traveling exhibitions related to their mission. The Discovery Center (which closes an hour before the museum) offers hands-on art activities for visitors of all ages along with a lineup of classes and special programs. The museum is very invested in the Casper community and often serves as host to some favorite local events. In summer the **Casper Downtown Farmers Market** (5pm-7:30pm Tues. mid-July-mid-Sept.) is held on the museum grounds. A wonderful festival, **Nic Fest,** takes place over a weekend in early June and offers artist booths, live music, and activities for kids. The museum's annual art auction and ball is held in early September, and over the winter holidays, The Nic hosts free open houses with ornament making, photo ops, and a screening of *How the Grinch Stole Christmas*.

Tate Geological Museum

A great little free museum associated with Casper College since 1980 is the **Tate Geological Museum** (125 College Dr., 307/268-2447, www.caspercollege.edu/tate, 10am-4pm Mon.-Sat., free), which houses nearly 3,000 fossil and mineral specimens. The museum is also home to "Dee," an 11,600-year-old Columbian mammoth (the oldest and largest mounted specimen in the world), who was likely 65 or 70 years old when he died. The collection includes dinosaur bones and fossilized footprints found in Wyoming. A fossil prep lab allows visitors to watch and ask questions of working paleontologists, and an interactive "Dino Den" will delight kids.

Fort Caspar

Positioned at a critical river crossing for the Oregon, Mormon, Pioneer, California, and Pony Express Trails, **Fort Caspar** (4001 Ft. Caspar Rd., 307/235-8462, www. fortcasparwyoming.com, museum 8am-5pm and fort buildings 8:30am-4:30pm daily May-Sept., museum 8am-5pm Tues.-Sat. Oct.-Apr., $4 adults, $3 children 13-18 and seniors 62 and up, half price when fort buildings are closed Oct.-Apr., always free for children under 13) was built in 1862 to protect travelers through the area and was occupied by the military until 1867. When the army decommissioned the site and took as many of the materials as they could with them to build Fort Fetterman in 1867, Native Americans burned what remained to the ground. In 1936, a Works Progress Administration crew rebuilt several of the buildings on the original site. The fort and museum are operated by the city of Casper.

Exhibits at the fort include reconstructions of the Mormon Ferry, Guinard Bridge, and Richard Bridge that predated the fort, as well as fort history, pioneer trail history, and other agricultural, oil, and gas exhibits related to the region. The museum also hosts interesting traveling exhibitions.

★ National Historic Trails Interpretive Center

Among the state's most renowned museums, the **National Historic Trails Interpretive Center** (1501 N. Poplar St., 307/261-7700, www.nhtcf.org, 9am-4:30pm daily winter, check website for expanded summer hours, free) tells the gritty story of Manifest Destiny and westward expansion on the historic pioneer trails through interactive exhibits and multimedia presentations. The museum's exhibits are both indoors and out, and they succeed in giving visitors a real sense of what day-to-day life was like for the early pioneers. The museum's seven distinct galleries are dedicated to four of the trails that cut through the region, as well as Native Americans, mountain men, explorers, and the trails today. There's even a virtual river crossing experience. Wyoming's BLM manages more than 340 miles (545 km) or 60 percent of the Oregon, California, Mormon, Pioneer, and Pony Express Trails in the state, and this museum celebrates both the heritage of those trails and the remarkable ability to still see and experience them in much the same way.

Ayres Natural Bridge

Some 50 miles (80 km) southeast of Casper and 10 miles (16 km) west of Douglas is one of Wyoming's earliest tourist attractions, **Ayres Natural Bridge** (208 Natural Bridge Rd., 307/358-3532, 8am-8pm daily Apr.-Oct., free), a natural arch where LaPrele Creek worked its way through a 100-foot-long, 50-foot-high solid rock wall over the centuries. It is set in a lovely 22-acre park. The Native Americans of the region thought of the natural bridge as a sinister place because of a tale about a young brave being struck by lightning in the canyon. The legend developed until it was widely believed among the Indians that an evil spirit lived beneath the bridge. Travelers on the Mormon Trail, which crossed the creek 2 miles (3.2 km) north of the site, discovered the bridge and the legend, and often visited the area to escape the Native Americans.

There are 12 beautiful campsites (free) within the park boundaries and a limited number of spots for RVs less than 30 feet (9 m) long; pets are not allowed in the park.

★ Casper Mountain

When Casper residents are eager to flee the city, particularly in the heat of summer, they head to **Casper Mountain,** an alpine oasis just minutes from town. In addition to the popular **Hogadon Ski Area,** several

campgrounds and parks, and miles of beautiful, forested hiking and biking trails, Casper Mountain is also rich with history and culture.

An early settler from Missouri, Elizabeth "Neal" Forsling, fled a horrible marriage with her two young daughters to homestead on the top of Casper Mountain in the 1920s. An artist and writer, Forsling was strong, independent, and loved the mountain with all of her being. She fell in love with and married a local rancher, Jim, who joined her in her happy life on the mountaintop, but when he froze to death at the age of 38 while skiing home from town with supplies, Neal dedicated herself even more to the land on which she lived. She painted and wrote stories about the spirits, trolls, fairies, and other beings that lived on Casper Mountain. She hosted a summer solstice party in 1930 that would become the **Mid-Summer's Eve Celebration** that continues today. Singlehandedly, Neal Forsling created a mythical culture on the mountain that persists today.

Forsling donated her land and cabin to Natrona County in 1973. She died a few years later, and the county turned her home into a wonderful museum named for the book of stories she created about the mountain: The **Crimson Dawn Museum** (1620 Crimson Dawn Rd., 307/235-1303, www. crimsondawnmuseum.org, museum 10am-7pm Sat.-Sun. June-Sept., park 8am-8pm daily June-Sept., free) is at the center of the Mid-Summer's Eve Celebration.

SPORTS AND RECREATION
Hiking and Biking

In addition to the abundance of hiking and biking trails just outside the city in places like Casper Mountain, there are a number of green trails within city limits. The **Platte River Trails** (www.platterivertrails.com) wind 11 miles (18 km) along the river's edge and can be accessed in a number of parks, including **Morad Park** and **Casper Whitewater Park**, as well as at the Holiday Inn on the River. **Rotary Park**, just south of town at the base of Casper Mountain, is home to the beloved Garden Creek Falls and 4.5-mile (7.2-km) **Bridle Trail**, which climbs 1,200 feet (366 m) and offers views of the falls and the city below.

Just 6 miles (10 km) east of town on Highway 252, **Edness K. Wilkins State Park** (8700 E. Hwy. 20/26, Evansville, 307/577-5150, http://wyoparks.state.wy.us, 7am-10pm daily Apr.-Sept., 8am-8pm Oct.-Mar., daily use $12 nonresidents, $7 residents) is a serene spot with giant cottonwoods, swimmable river access, ideal picnic spots, fishing, boat access, and a playground. There are also 2.8 miles (4.5 km) of paved trails for walkers, and birders will delight in the more than 40 species that can be counted in a single day in the park.

With more than 50 miles (80 km) of well-marked trails of varying difficulty, **Casper Mountain** is the best place for serious hiking and biking. Among the many popular trails in the area is the unique **Lee McCune Braille Trail** for both sighted and visually impaired hikers. The **Casper Mountain Outdoor Center** (McMurry Mountain Park, 1110 East End Rd., 307/215-4054, www.facebook. com/CMOutdoorCenter) offers more than 24 miles (39 km) of trails for hiking, mountain biking, fat biking, and skiing. The trails are free spring through fall, but a day pass ($10) is required in winter and can be purchased online (www.natrona.net/347/Casper-Mountain-Trails-Pass) or at a handful of vendors in town. For in-town biking, the Crossroads Park Trail is easily accessible at Mike Lansing Field (330 Kati Ln.) or near several downtown hotels. The single-track dirt trail along the North Platte is perfect for beginners and intermediate riders.

Avid bikers who need a repair, some equipment, or just good advice can stop by **Mountain Sports** (543 S. Center St., 307/266-1136, www.caspermtnsports.com,

---

1: Nicolaysen Art Museum and Discovery Center
2: cabin at Casper Mountain 3: spring on Casper Mountain 4: the North Platte River

10am-6pm Mon.-Sat., noon-4pm Sun.). Great gear and rentals are available at **Gear Up and Get Out There** (254 W. 1st St., 307/235-6353, www.gearupandgetoutthere.com, 9am-6pm Mon.-Fri., 10am-4pm Sat., from $45/day). They also rent kid carriers ($34), stand-up paddleboards ($40), and snowshoes ($14 adults, $10 children).

Skiing

Casper's easy access to the mountains makes this town an ideal winter getaway. Just 15 minutes from town is **Hogadon Ski Area** (2500 W. Hogadon Rd., Casper Mountain, 307/235-8499, www.hogadon.net, 9am-4pm Wed.-Sun., full day $55 adults 19-64, $47 youth 13-18, seniors 65 and up, and active military, $37 children 6-12; half day $45 adults, $40 seniors youth, and active military, over 70 and under 5 ski free), a small, family-friendly mountain that offers 20 percent beginner terrain and 40 percent each intermediate and advanced. There are 28 trails and two lifts, and a snowboard terrain park for more adventurous riders. Group and private lessons are available, as are rentals. Night skiing is available, and in summer, the mountain is open to mountain bikers and hikers.

For Nordic skiers, the **Casper Mountain Trails Center** (9301 S. Circle Dr. on Casper Mountain, 307/237-5014 or 307/259-0958, www.natrona.net/238/trails-center, sunrise-10pm daily, day pass $10) offers 26 miles (42 km) of groomed trails for both classical and skate skiers, in addition to a 0.7-mile (1.2-km) lighted loop. There are an additional 30 miles (48 km) of backcountry and snowshoe trails in the area as well. Day passes can be purchased online at www.natrona.net/347/Casper-Mountain-Trails-Pass or at a handful of vendors in town. A map of Casper Mountain Nordic trails is available at www.natrona.net. The lodge was entirely rebuilt in 2021-2022.

For equipment rentals in Casper head to **Gear Up and Get Out There** (254 W. 1st St., 307/235-6353, www.gearupandgetoutthere.com, 9am-6pm Mon.-Fri., 10am-4pm Sat.).

Rock Climbing

As Casper's status among outdoor junkies continues to climb, rock climbing is another of the region's well-known offerings. **Fremont Canyon** (www.fremontcanyon.com) has world-class granite climbing for people of all ability levels (5.6-5.13d in difficulty), with cliffs ranging 40 feet to over 400 feet (12 m to over 122 m). The area is known for its steep crack climbs but does offer some sport climbing and bouldering problems. To get to the canyon, which overlooks Alcova Reservoir, head south from Casper on Highway 220 to the town of Alcova; the canyon is 10 miles (16 km) farther south, accessed by the Fremont Canyon Bridge.

For professional guide service for both rock and ice, check out the awesome instructors at **Wyoming Mountain Guides** (www.wyomingmountainguides.com, 307/431-1741). Intro to alpine climbing classes start at $500; intro to ice climbing classes start at $285. This guide service can create custom trips for you across the state almost anytime of year.

Fishing

Fishing in the cold waters of the **North Platte River** is something of a comeback story. Around the turn of the 20th century, the North Platte was known as one of the great trout fisheries of the West; as an example, a celebration in Saratoga in 1907, known as the Railroad Days Celebration and Fish Fry, required more than 3,000 fish to be caught in two days to feed visitors. The river was thick with trout, and anglers flocked to the area to catch them. As industrialization spread across the country, feedlots and oil refineries increasingly dotted the landscape and polluted the North Platte until it was nearly uninhabitable. Only since 1997 have sweeping measures been taken to restore the river, an effort that has, by all accounts, been enormously successful. In fact, the Grey Reef section of the North Platte River has ranked among the best big fisheries in the world since 2005. The area is widely considered the best rainbow trout tailwater in the Lower 48. The largest trout caught in the North Platte, in the fabled Grey Reef section, was a 22-pound (10-kg) brown trout. Average rainbows in this river weigh upward of 5 pounds (2.3 kg) and measure 16-18 inches (41-46 cm), and trophies range 25-30 inches (64-76 cm).

Today, in part because of its shallow depth and slow current, the river can be fished for hundreds of miles, and anglers can expect to see the noses of rainbows, browns, Snake River cutthroats, walleye, and the occasional cutbow, a rainbow-cutthroat hybrid.

Casper offers an abundance of fly shops and guides. A good place to start for a license and regulations is **Wyoming Game and Fish** (3030 Energy Ln., Ste. 100, 307/473-3400, http://wgfd.wyo.gov, 8am-5pm Mon.-Fri.). For gear or guided trips, contact the **Ugly Bug Fly Shop** (240 S. Center St., 307/234-6905, www.crazyrainbow.net, 9am-5:30pm Mon.-Fri., 8am-4pm Sat.), which has full-day ($525-575/boat) and half-day ($425/boat) guided fly-fishing trips guided by the shop's **Crazy Rainbow Fly Fishing**. A full-day guided float trip on the Miracle Mile is $550 per boat. Discounts are available in the off-season (Nov.-Mar.), when the weather can be lousy but the fishing great. The **Platte River Fly Shop** (7400 Hwy. 220, 307/237-5997 or 307/277-6282, www.platteriverguides.com, 9am-4pm Mon.-Fri., 9am-2pm Sat. summer, 8am-5pm Mon.-Fri. winter) offers all-day guided trips in boats ($550-595 for 2 anglers) or wade fishing ($550-595 for 2 anglers). Single anglers and off-season trips are discounted. And trips can center around the Grey Reef, the Miracle Mile, and Fremont Canyon. Two-day trips ($575 wading for 2 anglers, $625 float for 2 anglers) can be arranged on the Bighorn River.

Golf

Casper has 90 holes for avid golfers, including a world-class course designed by Robert Trent Jones Jr. built on an old remediated oil refinery: The **Three Crowns Golf Club** (1601 King Blvd., 307/472-7696, www.threecrownsgolfclub.com, $80 for 18 holes on weekday morning, $84 for 18 holes on weekend morning, $49 for 9 holes on weekday morning, $15 carts 9 holes, $25 carts 18 holes, discounts for weekday, afternoon, pre- and post-season play) is a par-72 course that opened in 2005 and has a resort-like feel.

Another course worth playing is the **Casper Municipal Golf Course** (2120 Allendale Blvd., 307/223-6620, www.casperwy.gov, $32 for 18 holes, $20 for 9 holes Mon.-Fri., $34 for 18 holes, $22 for 9 holes Sat.-Sun.), which has 27 holes on three distinct nines. Opened in 1929, the course is consistently ranked among the best municipal courses in the state.

ENTERTAINMENT AND EVENTS
Theater
Performing in an intimate theater-in-the-round, Casper's **Stage III Community Theatre** (904 N. Center St., 307/234-0946, www.stageiiitheatre.org) is an entirely volunteer organization that produces six productions annually between September and June. The company has been entertaining Casper since 1980, with evening and matinee offerings ranging from classic dramas to mysteries and comedies.

Founded in 2014, **Casper Theater Company** (735 CY Ave., 307/267-7243, www.caspertheatercompany.net) is a semiprofessional theater company offering four productions each season, including original works.

Rodeos
Rodeo is serious business in this part of the state—or anywhere in Wyoming, for that matter. One of the biggest is the **College National Finals Rodeo** (509/529-4402, www.cnfr.com), held annually at the Casper Events Center (800/442-2256) in mid-June. More than 400 cowboys and cowgirls from 100 universities and colleges compete for champion status in saddle bronc riding, bareback riding, bull riding, tie-down roping, steer wrestling, team roping, barrel racing, breakaway roping, and goat tying.

Another big rodeo in Casper is the **PRCA Rodeo** held annually in conjunction with the **Central Wyoming Fair** (1700 Fairgrounds Rd., 307/235-5775 or 888/225-2600, www.centralwyomingfair.com) in mid-July. The fair has been in operation since 1904 and comes with all the hoopla and community spirit you'd expect.

Mid-Summer's Eve Celebration

Held each year on June 21, the summer solstice, the **Mid-Summer's Eve Celebration** (Crimson Dawn Park, 1620 Crimson Dawn Rd., 307/235-9311) is a unique event that showcases the history and spirit of Casper. The stories around this event, started in 1930 by Casper Mountain resident, artist, and author Neal Forsling, are considered by some to be Wyoming's only folklore. The event starts with a storytelling walk through the forest, amid a network of rock shrines, and culminates with a bonfire that everyone is invited to throw red dirt into, in hopes of seeing their fondest wish granted. It is a charming celebration of the witches, spirits, and trolls said to inhabit the mountain.

Beartrap Summer Festival

Undoubtedly one of the best outdoor music festivals in the region, the **Beartrap Summer Festival** (307/266-5252, www.beartrapsummerfestival.com) brings Casper Mountain to life with bluegrass music the first weekend in August. The event hosts big-name bands and musicians for two days midmorning-dusk. Rounding out the festival are musical workshops, an arts and crafts marketplace, an open-air food court, and supervised children's activities. Pets are welcome on a leash. Discounted tickets can be purchased in advance by phone.

SHOPPING

A central shopping locale for much of the region, Casper has every sort of shopping imaginable, from big malls and shopping centers to box stores and downtown boutiques. The largest facility in the region by far is the **Eastridge Mall** (601 SE Wyoming Blvd., 307/265-9392, www.shopeastridge.com), anchored by Target, Best Buy, Bed Bath and Beyond, Dick's Sporting Goods, and J. C. Penney.

Some smaller stores should not be missed. **WYOMade** (8500 Airport Pkwy., 307/277-3070, www.wyomade.com, hours vary so call ahead) sells beautifully designed apparel, gifts, jewelry, candles, and art, all made in Wyoming. Everyone needs a bison T-shirt that says "Don't pet the fluffy cows." A terrific place to find work by local artists is the **Casper Artists Guild/Art 321** (321 W. Midwest Ave., 307/265-2655, www.art321.org, 10am-6pm Tues.-Fri., 10am-4pm Sat.), which hosts regular shows in a variety of media as well as active workshops for artists and beginners alike. The gift shop is an excellent place to pick up one-of-a-kind works by local artists.

For real Western duds, and fantastic outdoor clothing, visit the behemoth **Lou Taubert Ranch Outfitters** (125 E. 2nd St., 800/447-9378, www.loutaubert.com, 10am-5pm Tues.-Sat., noon-4pm Sun.), which spreads across nine floors. An important Western retailer since 1919, Lou Taubert is the place to go for boots, hats, saddle and tack, Wyoming-made goodies, gifts of all sorts, and sportswear.

For a sweet tooth or an espresso with a side of chocolate, the best spot in Casper is **Donells Candies** (201 E. 2nd St., 307/234-6283, www.donellschocolates.com, 9am-6pm Mon.-Fri., 11am-3pm Sat.), which has been churning out delectable handmade chocolates, savory nuts, and all flavors of popcorn since 1956. The store is still owned and operated by the founding family, and with brisk Internet sales it has found admirers the world over. The Donells expanded the downtown store and added an espresso bar where candy lovers can also order hand-dipped ice cream.

FOOD

Casper is a breakfast lover's town: You'll find a number of great places to start the day right. **Eggington's** (229 E. 2nd St., 307/265-8700, www.eggingtons.com, 6am-2pm Mon.-Sat., 7am-2pm Sun., breakfast $7.50-11.50, lunch $10-13) serves breakfast and lunch to a bustling crowd. It offers everything from omelets and pastries to burgers and salads. A somewhat hidden but marvelous spot for lunch is ★ **The Cottage Café** (116 S. Lincoln St., 307/234-1157, www.cottagecafe.com, 11am-1:30pm Tues.-Fri., $12-14), which is tucked into a residential neighborhood and serves delicious homemade soups, paninis, pastas, and more. Another weekday-only place that offers up great, classic breakfasts and lunches is **Sherrie's Place** (310 W. Yellowstone Hwy., 307/235-3513, 6am-2pm Mon.-Fri., $4-11). From cinnamon rolls and stuffed French toast to fried chicken and good old-fashioned malts, this place is the real deal.

For good Mexican food, which southern Wyoming seems to have no shortage of, try **Guadalajara** (3350 CY Ave., 307/234-4699, www.guadalajaramexicanwyoming.com, 11am-9pm Sun.-Thurs., 11am-10pm Fri.-Sat., $10-17). **Bosco's** (847 E. A St., 307/265-9658, 11am-1:30pm and 5pm-8:30pm Tues.-Sat., lunch $8-10, dinner $12-23) serves wonderful Italian meals (including gluten-free options) in an intimate setting. Another favorite in town is the Wyoming/Dakotas chain **Sanford's Grub & Pub** (61 SE Wyoming Blvd., 307/315-6040, www.thegrubandpub.com, 11am-9pm Sun.-Thurs., 11am-10pm Fri.-Sat., $10-31), which has an outrageously big menu featuring Cajun twists on American food, along with plenty of beer; its $1 pints are well known among beer lovers. Kids will delight in the fact that every square inch of wall is covered with memorabilia and garage sale finds. For a high-end steak, chops, and seafood place, try the **FireRock Steakhouse** (6100 E. 2nd St., 307/234-2333, 11am-10pm Mon.-Thurs., 11am-11pm Fri.-Sat., 11am-9pm Sun., $11-40), serving aged steaks cooked over a wood-fired grill, rack of lamb, pork chops,

and all sorts of toppings and sides including shrimp and lobster. They also offer a nice selection of burgers, sandwiches, salads, and pasta. FireRock Steakhouse also has a full-service bar.

Silver Fox Steakhouse (3422 Energy Lane, 307/235-3000, 4:30pm-9pm Mon., 11am-2pm and 4:30pm-9:30pm Tues.-Thurs., 11am-2pm and 4:30pm-10pm Fri., 4:30pm-10pm Sat., 4:30pm-9pm Sun., lunch $13-28, dinner $13-39) serves up a modern take on the classic supper club seafood and steaks. From mouthwatering burgers and French Dip to prime rib and Alaskan King Crab, Chef Bernard has been making magic in the kitchen here for more than 40 years. It's both a comfortable place, and delicious.

Part Asian bistro and part sushi bar, **Dsasumo** (320 W. 1st St., 307/237-7874, www.dsasumo.com, 11am-2:30pm and 4:30pm-9pm Mon.-Fri., 11am-9pm Sat., noon-9pm Sun., $12-22) is a great find in Casper. Most of the food is Thai, but there are plenty of fusion choices and a great sushi menu. Don't miss the specialty cocktails.

There was a big hole to fill when the C85 Wonderbar closed overnight in 2019. The place, open since 1942, was famous for having cowboys ride in for a beer without ever dismounting their horses. And their slogan was "It's more fun to eat in a bar than drink in a restaurant." RIP. Though there aren't any horses in **Wyoming Ale Works** (5900 E. 2nd St., 307/472-5900, www.wyomingaleworks.com, 11am-11pm Mon.-Thurs., 11am-midnight Fri.-Sat., 11am-9pm Sun., lunch $12-15, dinner $20-30) there is plenty of excellent beer—40 craft beers on tap—and equally good grub. From mussels and flatbread to burgers, pulled pork, wood-fired pizza, and seasonal salads, to duck gumbo and bison chili, everything is fresh and delicious.

From the unique self-pour system at pay-by-the-ounce **Frontier Brewing** (117 E. 2nd St., 406/337-1000, www.frontierbrewingcompany.com, 3pm-10pm Wed.-Fri., 11am-10pm Sat.) and the welcoming **Gruner Brothers Brewing** (1301 Wilkins Circle, 307/439-2222, www.grunerbrewing.com, 3pm-9pm Tues.-Thurs., 3pm-10pm Fri.-Sat.), offering great food and regular live music, to the tiny and delicious **Skull Tree Brewing** (1530 Burlington Ave., 307/277-3764, 3pm-8pm Tues.-Sat.), which can seat a maximum of two people at the bar but serves great lunches and dinners, Casper has quite a brewing and distillery scene for those who like to tip one back. In fact, there are five breweries and a distillery in town. To learn about Casper's craft renaissance, visit www.visitcasper.com/restaurants/breweries-distilleries.

In Casper's Old Yellowstone District, **Racca's Pizzeria Napoletano** (430 S. Ash St., 307/337-2444, 11am-9pm Sun.-Thurs., 11am-10pm Fri.-Sat., $12-19) is an elegant place that serves hearty Italian fare, including thin-crust Neapolitan style pizza from their wood-fired oven. There's a long list of starters that should not be overlooked, plus soup, salad, sandwiches, and entrées including chicken or eggplant parmesan, lasagna, rigatoni alfredo, and more. Wine and beer is available as well.

ACCOMMODATIONS

Casper has no shortage of places to stay, and many chain hotel options are available. But for stunning scenery, nothing beats the **Red Butte Ranch** (8550 S. Bessemer Rd., 307/472-3784, www.redbutteranchlodging.com, from $150/night), just five minutes from Casper. The private ranch cottage (which sleeps up to 6), bed-and-breakfast rooms (call for rates), and the five-bedroom lodge (from $300/night) boast extraordinary views of Casper Mountain and the namesake Red Butte. The accommodations aren't fancy in any way, but in this setting you won't want to be spending much time indoors. The river runs through it, and the ranch can arrange e-bike rentals (from $40 half day, $75 full day), fishing, hunting, river shuttles, and more. Plus the lodge makes a point of announcing they are LGBTQ friendly, which is reassuring in this part of the country.

For fishers, the waterfront **Dry Fly Lodge** (7630 Spencer Rd., 307/237-5997, www.

platteriverguides, $175-356) is a dream. There are cozy cottages with decks and a beautiful home with five bedrooms, all right on the water and just two minutes from the fly shop.

The **Best Western Ramkota Casper** (800 N. Poplar St., 307/266-6000 or 800/528-1234, www.casper.ramkota.com, $106-165) is a large facility that caters both to business travelers (in-room desks, free Wi-Fi, and a business center) and to families with the **Water Playland,** geared to young children. The pet-friendly hotel also offers complimentary breakfast. Among the other chain hotels in Casper are **C'mon Inn** (301 E. Lathrop Rd., 307/472-6300 or 866/782-2690, www.cmoninn.com/casper, from $110), with king Jacuzzi suites and pillowtop beds; the newer 100-room **Courtyard by Marriott** (4260 Hospitality Ln., 307/473-2600, www.marriott.com/cprcy, $104-151); **Holiday Inn Express** (4250 Legion Ln., exit 185 on I-25, 307/237-4200, www.hiexpress.com, from $109); and the pet-friendly **Super 8** (www.wyndhamhotels.com, 3838 CY Ave., 307/266-3480, from $69).

The pet-friendly **Residence Inn** (4930 E. 2nd St., 307/234-9008, $146-269, $100 pet fee for first pet, $50 each additional pet) on Casper's East side is new, exceedingly comfortable, and convenient with a fully equipped kitchen and living room in every suite.

A more budget-friendly option downtown is **The Royal Inn** (440 E. A St., 307/234-3501, from $40), which offers basic rooms with microwaves and refrigerators, free Wi-Fi, and on-site laundry machines. The inn, which is undergoing renovations, also provides gas grills and a briquette grill for guests who want to cook out.

CAMPING

The closest public camping in the vicinity of Casper is 10 miles (16 km) south of town on **Casper Mountain,** a breezy, forested all-season playground for locals. There are four campgrounds on the mountain; **Beartrap Meadow** (Casper Mountain Rd., 307/235-9311, www.natrona.net, $10) is the only one with water and also the nicest of the four.

Various campsites maintained by the **Bureau of Land Management** (307/261-7500, www.wy.blm.gov, from $18) include the **Rim** and **Lodgepole Campgrounds** in the Muddy Mountain Environmental Education Area, which can be accessed from gravel roads off Casper Mountain Road. Both have vault toilets, and the campgrounds are connected by a 2-mile (3.2-km) interpretive nature trail.

For a scenic lakeside locale 28 miles (45 km) west of Casper on County Road 407, off Highway 220, **Alcova Reservoir** has numerous **campgrounds** (County Rd. 407/ Kortes Rd., 307/235-9311, www.natrona.net, from $35 full hookups, $10 unserviced), including **Westside Campground, Black Beach,** and **Cottonwood.** Unserviced sites are first-come, first-served, and sites with hookups are by reservation only.

A few private campgrounds and RV parks are also available right in town. Set along a bend in the North Platte River, the **Fort Caspar Campground** (4205 Fort Caspar Rd., 307/247-9399, www.ftcasparcamp.com, call for rates) offers basic tent and RV sites on gravel, a lodge, ponds, and several walking trails; it also provides free Wi-Fi.

INFORMATION AND SERVICES

The **Natrona County Travel and Tourism Council** (139 W. 2nd St., Ste. 1B, 307/234-5362, www.visitcasper.com, 8am-5pm Mon.-Fri.) has a wealth of information for visitors. The **Casper Area Chamber of Commerce** (500 N. Center St., 307/234-5311 or 866/234-5311, www.casperwyoming.org, 8am-5pm Mon.-Fri. summer, 9am-3pm Mon.-Fri. winter) is an excellent resource for local businesses and relocation information.

Post offices are located at 411 North Forest Drive (307/237-8556, 8:30am-5pm Mon.-Fri., 9am-noon Sat.) and at 150 East B Street (9am-5:30pm Mon.-Fri., 9am-noon Sat.).

The **Natrona County Public Library** (307/577-7323, www.natronacountylibrary.org, 9am-7pm Mon.-Thurs., 9am-5pm Fri.-Sat., 1pm-5pm Sun.) is at 307 East 2nd Street.

Wyoming Medical Center (1233 E. 2nd St., 307/577-7201 or 800/822-7201, www.wyomingmedicalcenter.org) is the largest health care facility in the state and offers everything from 24-hour emergency medicine to highly specialized care.

Laundry facilities are available at **Hilltop Laundromat** (2513 E. 3rd St., 307/234-7331, 24 hours daily) and **CY Laundromat** (2300 CY Ave., 307/696-2821, 7:30am-8pm daily).

TRANSPORTATION
Getting There

The **Casper/Natrona County International Airport** (CPR, 8500 Airport Pkwy., 307/472-6688, www.iflycasper.com) is on US 20/26 approximately 9 miles (14.5 km) west of downtown. Two carriers, **United** and **Delta,** provide daily flights to and from Denver and Salt Lake City.

Car-rental agencies at the airport include **Enterprise, National, Hertz, Avis,** and **Budget.**

Regular bus service to and from Casper is available on **Greyhound** (601 N. Center St., 307/265-2353) and **Arrow/Black Hills Stage Lines** (601 N. Center St., 307/265-2353, www.expressarrow.com).

By car, Casper is 145 miles (233 km) east of Lander, 148 miles (238 km) north of Laramie, 178 miles (290 km) northwest of Cheyenne, 240 miles (385 km) northeast of Green River, 242 miles (385 km) south of Gillette, 284 miles (460 km) east of Jackson, and 267 miles (425 km) southeast of Yellowstone National Park.

Getting Around

The easiest public transportation in Casper is **Casper Area Transit Link** (307/235-8287, www.casperwy.gov, 6:30am-6:30pm Mon.-Fri., 7:30am-3:30pm Sat., $1 general, $0.75 students, $0.50 reduced for elderly and disabled, free for children 5 and under), a fixed-route transit system.

Local taxi service is provided by **Casper Cabs** (307/577-7777, www.caspercabs.com) and **Share a Ride Wyoming** (307/696-6116).

Laramie

Nestled in a high basin between the Laramie and Medicine Bow Mountains, Laramie (pop. 31,407, elev. 7,173 ft/2,186 m) is a charming combination of Old West frontier town and sophisticated university town, all with immediate proximity to the natural rocky playground that envelops the city.

Even with a relatively lawless history, Laramie continues to be among the most progressive cities in the state, although it hasn't lost any of its cowboy swagger. The 150-year-old downtown buildings are beautiful and authentic examples of the finest frontier architecture. From old-school quilt shops to herb stores, cowgirl yarn shops to outdoor stores, downtown Laramie is a charming mix of the Old and New West. For proof, look no further than Ivinson and 1st Streets, where cowboy and motorcycle bars share customers with a vegetarian café and a global cuisine bistro. The town is full of important historic sites and an arresting spectrum of museums. The university gives Laramie just enough academic culture to keep the town young and vibrant with concerts, lectures, sports, and coffeehouses, and the surrounding wilderness is well used without becoming overcrowded.

HISTORY

Like so many cities in the region, Laramie can trace its roots back to a fort: Fort John Buford, built in 1866 to protect travelers on the pioneer trails, most notably the Overland Trail. In 1867, railroad workers plotting the course through the Laramie Valley rumbled into town, bringing with them numerous businesses to support their way of life. When the first passengers disembarked from the Union Pacific train in Laramie City in 1868, there were 23 saloons ready for them to wet their whistles.

Fort John Buford, by then known as Fort

Sanders, was abandoned in 1882, but other significant structures had been built in Laramie. The Wyoming Territorial Prison was first built in 1872 as a response to the lawlessness of the area. And in 1887, Wyoming University, now known as the University of Wyoming, opened its doors to both men and women. It's worth pointing out that women in Laramie were the first in the United States to sit on a jury and to vote, both in 1870.

SIGHTS

American Heritage Center

Established in 1945, the **American Heritage Center** (2111 Willett Dr., 307/766-4114, www. ahc.uwyo.edu, 8am-7pm Mon., 8am-5pm Tues.-Fri., 2nd-floor loggia only, free) houses one of the most extensive nongovernmental historical collections in the country. In addition to the manuscripts collections, a rare book center has more than 55,000 items that date back to medieval times. Topics range from the American West, an obvious and natural specialty, to British and American literature, natural history, conservation, women authors, and book arts, among countless others. The center is open to the public and is utilized constantly by scholars from all over the world. The center also hosts an array of fascinating events from lectures and symposia to rare and important exhibits. The website offers viewers a meaningful look into the digital collection, audiovisual collection, and virtual exhibits.

University of Wyoming Art Museum

Housed in the same architecturally interesting complex as the American Heritage Center, the **University of Wyoming Art Museum** (2111 Willett Dr., 307/766-6622, www.uwyo. edu/artmuseum, 10am-5pm Mon.-Sat. May-Aug. and Dec.-Jan., 10am-7pm Mon. and

Laramie

© MOON.COM

10am-5pm Tues.-Sat. Feb.-Apr. and Sept.-Nov., free) brings art from around the world to Wyoming. Its permanent collection houses more than 7,000 objects, including European and American paintings, prints, and drawings; 19th-century Japanese prints; 18th-to 19th-century Persian and Indian miniature paintings; 20th-century photography; and African and Native American artifacts. The museum also hosts important exhibitions focused on everything from regional art to international museum collections.

University of Wyoming Geological Museum

In a university with several compelling museums covering everything from anthropology to insects, another great one is the **University of Wyoming Geological Museum** (West Campus, 200 N. 9th St., 307/766-2646, www.uwyo.edu/geomuseum, 10am-4pm Mon.-Sat., free). The museum houses some of the best fossils in the country and dedicates plenty of space to Wyoming's earliest inhabitants: the dinosaurs. In addition to the usual suspects—from the allosaurus to the T. rex—the museum lays claim to one of only six apatosaurus skeletons on display worldwide. This one is 145-160 million years old and was discovered in Albany County in 1901. There are also skeletons of *Diatryma gigantea,* a prehistoric carnivorous flying dinosaur more than 7 feet tall, found in 1876. One unique exhibit is the fossilized remains of a dinosaur that died giving birth. The bones of the baby are clearly visible. Dozens of displays tell the stories of the more than 50 species of dinosaur whose remains have been found in Wyoming soil. And when displays are missing here, they are often on loan to the Museum of Natural History in New York City. These are serious bones in a very unassuming package.

1: downtown Laramie 2: the Wyoming Territorial Prison State Historic Site 3: Ivinson Mansion 4: Vedauwoo is a great place for camping, climbing, and hiking.

★ Laramie Plains Museum at the Historic Ivinson Mansion

Entrepreneur and banker Edward Ivinson was a local hero in Laramie, not only for his ethical business practices and his community-minded role in the construction of the prison and the university, but also for the home that he built in 1892, the same year he lost the Wyoming gubernatorial race. Indeed, the **Ivinson Mansion** (603 E. Ivinson Ave., 307/742-4448, www.laramiemuseum.org, tours 9am-5pm Tues.-Sat. and 1pm-4pm Sun. summer, 1pm-4pm Tues.-Sat. fall-spring, hours can change for private events, $10 adults, $7 seniors, $5 students and military, $25 families, free for children under 6) is among Laramie's most impressive buildings. The house was designed by architect W. E. Ware and built for $40,000 with then-unheard-of amenities that included central heating, electricity, and running water. Jane Ivinson, Edward's wife, decorated the home with elegant appointments from around the world. After his beloved wife died, Ivinson donated their regal residence to the Episcopal Missionary District of Wyoming with the understanding that it be used as a school and home for teenage ranch girls who otherwise might not be educated. The school operated until 1958, at which point the house sat vacant at the mercy of vandals for more than a decade.

In 1972 the Episcopal Church sold the mansion to the Laramie Plains Museum Association. Under the museum's care, the home has been beautifully restored and is open to the public as the Laramie Plains Museum. The home is filled with artifacts from all over the state, including the largest collection of Wyoming Territorial Prison furnishings, gorgeous wood pieces made by Swedish prisoner Jan Hjorth, a regional gun collection spanning more than a century, period furnishings, and more. Seeing the artifacts in such a stunning home setting makes this museum absolutely worth seeing. The only way to see the house is on a docent-led tour.

★ Wyoming Territorial Prison State Historic Site

Built in 1872 to deal with the ruffians in lawless Laramie, the **Wyoming Territorial Prison** (975 Snowy Range Rd., 307/745-6161, http://wyoparks.state.wy.us, 9am-4pm daily May-Sept., 10am-3pm Wed.-Sat. Oct.-Apr., $9 adults, $4.50 children 12-17, free for children under 12) was restored in 1989 and made into a 190-acre State Historic Site. The prison was in use 1872-1903, during which time more than 1,000 men and 12 women were imprisoned there. Among the most famous residents was Butch Cassidy. When Wyoming achieved statehood in 1890, work was already underway on a new state prison in Rawlins. When the Wyoming Frontier Prison opened in 1901, the transition began, and prisoners in the territorial prison were slowly replaced by animals from the University of Wyoming's experimental stock farm, which were housed in the prison for more than 70 years.

Rounding out the historic site are buildings in various stages of restoration, including the broom factory where many of the prisoners worked, an entirely re-created frontier town, authentic pioneer cabins, a schoolhouse, and agricultural buildings where kids can stick their arms into a simulated (and gooey!) cow's belly.

Still, the prison is the main attraction, and visitors should plan to spend at least 90 minutes touring the facility. A brochure in the gift shop provides a self-guided tour through furnished cells, the prisoner dining room, guards' quarters, women's quarters, the warden's office, and other rooms and exhibit galleries. The warden's house on the grounds can also be toured.

Several things make this experience both unique and unforgettable. For starters, willing visitors are assigned the identity of a former prisoner upon entering and can find out about their prisoner throughout the facility, something that keeps kids fully involved.

The prisoner ID card can be stamped at the end of the visit for a fun take-home souvenir. The museum itself is spotlessly clean and easy to explore. Numerous volunteers throughout the property, dressed as late 19th-century prisoners, answer questions and tell fascinating stories. This is just a wonderful place to spend an afternoon.

SPORTS AND RECREATION

Rock Climbing

A mecca for rock climbers and nature lovers alike, **Vedauwoo** (off I-80 exit 329, about 20 mi/32 km east of Laramie, 307/745-2300, www.vedauwoo.org) is an otherworldly jumble of enormous boulders that offer some of the best wide-crack climbing in the West. More than 500 sport climbs were documented in the first guidebook for the area, written in 1994 and no longer available. Today there are more than 900 climbs, many of which are detailed on the Vedauwoo website, and the number continues to grow. Those who want to learn and climb with a guide can contact **Wyoming Mountain Guides** (www.wyomingmountainguides.com, 307/431-1741). Intro to alpine climbing classes start at $500; intro to ice climbing classes start at $285. This guide service can create custom trips for you across the state almost anytime of year.

For nonclimbers, the area is ideal for hiking, trail running, and even wildlife-viewing. Among the animals sighted here are pronghorn, deer, moose, and even black bears and cougars. A U.S. Forest Service campground (Forest Rd. 720, Buford, 307/745-2300, www.fs.usda.gov, June-Oct. depending on weather, $10/night) is available at the site. The elevation is surprisingly high, at 8,200 feet (2,499 m) above sea level.

Hiking and Biking

Although it is primarily known for its climbing opportunities, Vedauwoo offers excellent hiking for those who like to stay in contact with the ground. The **Turtle**

Rock Loop is a 2.8-mile (4.5-km) trail that climbs only 314 feet (96 m) through forest and alongside the famed red rocks. The trail got its name from its proximity to the base of Turtle Rock, an outcrop of Sherman granite that is as old as the Rocky Mountains. Along the route, the Snowy Mountains are visible to the east. To get to the trailhead from Laramie, drive east on I-80 for 12 miles (19 km) to Vedauwoo Road. Turn left and cross under the interstate. Stay on Vedauwoo Road for 1.2 miles (1.9 km) to the campground entry gate. Turn left into the campground and continue 0.5 mile (0.8 km) to a small gravel parking lot on the left.

Accessed from a trailhead at West Garfield Street and South Spruce Street, the **Laramie River Greenbelt Park** offers 5.8 miles (9.3 km) of paved walking, running, biking, and inline skating paths.

In addition to meandering hikes in town along the Laramie River Greenbelt and at nearby Vedauwoo, the **Pole Mountain Area** (Forest Rd. 705, off I-80 exit 323, 13 mi/21 km east of Laramie) in the Sherman Mountains offers terrific trails for hiking and biking. The **Headquarters National Recreation Trail Loop** can be a 4-mile (6.4-km) or 8-mile (12.9-km) round-trip loop, depending on your time and energy level. The trail winds through a number of environments, from sage and grassy meadows to pine forests, and there is plenty of opportunity for bouldering among the pink granite rocks that are reminiscent of Vedauwoo. A brochure, *Pole Mountain Summer-Use Trails,* is available at the **Laramie Ranger District** (2468 W. Jackson St., 307/745-2300, 8am-4:30pm Mon.-Fri.).

You'll have to bring your own bike to Laramie, unless you are a student or faculty member of the University of Wyoming, in which case you can rent from the ingenious Bike Library through the **Outdoor Program** (307/766-2402), but if you need service, repairs, or just some good advice, head into the **Pedal House** (207 S. 1st St., 307/742-5533, www.pedalhouse.com).

Fishing

While Laramie isn't quite the hotbed of fishing that can be found in other parts of the state, its location makes access to varied waters relatively easy. For lake fishing, options include **Laramie Plains Lakes** (15 mi/24 km west of town off Hwy. 230) and **Lake Hattie** (20 mi/32 km southwest of Laramie off Hwy. 230). Nearby rivers filled with trout include the **Big Laramie River** and the **Upper North Platte River.** For fishing gear or guided trips, contact **Four Seasons Angler** (334 S. Fillmore St., 307/721-4047, www.fourseasonsanglers. com, 7am-7pm daily). Half-day wade trips for two anglers start at $400; full-day trips for two start at $500 including lunch.

Golf

Golfers can hit the links in Laramie at the nine-hole **Fox Run** (489 Hwy. 230, 307/745-4161, www.foxrunlaramie.com, $35 for 18 holes, $25 for 9 holes, cart rentals $20 for 9 holes, $30 for 18 holes) or the **Jacoby Park Golf Course** (3501 Willett Dr., 307/745-3111, www.uwyo.edu/jacobygc, $40 for 18 holes, $32 for 9 holes) on the University of Wyoming campus.

Skiing

Thirty-two miles (52 km) west of town in the Medicine Bow-Routt National Forests, **Snowy Range Ski Area** (3254 Hwy. 130, Centennial, 307/745-5750, www. snowyrangeski.com, full day $49-64 adults 18-69, $42-57 teens 13-17, $30-45 children 5-12, free for kids under 5 and seniors 70 and over, higher prices for weekend and peak ski days) has four ski lifts covering 27 trails on 250 acres: 7 beginner trails, 12 intermediate trails, 8 expert trails, and 2 terrain parks. The area receives an average of 245 inches (622 cm) annually, with a base elevation of 8,798 feet (2,682 m) and summit of 9,663 feet (2,945 m).

While Laramie is not known as a cross-country ski destination, there are miles upon miles of groomed trails just 15 minutes from town. **Tie City** and **Happy Jack Trailheads,** which give skiers access to some 30 miles (48 km) of trails, are found off I-80, exit 323, then north on Happy Jack Road for 1 mile (1.6 km). A $5 parking fee is required. More information and maps for these trails and others can be found online at www.visitlaramie. org and www.medicinebownordic.org. A terrific store for all kinds of gear, daily or weekly rentals, ski-tuning services, and first-rate advice for Nordic skiers is **Laramie's Basecamp** (220 S. 2nd St., 307/703-0172, www.laramiesbasecamp.com, 9am-6pm Tues.-Sun.). They have another location for ski stone-grinding services (1404 Skyline, 307/703-0358, by appointment).

Spectator Sports

When it comes to recreation, one cannot forget that Laramie is a college town and somewhat fanatical about its football. Attending a **Wyoming Cowboys** game at War Memorial Stadium (E. Grand Ave. and N. 22nd St.) is a true Wyoming experience. It's likely the only place in Wyoming you'll ever feel crowded. For schedule and tickets, contact the **Athletic Ticket Office** (307/766-7220, www. gowyo.com).

Recreation Centers

When the wind blows in Laramie, and it will, the **Laramie Community Recreation Center** (920 Boulder Dr., 307/721-5269, www. cityoflaramie.org, 5am-8pm Mon.-Fri., 7am-6pm Sat., 11am-6pm Sun., nonmember fitness class $8 adults, daily visit $6.50 adult 29-59, $6.25 seniors 60 and over, $5.50 children 12-19, $3.75 children 3-11, free for kids under 3) offers an indoor leisure pool, an eight-lane lap pool, an outdoor pool with water slides and a lazy river, a full-court gymnasium, weights, an indoor playground, and an abundance of classes and activities. Check the website for pool and gym hours.

When winter comes to town, the **Laramie Community Ice and Event Center** (3510 Garfield St., 307/721-2161, www.cityoflaramie. org, 5:30am-8am and 11:30am-10pm Mon., 5:30am-8am and 2:45pm-10pm Tues. and Thurs., 6am-7am and 11:30am-10pm Wed.,

11:30am-10pm Fri., 10am-10pm Sat., 10am-8pm Sun., weekly schedules posted online, $5 nonresident adults, $2.50 children 5 and under, drop-in figure skating $7 nonresidents, drop-in hockey $7 nonresident adults 18 and up) offers ice-skating, private skating lessons, broomball, curling, and skate rentals. When there is no ice (mid-Mar.-Sept., usually), roller-skating is available.

ENTERTAINMENT AND EVENTS

With such a young, vibrant population, Laramie has loads of events going on year-round. From scholarly lectures on campus to concerts and meditation gatherings, offerings are plentiful and diverse. A great way to get warmed up to the history of the region is with the living history tour **Legends of Laramie** (www.visitlaramie.org), available on your smartphone or tablet. Organized by the Albany County Tourism Board, the tour includes 16 stops around Laramie highlighting everything from railroad romances and shootouts to the Bucket of Blood Saloon.

On Wednesday nights throughout summer, the **Laramie Municipal Band,** made up primarily of students and teachers from the university, puts on free concerts in Washington Park (Sheridan St. between S. 18th St. and S. 21st St.) starting at 7:30pm. On Fridays July-September, the town comes downtown for the weekly and festive **farmers market** (307/742-3774, parking lot north of Depot Park on S. 1st St., www.laramiemainstreet.org, 3pm-7pm). For cultural events held throughout the year at the university, including the **University of Wyoming Symphony Orchestra,** theater and dance performances, and major concerts, contact the **Fine Arts Box Office** (307/766-6666, www.uwyo.edu/finearts).

Since 1940, **Laramie Jubilee Days** (www. laramiejubileedays.com) has been the annual hometown celebration that draws revelers from across the region. Often scheduled in the week leading up to the anniversary of Wyoming's statehood on July 10, the event offers Fourth of July celebrations, including the biggest fireworks display in the state. Other Jubilee Days events include street dances, a classic parade, bull riding, and three nights of professional rodeo.

The **Albany County Fair** is held annually late July-early August at the fairgrounds (3510 S. 3rd St., 307/742-3224, www.albanycountyfair.org) and has all the family-friendly fun visitors expect from a Western fair, including a carnival, entertainment, and 4-H activities.

SHOPPING

While the shopping options are quite varied around town, from marvelous bookstores to hippie outposts and classic Western saddleries, the experience of shopping in Laramie's historic and charming downtown cannot be beat. **The Second Story** (105 E. Ivinson Ave., 307/745-4423, 10am-6pm Mon.-Sat., Sun. during Christmas season only), for example, is a gem of an independent bookstore housed in a public hall built in 1889. Since then, it has been a hotel, a bordello, a saloon, a senior center, and now a bookstore. The children's book selection is particularly good. As a bonus, with every book purchase comes a free espresso drink, made to order. Watch their Facebook page for special events. Right next door, **Night Heron Books & Coffeehouse** (107 E. Ivinson Ave., 307/742-9028, www.nightheronbooks.com, 7am-7pm daily) offers a great selection of rare and used books. Plus, the coffee shop serves up a rotating menu of quiche, soups, sandwiches, and baked goods.

For a delectable treat, stop by **The Chocolate Cellar** (113 Ivinson Ave., 307/742-9278, 10am-6pm Mon.-Sat., noon-4pm Sun.), which has been creating handcrafted goodies since 1982. Plus they have an extensive collection of gifts, including chocolate and candy tins. **Mountain Woods Furniture** (retail shop 206 S. 3rd St., 307/745-3515 or 866/689-6637, www.mountainwoodsfurniture.com, 10am-6pm Mon.-Sat.) sells rustic log furniture handcrafted by artisans from across North America.

Chalk n' Cheese (209 2nd St., 307/742-1800, www.chalkncheesewy.com, 11am-6pm Tues.-Sat.) is a great cheese and gourmet food shop that sells kitchenware and antiques, as well as offering fun cooking classes. Stop by on Thursday and Friday evenings to taste from their elaborate charcuterie platters. Who doesn't want to shop for antiques in the Old West? There are treasures to be found at **Augusta Mizzelwitt's Back of the Wagon Antiques** (207 S. 2nd St., 307/721-3939, 10am-6pm Mon.-Sat.), where you'll find three floors of "a little bit of everything."

Works of Wyoming (300 S. 2nd St., 307/460-3304, www.worksofwyoming.org, 10am-6pm Mon.-Sat.) has an excellent selection of fine art, crafts, and gifts made by Wyoming artists and artisans. **Sweet Pickles** (117 E. Ivinson St., 307/745-4114, 10am-6pm Mon.-Sat., noon-4pm Sun.) is a wonderful spot for kids, with both toys and clothes. And if the shopping wears you out, there's wonderful homemade ice cream at **Big Dipper Ice Cream** (111 E. Ivinson St., 307/460-3358, 11am-8pm Mon.-Sat., noon-8pm Sun.) a few doors down.

FOOD

Like all college towns worth their salt, Laramie has an abundance of good, relatively cheap places to enjoy a meal. For breakfast or lunch, a local favorite is the pink **J's Prairie Rose Café** (410 S. 2nd St., 307/745-8140, 7am-2pm Mon.-Fri., 7am-3pm Sat., 7am-noon Sun., $6-12). The Prairie Rose, as it is known, has the best green chili in town, plus phenomenal breakfast burritos, Philly cheesesteaks, and, like all good diners, homemade pie. Its off-menu specials include everything from Italian dishes to eggs Benedict. Breakfast is served all day.

For a smattering of reasonably priced global cuisine, try ★ **Jeffrey's Bistro** (123 E. Ivinson Ave., 307/742-7046, www.jeffreysbistro.com, 11am-9pm Tues.-Sat., $10-16), which offers hearty salads, creative daily specials like ancho-cherry barbecue chicken or hot-and-spicy Thai shrimp, and delicious entrées such as pot pie, enchiladas, Thai burritos, and jambalaya, many of which can be made vegetarian. For serious vegetarians, **Sweet Melissa Vegetarian Café** (213 S. 1st St., 307/742-9607, 11am-9pm Tues.-Thurs., 11am-10pm Fri.-Sat., $6-14) is like green heaven in the middle of cow country. In fact, their ad hoc motto is "comfort food for the homesick vegetarian." Tons of salads, pastas, and sandwiches are on the menu, as expected, but there are also plenty of gluten-free options as well as good old-fashioned comfort food like smothered sweet potato and black bean burritos, seitan fajitas, caprese linguini, and Thai peanut stir-fry with tofu. There's a kids' menu, and the desserts include specialties like fried banana bread, peanut butter pie, and vegan chocolate cake. Check Facebook for daily specials and events. The fact that Sweet Melissa adjoins a popular watering hole, **Front Street Tavern** (11am-close Mon.-Sat.), is Laramie in a nutshell, and icing on the cake.

Serving upscale brewpub cuisine that ranges from the traditional (hickory burgers, seafood pasta, bacon-wrapped tenderloin, and cedar-plank salmon) to the unusual (Vietnamese barbecue, orange-braised pork loin, and Thai salmon burgers), **Altitude Chophouse & Brewery** (320 S. 2nd St., 307/721-4031, www.altitudechophouse.com, 11am-10pm Mon.-Sat., lunch $8-16, dinner $12-35) perfectly pairs sensational beer with delicious and creative cuisine. There's a kids' menu, plenty of options for vegetarians, and even a vegan menu. For burgers, brews, and wings (12 varieties and 16 sauces!), head to **Born in a Barn** (100 E. Ivinson, 307/460-3604, www.borninabarn307.com, 11am-9pm Sun.-Wed., 11am-10pm Thurs.-Sat., $8-20). Or for burritos and street tacos with a craft cocktail, try **Speedgoat** (213 Grand Ave., 307/460-3396, www.speedgoatlaramie.com, 11am-8pm Tues.-Thurs., 11am-9pm Fri.-Sat., $3.25-16), named for the moniker of the pronghorn antelope.

Set in the lovely, tree-lined university area, **Turtle Rock Coffee & Café** (270 N. 9th St., 307/745-3741, www.turtlerockcoffee.com, 7am-9pm Mon.-Thurs., 7am-8pm Fri.-Sat., 8am-6pm Sun.) serves up yummy sandwiches, pastries, ice cream, and, of course, the requisite college coffee. The outdoor seating is delightful, and the Geological Museum at the University of Wyoming is just steps away.

ACCOMMODATIONS

Laramie has more than 2,000 guest rooms in town, of which several hundred are just a handful of years old. Accommodation options include hotels, motels, bed-and-breakfasts, and guest ranches.

For the best value in town, the **Americas Best Value Inn** (523 S. Adams St., 307/721-8860, www.redlion.com, from $55) offers clean, no-frills guest rooms with air-conditioning and free Wi-Fi. Another good budget option is the **Laramie Valley Inn** (1104 S. 3rd St., 307/742-4200, www.laramievalleyinn.com, $79-109) owned by University of Wyoming alumni. Most of the rooms have been renovated; those that haven't are less expensive. Pets are welcome in a few rooms.

At the other end of the spectrum, the ★ **Hilton Garden Inn** (2229 Grand Ave., 307/745-5500, www.uwconferencecenter.com, $93-236) offers all the frills you are going to find in Laramie. From Egyptian cotton sheets and ergonomic chairs to flat-screen TVs and cushy bathrobes, this hotel sets the standard for luxury. There's also a newer **Fairfield Inn & Suites** (1673 Centennial Dr., 307/460-2100, www.marriott.com, from $104), which offers sitting rooms and pull-out sofas in all their extended suites.

Standard chain hotels in town include the newer **Holiday Inn Laramie** (204 S. 30th St., 307/721-9000, www.ihg.com, from $104), the pet-friendly **Days Inn** (1368 McCue St., 307/745-5678, www.wyndhamhotels.com, $60-195), and **Super 8** (1987 Banner Rd., 307/223-5230, www.wyndhamhotels.com, from $59).

A few unique lodging options are the fabulously quirky **Mad Carpenter**

Inn (353 N. 8th St., 307/742-0870, www. madcarpenterinn.net, $95-125), a B&B near the university where the creative and delightful innkeepers have a passion for carpentry, cooking (a gourmet continental breakfast is included), and poetry. In addition to three rooms, there is a three-bedroom house (from $145/night) available.

For those who want more of the rustic, backwoods-type experience, **Brooklyn Lodge** (3540 Hwy. 130, Centennial, 307/742-6916, www.brooklynlodge.com, from $220) is the ticket. Designated a National Historic Site and set in the Medicine Bow-Routt National Forests right near the ski area, the two rooms with king beds at this bed-and-breakfast are cozy, rustic, and abundantly comfortable. Although pets are not allowed, horses can stay for $25 per night. Also in Centennial, the **Mountainview Historic Hotel** (2747 Hwy. 130, 307/742-3588, www.themountainviewhotel.com, call for rates) has six rooms and a family suite with full kitchen. There's a café and coffee shop on-site and miles of wide-open country just outside the door.

In town right across from the Ivinson Mansion, the two **Mason Loft Condos** (611 E. University Ave., 307/742-4266, www.laramiemuseum.org, call or email djpowell@bresnan.net for rates) are built in the historic stone stable, and each has two bedrooms, a loft with two beds, and 2.5 baths. The structure was built in 1883 and has been completely and beautifully renovated. All proceeds go to the Laramie Plains Museum Association.

CAMPING

There are plenty of fantastic opportunities for camping or renting a cabin in the **Medicine Bow-Routt National Forests,** which surround Laramie to the east (Pole Mountain) and west (Snowy Range). The closest public campgrounds to town are the nicely forested **Yellow Pine Campground** (Forest Rd. 719, 13.2 mi/21.2 km west of Laramie, 307/745-2300, www.fs.usda.gov, $10) and otherworldly **Vedauwoo**

Campground (Vedauwoo Rd., 17.3 mi/27.8 km east of Laramie, 307/745-2300, www.fs.usda.gov, $10). Both campgrounds have potable water.

Equidistant between Laramie and Cheyenne is **Curt Gowdy State Park** (1264 Granite Springs Rd., Cheyenne, 307/632-7946 or 877/996-7275, http://wyoparks.state.wy.us, $7 day use residents, $12 day use nonresidents, camping $17 residents, $30 nonresidents, camping rates include day use), 24 miles (39 km) east of Laramie at the edge of the Laramie Mountains. Historically, the area served as prime hunting and camping grounds for numerous Native American tribes. There are 35 RV sites that can be reserved, 15 with water hookups, none with electricity. The remaining sites are first-come, first-served. Set on three lovely reservoirs, the park offers trout and kokanee salmon fishing as well as hiking and biking trails and prime picnicking spots. Dogs are not permitted off-leash or in the water.

For information on sites in the Laramie Ranger District or other nearby areas, contact the **U.S. Forest Service** (2468 W. Jackson St., 307/745-2300, 8am-4:30pm Mon.-Fri.).

Just north of I-80, the **Laramie KOA** (1271 W. Baker St., 307/742-6553 or 800/562-4153, www.koa.com) has tent sites ($34-41), RV sites ($45-73.50), and cabins ($74-85) in addition to free Wi-Fi, organized activities, and a playground.

INFORMATION AND SERVICES

The **Albany County Tourism Board** (210 E. Custer St., 307/745-4195, www.visitlaramie.org, 8am-5pm Mon.-Fri., 9am-1pm Sat. June-Sept., 8am-5pm Mon.-Fri. Oct.-May) operates a convention and visitors bureau and is happy to send a visitors guide in advance of your trip. The **Laramie Area Chamber of Commerce** (528 S. Adams St., 307/745-7339 or 866/876-1012, www.laramie.org, 8am-4:30pm Mon.-Fri.) can provide useful information on local businesses and relocation.

For information on recreation in the

nearby **Medicine Bow-Routt National Forests** and the **Thunder Basin National Grassland,** which are managed by the U.S. Forest Service, visit the **headquarters** (2468 W. Jackson St., 307/745-2371, 8am-4:30pm Mon.-Fri.).

The **Albany County Public Library** (310 S. 8th St., 307/721-2580, www. albanycountylibrary.org, 10am-6pm Thurs.-Tues.) has nine Internet terminals available for free.

The main **post office** can be found at 152 North 5th Street (307/721-8837, 8am-5:15pm Mon.-Fri., 9am-1pm Sat.).

Ivinson Memorial Hospital (255 N. 30th St., 307/742-2141, www.ivinsonhospital.org) offers 24-hour emergency care plus specialized medicine. Another option is **Grand Avenue Urgent Care** (3236 E. Grand Ave., 307/760-8602, www.grandaveurgentcare.com, 9am-8pm Mon.-Fri., 9am-6pm Sat., 9am-4pm Sun.).

This is a college town, with no shortage of laundries, including **Spic and Span Laundromat** (272 N. 4th St., 307/745-3939, 7:30am-10pm daily, last load in by 8:30pm), which offers plasma TVs, Wi-Fi, and double- and triple-load machines.

TRANSPORTATION
Getting There
The **Laramie Regional Airport** (LAR, 555 General Brees Rd., 307/742-4164, www. laramieairport.com) offers daily 40-minute flights to and from Denver on **United Express.**

The only car-rental agency at the airport is **Hertz** (307/745-0500). **Enterprise** (517 S. 3rd St., 307/721-9876) has a location in town.

Greyhound serves Laramie from the Diamond Shamrock Gas Station (1952 Banner Rd.).

By car, Laramie is 49 miles (79 km) west of Cheyenne, 130 miles (209 km) north of Denver, 148 miles (238 km) southeast of Casper, 207 miles (340 km) east of Rock Springs, 380 miles (610 km) southeast of Yellowstone National Park, and 383 miles (620 km) southeast of Jackson.

Getting Around
Laramie's taxi service is provided by **Snowy Range Taxi** (307/343-2323, www. snowyrangetaxi.com, 6pm-6am Tues.-Sat., $12 flat rate within Laramie) and **Laramie Taxi** (307/761-9891, www.laramietaxi.com, $3 pickup and $5 per mile).

Cheyenne

Just a few miles from the Colorado border is Cheyenne (pop. 65,132, elev. 6,062 ft/1,848 m), the state capital and an important historical and modern crossroads. The town was named by the Sioux, who used the word to define another tribe, which we know as the Cheyenne, that they considered alien. A settlement sprang up on July 4, 1867, in advance of the Union Pacific Railroad's arrival; the town's population thrived and culture flourished. Influential people and performers traveling across the West by train often stopped in Cheyenne, making it a rather progressive town. Today I-80 and I-25 cross in Cheyenne,

bringing visitors from every direction into its historic folds.

The city's defining event, Frontier Days, was founded in 1897 and today brings nearly 250,000 people (and 6,000 animals!) to town for 10 days in late July. Cheyenne is still a rodeo town, with one of the only visitor bureaus that lists horse-boarding stables along with hotels and motels. After all, if you're coming to Cheyenne, why not bring your horse?

High and windswept, Cheyenne is not a classic Wyoming beauty in the same way as Jackson or Sheridan, but it has a compelling setting with more urban culture than in most of the state, some wonderful museums, and a smattering of ways to enjoy the great outdoors.

HISTORY

The first makeshift railroad town to be settled in Wyoming was Cheyenne in July 1867. Initially a boisterous, mayhem-filled tent city, it soon began to blossom. By November, when the railroad arrived, it had 4,000 residents and was dubbed the "magic city" for its large population boom. Because Cheyenne was an "end-of-tracks town" for longer than any other Wyoming town, it was marked by rapid growth and lawlessness. Fort D. A. Russell was established nearby, and the military presence helped to settle things down.

In 1869, Cheyenne was named the territorial capital, a title challenged unsuccessfully by Laramie and Evanston. The cornerstone for the Wyoming Capitol was laid in May 1887. After the arrival of both sheep and cattle in the 1870s, Cheyenne became an important shipping center, exporting cattle and supplies to the East and importing the latest fashions and desirables. Thanks to the cattle barons, by the 1880s Cheyenne was considered one of the wealthiest cities per capita in the world.

SIGHTS

As a wonderful prelude to this historic city, jump on the **Cheyenne Street Railway Trolley** (121 W. 15th St., 307/778-3133 or 800/426-5009, www.cheyenne.org/things-to-do/cheyennetrolley, 90-min. tours daily May-Sept., check schedule; 1:30pm Sat. Oct.-Mar., 1:30pm Fri.-Sun. Apr., $15 adults, $6 children 2-12), departing from the beautiful old rail depot (121 W. 15th St.). The ride gives visitors a narrated overview of the city, stopping by many of the best sights, including the Nelson Museum, Wyoming State Museum, the state capitol, Cheyenne Botanic Gardens, Old West Museum, and Historic Governors' Mansion.

Wyoming State Capitol

The cornerstone of the **Wyoming State Capitol** (200 W. 24th St. and Capitol Ave., 307/777-7220, www.wyomingcapitolsquare.com, 8am-5pm Mon.-Fri.) was laid on May 18, 1887, when Wyoming was still a territory. Modeled after the capitol in Washington DC, this National Historic Landmark—one of 20 state capitols designated such—went through various phases of construction, the last being the addition of the senate and house chambers, completed in 1917. The building measures 300 feet in length, and its gold dome is 146 feet high. The capitol underwent a $7.6 million renovation during the 1970s, and the dome has been gilded six times, most recently in 1988. When celebrating its centennial in 1987, the original cornerstone was removed, and the documents that had been buried inside—a map and list of territorial officers, among others—were removed and entrusted to the state archives. In December 2015, the capitol was closed to the public for a nearly four-year restoration. The capitol reopened with much fanfare on July 10, 2019.

Visitors enter the rotunda on the 1st floor and can gaze up three stories to the dome, created from stained glass imported from England. A full video tour is available on YouTube (https://youtu.be/zFJnNwWx0Gw). The governor's office is off the rotunda on the 1st floor. The 2nd floor houses the legislative chambers, decorated by four large Western murals with ceilings of Tiffany stained glass inlaid with the state seal. The balconies on the 3rd floor are always open, and visitors can view the senate and house chambers while they are in session. From the 3rd floor it is also easy to appreciate the Renaissance-revival architecture of the entire building. Don't miss the 1,000-pound Tiffany chandelier in the conference room, and look at the ornate hinges on the large cherrywood doors.

Union Pacific Railroad Depot

At the southern end of Capitol Avenue sits the historic **Union Pacific Railroad Depot**

Cheyenne

To Chugwater and Wheatland

RIDING CLUB

FRANCIS E.

ROUNDTOP RD

FOUR MILE

WARREN

STOREY BLVD

WYOMING GAME AND FISH

BLM OFFICE

EXIT 12

AIR

FRONTIER DAYS

AIRPORT GOLF CLUB

CHEYENNE FRONTIER DAYS OLD WEST MUSEUM

CHEYENNE MUNICIPAL AIRPORT

CHEYENNE COUNTRY CLUB

Lions Park

CENTRAL AVE

Frontier Park

RANDALL AVE

8TH AVE

CHEYENNE BOTANIC GARDENS

FORCE

W PERSHING BLVD

SEE DETAIL

WARREN AVE

CENTRAL AVE

CAREY AVE

BASE

To Curt Gowdy State Park, Bit-O-Wyo Ranch, Bunkhouse Bar and Grill, and Laramie

HAPPY JACK RD

210

FAIRFIELD INN & SUITES SOUTHWEST

LITTLE AMERICA HOTEL RESORT

SUPER 8

LUXURY DINER

9TH ST

CAROL'S CAFÉ

HOLIDAY INN EXPRESS HOTEL & SUITES

ANONG'S THAI

LITTLE AMERICA

To Laramie

80

EXIT 358

EXIT 359

EXIT 8

OTTO RD

PARSLEY BLVD

225

25

87

WYOMING TRAVEL INFORMATION CENTER

AB CAMPGROUND

To Terry Bison Ranch and Denver, CO

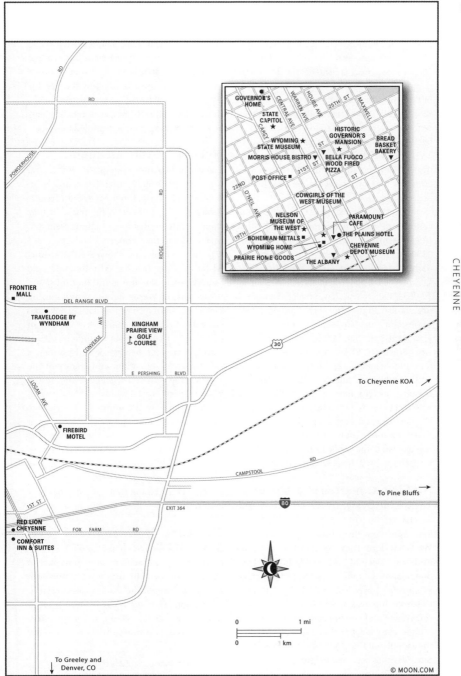

(121 W. 15th St., 307/632-3905, 9am-6:30pm Mon.-Fri., 9am-5pm Sat., 11am-3pm Sun. May-Sept., 9am-5pm Mon.-Fri., 9am-3pm Sat., 11am-3pm Sun. Oct.-Apr.). Built in 1886, this was once considered the finest train depot between Omaha and Sacramento. The building occupies an entire city block and was reopened in 2004 after undergoing a major renovation. It has been restored to its original beauty, and the sandstone structure is worth a visit just to appreciate the architecture and design. During the summer, free evening concerts and other events are held in the depot plaza.

In addition to housing the Cheyenne visitor center and a fun restaurant, **Accomplice Beer Company** (115 W. 15th St., 307/632-2337, www.accomplicebeer.com, 8am-9pm daily, $8-15), the structure is also home to the **Cheyenne Depot Museum** (121 W. 15th St., 307/632-3905, www.cheyennedepotmuseum. org, 9am-6:30pm Mon.-Fri., 9am-5pm Sat., 11am-3pm Sun. May-Sept., 9am-5pm Mon.-Fri., 9am-3pm Sat., 11am-3pm Sun. Oct.-Apr., $8 adults, $7 seniors and military, free for children under 12). The museum focuses on the important role the railroad played in the city's development and to the West as a whole. There are fantastic old photographs, an incredible narrow gauge model railroad that took more than 30 years to build and was opened to the public in 2012, and artifacts from the station's busiest railroad days.

Historic Governors' Mansion

The **Historic Governors' Mansion** (300 E. 21st St., 307/777-7878, 9am-5pm Mon.-Sat., 1pm-5pm Sun. June-Sept., 9am-5pm Wed.-Sat. and Tues. by appointment only mid-Nov.-Dec. 24 and mid-Jan.-May, free, donations welcome) was home to each of Wyoming's governors 1905-1976. Although the mansion was never intended to be a showplace and was intentionally built in a middle-class neighborhood just blocks from the capitol building, today it is a State Historic Site. Visitors will see original decor from 1905, 1937, 1955, and the 1960s. The home was the height of modernity when it was constructed in 1905, with indoor plumbing, hot water, central heating, and electrical and gas fixtures. The most interesting tidbit about this Georgian-style building is that it housed the country's first woman governor, Nellie Tayloe Ross, 1925-1927. Visitors can view a short video about the house and its residents before beginning their self-guided tour.

Wyoming State Museum

The **Wyoming State Museum** (2301 Central Ave., 307/777-7022, http://wyomuseum. state.wy.us, 9am-4:30pm Mon.-Sat., free) is dedicated to documenting the state's history from its earliest inhabitants to the present day. In addition to the permanent collection, 3-4 traveling exhibits are showcased at a time. Always on display are exhibits dedicated to prehistoric Wyoming and its dinosaurs, the wildlife of Wyoming, the state's mining history (including an explanation of how coal is created in nature), and a social history of the state. Other exhibits include beautiful Native American beadwork and pottery, a vast firearms collection, and a copy of the act granting women the right to vote in the Wyoming Territory. A hands-on history room for children is well equipped with vintage clothing, a child-size tipi, a chuck wagon, a dinosaur, and other interactive displays. As you tour the museum, you can dial up an audio tour at 307/316-0077. The museum also holds a free Family Days program geared to younger children the first Saturday of every month.

Cheyenne Frontier Days Old West Museum

Frontier Days is such an important part of Cheyenne's local history that a museum was created to tell the story of this Western celebration. The **Old West Museum** (4610 Carey Ave., 307/778-7290, www.cfdrodeo. com/cfd-old-west-museum, 9am-5pm daily

---

1: Wyoming State Capitol **2:** a chuckwagon at Frontier Days **3:** downtown Cheyenne

year-round, 8am-6pm daily during Frontier Days, $12 adults, $11 seniors and military, $6 children 6-12) is filled with memorabilia from the rodeo and focuses on frontier life in Wyoming. It has more than 150 horse-drawn carriages and wagons dating back over a century, along with large Western art exhibits and some 60,000 artifacts. A fun children's history room has clever interactive displays. The museum has extended hours during the Frontier Days festival and is conveniently located in Frontier Park adjacent to the rodeo. A terrific store is also on-site for gift shopping.

Nelson Museum of the West

If you are interested in viewing more cowboy and Native American memorabilia, head over to the **Nelson Museum of the West** (1714 Carey Ave., 307/635-7670, www. nelsonmuseum.com, 9am-4:30pm Mon.-Sat. June-Aug., 9am-4:30pm Mon.-Fri. May and Sept.-Oct., $5 adults, $4 seniors, free for children under 13). There are more than 20 exhibits created from the eclectic personal collection of Robert C. Nelson, including art of the Plains Indians, firearms of the West, and furnishings from the homes of cattle barons. Look for the stuffed big-game animals scattered throughout the three floors.

Audio tours are available on your phone at 307/316-0069.

Cheyenne Botanic Gardens

Should the days get hot and dusty in Cheyenne, find a stunning oasis at the **Cheyenne Botanic Gardens** (710 S. Lions Park Dr., 307/637-6458, www.botanic.org, grounds dawn-dusk daily, conservatory and children's village 10am-5pm Tues.-Sat. year-round and Sun. noon-5pm June-Aug., free). The plant diversity is stunning, and there is a unique children's village with drop-in activities, a pond and labyrinth, a solar conservatory, community gardens, and more.

★ Fort Laramie National Historic Site

An indelible part of Wyoming's history, **Fort Laramie** (965 Grey Rocks Rd., 307/837-2221, www.nps.gov, 9am-7pm daily Memorial Day-Labor Day, 8am-4pm daily Labor Day-Memorial Day, free) sits at the confluence of the Laramie and North Platte Rivers. It was a major trading center, a military garrison, and the site where the infamous Treaty of 1868 between the U.S. government and the Plains Indians was signed. People from all walks of life, including Native Americans,

Fort Laramie National Historic Site

trappers, missionaries, and homesteaders, passed through the fort during its almost 50 years of existence.

Today there are 22 original structures on the 830 acres of this National Historic Site. The first stop at the fort should be the **visitor center** in the old commissary building. An 18-minute video describes the fort's rich history, and exhibits display artifacts from frontier times, including weapons, uniforms, and historical photos. A free brochure is available to help visitors with a self-guided tour, or experience the audio tour, which includes voices and sounds from the past.

While at the fort, visit the **cavalry barracks,** which give a clear sense of the cramped living quarters of the soldiers, and **Old Bedlam,** initially the fort headquarters and later used as officers' quarters. The officers were known to host wild parties in the building, hence its name. Also on the grounds is an old stone **guardhouse** where prisoners were kept, a model of the original **Fort John** building erected in 1841, and the old fort **bakery.**

To get to the fort from Cheyenne, head north on I-25 for 81 miles (130 km) to US 26 (exit 92) for Guernsey and Torrington. Drive east for 28 miles (45 km), turn right onto Highway 160, and follow the signs. The drive is just over 113 miles (182 km) and should take about an hour and 45 minutes.

SPORTS AND RECREATION

For a city known for its rodeo, Cheyenne has a vast array of recreational opportunities beyond the chutes.

Hiking and Biking

For being in the middle of a high desert, Cheyenne has a remarkable number of green parks to explore and enjoy on two feet or two wheels. The **Greater Cheyenne Greenway** links several of the parks with 39 miles (63 km) of 10-foot-wide (3-meter) paved trails open to hikers and bikers. Sections of trail wind through Crow Creek, Dry Creek, Sun

Valley, Lions Park, and Allison Draw, among other parts of town. The trails also serve as a wildlife corridor, so keep your eyes peeled.

Halfway between Cheyenne and Laramie is **Curt Gowdy State Park** (1264 Granite Springs Rd., Cheyenne, 307/632-7946 or 877/996-7275, http://wyoparks.state.wy.us, $7 day use residents, $12 day use nonresidents, camping $17 residents, $30 nonresidents, camping rates include day use). The park contains more than 35 miles (56 km) of trails connecting three reservoirs as well as four open free-ride areas. The trails were given an Epic designation by the International Mountain Biking Association, and all are open to both hikers and bikers. Among the longer trails are **Canyon's Trail** (5.4 mi/8.7 km), **Stone Temple Circuit** (3.8 mi/6.1 km), **Lariat** (2.9 mi/4.7 km), and **Shoreline** (2.6 mi/4.2 km). The area is also open to horses. A map is available online or at the park. Pets are not permitted in the water at Gowdy, and the area is usually packed on warm weekends with campers and recreationists.

Golf

Cheyenne has a few golf courses, including the 18-hole **Airport Golf Club** (4801 Central Ave., 307/638-3700, $25 for 18 holes, $18 for 9 holes, twilight and off-season discounts), the 9-hole municipal **Kingham Prairie View Golf Course** (3601 Windmill Rd., 307/637-6420, $12), and 9-hole **Little America Golf Course** (2800 W. Lincolnway, 307/775-8500, $23-28 for 9 holes, $38-42 for 18 holes, carts $18 for 9 holes, $28 for 18 holes).

ENTERTAINMENT AND EVENTS
★ Frontier Days

The biggest event in Cheyenne—the biggest in Wyoming—is **Frontier Days** (www.cfdrodeo com), an affair that has been defining Wyoming's capital city since 1897. The largest outdoor rodeo in the country today, the celebration's origins are rather humble. Union Pacific passenger agent F. W. Angier and the editor of the local Cheyenne

The Grand Old Post

Originally built as a fur trading post in 1834, **Fort Laramie** was established as a military fort in 1849 when the U.S. government purchased the old Fort John. As was true of most of the forts across the region, its mission was to ensure the safety of pioneers traveling west on the established trails, the closest of which was the Oregon Trail. The second military fort constructed for this purpose, Fort Laramie was unique in that it was always an open fort, meaning there was no wall or fence enclosing the structures.

In 1854, three years after the Treaty of 1851, which was meant to bring peace between the Native Americans and the United States, 29 soldiers from Fort Laramie, an officer, and an interpreter were killed in the Grattan Fight. The event fueled a new ferocity in the war that raged throughout the 1860s and 1870s between Native Americans and the U.S. military. As the battles grew larger, Fort Laramie was often a staging ground and command post.

By the late 1880s, when the Indian Wars were mostly a thing of the past, Fort Laramie became more of a village than a fort. Trees were planted on the otherwise barren landscape. Boardwalks were built in front of the officers' quarters. In March 1890, when the Union Pacific Railroad was routed south of the fort, with no enemy to fight and no trails to protect, the military decommissioned the fort and sold many of its buildings at auction.

For decades, Fort Laramie existed as a small village, attracting a few curious history buffs, but not much else. Three homesteaders secured and used some of the existing buildings for businesses or agricultural purposes, preventing them from the fate of many of the buildings, which were to be stripped and sold for lumber and other materials. By the numbers, nine original buildings survived by being useful while more than 50 were demolished, moved, or stripped. In 1938, after much wrangling among federal and state officials and private landowners, including a battle over turning the fort into a golf resort, the 214 acres that had once been Fort Laramie were made a national monument. In 1960, the monument was increased to 571 acres and named a National Historic Site by Congress. A great deal of restoration took place at the fort 1950-1970.

Today, visitors can amble around the grounds and peek into several of the restored buildings. Admission is free. A very worthwhile audio tour, including readings from journals of people who lived at the fort, is available at the **visitor center** (9am-7pm daily Memorial Day-Labor Day, 8am-4pm daily Labor Day-Memorial Day). The fort offers a Living History Military Weekend (visit www.nps.gov for dates and details), which brings the fort to life with reenactments and various educational events. The weekend is also the time for the annual Moonlight Tour. Other events throughout the year include Haunted Prison Tours in October and Horse Barn Dinner Theater evenings in summer.

newspaper claimed to have dreamed up the idea based on Greeley, Colorado's "Potato Day."

The first Frontier Days was held on September 23, 1897, and drew a substantial crowd for events that ranged from a bucking horse contest to a mock stagecoach robbery and mock hanging. The troops from Fort Russell lit cannons, and the crowd quickly followed suit by firing their own guns, sending horses and other livestock into a panic. No one was killed, and the event only reinforced Wyoming's reputation for rowdiness.

By far the most popular event at early

Frontier Days was the bucking bronc contest, which allowed ranchers to pit their cowboys against each other to determine who had the best ones. Although riders could use a saddle, they had to wait until the horse came to a complete standstill before finishing their ride. They weren't allowed to hold on to any part of the saddle, but they could fan the horse with their hats, whip it, or use their spurs.

More than 125 years later, Frontier Days carries on with much the same spirit. It is now a 10-day event spanning two weekends. In recent years more than 250,000 people have shown up to attend events that include parades, major rock and country music concerts, free pancake breakfasts, tours of an Indian village, a Western art show, a carnival, dances, and nine days of PRCA rodeo. This event has clearly earned its nickname, "the daddy of 'em all."

The event is held annually the last two weekends in July at the rodeo grounds (4610 Carey Ave.) and around town. For more information, contact the **Frontier Days office** (307/778-7222, www.cfdrodeo.com, 9am-5pm Mon.-Fri.).

Other Events

At the end of May and beginning of June is the **Hispanic Festival** (www.facebook.com/HispanicFestival), celebrating Hispanic culture with educational exhibits, games, mariachis, food and craft vendors, and live performances. It's free and fun for the whole family.

Happening over a weekend each year in mid-June, Cheyenne gathers on the beautiful Depot Plaza to celebrate beer at the **Wyoming Brewers Festival** (www.wyobrewfest.com). The event includes a delicious Taster's Party, which pairs beer with food from Cheyenne's varied culinary scene. There is live music both nights and plenty of festivities. The proceeds from this event benefit the Cheyenne Depot.

For 13 days in early August, the **Laramie County Fair** (3801 Archer Pkwy., 307/633-4670, www.laramiecountyfair.com), which calls itself the oldest and largest county fair in the state, offers up family entertainment with everything from a demolition derby and dock diving for dogs to horse events and 4-H. After all the flash and sparkle of Frontier Days, the Laramie County Fair is bunny shows over bronc riding, a refreshingly traditional small-town event.

In mid-August, the **Cheyenne Arts Celebration** (www.artscheyenne.com, 307/222-4091) is a three-day event with artist booths, live music, food trucks, and art workshops.

SHOPPING

Because of its size, Cheyenne has plenty of the major superstores, but there are also some smaller and wonderful boutiques to check out. **Bohemian Metals** (314 W. 17th St., 307/778-8782, www.facebook.com/BohemianMetals, 10am-6pm Mon.-Fri., 10am-5pm Sat.) specializes in handmade jewelry, including vintage Native American pieces, gemstones and minerals, and fossils.

A wonderful place for browsing and shopping is the **Cowgirls of the West Museum & Emporium** (205 W. 17th St., 307/638-4994, www.cowgirlsofthewestmuseum.com, 11am-4pm Tues.-Fri., 11am-3pm Sat. May-Aug., extended hours during Frontier Days, free), a nonprofit museum dedicated to informing visitors about the contribution that women made to the settlement of the Old West and the contributions being made by women today. The gift shop features Wyoming-made collectibles, jewelry, Western art, antiques, and wonderful kids' items. In a beautiful, historic building, **Wyoming Home** (216 W. Lincolnway, 307/638-2222, www.wyominghome.com, 9am-6pm Mon.-Fri., 9am-5pm Sat., noon-5pm Sun. summer, 10am-6pm Mon.-Fri., 10am-5pm Sat. fall-spring) has an enormous selection of Wyoming-made gifts and housewares. Another wonderful spot for Wyoming gifts is **Prairie House Home Goods** (309 W. Lincolnway, 307/369-2004, www.prairiehousehomegoods.com, 10am-5:30pm Tues.-Fri., 11am-4pm Sat.), which is an elegant, clean space showcasing candles, clothing, bath and body, Wyoming-made gifts, pocketknives, gourmet foods, antiques, and more.

The largest shopping mall in the region is **Frontier Mall** (1400 Dell Range Blvd., 307/638-2290, www.frontiermall.com, 10am-9pm Mon.-Sat., 11am-6pm Sun.), which has more than 80 stores.

FOOD

As Wyoming's largest city by far, Cheyenne has quite a few restaurants and no shortage of chain establishments to choose from, and there are some wonderful gems worth seeking out. As an important aside, the city's tourism website is the only one I've ever seen with a restaurant category for "bison on the menu." You gotta love Wyoming!

One of the best local spots for breakfast or lunch is **Luxury Diner** (1401 W. Lincolnway, 307/514-0488, 6am-2pm Mon.-Thurs., 6am-3pm Fri.-Sun., breakfast $5-12, lunch $8-14), a tiny railroad-themed place announced by a "Wyoming Motel" sign nearly as large as the restaurant. Supposedly, the place operated as a trolley on the mean streets of Cheyenne from 1894 to 1912. Today it's crowded but completely delightful, and the food explains the wait; try the corned beef hash and eggs or Santa Fe breakfast burrito. The **Bread Basket Bakery** (1819 Maxwell Ave., 307/432-2525, www.breadbasketbakery.com, 6am-4pm Tues.-Fri., 7am-3pm Sat., $3.50-10.25) offers wonderfully fresh pastries, breads, cakes, and other goodies along with a selection of sandwiches and soups. Serving breakfast, lunch, early supper, and espresso all day in a classic movie theater, the **Paramount Café** (1607 Capitol Ave., 307/634-2576, www.paramountcafecheyenne.com, 7:30am-5pm Mon.-Sat., 9am-5pm Sun.) offers a great taste of Cheyenne, and right next door, the **Paramount Ballroom** serves some of the city's best craft cocktails and small plates. Another good spot for a quick bite, cup of joe, or delicious frappe is **Carol's Café** (2800 W. Lincolnway, 307/775-8400, www.cheyenne.littleamerica.com, 6am-3pm daily) in the Little America Hotel & Resort. You might have seen billboards across the state touting their 75-cent cones.

Just across from the historic depot on the corner of 15th and Capitol, **The Albany** (1506 Capitol Ave., 307/638-3507, www.albanycheyenne.com, 11am-2pm and 5pm-9pm Mon.-Sat., $12-31) has been serving locals since 1942. Owned by the same family all those years, The Albany looks more charming from the outside than it does the inside, but the food is good and hearty, from burgers, salads, sandwiches, and Mexican fare to steaks, chops, and seafood. The chicken-fried steak and Jack Daniel's bread pudding earn regular raves. There are extensive offerings for vegetarians and gluten-free sandwiches. Another old Cheyenne standby is the **Bunkhouse Bar & Grill** (1064 Happy Jack Rd., 307/632-6184, www.bunkhousebar.com, 11am-9pm Sun. and Wed.-Thurs., 11am-11:30pm Fri.-Sat., burrito drive-through open 5:30am-9:30am Mon.-Fri., lunch $8-17, dinner $10-30), which has been dishing up such classic Western fare as Rocky Mountain oysters, steak sandwiches, beef Wellington, and country fried steak since 1898. This is a Western honky-tonk, a good old-fashioned Wyoming roadhouse.

Despite the fact that **Anong's Thai** (620 Central Ave., 307/638-8597, www.anongthai.com, 11am-3pm and 5pm-9pm Mon. and Wed.-Sat., 11am-3pm and 5pm-8pm Sun., $12-20) looks like a strip club from the outside, with only two tinted windows and lots of attention-grabbing signage, the dishes here are authentically delicious, and the service is excellent. Anong's Thai has two other locations, one in Laramie and the other in Rawlins. Thai food lovers won't be disappointed by the big menu and wonderful cuisine at any of the three. Travelers with a hankering for Neapolitan thin-crust pizza will do well at **Bella Fuoco Wood Fired Pizza** (2115 Warren Ave., 307/514-2855, www.bellafuocopizza.com, 11am-2pm and 5pm-9pm Tues.-Fri., 5pm-9pm Sat., $9-25). Like Anong's, this restaurant doesn't look like much from the outside, but the artisan pizza, pasta, calzones, paninis, and more are mouthwatering.

For a rustic Western dinner theater experience, try the **Bit-O-Wyo Ranch Horse Barn Dinner Show** (470 Happy Jack Rd., 307/638-6924, 6pm Sat. July-Aug., and Wed. during Frontier Days, call for pricing, reservations required), which includes a classic chuck wagon dinner of steak, baked beans, and applesauce, followed by a two-hour performance of cowboy music and comedy.

The entire season is often sold out by July so be sure to book ahead.

ACCOMMODATIONS

A cornerstone of the Cheyenne community since 1911, **The Historic Plains Hotel** (1600 Central Ave., 307/638-3311 or 866/275-2467, www.facebook.com/thehistoricplainshotel, from $150) is a handsome establishment with 130 lovely rooms and suites. The hotel is decorated with art by Wyoming artists and offers a full restaurant, **Taste of the Plains and Wigwam**, a bar, coffee shop, and an on-site fitness center and spa. A multimillion-dollar renovation in 2003 restored the hotel to its glory, and The Historic Plains is an excellent value for your money in Cheyenne.

The official home of the governor in the 1930s, the **Governor's Home** (108 W. 27th St., 307/222-8267, www.governorshome.com, rooms from $210, entire villa from $390/night) is a comfortable and unassuming boutique hotel. There are four rooms, each with Wi-Fi and smart TVs, plus a living room, dining room, and fully equipped kitchen. Once you book one or more rooms, the hotel will not be available to other guests. The more rooms you book, the less expensive your individual room rate. Set in a quiet residential neighborhood not far from the capitol, this home makes a wonderful home base for families and people traveling together.

Undoubtedly one of the coolest signs at any motel just about anywhere is the one at the **Firebird Motel** (1905 E. Lincolnway, 307/632-5505, call for current rates). The dated rooms are as basic as can be, and the motel has been hit hard by the economic downturn, but the sign is worth seeing. A good and more reliable budget-friendly choice in town is the **Travelodge by Wyndham** (1625 Stillwater Ave., 307/274-3666, from $76).

Cheyenne also has comfortable, convenient chain hotels. Both the **Red Lion Cheyenne** (204 W. Fox Farm Rd., 307/638-4466, www.redlion.com, from $97) and **Holiday Inn Express Hotel & Suites** (1741 Fleischli Pkwy., 307/433-0751 or 800/315-2621, www.

ihg.com, from $103) are good choices. **Comfort Inn & Suites** (201 W. Fox Farm Rd., 307/514-6051, www.choicehotels.com, from $87) and **Super 8** (1900 W. Lincolnway, 307/635-8741, www.wyndhamhotels.com, from $71) are a bit more budget-friendly.

Both close to the downtown area, **Fairfield Inn & Suites Southwest** (1820 W. Lincolnway, 307/634-0401 www.marriott.com, from $107) and the pet-friendly **Tru by Hilton & Suites** (423 W. Fox Farm Rd., 307/2222-3600, www.hilton.com, from $106) were built in 2016 and 2017, and are newer, sleeker, and more upscale.

The website for the **Cheyenne Convention and Visitors Bureau** (800/228-6063, www.cheyenne.org) has a handy tool where travelers can input their Frontier Days travel dates starting around March to see all available accommodations in the city.

CAMPING

Thanks to the massive numbers of people that roll into town for Frontier Days, Cheyenne has abundant RV and tent campgrounds, not all of which are necessarily great. Among those that are really special is ★ **Curt Gowdy State Park** (1264 Granite Springs Rd., Cheyenne, 307/632-7946 or 877/996-7275, http://wyoparks.state.wy.us, $7 day use residents, $12 day use nonresidents, camping $17 residents, $30 nonresidents, camping rates include day use), 24 miles (39 km) west of Cheyenne, at the edge of the Laramie Mountains. There are 35 sites that can be reserved, 15 RV sites with water hookups, none with electricity, and the remaining sites are first-come, first-served. In addition to camping and picnicking spots, the park—set on three lovely reservoirs—offers trout and kokanee salmon fishing as well as hiking and biking trails. Remember that all dogs must be leashed in the park and are not allowed on the beaches or in the water.

Another worthwhile camping spot, particularly for families with children, is the **Terry Bison Ranch Campground** (51 E. I-25 Service Rd. E., 307/634-4171, www.

terrybisonranch.com), just 7 miles (11 km) south of Cheyenne. There is an abundance of activities available, including horseback riding, fishing, train tours to see the ranch's population of bison, ostriches, and camels, and even bison hunts in winter. With a restaurant on-site, the place is fully self-contained. Accommodation options include cabins ($120, or $250 during Frontier Days), 84 full-hookup RV sites ($55/night year-round, $100 during events, and $125/night during Frontier Days), dry, water/electric, and big rig sites ($40-65/night year-round, $42-135 during Frontier Days), and tent sites ($40-42/night year-round, $100/night during events). You can board your horse here too. Indoor stalls are $25/night and outdoor stalls are $20/night. Wood chips are $10/bag, and after-hours check-in (7pm summer, 5pm fall-spring) is $25 or $100 if you and your steed arrive after midnight.

Other options right in Cheyenne are the nicely shaded **A.B. Campground** (1503 W. College Dr., 307/634-7035, www.campcheyenne.com, Apr.-mid-Oct., $23 tent sites, $44-55 RV sites), which offers nightly barbecues, and **Cheyenne KOA** (8800 Archer Frontage Rd., 307/638-8840 or 800/562-1507, www.koakampgrounds.com, $37-44 tent sites, $56-63 RV sites, from $85 cabins w/o bathrooms), which has an outdoor swimming pool in summer.

INFORMATION AND SERVICES

Cheyenne's well-organized convention and visitors bureau has a downtown **visitor center** (121 W. 15th St., Ste. 202, 307/778-3133 or 800/426-5009, www.cheyenne.org, 8am-7pm Mon.-Fri., 9am-5pm Sat., 11am-3pm Sun. summer, 8am-5pm Mon.-Fri., 9am-1pm Sat. fall-spring).

The **Southeast Wyoming Welcome Center** (5611 High Plains Rd., 307/777-7777 or 800/225-5996, 8am-5pm daily June-Sept., 7:30am-4:30pm daily Oct.-May) is headquartered at the rest area at exit 4 on I-25 and offers abundant parking, a dump station, fresh water, clean bathrooms, picnic tables, and more information than you could possibly take in.

The main downtown **post office** (307/772-7080, 7:30am-5:30pm Mon.-Fri.) is at 2120 Capitol Avenue.

The **Laramie County Library** (307/634-3561, www.lclsonline.org, 10am-9pm Mon.-Thurs., 10am-6pm Fri.-Sat., 1pm-5pm Sun.) is at 2200 Pioneer Avenue.

The **Cheyenne Regional Medical Center** (214 E. 23rd St., 307/634-2273, www.cheyenneregional.org) is a major medical facility with 24-hour emergency care. Another option is **NextCare Urgent Care** (2030 Bluegrass Cir., 307/635-3500, 7am-7pm Mon.-Fri., www.nextcare.com, 8am-5:30pm Sat.-Sun.).

Wash clothes at **Easy Way Laundry** (900 W. Lincolnway, 307/638-2177, 8am-9pm daily).

TRANSPORTATION
Getting There

Though commercial service ended for a while starting in 2018, as of November 2021, the **Cheyenne Regional Airport** (CYS, 200 E. 8th Ave., 307/634-7071, www.cheyenneairport.com) offers two flights daily to Denver on United Express. For regular shuttle service to Denver, contact **Groome Transportation** (307/459-4433 or 888/472-6656, www.greenrideco.com, $57 one-way, reservations required), which offers four shuttles per day.

Car rentals are available at the airport from **National** (307/635-1909) and **Hertz** (307/634-2131). **Enterprise** has an agency in town.

By car, Cheyenne is 49 miles (79 km) east of Laramie, 100 miles (161 km) north of Denver, 256 miles (410 km) east of Rock Springs, 291 miles (465 km) southwest of Rapid City, 393 miles (635 km) southeast of Cody, 429 miles (690 km) southeast of Yellowstone National Park, and 456 miles (735 km) southeast of Billings.

Daily bus service in and out of Cheyenne

is provided from the Super Pumper Sinclair Station by **Greyhound** (3306 W. College Dr., 307/635-1327, www.greyhound.com) and **Express Arrow** (3306 W. College Dr., 877/779-2999, www.expressarrow.com).

Getting Around

Local public transportation is available in Cheyenne from **Cheyenne Transit** (307/637-6253, www.cheyennecity.org). Taxi companies include **Cowboy Shuttle** (307/638-2468) and **TI Shuttle** (307/778-4066).

Sweetwater County

Sweetwater County in the southwest corner of Wyoming is a mix of the desert Southwest—think kaleidoscopic rock formations, mesas, and canyons—and the rugged Western appeal of rodeo, wild mustangs, and vast open spaces. Though not a tourist destination in the way that northwest Wyoming is—the region is shifting with the boom-and-bust of the energy sector—this part of the state offers constant and abundant recreational opportunities. This is not so much cowboy country as mining country, mountain biking country, and river rafting country.

A high-alpine desert, Rock Springs (pop. 23,526, elev. 6,271 ft/1,911 m) parallels Gillette in some ways—it is in the thick of an energy boom-and-bust cycle—but it is located next to some pretty phenomenal country, including the unrivaled and scenic **Flaming Gorge National Recreation Area.** The city itself has a few good museums and an interesting international flavor that dates back to coal mining and railroad development around the turn of the 20th century.

Green River (pop. 11,439, elev. 6,109 ft/1,862 m) is an old railroad town that got its start as a station along the Overland and Pony Express routes. It has a rather industrial history spanning the railroads and mines in the region, but it is best known for its namesake river, which runs right through town. The Green River forms the headwaters of the Colorado River basin and was for years a prime shipping route for timber. Major John Wesley Powell launched two of his biggest expeditions from here, including his first into the unexplored Grand Canyon in 1869.

Surrounded by magnificent multicolored buttes and outcroppings, the town is still very much centered around the river and a popular launching spot for raft and kayak expeditions.

SIGHTS
Museums

There are a number of museums in this region worth a visit. The **Sweetwater County Historical Museum** (3 E. Flaming Gorge Way, Green River, 307/872-6435, www.sweetwatermuseum.org, 10am-6pm Mon.-Sat. mid-May-mid-Oct., 9am-5pm Tues.-Sat. mid-Oct.-mid-May, free) will surprise visitors with its vast and thorough displays. The museum has done a good job of documenting the history of the region and exhibits many artifacts from the daily life of ranchers, miners, and the numerous immigrants who came here. Visitors can see everything from a dinosaur's fossilized footprint to a rifle from Butch Cassidy's gang to an RCA Victor Victrola phonograph and a wedding dress from 1903. There is also an engaging video and display about the horrific Chinese Massacre in Rock Springs.

In Rock Springs, the **Rock Springs Historical Museum** (201 B St., 307/362-3138, www.rswy.net, 10am-5pm Mon.-Sat., free) is situated in the stately city hall, built from sandstone in 1894 for a total cost of $28,200. The museum documents the city's diverse immigrant population, its coal-mining history, and the illegal activity and outlaws it also attracted. The **Western Wyoming Community College Natural History Museum and Weidner Wildlife Museum**

(2500 College Dr., 307/382-1600, 8am-10pm daily Sept.-May., 8am-10pm Mon.-Thurs. June-Aug., free) houses a small collection of fossils, minerals, replica Moai statues like those on Easter Island, and Native American artifacts from the area. A large number of big-game heads and full-body mounts from around the world are on display in the Weidner Wildlife Museum. The **Community Fine Arts Center** (400 C St., 307/362-6212, www.cfacf4art.com, 10am-6pm Mon.-Thurs., noon-5pm Fri.-Sat., free) is an unexpected gem with works by Norman Rockwell, Conrad Schwiering, and Grandma Moses, among other prominent American artists.

Pilot Butte Wild Horse Scenic Tour

There are 1,100-1,600 wild horses roaming the stark landscape of the 392,000-acre **White Mountain Herd Management Area** around Rock Springs and Green River. Although they can often be spotted from I-80, a scenic road affords better opportunities for wild horse sightings. County Road 53 can be accessed either from Rock Springs or Green River; it is a 24-mile (39-km) gravel road that takes about 90 minutes to drive as it winds across the White Mountains with spectacular vistas. The most likely view of the horses comes between Rock Springs and 14-Mile Hill and all the way across the top of White Mountain. Early morning and late afternoon are the best times to view wildlife. The road is only open May-October. For more information about the scenic drive, contact the Bureau of Land Management's **Rock Springs Field Office** (280 Hwy. 191 N., 307/352-0256, www.blm.gov).

Rich Nobles and Mark Rasmussen of **Light Chase Wild Horse Tours** (307/875-2923 or 307/875-5711, www.wildhorsephoto.com, call for schedule and rates) work hard to get their guests views of the iconic wild mustangs for the best photo ops. They take aspiring photographers off the normal route in Nobles's imported all-terrain vehicle to

view the wildlife up close. Single-day trips usually cover about 70 miles (113 km) and can last up to six hours. Multiday and custom trips are available too. You'll learn fascinating facts about wild versus feral horses, and how to tell the difference. And you may go home with some breathtaking shots.

White Mountain Petroglyphs

Some 26 miles (42 km) north of Rock Springs on County Road 4-17 is one of the state's premier rock art sites, the **White Mountain Petroglyphs**. On a 300-foot cliff, hundreds of images—portraying everything from bison and elk hunts to geometric shapes and even tiny footprints—tell the stories of the Plains and Great Basin Indians who lived and traveled through the region as many as 1,000 years ago. Depictions of horses and swords suggest the natives' first contact with Europeans. The site is remote and primitive with no facilities. Pack plenty of water and food. Four-wheel drive is recommended, and you will be on foot for the last 0.25 mile (0.4 km) to the site. For more information, contact the Bureau of Land Management's **Rock Springs Field Office** (280 Hwy. 191 N., 307/352-0256, www.blm.gov).

Seedskadee National Wildlife Refuge

The **Seedskadee National Wildlife Refuge** (307/875-2187, www.fws.gov) sits along 36 miles (58 km) of the Green River and encompasses more than 26,000 acres of land. The Shoshone first called the Green River "Sisk-a-dee-agie," or "River of the Prairie Chicken." Fur traders changed the name to Seedskadee. The refuge consists of marshes, wetlands, and uplands, and more than 200 different bird species have been sighted in the area. The riparian areas have become important nesting grounds for migratory birds, including Canada geese, great blue herons, and swans. In springtime, the prairie is filled with the strange pops and whistles of the greater sage-grouse males, pining for mates. The

The Chinese Massacre

MINING AT ROCK SPRINGS AND CARBON

Mining was essential to the success of the Union Pacific Railroad: Closed mines threatened coal supplies and trains required a steady supply of fuel to meet their schedules. In 1875, when miners in Rock Springs and Carbon organized to demand better wages, their strike shut down Union Pacific's two largest mines. It was no surprise the railroad looked for a quick yet cheap solution. Until this point, all the miners in Rock Springs had been white, but two weeks after the strike started, Union Pacific brought in 150 Chinese men to work the mines. By month's end, some 50 white miners had returned to work, strike organizers had been fired, and the two races were expected to work side by side. Although there was underlying resentment and racism—Chinese miners worked for less, plus this was the era when the Chinese Exclusion Act of 1882, restricting immigration and barring those already in the country from obtaining U.S. citizenship, was passed—tensions did not come to a head until a decade later.

RISING TENSION

By 1885 the number of Chinese miners outnumbered whites as much as 2:1. Since they were paid by the ton, mine assignments were important. On September 2, some white miners were upset that Chinese miners had been assigned to prime areas. They met the Chinese men outside the mine and prevented them from entering. The altercation quickly turned violent, with one Chinese miner dying from his injuries. The mob mentality quickly picked up momentum. Many Chinese victims were scalped, mutilated, dismembered, and even burned alive. In an effort to escape the violence, many Chinese miners fled into the surrounding desert.

VIOLENCE AND RACISM

The white miners entered Chinatown, attacking its occupants and setting fire to the buildings. The entire neighborhood burned to the ground: 79 homes were destroyed, 28 Chinese people were killed, and 15 were injured. The violence shocked the nation, but it also ignited anti-Chinese violence in other small towns in the West. Reaction in Wyoming was mixed. The local newspaper supported the attacks; other papers criticized the massacre while empathizing with the plight of the white miners. The territorial governor, Francis E. Warren, requested federal help to restore peace.

When the mines reopened, 45 men were fired for their role in the violence. Sixteen men were arrested and held in Green River. Although a grand jury was called, no indictments were handed out, and the men were released a month later to a heroes' welcome.

REPARATION ATTEMPTS

The only form of justice came as a response by the U.S. government to appease the Chinese government. With much finagling, President Grover Cleveland persuaded Congress to issue financial compensation to China for $149,000. During the 1920s and 1930s, the Union Pacific Coal Company paid retirement packages and purchased tickets for retired miners to return to China. Only one of the miners chose to live his final days in Rock Springs.

For more information on the Chinese Massacre or other episodes in Wyoming's storied history, visit www.wyohistory.org, an outstanding resource.

refuge is a popular spot for fishing, wildlife-viewing, and short float trips. It is 37 miles (60 km) north of Green River on Highway 372. The refuge headquarters is just 2 miles (3.2 km) north of the junction of Highways 372 and 28.

Killpecker Sand Dunes

Thirty-seven miles (60 km) from Rock Springs is one of Wyoming's most unique natural wonders, complete with a herd of rare desert elk not found anywhere else in the United States. The 109,000-acre **Killpecker Sand**

Dunes are the largest active dunes in the United States. The massive hills of white sand stretch more than 55 miles (89 km) and offer a fun playground for hikers. They're known as "singing" sand dunes because the grains are rounder and more polished than others, and when the wind passes over or a person walks across the sand, the sliding movement creates a rare "singing" sound.

There are two wilderness study areas in the dunes—Buffalo Hump and Sand Dunes—but elsewhere on the shifting sands, off-road vehicle enthusiasts can explore this natural playground. However, go prepared with water, food, a compass, and a map—people can easily get disoriented in the desert setting. If approaching the dunes from Rock Springs, you will pass the area office of the **Bureau of Land Management** (280 US 191 N., Rock Springs, 307/352-0256); it's worth stopping in to get more information and a map of the area. Don't forget to ask about the wild horses and how you can have the best chance of seeing them in their desert habitat. Sightings often occur in the Leucite Hills area.

Also at the dunes, rock-climbing enthusiasts and photographers alike will enjoy a visit to the volcanic plug known as **Boar's Tusk.** This towering rock formation measures 400 feet in height; Devils Tower is the only other geological feature like this in the state.

Fossil Butte National Monument

Known as "America's Aquarium in Stone," **Fossil Butte National Monument** (864 Chicken Creek Rd., Kemmerer, 80 mi/129 km west of Green River, 307/877-4455, www.nps.gov, free) sits in the middle of what was once a subtropical habitat. During the Eocene epoch, 50 million years ago, this was a large lake area, home to alligators, turtles, fish, and even palm trees. Over the eons, animal and plant remains sank to the bottom of the lake bed, where they were covered with sediment

and fossilized. When the lake dried up and the bed was eventually pushed to the surface, some of the best-preserved fossils in the world were revealed.

The **visitor center** (8am-4:30pm daily May-Memorial Day, 8am-5:30pm daily Memorial Day-Labor Day, 8am-4:30pm daily Labor Day-Oct., 8am-4:30pm Mon.-Sat. Nov.-Apr.) displays more than 80 fossils, including two types of bats, numerous species of fish, and even a 13-foot crocodile. There is also an area where visitors can handle the fossils and make rubbings of them. During summer, experts conduct fossil preparation demonstrations and take questions from the public. Two short trails take visitors through the unique history of the park and allow for some wildlife-viewing. From late June through August, plan to visit 11am-3pm Friday-Saturday to assist paleontologists as they collect fossils at the research quarry. Plan to spend about 90 minutes at the quarry, and note that there are no bathrooms and no shade. Bring your own water, sunscreen, and bug repellent.

★ Flaming Gorge National Recreation Area

The **Flaming Gorge National Recreation Area** is full of beautiful rock formations, spectacular land, and rich natural colors. The area was aptly named by a group led by John Wesley Powell, who started their famous journey down the Green River from where the town of Green River now stands. The explorers floated through the rocky canyons and were stunned by the striking red hues, particularly in Utah.

The area consists of more than 200,000 acres and crosses southwestern Wyoming into northeastern Utah. The landscape in Wyoming is primarily high desert, and the more impressive and dramatic sights are found over the border in Utah. Three roads—Highway 530, US 191, and UT 44—connect to form a loop around the national recreation area. The visitor center is on the Utah side at Red Canyon.

1: Fossil Butte National Monument 2: Killpecker Sand Dunes

Flaming Gorge National Recreation Area

Activity in Wyoming is largely based around the 91-mile-long (147-km) **Flaming Gorge Reservoir,** with more than 300 miles (485 km) of shoreline. Constructed in 1964, the reservoir is a popular destination for waterskiing, fishing, camping, and boating. Its trout-filled waters make it an attractive year-round fishing spot; licenses can be bought in Wyoming or Utah. There are also campgrounds nearby (43 campgrounds with 700 individual sites and more than 30 group sites in the entire recreation area) and many boat launches around the reservoir.

If approaching the reservoir from Highway 530 south of Green River, the road follows the west side of the lake just a few miles from the shore. Various dirt-road turnoffs lead to the water, and many end at isolated beaches where you can camp for free. There are also commercial services, including **Lucerne**

Valley Marina (5570 E. Lucerne Valley Rd., off Hwy. 530, 435/784-3483, 8am-6pm daily in season, www.flaminggorge.com) and **Buckboard Marina** (Hwy. 530, 25 mi/40 km south of Green River in McKinnon, 307/875-6927, www.buckboardmarina.com), that take visitors to the recreation area's campsites and docks. If you continue south, heading to Utah, the road passes **Haystack Buttes,** rocky mound-like formations that resemble haystacks, and **Devil's Playground,** a barren badlands of rough terrain.

The loop can also be started at US 191, heading south from Rock Springs. This approach is more mountainous and therefore more scenic, but it is also farther from the reservoir. Early on, a paved road turnoff will take you to **Firehole Canyon.** Here you can see the rocky spires known as **North and South Chimney Rocks** and other interesting geological features. US 191 continues south, climbing 8,000 vertical feet (2,438 m), and has good views of the rolling hills and valleys to the east and west. From here the reservoir is about 15 miles (24 km) from the road. However, when crossing Spring Creek, the water becomes visible, and there is a turnoff leading 4 miles (6.4 km) to the shore.

Both routes cross the Wyoming-Utah border and lead to Utah Highway 44, which takes visitors through the dramatic canyons. One other approach to the loop is from Highway 414, heading southeast from the town of Mountain View. This road traverses badlands, fields filled with sage and juniper, and large open pastures and leads to Henry's Fork, the site of the first mountain man rendezvous in the country.

SPORTS AND RECREATION
Recreation Centers

Thanks to the energy boom around the turn of the 21st century and subsequent growth of the tax base, Rock Springs built plentiful facilities, so recreational opportunities abound. The **Rock Springs Family**

Recreation Center (3900 Sweetwater Dr., 307/352-1440, www.rswy.net, 5am-9pm Mon.-Thurs., 5am-4pm Fri., 10am-4pm Sat.-Sun., $7 adults, $4 students 7-18, $2.50 seniors 62-74, $1.25 seniors 75-79, free for children under 7 and seniors 80 and up) offers an indoor swimming pool with a fun splash area for little ones and slides for bigger ones; a full-size ice arena; a full gym with basketball, volleyball, racquetball, and handball courts; an indoor putting course; and classes and fitness programs.

Golf

Golfers can tee off at the 27-hole championship **White Mountain Golf Course** (1501 Clubhouse Dr., Rock Springs, 307/352-1415, www.rswy.net, sunrise-sunset daily late Mar.-early Nov.), considered among the best public golf courses in the state. Nonresidents pay $75 for 18 holes with cart or $43 for 9 holes with cart. There is also an 18-hole course in Green River, the **Rolling Green Country Club** (29 Country Club Rd., 307/875-6200, call for tee times and greens fees).

Hiking and Mountain Biking

Although this is wide-open desert, there are some interesting places to hit the trail. For starters, the **Green Belt** and **Scotts Bottom Nature Area,** running through Green River, offer lovely trails to stretch your legs and enjoy the views. The trails are easily accessed from **Expedition Island,** the launching point for Powell's famous river trips through the Grand Canyon.

For more of an adventure, Sweetwater County has more still-visible pioneer trails running through it than anywhere else in the country, and hikers and mountain bikers can follow the double ruts at a variety of points in the big open countryside. Trails in the region include the Oregon and California Trails, the Mormon Trail, and the Pony Express Trail. All adventurers need to be well prepared for the vast undeveloped stretches of land and should bring maps, adequate clothing, and plenty of water.

The mountain biking in the area is sublime, with hundreds of miles of trails ranging from the scenic to the gnarly. Green River is known for some of its hairier trails, including the extremely technical 4-mile (6.4-km) **Lunatic Fringe** (with lots of ladder bridges and areas of exposure) and the slightly less insane 5-mile (8-km) **Macbones Trail,** both of which can be scouted on www.singletracks.com. The 20 miles (32 km) of single-track

Flaming Gorge National Recreation Area

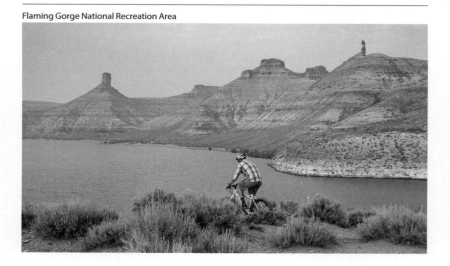

trails on **Wilkins Peak** offer good intermediate terrain and see plenty of traffic.

Among the most popular areas for mountain biking near Rock Springs is the 32-mile (51-km) **Current Creek Mountain Bike Trail** (www.blm.gov/visit/current-creek-mountain-bike-trail, 307/352-0256) along existing two-tracks at the intersection of Highway 191 and County Road 4-34/Upper Sage Creek Road.

For excellent advice or service, visit **The Bike and Trike** (612 Broadway, Rock Springs, 307/382-9677, www.bikeandtrike.com, 9am-5pm Mon.-Fri., 9am-3pm Sat.). They also have a great coffee shop (7am-4pm Mon.-Fri., 9am-2pm Sat.).

Without a doubt, the **Flaming Gorge National Recreation Area** offers the densest concentration of recreational opportunities, including miles upon miles of trails for hikers and mountain bikers. The scenic 5-mile (8-km) **Canyon Rim Trail** is accessible from the Red Canyon Visitor Center and is open to both hikers and mountain bikers. The **Dowd Mountain-Hideout Canyon Trail** is significantly steeper and also open to both hikers and mountain bikers. A trail map for these and other trails in the gorge is available for free at the **U.S. Forest Service** offices in Green River (132 Buck Board Rd., 307/875-4641) and Manila, Utah (intersection of Hwy. 43 and Hwy. 44, 435/784-3445). For a list of other hiking trails, visit www.flaminggorgecountry.com. For **mountain bike rentals** in the Flaming Gorge, visit the **Red Canyon Lodge** (2450 W. Red Canyon Lodge, Dutch John, Utah, 435/889-3759, www.redcanyonlodge.com, $12/hour, $20/half day, $36/full day), 4 miles (6.4 km) west of the junction of Highway 44 and US 191.

Fishing

There are a couple of ways to fish this part of the state, but for anglers looking to hook the big one—the really big one—**Flaming Gorge Reservoir** is the place to go. The lake trout in the reservoir can grow to weigh more than 50 pounds (23 kg), and 20-pounders (9 kg) are common. Lake trout generally like deeper waters and are more easily fished from boats. The rainbows in the reservoir, on the other hand, can be fished from shore. Other fish in the reservoir include smallmouth bass, kokanee, and burbot. The reservoir drops into Utah, and fishing licenses are required in both Wyoming and Utah; special-use stamps are available for fishing in both states.

The fishing on the **Green River** around its namesake town produces cutthroat, lake trout, and the occasional whitefish. For current conditions, information, and licenses, visit the **Wyoming Game and Fish Department** (351 Astle Ave., Green River, 307/875-3223, http://wgfd.wyo.gov).

For equipment and guided fishing trips on the Green River, contact **Trout Creek Flies** (1155 Little Hole Rd., Dutch John, Utah, 435/885-3355 or 435/885-3338, www.troutcreekflies.net, 7am-7pm daily) at the corner of US 191 and Little Hole Road. In addition to being a full-service fly shop, Trout Creek Flies offers half-day ($525 for up to 2 anglers) and full-day ($625 for up to 2 anglers) float trips that are discounted November-March, plus lodging, shuttling, overnight camping trip options, and pretty much anything an avid angler might need, including boat rentals.

Rafting and Boating

For the high desert, Sweetwater County has an awful lot of ways to enjoy the water. Kayakers get their thrills at the **Green River Whitewater Park and Tubing Channel** (www.cityofgreenriver.org) near Expedition Island in Green River. In addition to the splash park, there is a 1,200-foot-long tubing channel for beginning boaters and swimmers with a series of 4.5-foot drops and three pools. In the main river, a white-water park with eight gates is geared to advanced boaters. The park and channel can close due to river conditions, so check the website or call the

Parks and Recreation Department (307/872-6148 or 307/872-6151) before you go.

Most of the boating action in the area, however, happens at Flaming Gorge, and boats can be rented at a number of locations: **Buckboard Marina** (Hwy. 530, 25 mi/40 km south of Green River, 307/875-6927, www.buckboardmarina.com), **Cedar Springs Marina** (2685 Cedar Springs Boat Ramp, off US 191, 2 mi/3.2 km from the dam, 435/889-3795, www.cedarspringsmarina.com), **Lucerne Valley Marina** (5570 E. Lucerne Valley Rd., off Hwy. 530, 435/784-3483, www.flaminggorge.com), **Flaming Gorge Resort** (1100 E. Flaming Gorge Resort, Dutch John, Utah, 435/889-3773, www.flaminggorgeresort.com), **Red Canyon Lodge** (2450 W. Red Canyon Lodge, Dutch John, Utah, 435/889-3759, www.redcanyonlodge.com), and **Trout Creek Flies** (1155 Little Hole Rd., Dutch John, Utah, 435/885-3355 or 435/885-3338, www.troutcreekflies.net, 7am-7pm daily). All three marinas also offer lodging options.

ENTERTAINMENT AND EVENTS

Known as **Wyoming's Big Show,** the **Sweetwater County Fair,** held annually at the **Sweetwater Events Center** (3320 Yellowstone Rd., Rock Springs, 307/352-6789, www.sweetwaterevents.com, $15 adults, $9 children 6-12, free for children under 6, discounts for advance purchase), is a 10-day event in late July and early August that includes rodeo action, 4-H livestock competitions, entertainment, and a carnival. Comparable in size to the Wyoming State Fair, the event attracts some 80,000 attendees annually. The Sweetwater Events Center is also home to rodeo events and stock-car, motocross, and BMX racing.

Rock Springs has a healthy representation of the performing arts, including the **Sweetwater County Concert Association** (307/350-5697 or 307/382-5035), which produces 4-5 musical performances annually

as well as fundraisers that pair music with festive dining. Check their Facebook page for events. The city also programs a solid lineup of musical performances, with **Rock Springs Concerts in the Park** (Friday nights at 7pm in Bunning Park, Evans St. between Elk St. and Noble Dr., 307/352-1500, www.rswy.net) June-August, as well as **Movies in the Park** (Bunning Park). Also in Bunning Park in mid-August is the **Annual Sweetwater Blues 'n Brews Festival** (307/352-1434, www.downtownrs.com, from $35 for concert tickets, unlimited tasting, and commemorative glass), which combines a daylong lineup of blues music with local hoppy libations.

As a nod to the town's 56 different ethnicities, the Rock Springs Chamber of Commerce hosts a free **International Day** (307/362-3771, www.rsinternationalday.com, free) in Bunning Park early to mid-July. The daylong family-oriented event includes international food and beer plus entertainment and activities.

In Green River, the biggest event of the year is **Flaming Gorge Days** (800/354-6743, www.fgdays.com), held annually the last weekend of June, though canceled in 2020 and 2021 due to the pandemic. The event includes a country concert and a rock concert along with basketball and volleyball tournaments, a parade, a festival in the park, and children's entertainment. Concert tickets are available in advance at discounted rates from the chambers of commerce in Rock Springs (1897 Dewar Dr., 307/362-3771, www.rockspringschamber.com, 8am-5pm Mon.-Fri.) and Green River (1155 Flaming Gorge Way, 307/875-5711, www.grchamber.com, 8:30am-5:30pm Mon.-Fri.) or at full price at the gate.

Another big event in Green River is the **Annual River Festival** (307/875-5711, www.grchamber.com) held in late August. This two-day event includes a Cajun shrimp boil, kids' games, a horseshoe tournament, a car and bike show, dog and bike events, a number of races including a marathon and half marathon, and plenty of food.

SHOPPING

With the major slump in both coal and oil prices, the economy in the region is hurting, and many of the local galleries and gift shops are shuttering. But there are pawn shops aplenty. Little gems remain, however.

In Green River, **Busy Bee Bath Essentials** (68 N. 1st E. St., Green River, 307/851-9862, www.busybeebathessentials. com, 10am-6pm Tues.-Fri., noon-4pm Sat.) is known for its handmade body care and beauty products, but it also features handmade crafts by local artists including jewelry, home decor, blankets, and unfinished wood.

In Rock Springs, **Tynsky's Rocks & Jewelry** (706 Dewar Dr., Rock Springs, 307/389-6868, noon-3pm daily or by appointment) has a nice selection of locally quarried rock, fossils, jewelry, and tumbling supplies. Owned by local painter and potter Andrew Kneeland, **Kneeland Fine Art** (203 D St., Rock Springs, www.kneelandfineart. com, 10am-6pm Mon.-Sat.) specializes in works that celebrate the Wyoming landscape, wildlife, and character through various media. Andrew often paints on-site and hosts workshops. His own work ranges from wildlife to landscape to gorgeous and finely detailed images of rocks and lichen.

Also in downtown Rock Springs, **Mack & Co** (623 Pilot Butte Ave., Rock Springs, 307/731-0384, www.mack-co-boutique.com, 11am-6pm Tues.-Fri., 11am-3pm Sat.) is an artisan boutique where you can find gifts for everyone—from clothing, home decor, bath and body, Wyoming merch, jewelry, candles, and more—including Fido. For travelers who don't love shopping, there's no place better to end up than **Sidekicks Wine & Books** (507 Broadway St., Rock Springs, 307/389-9727, www.sidekicksbookbar.com, 11am-6pm Mon.-Tues., 11am-7pm Wed.-Thurs., 10am-9pm Fri., 10am-7pm Sat.), which is even better than the name implies, if such a thing is possible. Inside the lovely book-filled space,

wine, espresso, appetizers, and desserts are served. You may never want to leave.

FOOD

For a relatively remote Wyoming town, Rock Springs has an impressive number of international eateries, the origins of which date back to the town's international population. **Bonsai** (1996 Dewar Dr., 307/362-1888, 11am-9pm Tues.-Sun., $7-16) feeds the community's appetite for Asian cuisine. In addition to Chinese and Thai specialties, the restaurant serves decent sushi. For good classic Mexican food in a warm, inviting setting, try **Casa Chavez** (744 Pilot Butte Ave., 307/362-3686, 11am-9pm Mon.-Sat., $7-13), which also serves beer, wine, and margaritas. The food is fantastic and the owners and servers are delightful and so focused on their customers.

For southwest Wyoming's favorite hamburgers, fries, and shakes, hit **Grub's Drive In** (415 Paulson St., Rock Springs, 307/362-6634, www.grubsdrivein.com, 6am-8pm Mon.-Fri., $4-10). It's not healthy, and you may have to wait in a good-size line, but the shamrock burgers are juicy, the fries come with a side of brown gravy, and the milk shakes are something to write home about.

Another local favorite in Rock Springs is **Cowboy Donuts** (1573 Dewar Dr. #4, 307/362-3400, www.cowboydonuts.com, 5am-2pm Mon.-Sat.), which serves 55 different varieties baked daily, from hand-chopped apple fritters to blueberry cake and glazed doughnut holes. It also offers an excellent selection of *kolaches*—slightly sweet butter bread stuffed with meats and cheeses. If you don't get your sugar fix with donuts, head down the road to **Cowboy Crepes & Café** (1977 Dewar Dr. G, 307/362-6299, www. cowboycrepesandcafe.com, 8am-8pm Mon.-Thurs., 8am-10pm Fri.-Sat., 9am-2pm Sun., $7-13), which serves delicious crepes, both sweet and savory, plus pasta and paninis, and a full espresso bar.

Among the hippest dining options in town is ★ **Bitter Creek Brewing** (604

Broadway, Rock Springs, 307/362-4782, www.bittercreekbrewing.com, 11:30am-7:30pm Tues.-Thurs., 11:30am-8:30pm Fri.-Sat., extended hours in season, lunch $10-16, dinner $10-21.50), which offers a large and varied menu—think chicken wings, Thai nachos, pizza, and mouthwatering baby back ribs—in a casual, fun, and family-friendly environment. There's a kids' menu too, and a fantastic selection of seasonal microbrews on tap.

In Green River, hungry diners head to **Penny's Diner** (1170 W. Flaming Gorge Way, Green River, 307/875-3500, ext. 550, 24 hours daily, $8-14), adjacent to the Oak Tree Inn, a classic 1950s-style diner open 24 hours a day that serves up everything from omelets and sandwiches to burgers and pie. Another local favorite is the family-friendly **Hitching Post Restaurant and Saloon** (580 E. Flaming Gorge Way, Green River, 307/875-2246, restaurant 6am-10pm daily, saloon 6am-2am Mon.-Sat. and 10am-midnight Sun., breakfast $7-13, lunch and dinner $9-26), which has an enormous menu with burgers, pasta, steaks, sandwiches, baskets, and a salad bar with more than 40 items to choose from. Hearty breakfast choices include skillets,

burritos, omelets, chicken-fried steak, and all the classics.

Another great place for a casual and delicious meal is the **Bird's Nest Restaurant** (71 Uinta Dr., Green River, 307/466-2013, www.birdsnest307.com, 6am-8pm daily, breakfast $7-11, lunch and dinner $8-25), which serves classic breakfasts using fresh ingredients, big, beautiful sandwiches and salads, burgers and baskets, pasta, steak and seafood. Their Saturday night prime rib is a hit with locals.

ACCOMMODATIONS

Rock Springs has a number of chain hotels, but among the best is the pet-friendly **Best Western Outlaw Inn** (1630 Elk St., Rock Springs, 307/362-6623 or 800/528-1234, www.bestwestern.com, $98-188), which has a variety of room configurations, standard amenities, a pool, an on-site restaurant, and complimentary breakfast. Another option in Rock Springs is the **Homewood Suites by Hilton** (60 Winston Dr., Rock Springs, 307/382-0764, www.hilton.com, from $92) which has spacious, modern rooms. A good budget-friendly option is the pet-friendly **Baymont by Wyndham** (2717 Dewar Dr., 307/362-1770, www.wyndhamhotels.com,

SOUTHERN WYOMING
SWEETWATER COUNTY

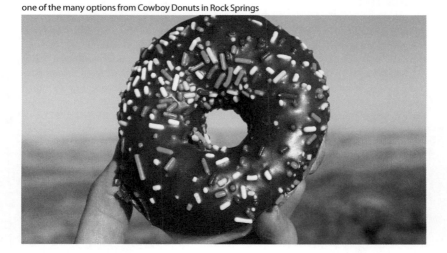

one of the many options from Cowboy Donuts in Rock Springs

from $72), which offers free breakfast, laundry facilities, an outdoor pool, and family rooms. The **Western Inn** (890 W. Flaming Gorge Way, Green River, 307/875-2840, from $40) offers clean but dated, no-frills accommodations with friendly staff, Wi-Fi, refrigerators, microwaves, and a continental breakfast included. Chains in Green River include the pet-friendly **Hampton Inn & Suites Green River** (1055 Wild Horse Canyon Rd., Green River, 307/875-5300, www.hamptoninn3.hilton.com, from $81), which has connecting rooms, an indoor pool, and free hot breakfast, and **Super 8** (280 W. Flaming Gorge Way, Green River, 307/875-9330, www.wyndhamhotels.com, from $49).

The most appealing place to stay in the region is actually over the border near Dutch John, Utah. The ★ **Red Canyon Lodge** (2450 W. Red Canyon Lodge, Dutch John, Utah, 435/889-3759, www.redcanyonlodge. com, cabins $139-185) has attractive and cozy cabins with front porches perfect for enjoying the tranquil scenery. The resort offers excellent dining with stunning views and daily wild-game specials, plus a host of activities that range from horseback riding and mountain biking to boat trips and fishing tours. And it's pet friendly.

CAMPING

The **Rock Springs/Green River KOA** (86 Foothill Blvd., Rock Springs, 307/362-3063, www.koa.com) is open year-round and offers tent sites ($40) with electricity, RV sites ($46-72), and cabins with (from $145) or without (from $64) bathrooms. The campground also has Wi-Fi, a swimming pool, a playground, and a variety of games. Pets are not permitted in the cabins with bathrooms, but they are elsewhere through the campground.

From Green River, take Highway 530 south 22 miles (35 km) to the sign for **Buckboard Crossing Campground** (McKinnon, 877/444-6777, www.flaminggorgecountry. com/Buckboard, May-Sept., $16/night, $4 extra for electric). Turn left after the sign and go 1.3 miles (2 km) to the campground. The campground has 58 sites and is on the far northwest shore of Flaming Gorge Reservoir. Don't count on any cell coverage here, even under the wide open Wyoming sky.

There is phenomenal public camping in the Flaming Gorge National Recreation Area. Among the favorites is the ★ **Red Canyon Campground** (Forest Rd. 95/Red Canyon Rd., Dutch John, Utah, early May-late Sept., $22), which offers front-row seats for the area's spellbinding sunsets. There are lodgepole and ponderosa pines for shade, abundant wildflowers in summer, and nearby Greens Lake for recreation. The red Canyon Rim Trail starts nearby and is excellent for hikers and mountain bikers. To reserve one of the more than 700 campsites throughout Flaming Gorge, visit www.recreation.gov or call 877/444-6777. To read more about individual campsites in the recreation area, go to www.flaminggorgecountry.com.

INFORMATION AND SERVICES

The **Rock Springs Chamber of Commerce** (1897 Dewar Dr., Rock Springs, 307/362-3771, www.rockspringschamber.com, 8am-5pm Mon.-Fri.) doubles as a visitor center. The **Green River Chamber of Commerce** (1155 W. Flaming Gorge Way, Green River, 307/875-5711, www.grchamber.com, 8:30am-5:30pm Mon.-Fri.) also operates as a visitor center. The **Explore Rock Springs & Green River Visitor Center** (1641 Elk St., Rock Springs, 307/382-2538, www.tourwyoming.com, 11am-3pm Mon.-Fri.) is an excellent resource for current happenings and adventure planning.

There are **post offices** in Rock Springs (2829 Commercial Way, 307/362-9792, 9am-5pm Mon.-Fri., 9am-noon Sat.) and in Green River (350 Uinta Dr., 307/875-4920, 8:30am-5:30pm Mon.-Fri., 9:30am-1pm Sat.).

Medical care is available 24/7 at **Memorial Hospital of Sweetwater County** (1200 College Dr., Rock Springs, 307/362-3711, www.sweetwatermemorial.com). Walk-in care is offered at **Sterling Urgent Care** (2761 Commercial Way, Rock Springs,

307/382-3064, www.sterlingurgentcare.com, 7am-7pm Mon.-Fri., 9am-5pm Sat.) and **Big Horn Urgent Care** (1453A Dewar Dr., Rock Springs, 307/382-2466, 8am-8pm Sun. only). In Green River, walk-in care is available at **Castle Rock Medical Center** (1400 Uinta Dr., Green River, 307/872-4500, www.castlerockmedicalcenter.org, 8am-5:30pm Mon.-Fri.).

In Rock Springs, wash clothes at two locations of **Sweetwater Laundry** (2528 Foothill Blvd., 307/382-6290, and 801 Powerhouse Dr., 307/354-6050, Rock Springs, www.sweetwaterlaundry.com, 24 hours daily). In Green River, big, clean machines (and a nice kids' play area) are available at **Wash and Play Laundromat** (1315 Bridger Dr., Green River, www.washandplay.biz, 307/364-0479, 24 hours daily).

TRANSPORTATION
Getting There
The **Rock Springs-Sweetwater County Airport** (RKS, 382 Hwy. 370, 307/352-6880, www.flyrks.com) has two daily nonstop flights to Denver on **United Express**.

Rental cars are available at the Rock Springs-Sweetwater County Airport from **Avis** and **Budget**.

Green River is 14 miles (22.5 km) west of Rock Springs, 113 miles (182 km) south of Pinedale, 209 miles (340 km) southwest of Thermopolis, 240 miles (385 km) southwest of Casper, and 247 miles (395 km) south of Yellowstone National Park.

Daily bus service is provided by **Greyhound** (1695 Sunset Dr., Ste. 118, Rock Springs, 307/362-2931).

Getting Around
Public transportation across Sweetwater County is available through **STAR Transit** (307/382-7827, www.ridestartransit.com), which is a combination of fixed route and demand response services.

For taxi service in and around Sweetwater County, contact **All City Taxi** (307/382-1100, www.allcitytaxiwy.com, 5am-2am daily or by appointment), **All Time Taxi** (307/382-3183), **Diamond Choice Taxi** (307/209-1716), or **Quick Response Taxi** (307/371-4510, www.quick-response-taxi.business.site).

Background

The Landscape

GEOGRAPHY

Wyoming is the least populous state in the union with only 576,851 people as of April 2020, but is 10th in land area—just over 97,000 square miles (251,229 sq km). One of only three states (Colorado and Utah are the others) that have borders along straight latitudinal and longitudinal lines, Wyoming is bordered on the north by Montana and on the south by Utah and Colorado. Nebraska and South Dakota border Wyoming on the east, while Idaho makes up most of the western border with a little slice of Utah. The western part of Wyoming is made up of mountainous terrain covered by coniferous forests, and similarly the Continental Divide continues its diagonal run through the state. Eastern Wyoming consists of the High Plains, an expanse of high-elevation prairie that is home to large cattle ranches and oil and gas wells. Wyoming is the third-highest state in the nation (behind Alaska and Colorado), with an elevation range of 3,125-13,804 feet (953-4,207 m). Gannet Peak in the Wind River Range is the highest point in the state at 13,804 feet (4,207 m).

GEOLOGY

Wyoming (as well as parts of Idaho) converge around the Greater Yellowstone Ecosystem, widely regarded as the largest biologically intact temperate ecosystem in North America. Centered around Yellowstone National Park, this 31,000-square-mile (80,290-sq-km) area, or nearly 20 million acres, consists of a diverse landscape with geothermal activity and native wildlife; it is considered by scientists to be a natural laboratory for landscape ecology, geology, and wildlife preservation.

Visiting the Greater Yellowstone area provides the opportunity to see a natural environment much like it was hundreds and even thousands of years ago. Yellowstone National Park itself is on a high plateau, the remnants of a volcano that last erupted more than 640,000 years ago, leaving a giant caldera. Yellowstone is one of the most geothermic places on earth, containing a majority of the world's types of geothermal features, including geysers, hot springs, mud pots, and fumaroles.

If you are worried that Yellowstone could erupt during your vacation, don't. Scientists are constantly measuring the amount of pressure in the magma chamber, which actually raises the floor of the caldera plateau—nearly 7 inches (18 cm) between 1976 and 1984, and almost 10 inches (25 cm) from 2004 to 2009. Since 2010, the rate of growth has significantly slowed down; by 2020, it was rising approximately 1 inch (2.54 cm) per year. But as if the caldera could breathe, the growth is up and down. The dome rises and falls, then rises again. Theoretically, the volcano could erupt. but scientists agree there is little evidence that a cataclysmic explosion will occur anytime soon. Due to its volcanic nature, the Yellowstone area experiences upward of 1,000-3,000 measurable earthquakes each year, but you are unlikely to feel one.

Outside Yellowstone Park, the rest of the ecosystem is mountainous and filled with large tracts of roadless land, jagged peaks, broad valleys, and flowing rivers—exactly why many people live here and even more choose to visit. Wildlife abounds, offering a rare glimpse into the lives of everything from the pine marten to the grizzly bear. Of course, people live here too, and the interaction between humans and nature is important not only historically but in contemporary matters as well.

Large tracts of prairies contain mostly dry grasses and shrubs. The iconic big sagebrush plant can be found at nearly every elevation—more sage grows in Wyoming than anywhere else—and many land areas seem almost desertlike, right down to the tumbleweeds that roll along in the breeze. Wyoming includes two areas actually classified as desert: the Red Desert near Rock Springs and a large part of the Bighorn Basin.

CLIMATE

Generally, summers are hot and dry, often punctuated by brief but intense afternoon thunderstorms. Winters are cold and see a healthy amount of snow, particularly in the western portions of the states. Daytime highs in a Wyoming summer range between 75 and 90°F (21.1-32.2°C), with triple digits occasionally setting in. During winter, it can get downright cold. July and August are the warmest months, while January and February are the coldest. Snow can fall at any time of the year,

---

Previous: Jagged peaks soar skyward from this Wyoming high country basin.

but most occurs November-March. May and June are often the rainiest months. Humidity is generally on the low side, making the hot summer days a little more bearable. It's important to realize that when engaging in outdoor activities during the summer, you should always plan for bad weather—it can happen almost instantly at any time, even during the hottest part of the summer.

Temperatures decrease with higher altitude, so it's not uncommon in the mountains for the weather to be drastically different from lower elevations. Storms can move in without warning and can be fierce—driving hail in the summer and blizzard conditions in the winter. Rain in the valleys can often mean snow in the mountains, especially in the spring when a storm can dump several feet of heavy snow in a relatively short amount of time.

Chinook winds blow in the state. These unusually warm, dry winter winds blow down the east slopes of the Rockies and across the plains. They occur when moist Pacific air rises over the mountains, loses its moisture in the form of precipitation, and then warms rapidly on the leeward side. Chinooks can quickly melt snow and raise the temperature.

Casper and Cheyenne, Wyoming, all rank among the windiest cities in the country. Winter winds can turn an average cold day into a bone-chilling one, while summer gusts often keep outdoor event planners working overtime.

Plants and Animals

PLANTS

Wyoming encompasses a variety of habitats, ranging from grasslands and desert shrublands to forests, mountain meadows, and alpine tundra. Wyoming has some 2,200 plant species.

Trees

Forests account for roughly one-fifth of the state's land. In the lower-elevation mountains in the eastern part of the state, **ponderosa pine** is the primary species. Farther west, **Douglas fir** is prominent in the lower elevations. Higher up, where the climate is cooler and wetter, **lodgepole pine, Engelmann spruce, subalpine fir,** and **aspen** are among the most common species. Timberline in the northern part of Wyoming is at about 8,900 feet (2,713 m), and at about 11,500 feet (3,505 m) in the southern part of the state. **Engelmann spruce, subalpine fir, whitebark pine**— an important and rapidly dwindling food source for grizzly bears—and **limber pine** grow at high elevations as shrubs, rather than trees.

Flowers

What it lacks in fall foliage colors, thanks to an abundance of evergreens, Wyoming more than makes up for with spring and summer displays of wildflowers. Wyoming has more than 150 varieties, including purple **New England asters, bluebells, California poppies, camas, black-eyed Susans, fireweed, wild blue flax,** and **sticky geraniums.** The Indian paintbrush is the state flower of Wyoming.

Vegetation

Wyoming's alpine tundra, found above timberline, is home to a variety of grasses and other herbaceous plants that can tolerate freezing temperatures at any time of year. **Big sagebrush,** the most dominant of Wyoming's species of sagebrush, covers much of the western two-thirds of the state. Other plants with a wide range in Wyoming include **western wheatgrass, blue grama, needleleaf sedge, scarlet globemallow, fringed sagewort, phlox, milkvetch, rabbitbrush,** and **prickly pear cactus.** In the driest parts of the state, shrubs like juniper, mountain mahogany, saltbush, winterfat, and spiny hopsage occur alongside various species of sagebrush. The most abundant vegetation in this part of the state is found along rivers and streams and can include cottonwood trees and willows.

ANIMALS

Wyoming is known for its abundant wildlife, and it's only fitting that residents and visitors want to see them in their natural habitat. Both herbivores and predators roam the land, and with the right information a savvy traveler can seek out views of these animals. Keep in mind that it is not acceptable to approach wildlife for any reason—keep a safe distance away and never feed any animal. Stay 25 yards/meters from most wildlife, and at least 100 yards/meters from large animals, including bison and moose, and predators.

Bison

Two herds fluctuating from 2,300 to 5,500 bison roam within the borders of Yellowstone National Park, a far cry from the millions that once lived throughout central North America from Canada to Mexico. These massive creatures graze on grasses, and males can weigh up to 2,000 pounds (907 kg), while females can weigh as much as 1,000 pounds (454 kg). Bison can commonly be seen almost any time of the year in Yellowstone, often causing traffic jams as they stand on the road.

Elk

Elk are found throughout the mountainous region, and between 10,000 and 20,000 migrate through Yellowstone National Park in 6-7 different herds. These regal creatures are fairly common and can be found at higher elevations in the summer and lower elevations in the winter. The Northern Yellowstone elk herd numbered 6,249 animals in the 2020 count, compared to 2019's count of 5,800 and 2017's count of 5,349; the herd spends its winters just north of the park. The National Elk Refuge in Jackson, Wyoming, is home to 6,000-8,000 wintering elk, though 5,000 is the population objective.

Deer, Antelope, and Sheep

White-tailed deer and the large-eared mule deer, as well as pronghorn antelope, can be found throughout the region and are as often seen on the sides of highways as they are in the wild. Bighorn sheep are impressive, stocky animals. The rams (males) are known for their massive curled horns, which give the rugged creatures their distinctive look. Herds of bighorn sheep can be found in and around Yellowstone and the Whiskey Basin Habitat Area near Dubois.

Mountain Goats

Mountain goats inhabit many of the high peaks and can often be seen clinging to impossibly steep sides of rocky cliffs. Considered nonnative species, mountain goats were introduced to Yellowstone in the 1990s.

Moose

Some of the largest animals you'll encounter are moose, which typically inhabit river bottoms, wetlands, and willowed areas and graze on grasses, brush, and leaves. Moose can surprise you on the trail, as they are typically quiet and private creatures. Their docile nature can quickly turn deadly if they charge; give them plenty of room—at least 100 yards/meters—especially if you encounter a female with young.

Bears

Black bears can be found in forested areas and often see much more human interaction than their larger counterpart, the grizzly bear. Grizzlies once roamed the entire Northern Hemisphere, and when Lewis and Clark traversed the area, there were likely more than 50,000 grizzlies across the West. Although there are still healthy populations in western Canada and Alaska, grizzly numbers in the Greater Yellowstone Ecosystem dropped to as few as 136 animals in 1975. Since the U.S. Fish and Wildlife Service listed

The Wyoming Jackalope

As much a design staple as statewide lore, the famed jackalope is to Wyoming what Bigfoot is to the Pacific Northwest. Does it exist? Could it possibly? Stop into nearly any roadside tavern and you are bound to see a mount of the creature. Ask around and the locals will gladly play along.

Popularized by Douglas Herrick in 1939, the jackalope is supposed to be an extinct antlered rabbit species, a cross between a pygmy deer and some sort of killer rabbit. Among the beliefs surrounding these legendary creatures are that jackalopes can travel at speeds of 90 mph and can mimic human sounds when chased.

Sighted in Colorado, New Mexico, and Nebraska in addition to Wyoming, jackalopes have cousins in Germany (called the *wolperdinger*) and in Sweden (the *skvader*). Drawings of antlered rabbit-like creatures date back to the 16th century in scholarly European works, so it is not just the stuff of goofy Wyoming calendars.

Those who sit on the fence between believing and not believing cite a disease called papillomatosis, which indeed leads parasite-caused growths on the top of a rabbit's head to harden, perhaps resembling antlers.

For those who prefer lore to science, the story of Herrick, a taxidermist from Douglas, seems a believable origin. Herrick and his brother Ralph returned from a hunt one day and slid their catch onto the floor. A hare landed next to a set of antelope antlers, and a pop-culture idea was born. The brothers mounted the antlered bunny, and the rest is history.

Jackalopes became so popular in the 1940s that Douglas was known far and wide as the "Jackalope Capital of the World." The city has stayed true to the legend with public art and signage all over town, as well as an annual Jackalope Day in June. Each year the local chamber issues thousands of jackalope hunting licenses, which specify that hunters cannot have an IQ higher than 72 and can only hunt between midnight and 2am on June 31. In the works now? There's been talk for years of a giant 80-foot fiberglass jackalope sculpture to tower over I-25. So far, there's just a metal silhouette of a jackalope on a Douglas hilltop. This is a story so entwined with Wyoming culture that it will never fade away.

them as a threatened species, the population has recovered to include an estimated 728 bears in the region as of 2019. The Northern Continental Divide Ecosystem is believed to be home to the largest number of grizzlies—approximately 1,000 as of 2020. The grizzlies along the Rocky Mountain Front have, in the last several years, started coming out of their alpine habitat to regain their status as residents of the plains, something not seen since Lewis and Clark traveled the region at the turn of the 19th century. Indeed, grizzlies today have been reported east of Great Falls, more than 100 miles (161 km) from the nearest mountain range. But despite their successes, grizzlies in the region face enormous hurdles, including habitat destruction

and climate change, both of which put them in danger of human conflict. According to the United States Geological Survey (USGS), in 2020 there were at least 17 human-caused deaths for grizzlies in the Greater Yellowstone Ecosystem, with reasons ranging from road-kill and self-defense to management for livestock depredations and those mistaken by hunters for black bears. The number of human-caused grizzly deaths was up over 2019 and higher than the 10-year average. Add that to the fact that grizzlies are the second-slowest reproducing land mammal in North America, and the hurdles for their survival look insurmountable. Even so, in 2017 the U.S. Fish and Wildlife Service (USFWS) delisted the Yellowstone grizzly population, and while the bears will be protected inside park boundaries, a hunting season was slated for fall 2018 where both males and females could

1: bison 2: The Meadowlark is Wyoming's state bird. 3: grizzly bear 4: bighorn sheep be shot outside the park in Wyoming. More than 7,000 hunting permit applications were received, which is but a trickle compared to the 850,000 public comments submitted on the 2016 delisting proposal, 99 percent of which opposed delisting. The delisting was overturned in court in 2020, after a midnight stay before the first hunting season could begin, and it's a debacle that continues today. In late 2021, Wyoming petitioned the USFWS again to delist grizzlies. Time will tell what will happen in the courts. It's time for humans to protect grizzlies, and what is wild, or lose them forever.

Wolves and Coyotes

The reintroduction of the gray wolf is one of the greatest—and most controversial—wildlife success stories of the 20th century. Numbers went from zero—gray wolves were last seen in Wyoming in the 1930s—to more than 3,123 in some 300 packs living throughout Montana, Wyoming, and Idaho in mid-winter of 2020. Yellowstone National Park is the best place to catch a glimpse of the elusive wolf. The Lamar and Hayden Valleys are especially good places to view one of the 123 or so wolves that roam through Yellowstone in nine different packs.

You'll often see coyotes walking along the roadsides in Yellowstone or strolling in an open meadow stalking their prey. These dog-like predators have a longer and more pointed nose than wolves, a much fluffier tail, and are noticeably smaller and more delicate in appearance. Their numbers in Yellowstone decreased substantially with the reintroduction of the wolf, thanks to food competition and conflicts between the two species.

Mountain Lions

Mountain lions, also known as cougars, are present in the region. Though their numbers dwindled to almost zero with the predator removal campaigns in the early 1900s, they managed to hang on thanks to their shy nature. These elusive cats are becoming slightly more common, and human confrontations have risen over the years. The largest cat in North America, with a length of up to 7.5 feet (2.3 m) from nose to tail, male cougars can weight 145-170 pounds (66-77 kg), and females generally weigh 85-120 pounds (39-54 kg). If you see one in the wild, chances are it will be crossing the road on a late-night hunting excursion.

Pikas and Marmots

The high country is home to the smallish pika and the larger, fuzzier yellow-bellied marmot. Both can be spotted running along rocky outcrops and scree fields at higher elevations. Listen for their high-pitched chirp.

Birds

Attentive visitors can expect to see **bald** and **golden eagles, osprey, hawks, falcons, owls, woodpeckers, grouse, herons, pelicans,** and more. Smaller species include **jays, mountain bluebirds, warblers, western tanagers,** and **magpies.** There are excellent opportunities for bird-watching in Seedskadee National Wildlife Refuge, among many other hot spots. For information on the excellent birding opportunities, visit www. audubon.org.

Snakes

In addition to the prairie rattlesnake, found primarily east of the Rockies and typically in open arid country, Wyoming has an endangered population of its cousin, the **midget faded rattlesnake,** which lives only around the Flaming Gorge area. Prairie rattlesnakes tend to den on south-facing slopes with rock outcrops and consume rodents as their primary prey.

Environmental Issues

As in many Western states, the environment is a controversial topic in Wyoming. While the state is on the conservative side politically, many of the residents—both old-timers and newcomers—have a vested interest when it comes to land, air, and water issues.

MINING

In the early 2000s, Wyoming's mining and gas industries experienced a major boom. In 2004, Wyoming ranked 16th in the country in total nonfuel mineral production value and first in the production of coal, which is mined primarily in the Powder River Basin. Together, this was a $7.8 billion piece of the state's economic pie. The state has nearly 200 mines and is the country's largest producer of soda ash and bentonite clays. Wyoming also has the world's largest deposit of trona, from which soda ash is refined. By spring of 2016, the bust could not be ignored. When low natural gas prices damaged coal's dominance in the electricity sector, the country's largest coal mine, south of Gillette, laid off 15 percent of its workers, as did another major mine nearby. More than 1,000 mining jobs were lost and several mining companies in the area filed for bankruptcy amid the plummeting market. In all of 2017, only five full-time mining jobs were added in Wyoming. Even the companies that survived were still reducing production as of 2018. Even with a 20 percent decline in overall production from 2019, in 2020 Wyoming's 16 coal mines still produced 41 percent of the coal in the United States.

AIR POLLUTION

Air quality is another concern, in particular emissions from coal-fired power plants and, in places, ongoing tire burning. Proponents of banning snowmobiles in Yellowstone National Park succeeded in lowering the number of machines allowed to enter, as well as requiring all snowmobiles to be the cleaner four-stroke variety. This has divided towns where the winter economy has traditionally relied on the snowmobile tourism industry. Global warming has also affected Glacier National Park, as the number of glaciers larger than 25 acres has decreased from 150 in 1850 to 26 in 2015 and 25 by 2021—and some prediction models, based on a 2003 USGS study and 1992 temperature predictions, suggest that the park's glaciers could disappear altogether by 2030. A significant problem for air quality during most summers is smoke from massive forest fires. The Department of Environmental Quality (DEQ) (www.deq. wyoming.gov) monitors air quality.

WATER QUALITY

Major environmental issues in Wyoming also include water quality, especially associated with coal-bed methane, a form of natural gas. Wyoming is the country's third-largest coal-bed methane producer, much of it coming from the Powder River Basin in the northeast part of the state, and the ninth largest producer of natural gas in the country, 7 percent of which can be accounted for by coalbed methane. Wyoming was also the eighth-largest oil-producing state as of 2020, with five large refineries and the fourth-largest volume of oil reserves. Wyoming faces issues with hard-rock mining and coal-fired power plants. And as is true around the country, and the world, the process of fracking—extracting natural gas from shale rock layers using hydraulic fracturing—is stirring up significant controversy in these resource-rich states. Various reports on impaired waters are available through the state's DEQ (www.deq.wyoming.gov).

FOREST MANAGEMENT

Perhaps nothing divides Westerners more than how to use and manage the forests. As of 2016, Wyoming was just over 18 percent

Leave No Trace

Leave No Trace is an educational program that teaches outdoors enthusiasts how to protect the places they love from human-caused recreational impact. However, the Leave No Trace ethic extends far beyond backcountry and wilderness areas. As more and more people are recreating in "front country" settings, knowledge of how to apply Leave No Trace principles becomes increasingly important.

Planning ahead is the easiest way to protect outdoor places and to enjoy a safe visit. Use a map, bring a small first-aid kit, remember to bring additional clothing to keep you warm and dry, and wear suitable shoes or boots on the trails. When hiking, stay on designated trails, especially if they pass through private property. Shortcutting around corners causes erosion and damages trailside plants, especially if it's wet or muddy. Dispose of trash and biodegradable materials, such as orange peels, apple cores, and food scraps, in a bear-proof trash container. Remember, animals that become dependent on human food often have to be relocated or destroyed. Two easy slogans to remember are "Pack it in, pack it out," and "Leave it as you find it." By leaving the natural world as you find it, you will be protecting the habitat of plants and animals as well as the outdoor experience of millions of visitors.

In the backcountry, you must carry all trash out with you. Use a biodegradable soap when washing dishes, and avoid using soap within 200 feet (60 m) of a stream or spring. Allow others a sense of discovery by leaving rocks, plants, archaeological artifacts, and other objects of interest as you find them. Minimize campfire impacts by instead using portable camp stoves or fire pans. Use designated fire grates if available, and always make sure the fire is completely out before you leave camp. If you make a fire ring with rocks, disperse the rocks before you leave camp, and try hard to "leave no trace" of your being there.

Finally, always respect wildlife and be considerate of other visitors to help protect the quality of their experience. The last thing you want to do is ruin somebody else's trip of a lifetime. Keep noise to a minimum and let nature's sounds prevail; everyone will be happier for it.

forested. Whether the topic is the creatures that live in them, logging operations, forest fires, recreation, or potential wilderness, residents are passionate about their beliefs. Both sides of any issue typically have ardent followers, making legislation a painstaking process. Whether it's clear-cutting issues or motorized-vehicle access, forestry can be a touchy subject at the lunch counter. Check any newspaper in either state and you're bound to see articles and letters to the editor about these topics.

WOLF MANAGEMENT

Another contentious issue is the government-sponsored reintroduction of the wolf, which started in 1995 when 66 Canadian wolves were transplanted to Yellowstone National Park and central Idaho. The population rebounded and, in some people's minds, become a threat to humans and livestock. As of the last count in midwinter 2020, there were close to 3,123 wolves across three states and about 123 in Yellowstone National Park. Area ranchers say wolves prey on livestock and elk herds; environmentalists say the animals have a right to thrive on land that was once theirs. Wolves were relieved of their endangered-species status in Wyoming by 2012, but were re-listed in 2014 as a nonessential experimental population since the state could not abide by post-delisting rules. They were delisted again in 2017, and in the first hunt since 2013, 44 Wyoming wolves were killed. In Wyoming in 2020, 31 wolves were killed by hunters.

History

Wyoming is a young state with a long history. Cowboys and Native Americas, cattle barons and miners, railroads and ranching. As the least populous state in the union, some parts of Wyoming have remained unchanged since the first settlers came into the area, allowing those who live and visit today a glimpse into the state's rich and varied past.

Geology and Early Life-Forms

Wyoming's geologic history includes the creation of the Rocky Mountains and the impact of glaciers on the landscape. Of course, Yellowstone National Park is the state's biggest geologic claim to fame, created when a series of three massive volcanic explosions—2.1 million, 1.3 million, and 640,000 years ago—spewed gases and hot ash across North America. Some experts suggest the most recent blast alone was more than 10,000 times larger than the well-known 1980 eruption of Mount St. Helens in Washington. Geothermal forces are still at work underneath Yellowstone's surface, giving the park its trademark geysers, hot springs, fumaroles, and mud pots, making it the earth's most active geothermal area.

Wyoming is also a hotbed for dinosaur fossils. A fossil of a giant allosaurus—among the first meat-eating dinosaurs—was found in 1991, providing valuable insight into this carnivore that roamed the earth during the Jurassic period 130-190 million years ago. The excellent Wyoming Dinosaur Center (www.wyomingdinosaurcenter.org) in Thermopolis features more than 200 displays and more than 30 mounted skeletons of various dinosaurs. Fossils of fish, insects, birds, plants, and reptiles are on display at the Fossil Butte National Monument, a 50-million-year-old lake bed near Kemmerer that holds the largest deposit of freshwater fish fossils in the Western Hemisphere.

By most accounts, humans have inhabited what is now Wyoming for at least 13,000 years. Stone fossils have been found that indicate the presence of early human cultures, including the Plano, a tribe of hunter-gatherers that inhabited the Great Plains 9000-6000 BC. There is also evidence of the Clovis culture, people that lived in the area nearly 13,000 years ago. Their distinctive bone and ivory "Clovis points" have been found in Wyoming.

Native Americans and Mountain Men

Plains Indians didn't move into the area until the early 1600s, when Native Americans around the Great Lakes and Canadian plains were forced west. The arrival of horses and rifles created nomadic hunters who followed the massive herds of buffalo, and the cultures began to change as villages grew larger and tribes had more interaction. Indian society grew more turbulent by the 19th century, and was soon greeted by early American explorers who sought control of the state's vast geographic and natural resources.

Although French explorers crossed into northern Wyoming in the mid-1700s, two of the most famous names in Wyoming's early history are John Colter and Jim Bridger. Colter, a member of the Lewis and Clark expedition, was most likely the first person of European descent to enter the region in 1807, and he gave birth to the term *mountain man*. He explored what would become Yellowstone National Park and was one of the first non-Native Americans to see the Grand Tetons, spending a winter alone in the wilderness as he recorded his discoveries. Colter's most legendary story is when he escaped from a group of Blackfeet, running naked and evading capture for 12 days.

Another mountain man, Jim Bridger, had a profound effect on Wyoming's early frontier days in the 19th century. Bridger established the Rocky Mountain Fur Company in

1830 and spent the next 30 years in the West as a fur trader and guide, establishing a trading post on the banks of Wyoming's Green River. Bridger married Indigenous women—the last being the daughter of Shoshone chief Washakie—and discovered new trading routes, including shortcuts on the Oregon and Bozeman Trails. He later served as a U.S. Army guide and scout in their campaign against the Sioux and Cheyenne, who were attacking parties along the Bozeman Trail.

An interesting but still somewhat mysterious discovery in Wyoming was a giant medicine wheel in the north-central part of the state. Now the Medicine Wheel National Historic Landmark, this stone ring is thought to have been sacred to Indigenous people and believed to have been used for astronomical, teaching, and healing purposes. Constructed between 300 to 800 years ago, the wheel is roughly 80 feet (24 m) in diameter and is one of the best-preserved stone rings in the world.

Blazing Trails Across the State

The famous Oregon Trail passed through central and southern Wyoming on its way from Missouri to the Northwest. Today, Wyoming contains the longest and least-changed stretch of trail—487 miles (790 km)—that can be re-created by traveling on various state and federal highways. The Oregon Trail was one of the main trading routes for those migrating west and used by an estimated 400,000 people. Large wagon trains left Missouri as early as 1841 and usage peaked in 1850, but the trail practically disappeared when the first transcontinental railroad was completed in 1869.

With the arrival of the railroad, population gradually began to increase, and the Wyoming Territory was created in 1869. Yellowstone was made the country's first national park in 1872, and visitors slowly started trickling in from the East. Coal was discovered near Rock Springs in 1885, but no large deposits of minerals like gold or silver were ever discovered. Wyoming's lack of a gold rush limited its population growth, but in 1890 the territory was officially recognized as the 44th state.

Wyoming played a large role in the women's suffrage movement, being the first to grant women the right to vote in 1869. Wyoming also had the first female justice of the peace, the first female court bailiff, and the first female governor in the country.

Livestock, Energy, and Tourism

The devastation of the West's bison herds and the subsequent placement of Native Americans on reservations led to the development of what would become Wyoming's hallmark industry in the late 19th century: cattle. Millions of cattle were driven into Wyoming in the 1870s and 1880s, and cattle barons soon dominated the natural and political landscape, basically buying off any and all forms of government. Sheep soon followed, taking advantage of vast tracts of grasslands, and by 1902 there were more than six million sheep roaming throughout Wyoming. Conflicts between sheepherders and cattlemen often escalated into violence, but these died down as the government enacted policies and divided up the land.

Wyoming's first oil well was drilled in 1884, and by the time of the first oil boom in 1908, the state was pumping out nearly 18,000 barrels per year. Production continued to climb, peaking in 1970, when more than 150 million barrels were pumped. It has mostly declined since then, and for a while, leveled off at around 51-55 million barrels per year. In 2014, another boom bounced production up to 69 million barrels of crude oil annually. After reaching a 30-year high in 2019, the state's crude oil production fell sharply in 2020 as a result of the drop in demand from consumers and falling oil prices during the pandemic. The boom-and-bust oil cycle of the 1970s and 1980s had a profound effect in Wyoming as so-called oil-patch towns like Green River, Rock Springs, and Casper grew rapidly on the promise of high-paying oil jobs, then fell flat as the industry bubble collapsed in the early 1980s. It's a pattern the state has lived through time and again.

After its peak in the 1970s, the oil industry in Wyoming was surpassed by coal, of which the state is still the nation's leading producer by far. As of 2020, Wyoming provided 41 percent of the country's coal, much of which is located in the Powder River Basin and used for coal-fired power plants. The state produced some 218 million short tons of coal in 2020, down significantly from the 442.5 million short tons produced statewide in 2010, but still has billions, maybe even trillions, of tons in reserves. But the bust is obvious. Massive mine layoffs starting in 2016, plus bankruptcy filings for two of the largest coal producers, are in line with the significant decreases each year: Production decreased more than 46 percent between 2014 and 2020. After more than 6,000 mining job losses in 2020 and significant population reductions in Wyoming's biggest mining towns, things don't look good for the mining industry in Wyoming at present. It's worth noting that 2020 taxes paid to the state by mining companies were down 67 percent in places from 2019, creating serious shortfalls for counties relying on both jobs and the tax base. After Louisiana, Wyoming has the second most energy-intensive state economy, so both booms and busts create significant impacts statewide.

Even though Wyoming has two of the country's largest natural gas fields and produces more natural gas from federal leases than any other states, the natural gas boom of the first decade of the 21st century shows no signs of reoccurring, with production falling steadily—around 4.4 percent each year—starting in 2009. Production decreases across the state can be attributed to several things: lower prices in 2020, reduced consumer demand in part because of the pandemic, a national supply glut, and natural production declines in aging wells.

In 2020, 15 percent of Wyoming's electricity was generated by renewable energy sources, including wind power, which accounted for 80 percent of the state's renewable electricity. Even with the state's significant wind resources, wind energy hit a wall in Wyoming in 2015 because of the expense of building transmission lines. The production is easy, but how to get it moved out of state? In 2020 however, the amount of wind-powered generating capacity installed in Wyoming nearly doubled to almost 1,800 megawatts. There are several large wind projects in development or under construction across the state, and several large transmission projects in the works too, allowing Wyoming to sell and transport wind energy to other states. Both hydroelectric and solar power accounted for about 3 percent each of the state's renewable energy generation in 2020.

Just as people migrated west and settled in Wyoming hundreds of years ago, people today come to visit Yellowstone National Park, travel the Oregon Trail, or climb one of the majestic peaks of the Teton Mountains. Tourism is the state's second-largest industry behind mineral extraction, worth more than $3.5 billion annually. In 2017, Wyoming saw 8.7 million visitors, nearly doubling the national average visitation growth rate. Visitation in Wyoming had gone up 48 percent in the last decade, until COVID-19 caused a 23 percent decline in the travel economy, compared to a decline of 36 percent nationally. Towns like Jackson Hole and Cody reap the benefits of being adjacent to Yellowstone, while the park itself attracted nearly 4.5 million visitors in 2021. Statewide, tourism accounts for 7 percent of total employment, meaning one in every 10 jobs is tied to tourism.

Wyoming's balance among energy development, agriculture, and tourism is the face of the New West, where people move for a better quality of life while still trying to preserve the cultural heritage. Just like the settlers who established trading posts hundreds of years ago, these new immigrants are chasing a dream of living in an unspoiled part of the world and doing anything necessary to pay the bills.

Conservative State, Progressive Past

The political history of Wyoming are as colorful as the Wild West and have changed over the years to reflect the shifting populations, economies, and cultures that exist here.

Wyoming's political history is a study in contrasts. It was the first state to grant women the right to vote and the first state to elect a woman as governor. Yet the state remains largely conservative and has only voted for one Democratic president since 1960 (Lyndon B. Johnson in 1964). Even though more than half of Wyoming's residents consider themselves Republicans, and Republicans have held a majority in the state senate continuously since 1936 and in the state house since 1964, Democrats have owned the governor's seat for all but 18 years since 1975. Democratic governor Dave Freudenthal, in office 2002-2011, had one of the highest approval ratings in the country. Still, as recently as 2018, a Gallup poll ranked Wyoming as the most conservative state behind Mississippi.

As in many states in the West, Democratic strongholds tend to exist in slightly more urban areas or areas that have a large number of transplants and a younger population. In Wyoming, Teton County is the only reliably Democratic county, which is no surprise as it includes Jackson Hole. The town's population has boomed over the years, boosted by younger transplants from more liberal parts of the country who come for the skiing, fly-fishing, and outdoor lifestyle the town offers. Albany County, which includes both Laramie and the University of Wyoming, was the only other county in the state where Biden got more votes than Trump in 2020.

Government

Wyoming Territory was formed in 1869, but the road to statehood did not begin until 1888. After a few statehood bills failed to pass, the House finally approved the bill on March 27, 1890, making Wyoming the 44th state after President Benjamin Harrison signed the bill into law soon after. Its capital is Cheyenne.

During the territorial era, the Wyoming Legislature played a pivotal role in the U.S. suffrage movement. In 1869, just 4 years after the Civil War and 35 years before women's suffrage became a highly visible political issue in the United States, Wyoming granted all women age 21 and older the right to vote; the territorial government was the first in the world to secure this right for women. Democrat Nellie Tayloe Ross became the first female governor in the country when she won a special election in 1924 after then-governor William Ross died in office. She later became the first woman to serve as director of the U.S. Mint, appointed in 1933 by President Franklin

D. Roosevelt, a position she held until her retirement in 1953.

Wyoming remains one of the few states that have a true part-time citizen legislature, meaning its members don't enjoy the same accommodations provided to full-time legislators in larger states. As of 2021, for example, legislators were still paid just $150 per day, when convening, after a proposal to raise payment to $175 per day was rejected. There are 60 state representatives elected for two-year terms, along with 30 state senators that serve four-year terms. There are no term limits. The state legislature meets in odd-numbered years beginning the second Tuesday in January. The general session is limited to 40 legislative days. The offices of governor, secretary of state, auditor, treasurer, and superintendent of public instruction are all elected every four years.

The Wyoming Legislature passed a bill limiting the office of governor to two consecutive terms after Democrat Edgar Herschler served three terms in the mid-1980s. In 1992

Header at top right with page number and vertical side text.

voters approved term limits in a ballot initiative, but neither action constituted an amendment to the Wyoming constitution. In 2004 two state legislators challenged the term-limit law in the courts, and the Wyoming Supreme Court subsequently invalidated the limits in a unanimous decision, ruling that a constitutional amendment would be required to establish such a law. Popular Democrat Dave Freudenthal, who served two terms as governor after being elected in 2002 and 2006, did not use the same challenge to seek a third term.

Freudenthal's election and popularity—his approval rating was a staggering 82 percent in the months before the 2010 election—defy Wyoming's Republican nature. In fact, the governorship in general has seen its fair share of Democrats, but Republicans have dominated both houses of the legislature almost since statehood. Wyoming has only voted for one Democratic president in the last half century (Lyndon B. Johnson in 1964), and Republicans have held a majority in the state senate continuously since 1936 and in the state house since 1964. Despite its tendency to elect Democrats as governor—though current governor Mark Gordon is a Republican—Wyoming is considered a red state at the national level and was named the country's second-most conservative state in a 2018 Gallup poll.

Dick Cheney is Wyoming's best-known political figure. Born in Casper, Cheney was the White House chief of staff during the Nixon and Ford administrations and was then elected to the U.S. House of Representatives in 1978. He served five terms and was then selected to be the secretary of defense during the first Bush presidency and later served as the vice president 2001-2009 under George W. Bush. In 2016, his daughter, Republican Liz Cheney, ran for Wyoming's lone seat in the U.S. House of Representatives and won, but in November 2021, after she spoke out against Donald Trump and his role in the January 6 attack

on the Capitol, the Wyoming GOP voted to no longer recognize Cheney as a Republican. Despite the fact that Donald Trump earned only 7 percent of the Republican primary vote, behind Ted Cruz at 66.3 percent and Marco Rubio at 19.5 percent, he beat Hillary Clinton handily with 70.1 percent of the vote to her 22.5 percent.

The Wind River Indian Reservation is home to the Eastern Shoshone Tribal Government, a sovereign government that operates under its own constitution. The Business Council of the Eastern Shoshone Tribe consists of a chair, vice chair, and four additional council members who are elected by the tribe. The tribal council chair is the administrative head of the tribe and serves a two-year term with the vice chairman and the other members of the council. Both the Eastern Shoshone and Northern Arapaho are represented.

INDIAN RESERVATIONS

The Native American population plays an important role in Wyoming government and politics. Tribal law prevails within reservation boundaries, and Indian reservations are federally recognized as independent political units with their own structure and legislation. As sovereign nations, tribes can have their own school systems, constitutions, police and court systems, and legislative councils. They can also regulate transport and trade within reservation boundaries. The state can't tax land or transactions that occur on reservations.

What does this mean to the visitor? Essentially, some state laws may not apply on reservations. Goods and services—mainly gasoline and tobacco—can be much cheaper on the reservations since there are no state taxes enforced. Not all land may be open to the public, and there may be additional fees for recreation, including hunting and fishing. It's best to inquire at a local store or gas station if you are traveling on reservation land in Wyoming.

Economy

Natural resource extraction, agriculture, and tourism play major roles in the economy. Oil production and coal and natural gas extraction fell dramatically in the middle part of the decade, making Wyoming's economy one of only four states in the country to shrink in the first half of 2015. In 2017, Wyoming current-dollar GDP was $40.3 billion, compared to $36.3 billion in 2007, ranking the state 49th and 46th respectively in the United States. In 2020, after hits across the board due to COVID-19, the real GDP was $36.47 billion, barely up over the 2007 figures. In 2020, Wyoming's largest industry was still mining, quarrying, and oil and gas extraction, followed by tourism, agriculture, and manufacturing, which has grown by nearly 50 percent since 2015.

Tourism is still one of the largest contributors of tax revenue to the state, providing the state government with more than $2 billion in annual revenue and employing 7 percent of the labor force as of 2020. In 2020, 6.9 million people visited the state, spending $3.05 billion. Because of the pandemic, the figures were down from 8.7 million visitors in 2017 but are expected to rebound as the pandemic eases. Leisure and hospitality is the largest employer among all private industries in the state. Yellowstone and Grand Teton National Parks play a big role in tourism for the state, and both broke records for visitation in 2021.

Since most of Wyoming can be classified as rural, it's no surprise that agriculture plays a vital role in the state's economy—more than $1.8 billion in cash receipts in 2019. There are more than 12,000 farms and ranches operating in Wyoming, occupying 29 million acres. Wyoming ranks 11th nationally in total land in farms and ranches, and 1st in the United States for the average size of farms and ranches, which was 2,417 acres in 2019. The number of ranches and farms peaked at more than 18,000 in the 1930s, then slowly declined,

but the industry has leveled off in the past few decades and is starting to grow again.

Hay is the leading crop in Wyoming, followed by sugar beets, barley, corn, wheat, and dry beans. Dryland winter wheat is grown primarily in the eastern part of the state. Other more specialized commodities in the state include oats, pinto beans, hogs, bison, and sunflowers.

The cattle industry produces the largest agricultural commodity—mainly beef cattle—and dates back to the mid-1880s, when settlers first came to the West. After the Civil War, cattle ranching flourished, and Cheyenne became a world trade center for the beef industry. Even today, there are three times as many cattle in Wyoming as there are people.

Wyoming's high plains and mountain meadows are recognized for their role in producing high-quality sheep. According to the National Agricultural Statistics Service, in 2020 Wyoming ranked fourth in the country in stock sheep and second in lamb crop and wool production. Wyoming's wool is among the most desirable in the world.

The University of Wyoming is the largest government employer in the state with 4,500 jobs. The largest private employer is Omega Probe, a Cheyenne-based tech firm with 2,200 employees and an annual revenue of more than $80 million. From 2015 to 2019, Wyoming's median household income was $64,049, with the annual per capita income being $33,366 for the same time period. Wyoming's economic recovery from the COVID-19 pandemic has been slower than most other states, with revenues in 2021 still lagging 10 percent behind pre-pandemic collections, despite small increases in fossil fuel prices and record-setting tourism numbers in both Yellowstone and Grand Teton National Parks. Even so, there is reason for optimism according to economists. Wyoming still lays claim to the country's largest "rainy day fund,"

Wind Power: Wyoming's Next Boom?

Having prospered from the boom and then endured the bust of energy production cycles countless times over the last century and more, Wyoming is at the forefront of what may be a renewable energy boom based on what has for eons been at the center of the state's frequently harsh climate: wind. Wind power technology as we now know it started in the early 1980s. As the seventh-windiest state, according to the American Wind Energy Association, Wyoming ranks 19th in installed wind capacity, and the numbers are growing steadily. In 2017, wind energy provided 9.4 percent of all in-state electricity production, or enough to power 408,700 homes. By 2021, the figures had more than doubled: 1 million homes can now be powered by clean energy produced in Wyoming. The DOE Wind Vision Scenario projects that wind energy from Wyoming could power the equivalent of 3.4 million average American homes by 2030. In addition to constant wind, the vast tracts of public land and low population density make Wyoming an ideal wind energy producer. Benefits of wind power to Wyoming include jobs—though not nearly as many as either exist or have been lost in mineral extraction—and electricity produced without greenhouse gases.

One of the challenges has been trying to sell that wind energy to major urban areas that need it, such as Las Vegas and locations in California and Arizona. The distances are vast, and transmission capacity has only been substantively addressed since 2020. A consortium of companies, some of them affiliates of the privately held Anschutz Corp., which is building the biggest wind farm in the country in Carbon County, proposed building three major transmission lines—Transwest Express, Zephyr, and Gateway West—to send the energy to the Southwest and California. Another not insignificant challenge has been the conservative state's reluctance to give up on fossil fuels—and the economy and culture that they've known for so long—in favor of clean energy. The fear is that growing the wind business in Wyoming will hasten the demise of the coal, oil, and gas industries, something Wyoming residents are loath to give up. In 2021, coal still accounted for 80 percent of the state's electric grid, and wind came in a distant second at just over 13 percent.

Spend a few days in Wyoming, particularly in the southern half of the state, and you will agree it has some of the most consistent wind in the country. As of 2021, more than $5 billion in capital has been invested in wind, solar, and energy storage projects in Wyoming. In 2020, there were just over 1,000 wind turbines installed in Wyoming, according to the American Wind Energy Association, and hundreds more were under construction. Estimates put the eventual tally as high as 10,000 towers across the state, which will clearly change the landscape of Wyoming.

Somewhat controversially, Wyoming is the first state to put a tax on wind energy production. Proposed by Governor Dave Freudenthal, the $1 per megawatt hour tax went into effect in 2012 after a sales tax exemption for renewable energy projects expired in 2011. In its first year alone, the tax generated roughly $2.6 million for the state. As of 2021, more than $36 million in tax revenue had been collected for the benefit of the state. In Carbon County, taxable sales increased by 108 percent in 2020, thanks to wind power projects, and they were one of only three counties in the state to end the year with a budget surplus. Experts expect tax revenue to grow significantly as the state's ability to sell and transport the energy expands. The crux of the controversy is that some feel this makes Wyoming unfriendly to wind power producers, but the governor and his supporters argued that the producers are going to make a lot of money but Wyomingites will bear the environmental—primarily visual—and socioeconomic burden. They pointed to the benefits gained statewide by tax revenues from oil, gas, coal, and coal-bed methane.

As the wind power boom takes off, there is something of a land rush in southeastern Wyoming, where the greatest number of wind farms exist, transforming the local agricultural and ranching culture. In an effort to prevent bad deals with a strength-in-numbers approach, ranchers and farmers have joined together to form associations to bargain collectively. Just as the massive wind turbines are undoubtedly altering the landscape of Wyoming, so too are the proactive ranchers and farmers working together to transform the business of agriculture. In 2021, lease payments to farmers and ranchers from wind companies totaled $17.3 million. Indeed, income from wind farms can often be the deciding factor in whether a family can hold on to their ranch or not. As a result, some argue that wind farms are in fact strengthening Wyoming's agricultural tradition by keeping farmers and ranchers on their land.

which can offset revenue declines with cash reserves for 353 days of operating costs. In addition, the state is working to cut spending and is attempting to diversify the economy.

Local Culture

The people and culture are largely tied to the settling of the West and the Native Americans who inhabited the area. It wasn't until the 1860s that settlers started building permanent communities as the gold rush, the railroad, and the Homestead Act lured those seeking a different and potentially lucrative way of life. Many areas were settled by immigrants and still retain their European heritage.

Wyoming is considered a conservative state and has a population that is around 90 percent white. More than 10 percent of Wyoming's population is listed as Hispanic or Latino in origin.

NATIVE AMERICANS

Although farming, ranching, and natural resource extraction certainly contributed to the growing cultural landscape, it's the rich Native American history that gives the state a proud and colorful representation of the past that transcends today's modern American culture. Before trappers and settlers came west, Indigenous people roamed freely across the land, following the huge bison herds that once covered the plains. Each tribe has unique customs and traditions. While Native Americans have worked to adapt to the changing world around them, they have also tried to keep the culture and traditions of their past alive. Their culture is celebrated through dance, songs, games, language, and religious ceremonies. This rich heritage contributes significantly to Wyoming.

Several museums in each state pay tribute to the American Indian, and many reservation towns host annual powwows, rodeos, and celebrations. Today, 2.4 percent of Wyoming's are classified as Native American.

There is only one reservation in Wyoming, which is home to two different tribes. The following is a list of the Native American groups and the reservations that they inhabit today.

Wyoming's Wind River Reservation, the seventh-largest in the country at more than 2.2 million acres, is home to more than 4,216 Eastern Shoshone and 9,862 Northern Arapaho. The Shoshone have been in Wyoming since the 16th century and were some of the first Indians to have horses. The eastern part of the tribe was pushed back west of the Laramie Mountains when their enemies—the Sioux, Crow, and Arapaho—invaded their territory.

Fort Washakie is home to the Shoshone Tribal Cultural Center and the cemeteries where both Shoshone chief Washakie and Lewis and Clark's Shoshone guide, Sacagawea, are buried. Originally called Fort Brown, the name was changed in 1878 to honor the chief who negotiated the treaty establishing the reservation. Ironically, the Shoshone ended up on the same reservation as their former enemies, the Arapaho, after the U.S. government temporarily placed them together—which soon became a permanent situation, betraying Chief Washakie's wishes to end the arrangement.

The Arapaho people ended up on Wyoming's Wind River Reservation along with their former enemies, the Shoshone, after the U.S. government placed them together, supposedly temporarily. Today, Wind River is home to more than 4,200 Eastern Shoshone and 9,800 Northern Arapaho.

Like many tribes, the Arapaho were forced out of Minnesota after the arrival of settlers and migrated to the Great Plains in the late 18th century. After many years of trying to fight back against the settlers, the tribe was decimated by the late 1800s and ultimately forced onto a reservation with the Shoshone. The Heritage Center at St. Stephens and the Arapaho Cultural Museum in Ethete both provide insight into the tribe and its traditions.

THE ARTS

Wyoming boasts vibrant and varied art scenes with an interesting and colorful history. Towns like Great Falls, Cody, and Jackson are meccas for Western art.

Wyoming has its share of standouts. Platte Valley resident C. J. Box is one of the top-selling mystery writers in the country, and Annie Proulx won a Pulitzer Prize for her novel *The Shipping News*. Other writers who call Wyoming home include James Galvin (The Meadow), Mark Spragg (*Where Rivers Change Direction*), Kathleen O'Neal Gear (*People of the Longhouse*), and Alexandra Fuller (Don't Let's Go to the Dogs Tonight). In addition, Ernest Hemingway spent a lot of time in Wyoming, where he worked on several novels, including *Death in the Afternoon* and *Green Hills of Africa*.

Fine Art

Not surprisingly, Wyoming is a hotbed for Western art lovers. Two of the West's premier art events—Jackson's Fall Arts Festival and Cody's Rendezvous Royale—take place each September in Wyoming. Much of the Cody event centers around the Buffalo Bill Center of the West, which houses the impressive Whitney Gallery of Western Art. Collections here include works from the early 19th century to contemporary times that commemorate the events, people, and landscape of the Rocky Mountain region.

Jackson features quaint streets lined with galleries and shops, offering everything from locally made stationery to the finest in Western photography, sculpture, and painting.

Its 10-day Fall Arts Festival is home to one of the region's largest auctions, and the Grand Teton Music Festival hosts some of the world's finest classical musicians each summer in nearby Teton Village. Jackson is also home to the National Museum of Wildlife Art, which boasts more than 5,000 works in its permanent collection, and to the Jackson Hole Center for the Arts, a vibrant community center that offers everything from nationally touring musical and dance acts to educational workshops.

Jackson's Off Square Theatre Company is a vibrant year-round company founded in 1998, and Casper's Stage III Community Theatre offers six productions each year September-June. In downtown Sheridan, the historic WYO Theater—which opened in 1929 as the Lotus—was saved from demolition and refurbished, opening again in 1989 as a nonprofit organization. Today it offers an array of musical concerts and theater productions that belie its small-town setting. The University of Wyoming is home to one of the most outstanding undergraduate theater programs in the country along with the University of Wyoming Fine Arts Studio, where some of the region's finest facilities are located. Indirectly, Wyoming is probably best known in the theater world as the setting for *The Laramie Project,* an award-winning play depicting the reaction to the 1998 murder of gay University of Wyoming student Matthew Shepard in Laramie. The play was produced by the New York-based Tectonic Theater Project and was also made into an HBO film of the same name.

Music

Many communities have free music nights, and local bars and taverns are usually good for a fun country band and the occasional touring act. Casper and Cheyenne are home to big arenas, while Cheyenne's Frontier Days rodeo offers nightly performances by favorite country music stars each July.

It seems nearly every small town has a bluegrass festival during the summer, and Wyoming's Grand Targhee Bluegrass Festival is one of the nation's best. The Grand Teton Music Festival hosts classical concerts and workshops June-August.

Matthew Shepard and *The Laramie Project*

Born in Casper, Wyoming, in 1976, Matthew Shepard was a political science major and the student representative for the Wyoming Environmental Council during his first year at the University of Wyoming in Laramie. Long a champion for equality and an admired peer counselor in high school, Shepard was the kind of kid who wanted to change the world. Tragically, it was his brutal 1998 murder that effected the change Shepard worked to inspire during his short life.

On October 7, Shepard, who was gay, was abducted from a bar in Laramie by Aaron McKinney and Russell Henderson. The two men drove Shepard to a remote area east of town where they robbed and viciously beat their victim with the butt of a handgun. Likely unconscious from countless blows to the face and head, Shepard was tied to a fence and left to die. He was found 18 hours later by a bicyclist who at first mistook Shepard for a scarecrow. Matthew Shepard died on October 12 from his injuries without ever having regained consciousness. Both murderers confessed their crimes using a gay-panic defense strategy and are serving consecutive life sentences in unidentified prisons.

What was a horrific tragedy for Shepard's tight-knit family was seen around the world as a hate crime, inflicted upon the 21-year-old because he was gay. Shepard's parents, Dennis and Judy, created the Matthew Shepard Foundation (www.matthewshepard.org) to honor the memory of their son and to "inspire individuals, organizations, and communities to embrace the dignity and equality of all people" through educational, outreach, and advocacy programs. Judy Shepard has turned her personal tragedy into a crusade for justice as she travels the world over, speaking on behalf of and advocating for lesbian, gay, bisexual, and transgender youth. To date, Judy has brought Matthew's message of acceptance to more than 300,000 people worldwide. In 2009, the Matthew Shepard and James Byrd Jr. Hate Crimes Prevention Act was passed into federal law, an expansion of the 1969 federal hate-crime law to include crimes motivated by a victim's actual or perceived gender, sexual orientation, gender identity, or disability. It was the first federal law to extend legal protection to transgendered people.

Another response to Shepard's murder was *The Laramie Project*, brought to fruition by Tectonic Theater Project. The small theater company traveled to Laramie and interviewed residents about the events surrounding Shepard's death. What they learned was transformed into a play, *The Laramie Project*, and eventually a movie of the same name that ran on HBO and was seen by more than 30 million people nationwide.

Ten years after the murder, Moisés Kaufman and other members of the theater company traveled back to Laramie to see if and how the community had been transformed by the passage of time. In October 2009, *The Laramie Project Epilogue* premiered across the country in major theaters, as well as at high schools and colleges. Another documentary project, *Matt Shepard Is a Friend of Mine*, won an Emmy in 2016.

On the 20th anniversary of his murder, in 2018, Shepard's remains were interred at Washington National Cathedral. Activists say that the site is a symbol of the LGBTQ+ movement.

Essentials

Transportation

GETTING THERE

Flying into Wyoming is easier than you think, and it's by far the best way to get here. Flights into the larger airports are becoming increasingly frequent as the region gains ground as an incredible destination for visitors. Although getting here by train or bus is possible, it's not as convenient, and stops can be far from the main travel areas—best left to hardy travelers or those on a tight budget. If you live in the West, driving is a great way to get here—major highways will carry you into the state, and well-traveled back roads will lead you to your final destination.

By Air

Commercial flights are available to and from Casper, Cheyenne, Cody, Gillette, Jackson, Laramie, Riverton, Rock Springs, and Sheridan. Jackson has the best service, with jet flights from Atlanta, Denver, Salt Lake City, Dallas, Houston, Chicago, Minneapolis, Phoenix, New York City, Newark, Washington DC, San Francisco, and Los Angeles. Remember that the Jackson Hole Airport will be closed completely from April 11, 2022 until June 27, 2022. Some flights only operate during peak times in the winter and summer, and many people choose to fly into Salt Lake City (275 mi/445 km) or Idaho Falls (90 mi/145 km) and pick up a rental car for the scenic drive to Jackson. Major carriers with service to Wyoming include American, United, Frontier, and Delta.

If budget is your top priority, be sure to look into flights into nearby airports. They can be less expensive or more available during high-traffic seasons. That's not always the case; sometimes smaller airports can be even pricier with more limited schedules, but it's worth looking into. Keep in mind that drivers will often encounter wildlife on the roads, particularly late at night. And weather conditions can be sketchy, especially during winter. In other words, make sure the money saved on the flight is worth your time on the road. And pay attention to arrival and departure times, particularly in winter, when the nights are long and dark.

By Car

I-80 runs across the state from Nebraska to Nevada, while I-25 heads north from Colorado up to its intersection with I-90 in Buffalo, then on to Billings, Montana. US 89 is a popular and scenic route to Jackson from

Salt Lake City and heads up through Grand Teton and Yellowstone National Parks.

By Train

For a state that was quite literally built by the railroads, train service today is spotty at best. There is no passenger train service in Wyoming on Amtrak, but Amtrak buses pick up in Casper and Laramie and can transport travelers to train stations in Utah and Colorado. In Montana, there is bus service from Livingston to train stops in the northern part of the state.

By Bus

Greyhound has service to all major cities and many smaller Wyoming towns, including Buffalo, Casper, Cheyenne, Evanston, Gillette, Jackson, Laramie, Rawlins, Rock Springs, Sheridan, and Wheatland. Bus service is also available on **Jefferson Lines** (800/451-5333, www.jeffersonlines.com) from Buffalo (stop is unstaffed), Gillette, and Sheridan.

Alltrans/Jackson Hole Express (307/733-3135 or 800/443-6133, www.jacksonholealltrans.com) provides daily shuttle service between Salt Lake City, Idaho Falls, Pocatello, and the resort town of Jackson, as well as transfers to and from the Jackson Hole Airport.

The **Wind River Transportation Authority** (307/856-7118, www.wrtabuslines.com) offers fixed-route and airport shuttles in summer between Riverton, Ethete, Hudson, Fort Washakie, Kinnear, and Lander.

GETTING AROUND

By far the best way to get around once you're here is by car. Rental cars are available at the major airports. Consider an all-wheel-drive vehicle even if you travel only during the summer, as many of the region's most scenic roads are gravel. In addition to better traction, these vehicles typically offer higher clearance.

Previous: painted horses at the Green River Rendezvous in Pinedale, Wyoming.

By Car

I-80 runs across the state, while I-25 is primarily a north-south highway that intersects with I-90 in Buffalo, then goes on to Billings, Montana. US 89 is a popular and scenic north-south route that passes through Jackson and then up through Grand Teton and Yellowstone National Parks into Montana.

CAR RENTAL

If you plan on renting a car, reserve one well in advance. Unless you will be driving entirely on paved roads, which is doubtful, a high-clearance or all-wheel-drive vehicle is a good idea. Many Forest Service campgrounds are located along gravel roads, and anytime you venture off the beaten path, you're bound to encounter some type of gravel or dirt road. In the winter, all-wheel drive is a must. And be aware that rock chips on the windshield are common occurrences at any time of year. Make sure your insurance will cover it, or consider paying for added insurance from the car-rental agency.

Car-rental agencies include **Alamo** (800/227-7368, www.alamo.com), **Avis** (800/352-7900, www.avis.com), **Budget** (800/527-0700, www.budget.com), **Dollar** (800/800-5252, www.dollar.com), **Enterprise** (800/261-7331, www.enterprise.com), **Hertz** (800/654-3131, www.hertz.com), **National** (888/868-6204, www.nationalcar.com), and **Thrifty** (800/847-4389, www.thrifty.com).

HIGHWAY SAFETY

A few considerations apply when you are planning a road trip. In general, interstates and major highways are in good condition across the region, although short summers mean road construction can be expected at any time of the day—or night, in some cases. State highways are often narrow and winding, not compatible with drowsy or inattentive drivers. Wildlife is a concern on any road, particularly at twilight and dark, and fallen rocks can be a problem in mountainous areas. For road conditions, the **Wyoming Department of Transportation**

(888/996-7623, www.wyoroad.info) has a wealth of information.

Distances between settlements can be great, especially in the eastern parts of the state. Planning ahead is critical. Don't wait until your gas light is on to fill up your tank, and make sure your spare is inflated. Carrying emergency gear is recommended. Rest areas—even on major highways and interstates—can be hundreds of miles apart. Most major towns and cities have reliable mechanics and car dealerships, but don't expect to find parts for your old Porsche roadster in very many places.

In general, the speed limit is 80 mph on interstates and 70 mph on most two-lane highways, although it can vary quite a bit depending on location and time of day. Many two-lane roads have numerous turnouts, where slower-moving vehicles can pull over and let cars pass. Wyoming drivers are used to driving faster on these roads, so if you're getting tailgated by a local, just pull over and let them go by. Increasingly, passing lanes are being incorporated into many state highways, particularly on roads over mountain passes. Slow down and change lanes for stopped emergency or maintenance vehicles. Courtesy would suggest you do the same for any vehicle stopped alongside the road.

WINTER TRAVEL

Winter driving takes special care, focus, and—at times—lots of caffeine. Roads can be rendered impassable in a matter of minutes by snow and wind, and mountain passes are especially susceptible to fast-changing conditions. Because of the area covered, it may take a while before snowplows clear the roads. And be extremely cautious when driving behind or toward a snowplow, as visibility can be diminished to nothing. Be aware that because of wildlife, salt is rarely used on roads. Instead, the roads are graveled to provide better traction in icy conditions. Loose gravel often translates into cracked or chipped windshields, so drive with caution, and never get too close to a graveling truck.

Snow tires are a must in many places, and

Laws of the Wild West

Because Wyoming was born of the Wild West, in many cases there still exists a hands-off, "we don't need no government" mentality. While this may work in some areas, some outdated laws and rules are being updated or eliminated.

Currently, the speed limit for automobiles is 80 mph on interstates, 70 mph on most two-lane highways, and 65 mph on most interstates within urban areas. In places, nighttime speed limits are lower than daytime.

Believe it or not, it used to be legal to operate a vehicle in Wyoming with an open container of alcohol, whether you were driving or just along for the ride. In states where distances are often measured in "six-packs," this was a big deal.

Wyoming passed a weak open-container law in 2002, which became known as the "Here, hold my beer while I talk to this officer" law, but passed a stricter version in 2007. It is taken much more seriously these days.

Speaking of alcohol, Wyoming is one of the few states where you can still buy a bottle from a drive-through liquor store—just don't open it in the car. And they no longer serve "to go" cocktails.

Make sure you close the gate if you cross a river or onto private land; otherwise it could cost you $750.

---

carrying emergency supplies is strongly recommended. A good emergency kit includes a shovel, a first-aid kit, jumper cables, a flashlight, signal flares, extra clothing, some food, water, a tow strap, and a sleeping bag. Don't rely on your cell phone to save you—although service is improving, there are many dead zones.

The state's transportation website (www.wyoroad.info) has links to current and projected weather patterns, and toll-free information numbers are updated regularly. Carry these numbers in your car. Occasionally weather information can be found on the AM band of your car radio—you'll notice signs along roads indicating where this is possible.

TRAVEL MAPS

Free road maps can be found at visitors centers and rest areas, while an excellent supplement is the **Delorme Gazetteer series** (www.delorme.com), available at bookstores and in many gas stations. These oversize companions are a must for those venturing off the beaten path, as they include topographic data, Forest Service roads and trails, camping and hiking information, fishing areas, scenic drives, and more. Sporting goods stores offer more specialized maps, from national forests and wilderness areas to Bureau of Land Management lands and mile-by-mile river guides. The free road maps you get when you enter the national parks are sufficient to use during your stay.

By Bike

Numerous back roads and accessible campgrounds make for some fun trips, but be prepared for long-distance rides and not much company. The Wyoming transportation website (www.wyoroad.info) offers excellent information for cyclists. Information can also be found on www.cyclingwyoming.org.

Recreation

Wyoming offers some of the best recreational opportunities in the West, from mountain biking and fishing to boating and horseback riding. Vast areas of untouched land make for scenic beauty that can take a lifetime to explore, luring visitors back time and again to experience the outdoors.

In the summer, rivers come alive with white-water boaters, and smaller streams entice fly-fishers seeking solitude. Wilderness areas and national forests offer miles of hiking trails, while national parks host visitors from around the world. Lakes buzz with the sound of motorboats, campgrounds are full, and everyone seems to be outside doing something. Summers are short, so people take advantage of them.

It's no surprise, then, that winters are particularly long, but residents take advantage of it by enjoying some of the finest and least-crowded ski slopes in the country. Great snow and majestic mountain trails make snowmobiling extremely popular, and Nordic ski centers and trails can be found in most mountain areas. Ice fishing, dogsledding, and backcountry skiing and snowboarding are other activities that keep folks busy when the snow flies.

NATIONAL PARKS

Most of **Yellowstone National Park** (www.nps.gov/yell) is in Wyoming, but three of the park's entrances are found in Montana. Just below Yellowstone in Wyoming is **Grand Teton National Park** (www.nps.gov/grte). Visitors will find a variety of accommodations in the parks, including rustic cabins, grand lodges, and tent and RV campgrounds. Popular activities include hiking, boating, fishing, and wildlife-viewing. Informational visitors centers and museums are sited in each park and offer excellent resources for history buffs.

The entrance fee in the summer for each park is $35 for automobiles, which is valid for seven days. An annual America the Beautiful national parks and federal recreation lands annual pass, which permits entrance to more than 2,000 federal recreation sites, costs $80. Campground and other lodging fees are extra. Annual passes for any of the three parks are available for $70.

STATE PARKS

Wyoming manages **12 state parks** (www.wyoparks.wyo.gov) plus historic sites and landmarks, ranging from battlefields and museums to parks with hot mineral soaking springs. Daily use fees are $4 per adult for historic sites (kids under 18 are free) and $7 per vehicle (nonresident) for state parks. Overnight camping permits start at $17 for nonresidents and include the daily use fee. Camping cabins and yurts start at $60 per night (plus a $50 deposit, $7 daily use fee, and $11 camping fee). Sites can be reserved online (www.wyoparks.wyo.gov) or by calling (877/996-7275).

NATIONAL FORESTS

Much of the public land in Wyoming's mountainous areas is administered by the U.S. Forest Service (www.fs.fed.us), including 9.7 million acres in 8 national forests in Wyoming. The Forest Service is a branch of the United States Department of Agriculture (USDA) and manages much of the nation's forest and rangelands. All national forests contain developed hiking and biking trails, and in the winter the roads and trails can often be used for cross-country skiing. Forest Service ranger stations are good places to obtain information on camping and recreation, while most sporting goods stores sell excellent maps that pertain to specific areas. **Beartooth Publishing** (www.beartoothpublishing.com) offers a popular series of waterproof maps that highlight national forest roads, trails, campgrounds, picnic areas, and fishing access sites. For reference, Wyoming is located in Region 2 (Rocky Mountain Region) and Region 4 (Intermountain Region). You'll notice signs along the highways that indicate when you enter and leave a particular national forest.

Forest Service campgrounds are widespread and offer some of the finest camping available. Fees range free-$17, depending on the type of site and the amenities offered. Free sites are often very remote and offer limited services. The Forest Service also rents some rustic cabins and lookouts starting at $25 per night. These can be a great way to enjoy the outdoors, as most are in prime locations. These cabins, as well as most campgrounds, can be reserved in advance (with additional fees) at www.recreation.gov.

WILDERNESS AREAS

As of 2021, there are 14 federally designated wilderness areas in Wyoming. These are roadless and closed to mechanized use, including mountain bikes. Wilderness areas generally offer solitude and amazing scenery, although some areas may be more heavily used than remote non-wilderness areas. Some wilderness areas may fall under Native American

jurisdiction, so make sure you have the necessary permits before hiking, hunting, or fishing in these locations.

BLM PUBLIC LAND

The rest of the public land falls under purview of the Bureau of Land Management (BLM), which offers everything from camping and boating to caving and backcountry scenic byways. The BLM manages multiple resources and uses, including energy and minerals; timber; forage; recreation; wild horse and burro herds; fish and wildlife habitat; wilderness areas; and archaeological, paleontological, and historical sites. There are just about 17.5 million acres of BLM land in Wyoming. You can find out more about the BLM offerings at www.blm.gov.

HUNTING

Wyoming is a popular destination for those hunting elk, deer, black bears, bighorn sheep, pronghorn, pheasants, and mountain lions.

For more information on hunting in Wyoming, contact the **Wyoming Game and Fish Department** (307/777-4600, http://wgfd.wyo.gov). If you would like to enlist a hunting guide, check the websites for recommendations on established outfitters

fly-fishing in Grand Teton National Park

Forest Service Cabins and Lookouts

Imagine waking up in your own rustic cabin, nestled in the woods next to a rambling stream. You stoke the fire, mix up a pot of cowboy coffee, and enjoy a sunny breakfast on the porch with a 10,000-foot (3,000-m) peak looming overhead. There is no one else around. Now imagine that you have to pay less than $100 per night for this. Too good to be true? Well, thanks to the U.S. Forest Service cabin rental system, it isn't.

Literally hundreds of these cabins exist, most situated in locations that people would pay millions of dollars to own a piece of. Many are old ranger stations, very few are still used by the Forest Service, and all have their own unique charms. Cabins come in all different shapes and sizes, from extremely remote backcountry sites and mountaintop fire lookouts to larger cabins with electricity and motor vehicle access. Either way, they offer an unparalleled way to enjoy the outdoors.

Each national forest has cabins for rent. Your best bet in Wyoming is to search whichever of the eight national forests you want to explore, from the Bridger-Teton National Forest to the Bighorn National Forest. All cabins must be reserved online (www.recreation.gov), where you can enter when you want to stay and a list of available cabins will come up, or over the phone (877/444-6777 or 518/885-3639 outside the U.S.). Cabins range from $25 for small, one-room units to upward of $200 for larger rentals that sleep up to eight people. There are additional booking fees, both online and over the phone.

Cabins typically have bunk beds (bring your own bedding), wood stoves, wood, and pots and pans. Some have more, some have less. Toilet facilities are usually outside, and potable water is not always available. When you make your reservation, you'll get a list of what to bring as well as detailed directions.

Some of the more interesting rentals are historical fire lookouts, perched high atop a mountain with commanding views of the surrounding peaks. Sitting inside these lookouts, you can imagine backcountry rangers gazing out over the land trying to spot forest fires. These lookouts are especially beautiful at night, when you're out among the stars feeling like you're on top of the world. It's a must-do experience for those who want to get off the beaten path—and one you'll remember for a lifetime.

or contact the **Wyoming Outfitters and Guides Association** (307/265-2376, www.wyoga.org).

FISHING

Wyoming is known throughout the world as premier fishing destinations, mainly due to the popularity of fly-fishing on beautiful rivers that flow throughout the region. Legendary trout streams lure anglers looking for lunkers, especially June-September. These rivers can be crowded during the summer, but luckily there are literally hundreds of other rivers and smaller streams on which to wet a line. And for die-hard anglers, plenty of secret spots are around—think spring creeks and alpine lakes—for excellent year-round fishing.

Lake fishing is also popular. In Wyoming, the Flaming Gorge and Buffalo Bill Reservoirs offer lake trout, kokanee salmon, and smallmouth bass. In addition, hundreds of backcountry lakes offer solitude and great fishing in a wilderness setting, and ice fishing is becoming increasingly popular during the winter.

Nonresident fishing permits cost $14 for one day or $56 for five days. Resident fishing licenses cost $27 per year or $6 per day. With the exception of a one-day license, you'll also need to purchase a Wyoming Conservation Stamp for $21.50, which is good for one calendar year. Youth under 14 do not need a license if fishing with an adult who has a valid fishing license.

It's important to remember that you need a separate license to fish in Yellowstone National Park. Anglers 16 years of age and older are required to purchase a $40 three-day,

Great Divide Mountain Bike Route

Created in 1998, the Great Divide Mountain Bike Route is the longest off-pavement bicycle route in the world, running 3,083 miles (4,962 km) from Jasper, Canada, down to Antelope Wells, New Mexico. Developed by the Adventure Cycling Association, the trail is roughly 90 percent unpaved and crosses the Continental Divide as many as 30 times. The elevation gains and losses are equivalent to 220,000 vertical feet (27,056 m), which compares to riding up Mount Everest nearly 10 times.

One stretch of the trail in southern Wyoming from South Pass City near Lander to Rawlins cuts through an area known as the Great Basin, since the water in this area does not drain into the Atlantic or Pacific but rather stays in the playa lakes here or evaporates in the heat. In fact, the Continental Divide splits and is on both sides of the Great Basin. It's the only portion of the route where the terrain is consistently level. But that doesn't make it easy. Riders will need to carry plenty of water on the 131-mile (211-km) stretch and will likely have to deal with significant wind. Temperatures in this high desert can plummet quickly, and rainstorms can make the double-track nearly impassable. Possible wildlife encounters in this stretch of the trail can include prairie dogs, pronghorn, coyotes, and even wild horses.

The Great Basin is a starkly picturesque place that will appeal to those who love wide-open spaces. For maps and detailed route information, start online at www.adventurecycling.org.

$55 seven-day, or $75 season permit. Children 15 and under may fish without a permit if fishing with an adult who has a valid park permit. Permits are available at park ranger stations, stores, and many businesses in the Greater Yellowstone area.

Outfitters and guide services are abundant in Wyoming. Although it's not necessary, using one of these outfitters is a good idea if you're new to angling or want to hone your fly-fishing skills. Guides also know the hot spots on the rivers, can tell you what is hatching on any given day, and may have access to private sites along various streams.

Two excellent private websites for general fishing information and a good overview of the region are **Big Sky Fishing** (www.bigskyfishing.com) and **Wyoming Fishing Network** (www.wyomingfishing.net).

For detailed fishing information, contact the **Wyoming Game and Fish Department** (307/777-4600, https://wgfd.wyo.gov).

TOUR OPERATORS

Wyoming covers a large geographic area, so it can be difficult to choose what to see in the time you have. There are many tour operators with well-researched itineraries that can cater to your specific needs and wishes. Many of these tours cater to families or a particular interest: biking, cultural and history tours, wildlife, and more. **Austin Adventures** (800/575-1540, www.austinadventures.com), for whom this writer used to guide, offers numerous multiple-sport trips (think biking, hiking, horseback riding, and rafting on one trip) in the region, including Yellowstone and Grand Teton National Parks. The Montana-based **Adventure Cycling Association** (800/755-2453, www.adventurecycling.org) offers self-contained and supported bicycle tours in Yellowstone and Grand Teton National Parks. **Backroads** (800/462-2848, www.backroads.com) offers multiple-sport tours throughout Greater Yellowstone. **Big Wild Adventures** (406/823-0337 www.bigwildadventures.com) offers backpacking and canoeing trips in Yellowstone and Grand Teton National Parks. **Yellow Dog Fly Fishing Adventures** (406/585-8667 or 888/777-5060, www.yellowdogflyfishing.com) offers custom trips around the area. In addition, operators in nearly every town offer specific adventures, such as white-water rafting, horseback riding, fly-fishing, hiking, biking, and more.

SPECTATOR SPORTS

Most communities in Wyoming have rodeos at least once during the summer, and some of the larger towns like Jackson, Cody, and West Yellowstone have nightly or weekly rodeos that showcase the sport's nonstop action. Some of the best rodeos are the smaller ones, often called "ranch rodeos," that feature real cowboys and cowgirls from area ranches competing against each other in real-life ranch activities. Many rodeos offer events for kids, such as greased-pig contests or wild-sheep riding. Generally speaking, rodeos are great family-oriented events, but the tenderest animal lovers may not be okay with several of the events, including roping, tying, and bronc riding.

Frontier Days (307/778-7222, www. cfdrodeo.com) in Cheyenne is the country's largest outdoor rodeo, with attendance of nearly 250,000 people each summer for the 10-day festival. The **Cody Stampede Rodeo** (307/587-5155, www.codystampederodeo. com) in Cody has had bucking broncs since 1919, and the family-friendly

Cody Nite Rodeo (307/587-5155, www. codystampederodeo.com) runs nightly June-August. Jackson Hole offers rodeos (307/733-7927, www.jhrodeo.com) twice weekly, on Wednesday and Saturday nights, Memorial Day-Labor Day, plus some Friday nights in July and August. West Yellowstone also hosts a rodeo (406/560-6913, www.westyellowstonerodeo.com) during each weekend in the summer June-August, and the **Professional Bull Riders** tour (719/242-2800, www.pbr. com) stops in Cheyenne.

With only one university in the state, it's no great surprise that the NCAA Division I **University of Wyoming Cowboys** (www. wyomingathletics.com) draw rabid fans to home games in Laramie. The annual "border war" match between Colorado State and Wyoming has been going on since 1899 and is considered the oldest interstate rivalry west of the Mississippi River. Since 1968, the winner of that game takes home the Bronze Boot, one of the best-known and most highly sought-after traveling trophies in college football.

Travel Tips

CANADIAN CROSSINGS AND CUSTOMS

Of the many roads in Montana that cross into Canada, only three border crossings are open 24 hours year-round—US 93 (Roosville) and I-15 (Sweetgrass/Eureka) are the busiest,, while the remote crossing near Raymond on Highway 16 sees much less traffic. U.S. citizens are now required to carry passports when crossing into Canada; Canadians entering the United States must have a passport, a NEXUS card, and an Enhanced Driver's License (EDL) or Enhanced Identification Card (EIC). Citizens of other countries must show their passports and appropriate visas and may be asked to prove that they have sufficient funds for their length of stay. U.S. citizens

returning to the United States by air must present a U.S. passport.

When heading north into Canada, travelers age 21 and older can import, duty free, a maximum of 40 ounces (1.2 liters) of liquor or 24 12-ounce (0.4-liter) cans of beer or ale into the country as personal luggage. Up to 50 cigars and 200 cigarettes may be allowed entry duty free for those age 18 or over. U.S. visitors spending more than 48 hours in Canada may bring $800CAD worth of duty-free goods back with them, or $200 if staying less than 48 hours. If you're carrying more than $10,000, you'll need to declare the amount. Handguns can't be taken into Canada, although hunting rifles are allowed. Bear spray and hunting knives are also prohibited.

As of December 2021, restrictions (www.

travel.gc.ca) at the Canadian border due to COVID-19 are tight and should be carefully reviewed before you attempt entry. Vaccinations are required for travel within and out of Canada. Testing, pre-registration for arrival, and proof of vaccination are required. Unvaccinated travelers will be tested on arrival and again on day 8, and are required to quarantine for a full 14 days in a designated facility. Even fully vaccinated travelers who have been anywhere but Canada or the U.S. within 14 days of entry can be selected for arrival testing, which requires quarantine in a suitable location until negative test results are confirmed. Changes can happen without warning, so be sure to study the requirements in advance.

TOURIST INFORMATION

Most chambers of commerce and visitors centers (listed for each town in this book) are good sources when driving around, but the online sites are where you should start your research. Visit **Wyoming Tourism** (307/777-7777, www.travelwyoming.com) for the latest information. You can check out the various towns (many of which have their own tourist information offices and vacation guides), attractions, and events, as well as order a **free vacation guide.**

COMMUNICATIONS AND MEDIA
Cell Phones

Cell phone coverage is overall very good and getting better each year. That being said, rural and mountainous areas may have spotty coverage, and plenty of places have none at all. Indeed, check the storefronts in some of the smaller towns in the region, and you'll see that cell-phone service is just being brought to the area. Verizon is the main carrier, although AT&T is increasingly available.

Internet Access

Many coffee shops and public libraries have computers available for Internet use, and most larger towns have business centers with computers and fax machines.

High-speed Internet connections are generally available, but the service is often slower and more problematic compared to larger metropolitan areas. Wireless Internet is frequently offered at coffee shops, libraries, hotels, and other public places.

Media

USA Today is the one national newspaper that can be found throughout the region, and the *Wall Street Journal* is also popular. If you want a national newspaper like *The New York Times* or the *Washington Post,* some larger towns still have smaller newspaper and magazine stores, or sections in bookstores, but you may get a copy that is a few days old at best. Large grocery stores typically have regional dailies.

In Wyoming, the larger newspapers include the *Casper Star-Tribune* (the only statewide newspaper) and the *Wyoming Tribune Eagle* in Cheyenne, which are the only two papers in the state that publish daily. Other popular papers include the *Jackson Hole Daily*, the *Northern Wyoming News* from Worland, and the *Laramie Daily Boomerang*, all of which publish five or six times a week. Other Wyoming publications to watch for include *Wyoming Magazine* (www.wyomingmagazine.com), which focuses on travel and adventure in the state, *Wyoming Wildlife Magazine* (https://wgfd.wyo.gov/magazine), which is a product of the Wyoming Game & Fish Department, and *Wyoming Lifestyle Magazine* (www.wyolifestyle.com).

One of best sources of local and national news is **National Public Radio,** which can be heard in even the smallest of towns. **Yellowstone Public Radio** (www.ypr.org) and **Wyoming Public Radio** (www.wyomingpublicradio.net) cover much of the state.

FOOD

One thing is certain: This is meat-and-potatoes country, which can be great for those craving a good steak, as you can find one in almost every town. Locally raised beef can be found on the menus of many restaurants, and bison is becoming increasingly popular as well. If you haven't had it, it's highly recommended, and beef lovers will generally enjoy bison. A good bison burger or tenderloin is hard to beat, but if you are asked how you like it cooked, never ask for anything more than medium. Medium rare is better, as lean wild meat can dry out more quickly. Wild-game dishes, mostly elk and venison, are also found at finer establishments, with pheasant and other regional game occasionally on the menu. If you enjoy trying new fare, this can be an exciting option.

With all the meat on the menu, you would think that vegetarians would be out of luck when dining out, but surprisingly, options abound, especially at higher-end restaurants. The "eat local" campaigns are in full swing out West, and many of the best restaurants get as much of their food as possible from local and regional growers. Despite the region being seriously landlocked, seafood is no longer necessarily a bad idea. Fresh seafood is flown in from Hawaii or Seattle daily in many places, and it is generally pretty good. Yes, there are even fresh sushi bars, and some are darn tasty.

You'll also see the standard fast-food establishments, especially near the interstates, but avoid these and try a local restaurant instead. You'll find the best food at the most random of places—and it will certainly be a more culinary and cultural experience. And remember, folks out here are friendly—if you stop and ask someone about the best place in town, they will happily point you in the right direction and will probably know the owner.

If you are traveling the back roads and small towns and get tired of ordinary bar-type food (burgers, burgers, and more burgers), consider a quest to find the best chicken-fried steak or the best piece of pie. Sometimes a personal challenge can relieve the boredom of limited options. Plus, who doesn't want an excuse to eat homemade pie for breakfast, lunch, and dinner?

ACCOMMODATIONS

It's no surprise that a wide variety of lodging options are available, from standard hotels and motels to luxury resorts and guest ranches. Generally speaking, all lodging is more expensive in the summer, and rooms fill rapidly—advance reservations are a must, especially around special events like Cheyenne's Frontier Days. Rooms, cabins, and even campgrounds in the national parks fill up several months—if not longer—in advance. Shoulder seasons (spring and fall) offer reduced rates and thin crowds, while rooms at the ski resort lodges fill up fast in the winter but may be wide open during the summer.

Most larger towns have numerous choices for chain motels, which are typically clustered around the interstate exits. Gateway towns to Yellowstone and Grand Teton National Parks also have chain hotels, as well as mom-and-pop motels sprinkled around town. Travelers used to standard hotels will be happy with these choices, but those who seek a more unique experience will want to try some of the smaller boutique hotels. It just depends on whether you would rather stay in the usual Super 8 or sleep in a room that once accommodated Ernest Hemingway or Annie Oakley. A good resource is **Historic Hotels of the Rockies** (www.historichotels.org).

Most bed-and-breakfasts in Wyoming are in the higher-traffic tourist areas. Many are located on the banks of a river or nestled in the pine trees and often make great escapes from the busier hotel atmosphere. A fairly comprehensive listing can be found at **BnBFinder** (www.bnbfinder.com). Very few hostels exist here, but **Hostels.com** (www.hostels.com) has a list of what might be available.

Guest ranches range from traditional horse-and-cowboy dude ranches to luxury "glamping" (a portmanteau of *glamorous* and *camping*) resorts that offer spa services and high-end cuisine. An excellent resource for those seeking a real Western working vacation is the **Wyoming Dude Ranchers' Association** (www.wyomingdra.com). Many of these are focused around horseback riding, fly-fishing, and family activities and often are booked in weeklong blocks. In the winter, many of these ranches offer cross-country skiing, snowshoeing, or dogsledding.

Higher-end guest ranches are becoming very popular, offering guests a chance to experience a more rustic atmosphere with upscale amenities. These are typically set in remote locations with beautiful surroundings and are private, in some cases gated from public access. Typically these are the priciest accommodations, ranging from several hundred to $1,000 or more per night.

Cabins and other vacation rentals are becoming increasingly popular, as many travelers are looking for that Western cabin experience. These can range from rustic— just beds, no plumbing—to luxurious— down comforters, a rock fireplace—and are perhaps the best way to stay. Sites like **Airbnb** (www.airbnb.com) and **VRBO** (www.vrbo.com) offer private homes and cabins for rent, while many resorts provide nightly cabin rentals. For Forest Service cabins—which can be quite primitive but in phenomenal locations—travelers can check availability and make reservations at www.recreation.gov.

Plenty of RV and tent camping sites are available for those on the road. From national forest campgrounds to large private RV resorts, there is something for everyone. RV campers will find private campgrounds in most towns, and most national forest campgrounds have room for all but the longest RVs. It's generally legal to camp on national forest land, unless you see a sign indicating that overnight camping isn't allowed. For something closer to backcountry experience without hoofing it, drive on a Forest Service road until you find a nice campsite, pull over, and set up camp. Not only is it often scenic, it's also free.

ACCESS FOR TRAVELERS WITH DISABILITIES

For the most part, Wyoming complies with state and federal guidelines for accessibility. Most hotels offer accessible rooms, and the national parks and even some state parks feature accessible trails. However, it's important to remember that many parts of the state are rural, and some features may be outdated, less accessible, or nonexistent. A list of trails that are easy to navigate and/or accessible to most wheelchairs is available at www.accessiblenature.info. Another resource for travelers with disabilities is **Rocky Mountain ADA** (800/949-4232, www.rockymountainada.org). In the national parks, wheelchair accessibility information can be found on their individual websites.

TRAVELERS OF COLOR

Wyoming is right around 90 percent white, with Native Americans, Latin American people, multiracial people, Black people, and Asian people accounting for the rest of the population, according to the 2020 U.S. census. With so few people of color, Black people and other minorities tend to be cautious when traveling in this part of the country, according to Judith Heilman, executive director of the Montana Racial Equity Project (www.themtrep.org). And for good reason: There are still a lot of sundown towns where people of color may not feel welcome or even safe. This doesn't mean you should expect to be intimidated or harassed, but it does mean you will have to be alert and aware of your surroundings.

The United States has a terrible record when it comes to land management and racial equity. People of color have been excluded from national parks—dating back to the founding of the National Park Service (NPS) in 1916 and the enforcement of segregation through Jim Crow laws—and other green settings for generations. Even though the country is becoming more and diverse, parks, green spaces, and conservation spaces are remaining white and somewhat elitist. An NPS poll taken in 2018 shows that even though people of color make up 42 percent of the U.S. population (and are expected to be the majority by 2044, according to the U.S. Census Bureau), only 23 percent of visitors to the national parks were people of color, and only 6 percent identified as Black. There are a multitude of social and economic reasons why this is true, and though the NPS is committed to addressing the racial disparity—by marketing to non-white communities, training staff on racial sensitivity, and working to hire rangers from more diverse backgrounds—the problem is real and poses an existential threat to our public lands. If we don't have a population that is willing to fund and fight for these natural spaces, they will cease to exist.

Which brings us back to the problem of Wyoming, a mostly white state with vast expanses of public land. It follows that people of color are underrepresented here and thus face real questions of both comfort and safety. The Montana Racial Equity Project encourages travelers of color to be alert and aware, and to document (and film, whenever possible) any mistreatment. Generally speaking, the larger towns have more people of color and thus may feel safer and more welcoming.

Consider connecting with communities—and there are several—that can offer insider advice for your specific destinations. A remaking of the *Green Book,* a travel guide published from 1936-1967 that identified businesses that were friendly to African American customers, the **Inclusive Guide** (www.inclusivejourneys.com) is a brand-new online community that lists safe and welcoming spaces for anyone who faces discrimination. There are also Instagram and Facebook pages targeted to people of color in the great outdoors. Outdoor Afro, Latino Outdoors, Brown People Camping, Natives Outdoors, and Black People Who Hike are but a few examples. **On She Goes** (www.onshegoes. com) is a travel website created by and for women of color. And **Travel Noire** (www. travelnoire.com), which has more than 100 articles that reference the region, is a digital media company geared to millennials of the African Diaspora. BIPOC journalist James Edward Mills started the **Joy Trip Project** (www.joytripproject.com), which focuses on outdoor recreation. There's an excellent list of anti-racism resources on the site related to justice, equity, diversity, and inclusion of BIPOC in parks and greenspaces. One such site is **Diversify Outdoors** (www.diversifyoutdoors.com), which promotes diversity in outdoor recreation and conservation.

WOMEN TRAVELING ALONE

Overall, Wyoming can be exciting for a woman traveling alone. For the most part, the West is full of independent and strong women, and you won't seem out of place because of your gender in most areas. A cursory Google search turns up a wealth of stories and blogs of women chronicling their solo travels across Wyoming. The reality is most of these women are probably white and the experience could be very different for a woman of color.

Of course, there is always the occasional weirdo, so if a place or a person makes you uncomfortable, the best thing to do is just leave. Use the same precautions and common sense that you would at home. Even in a quaint mountain town, it's probably not safe to be out, wandering alone, in the middle of the night. It's worth noting that bear spray can be just as effective on a creepy dude as it is on a curious grizzly.

LGBTQ+ TRAVELERS

It's safe to say that many people in Wyoming are socially conservative, and queer public displays of affection are not entirely common, although they are becoming more so. You shouldn't necessarily anticipate discrimination or hostility if you are LGBTQ+, but you'll want to be aware of your surroundings. You might not think much of expressing yourself at a back-road Wyoming bar, but you never know what the patrons in the corner are thinking. Sadly, this is where Matthew Shepard was brutally murdered in 1998 for no other reason than because he was gay. A lot of people in Wyoming still have a long way to go in terms of recognizing and celebrating alternative lifestyles. In general, "don't ask, don't tell" is the safest policy to assume when traveling here. And, as is expected, urban areas are often friendlier to LGBTQ+ travelers.

That being said, there are thriving—although often underground—gay communities in many Wyoming towns, particularly Laramie. An excellent resource for LGBTQ+ travelers is the **University of Wyoming's Rainbow Resource Center** (307/766-3478, www.uwyo.edu/RRC). **Wyoming Equality** (307/778-7645, www.wyomingequality.org) is an organization whose vision is "a Wyoming where the dignity and humanity of all LGBTQ Wyomingites are celebrated and protected." Each summer they host a Rendezvous camping weekend as a fundraiser for the important work they do across the state.

HOW TO GIVE BACK

I've spent the last year and a half working on my father's memoir, the one he wrote for eight years but didn't finish before he died in 2020. My dad had a knack for remembering obscure quotes, and a gift for repeating them at often wildly inappropriate times. I mean, who toasts a new bride with "I'd rather have a bottle in front of me, than a frontal lobotomy." Dad. There was none better.

But the saying that beats in me to this day, the one he learned as a boy, and lived his whole life, is this: Of them to whom much is given, much is required. It came from a bible verse and included an "unto" and a "whomsoever." But Dad liked the simpler version. And he offered it to me whenever a thing would go right in my life: a good grade, a lucky break, a new opportunity. What it did, and what I am grateful for even now, was to remind me to slow down, to think about where I'd come from, to tally all that I'd been given, and to figure out how I was going to make myself equal to it. These days, I say it to my daughters

as they go out into the world, to take it all in and to make their own marks. And now, I'm going to say it to you too.

You have a right to be here. Yellowstone and Grand Teton National Park. They belong to all of us. So do the millions of acres of national forests, the soaring peaks, and great expanses of plains and desert managed by the BLM. Public land is our birthright as Americans. Yours and mine. All of ours. But reaping the benefits of its beauty and solitude and rarity brings responsibilities.

So here is my ask: Slow down. Be a thoughtful traveler, a conscientious visitor. Don't just take what you want from this place, but honor it—the parts that belong to you, and the parts that don't. Find ways to give back, to make a place even better than when you found it, whether you participate in a trail cleanup or attend a gala that's raising funds for the local animal shelter, or maybe you just write a check to protect grizzly habitat and drop it in the mailbox.

There is advice in these pages: sharing proper powwow etiquette, teaching you how to be on a trail, and the ways to engage—or more often, not engage—with wildlife. But what I'm asking now is more than that. I'm asking you to do right by the wilderness here, and by the communities, by every last inhabitant and fellow visitor. I am asking you to be even better than you already are. To pay attention. To stay curious. To think bigger, feel deeper, and give more. I'm asking you to be worthy of all the gifts coming your way. Dad would have said it better, but you know what I mean.

Nonprofits

This is a short list of nonprofits in Wyoming. For ways to give back, you can start here.

- **Alliances for Historic Wyoming:** Started around a dining room table by two women who wanted to see Wyoming's heritage preserved, rather than sold off to special interest groups, Alliances for Historic Wyoming (307/333-3508, www.historicwyoming.org)

is dedicated to protecting historic and cultural resources in both the built and natural environments.

• **Black Dog Animal Rescue:** The mission of the Black Dog Animal Rescue (307/514-4024, www.bdar.org), Wyoming's largest, is to promote, provide, and advocate for the needs of companion animals. All the adoptable animals live off-site with a volunteer foster family, which means they have volunteers across the state.

• **Edible Prairie Project:** Based in Gillette, Wyoming, the Edible Prairie Project (307/228-0044, www.edibleprairieproject.org) works with family-scale agricultural and food-processing operations to improve the affordability and accessibility of high quality and nutritionally appropriate food for all members of the community.

• **Wind River Foundation:** Based in Jackson, the Wind River Foundation (www.windriverfoundation.org) cites as its mission "to advance philanthropy that will empower the Indigenous communities of Wyoming's Wind River Indian Reservation in their work toward cultural revitalization, social progress, and economic prosperity." Their programs focus on three priorities: youth and community leadership, cultural revitalization, and creating connections.

• **Food Bank of Wyoming:** The statewide Food Bank of Wyoming (307/265-2172, www.wyomingfoodbank.org) provides food and necessities to 160 hunger relief partners across the state. More than 3,400 volunteers serve some 54,000 totes filled with nutritious food for children and their families, in addition to supporting seniors and families in need.

• **Wyoming Arts Alliance:** Working from the idea that more art equals a better Wyoming, the Wyoming Arts Alliance (307/316-1277, www.wyomingarts.org) focuses on advocacy for arts and culture, and on art-based learning to create pathways for successful citizens and workers.

• **Wyoming Community Foundation:** For more than three decades, the Wyoming Community Foundation (307/721-8300, www.wycf.org) has connected people who care with causes that matter. They've granted nearly $100 million to charitable causes across the state and support a range of organizations.

Health and Safety

While medical services and health care in Wyoming towns are excellent—and in some cases on par with bigger cities—it's important to remember that when traveling around, you'll mostly likely be far away from emergency medical services. Rural and mountainous highways are especially troublesome, as cell phone coverage can be spotty. Most small towns have a local clinic, and services are available in the national parks. Refer to specific areas of the text for emergency numbers, and remember that calling 911 doesn't always work in rural areas.

In general, **weather, altitude,** and **insect bites** pose the greatest risk traveling here. The summer sun can get extremely hot, and it is easy to get dehydrated, so make sure to drink plenty of water during the day. Hiking—and just walking, for some people—can be a strenuous activity as the altitude increases. It's best to carry plenty of food and water, and take your time getting to your destination. Always let someone know where you are going and when you plan to be back. The earliest and most obvious sign of altitude-related health problems is a headache, and the best remedy is drinking water and moving to a lower elevation if possible.

The common insect nuisances are mosquitoes and ticks. Wyoming mosquitoes rarely carry any diseases, but they can be annoying at certain times during the summer. While West Nile virus is becoming an increasing threat to livestock across the West, human infection is less common. Still, carry bug repellent with DEET, especially when hiking or camping near water. Ticks can pose a small threat of Rocky Mountain fever or Lyme disease, and they seem to have become more pervasive in the last 10 years or so. Check every part of your skin after a day of hiking or fishing outdoors—places where you might encounter underbrush, dense trees, and grassy meadows. If you find a tick with its head stuck in your skin, pull gently with tweezers or your fingers until the tick works its way out. Don't forget to check your pets too.

A common backcountry illness is **giardia,** sometimes called "beaver fever," from a microscopic parasite that lives in mountain streams and can wreak havoc in your intestinal tract. Avoid drinking unfiltered or untreated water directly from streams, rivers, springs, or lakes. Carry a water filter or water-purifying tablets (iodine or similar products), and you'll have nothing to worry about.

If you're camping or staying in a cabin where mice have been active, **hantavirus** can be a concern. Hantavirus is a potentially fatal disease caused by contact with rodent droppings, particularly those of deer mice. Symptoms include fever, muscle aches, coughing, and difficulty breathing. Campers should avoid sleeping on bare ground, and avoid cabins if you see signs of rodents. For more information, visit the Centers for Disease Control and Prevention (www.cdc.gov).

Winter poses different types of health concerns, namely **hypothermia** and **frostbite.** If you or someone in your party shows any signs of hypothermia—uncontrollable shivering, slurred speech, loss of coordination—get them out of the wind and inside immediately. If you're camping, a dry sleeping bag is your best bet. Dress in layers, avoid cotton clothing, always bring a hat, and—most important—make good decisions *before* you put yourself in a situation where you could be stranded in the wind and cold. If you're outside in the winter, a sign of frostbite is the whitening and hardening of the skin. The best way to warm the affected area is with other skin, but avoid warming it too quickly because thawing can be quite painful.

WEATHER

The old saying is a tad cliché but often true: If you don't like the weather in Wyoming, just wait five minutes. What this means to the traveler is that weather in this part of the West can change dramatically in an unbelievably short amount of time. In the summer, extreme heat can dehydrate the human body rapidly, and in the winter, extreme cold can render your body useless in a matter of minutes. Sudden changes in the weather can happen at any time of the year in mountainous areas. It can snow, sleet, hail, and rain at a moment's notice. If you're heading into the backcountry or getting ready for a three-day river float, check the forecast, but don't rely on it; plan for the worst with extra gear and plenty of food and water.

In general, Wyoming has a semiarid climate. There is enough moisture at certain times of the year, but summers are typically dry and warm, with July and August being the hottest months. Mountainous areas see heavy snowfall during the winter (to the delight of skiers), while the east can seem downright desertlike much of the year.

WILDLIFE

Although many people visit Wyoming for the abundant wildlife, with so much human interaction, safety is a real concern. *Never* to approach wildlife, no matter what the situation. It's just a bad idea, and each year people are hurt or killed because they ignore this basic rule. Not only are they putting themselves in harm's way, but they are often precipitating imminent doom for the animal as well. The

Coronavirus in Wyoming

At the time of writing in 2022, Wyoming had emerged from periods of some of the highest Covid transmission rates in the country, but the situation is constantly evolving. With a Republican governor, Wyoming all but outlawed mask mandates, nor are vaccines required to enter either state. The majority of people you'll see do not wear masks when they are out and about, but plenty of businesses ask their employees to mask up. In general, you may feel uncomfortable in a mask, simply because you are likely to be one of only a few, but you should not expect to be harassed because of it. There are no travel restrictions in place due to Covid. But now more than ever, Moon encourages readers to be courteous and ethical in their travel. Be respectful to local residents and mindful of the situation in your chosen destination when planning your trip.

BEFORE YOU GO

- Check websites (listed below) for **state restrictions** and the overall health status of the destination and your point of origin. Check the local county health department website for the areas you intend to visit. If you're traveling to or from an area that is currently a COVID-19 hotspot, you may want to reconsider your trip. Moon encourages travelers to **get vaccinated** if their health status allows and to take a **coronavirus test** with enough time to receive the results before departure if possible. Check local requirements and factor these into your plans.

- If you plan to fly, check with your **airline** and the **local health authorities** for updated travel requirements. Some airlines may be taking more steps to help you travel safely, such as limiting occupancy; check their websites before buying your ticket. Flights may be more infrequent, with increased cancellations.

- Pack **hand sanitizer,** a **thermometer,** and plenty of **face masks.** Be prepared for possible closures and reduced services over the course of your travels.

- Assess the risk of entering **crowded spaces,** joining **tours,** and taking **public transit.**

- Expect **general disruptions.** Events may be postponed or cancelled. Some tours and venues may require **reservations,** enforce **capacity limits,** or operate during **different hours** than the ones listed. Other venues may be closed entirely.

RESOURCES

- The **Wyoming Department of Health** website (www.health.wyo.gov) shows current data on cases statewide and provides answers to a number of pandemic-related questions.

---

old adage, "A fed bear is a dead bear," can be applied universally to wildlife. The problem of humans getting too close to animals, particularly in Yellowstone National Park, gets plenty of coverage these days on YouTube and the evening news. Do not become a cautionary lesson for other travelers; keep your distance from wildlife. Period.

SAFETY IN BEAR COUNTRY

Grizzly bears and black bears live in many parts of the state, and although encounters are rare, it is necessary to learn what to do in case it happens to you. It is also important to know how to avoid the situation in the first place. No method is absolutely foolproof, but with caution and attentiveness you can avoid most of the common mistakes that lead to bear encounters.

When out in the backcountry, it's the unexpected bear encounter you really want to avoid. The best way to do this is to let them know you are present. Make noise in areas of dense cover and blind spots on hiking or biking trails. Immediately move away from any animal carcass you come across, as there may be a bear nearby protecting it. Avoid hiking or biking in the early morning or at dusk, and travel in larger groups; the more of you there are hiking together, the more likely a bear will sense you and move away. Making noise is a great way to let bears know you are near, and in most cases they will be long gone before you have the chance to get a glimpse of them. Be aware that dogs can provoke bears and bring them right to you. And, of course, never leave food out.

If you're camping in an area frequented by bears, look for bear signs (scat, overturned rocks, decimated fallen timber, claw marks and hair on trees) around the campsite. Since bears are attracted to all kinds of odors—food, toothpaste, soap, deodorant—your cooking, eating, and food storage area should be at least 50 yards/meters from your tent. It's tempting to bring tasty items like sausage, ham, tuna, and bacon with you, but these smell good to bears too. Freeze-dried foods are your best bet. Store foods in airtight bags, and be sure to hang all food at least 12-15 feet (4-5 m) off the ground and away from tree trunks. Some designated campsites have bear storage containers or food storage poles.

Carrying **pepper spray** (sold in most sporting goods stores, but it's worth noting that the Grizzly and Wolf Discovery Center in West Yellowstone is the only place you can buy bear spray at cost) is a must in bear country, and it has been proven useful in fending off bear attacks. These sprays only work at close range (10-30 feet/3-9 m) and can quickly dissipate in the wind or sometimes blow back in your face. Carry the spray in a holster or on a belt across your chest for easy access. It's important to note that these spray canisters are not allowed on commercial airplanes, they expire after a certain date, and they should not be left in a very hot place like a closed car. Also, test your container every now and then in light or no wind to make sure it works.

If you happen to encounter a bear, and it notices you, try not to panic or make any sudden moves. Do not run—bears can run more

than 40 mph in short bursts—or try to climb a tree. Make yourself visible by moving out into the open so the bear can identify you. Avoid direct eye contact with the bear, but talking in a low voice may convince the animal that you are human. If the bear is sniffing the air or standing on its hind legs, it's most likely trying to identify you. If it's woofing and posturing, this could be a challenge. Stand your ground if the bear charges; most charges are bluffs, where the bear will stop short and wander away.

If a grizzly does charge and knocks you to the ground, curl up in the fetal position with your hands wrapped behind your neck and your elbows tucked over your face. Keeping your backpack on may offer some protection. Remain as still as possible, as bears will often only sniff or nip you and leave. This is considered playing "active dead." If the bear rolls you over, as it will likely try to do, roll yourself back over on your stomach and keep your neck as protected as possible. Remain on the ground until you know the bear has vacated the area.

In general, black bears are more common and seem to have more interaction with people. In many places they can be a nuisance—getting into garbage, breaking into homes—but don't think that they are not dangerous. Black bears will generally try to avoid you and are easily scared away, but if you encounter an attacking or aggressive bear, this usually means it views you as food. In this case, most experts recommend fighting back with whatever means possible: large rocks or sticks, yelling, and shouting.

It's a rare event when a bear attacks sleeping campers in tents at night, but if you find yourself in that situation, defend yourself as aggressively as you can. In these circumstances, bears are viewing you as prey and may give up if you fight back. Never play dead in this case, and to thwart off an attack, always keep pepper spray and a flashlight handy.

Before you go into the backcountry, brush up on your **bear identification.** You can't tell what kind of bear you see by its color alone. Grizzlies are often larger and have a trademark hump at the top of their neck. Grizzlies also have more of a dish-shaped face profile, compared to a straighter profile of black bears.

OTHER WILDLIFE

Although bears get more press, there are other animals you need to be aware of when traveling around Wyoming. Moose are huge animals that are prone to sudden charges when surprised, especially females traveling with young. If you travel through Yellowstone National Park, you'll encounter numerous bison, large animals with sharp horns. Although it may be tempting to walk up to them, avoid doing so. While they are not vicious, bison can charge if provoked and have maimed and even killed visitors in the past. Statistically, bison injure more people in Yellowstone than any other animal. Be aware that these lumbering beasts can sprint the length of a football field in six seconds and can leap a 6-foot fence. Likewise, elk in the park can seem downright docile, but it's important to remember not to approach them. They too have attacked, stomped, and gored visitors who got too close.

Mountain lions generally keep a low profile, but as humans encroach on their habitat, encounters are becoming more frequent in the West. Most attacks have been on unattended children, and they rarely target adults. If you happen to find yourself in a situation with a mountain lion, be aggressive and fight back if necessary, or throw rocks and sticks to try to make it go away.

Rattlesnakes can be found in the central and eastern parts of Wyoming, especially in the drier prairies. Rattlesnake bites are rarely fatal (less than 4 percent when antivenin is used in time), and the snakes generally avoid humans. Be careful where you step when hiking around these areas, and pay attention if children are with you. If you surprise or step on a rattlesnake—chances are you'll hear its trademark rattle before you do—it may coil and strike. Any bite from a rattlesnake should be regarded as a life-threatening medical emergency that requires immediate hospital treatment by trained professionals. Bear in mind that dogs can get two doses of a rattlesnake vaccine in order to give them a better chance to get to the vet before the toxin kills them.

With all of the incredible wildlife-viewing opportunities around Wyoming, it can be easy for some people to get complacent when taking pictures or hiking around. Treat all wildlife with respect and care, and never feed or approach any type of wild animal. If you are lucky enough to see many of these critters, observe them in their natural habitat and then carry on. The last thing you want is to become a statistic.

Resources

Suggested Reading

INFORMATION AND TRAVEL

Fritz, William J. *Roadside Geology of the Yellowstone Country*. Missoula, MT: Mountain Press Publishing, 2nd edition, 2011. Even though it was first published more than 30 years ago, we're talking about rocks; a couple of decades doesn't make much difference, and this is a fantastic resource for anyone interested in the region's geology.

Kilgore, Gene. *Ranch Vacations: The Leading Guide to Dude, Guest, Resort, Fly Fishing, Working Cattle Ranches and Pack Trips*. Sonoma, CA: Ranchweb, 2016. The best resource for finding a ranch vacation perfectly suited to you and your family.

Pflughoft, Fred. *Wyoming Wild and Beautiful II*. Helena, MT: Farcountry Press, 2003. As in his first book in the series, photographer Fred Pflughoft captures the beauty of the Cowboy State.

Roberts, Stephen L., David L. Roberts, and Phil Roberts. *Wyoming Almanac*. Laramie, WY: Skyline West Press, 2001. Every factoid you could ever want to know about Wyoming.

Trevathan, Mary Ann. *More Than Meets the Eye: Wyoming Along I-80*. Glendo, WY: High Plains Press, 1993. As a marvelous and unique approach to traveling, this book focuses on the people who live and work along the highway and is imbued with the sense that people give places life.

HISTORY

Ehrlich, Gretel. *Heart Mountain*. New York: Penguin, 1989. This historical novel by one of Wyoming's best-loved writers is set in the Heart Mountain Relocation Camp.

Federal Writers' Project, James R. Dow, and Roger L. Welsch, photographs by Susan D. Dow. Wyoming Folklore: Reminiscences, Folktales, Beliefs, Customs, and Folk Speech. Lincoln, NE: Bison Books, 2010. This fun read was created by the members of the 1935 Federal Writers' Project, when President Roosevelt sent out-of-work teachers, writers, and scholars out across the country to document local lore.

Haines, Aubrey L. *Historic Sites Along the Oregon Trail*. St. Louis: Patrice Press, 1994. This volume, written by a well-respected historian, gives readers a look at the historic sites along the trail.

Harris, Burton. *John Colter: His Years in the Rockies*. Lincoln, NE: University of Nebraska Press, 1993. This book, first published in 1952, provides the best look at early explorer and legendary figure John Colter, considered the first non-Native American to lay eyes on Yellowstone.

Larson, T. A. *History of Wyoming*, 2nd edition. Lincoln, NE: University of Nebraska

Press, 1990. This massive volume covers it all and is considered the best single-volume history of the state in print.

Lightner Jr., Sam. *Wyoming: A History of the American West.* Jackson Hole, WY: Summits and Crux Publishing, 2020. This book hits all the highlights and puts them into context in the greater world.

Mcphee, John. *Rising from the Plains.* New York: Farrar, Straus and Giroux, 1987. McPhee masterfully parallels Wyoming's geology with frontier history.

Moulton, Candy. *Roadside History of Wyoming.* Missoula, MT: Mountain Press Publishing, 2003. An excellent guide, this book is organized by driving routes across the state.

Munn, Debra D. *Wyoming Ghost Stories.* Helena, MT: Riverbend Publishing, 2008. A fun read for ghost lovers, this short volume rounds up ghost stories from across the state.

Murray, Robert A. *The Bozeman Trail: Highway of History.* Boulder, CO: Pruett Publishing, 1988. Murray gives readers a short but meaty volume on the bloodiest settler route of them all.

Philipps, David. *Wild Horse Country: The History, Myth, and Future of the Mustang.* New York: W.W. Norton, 2017. A reporter for the *New York Times*, Philipps explores how wild animals captured the imagination of a nation and became central to American identity amid controversy.

Russell, Don. *The Lives and Legends of Buffalo Bill.* Norman, OK: University of Oklahoma Press, 1979. When it comes to biographies of the legendary figure, this is the bible.

Shepherd, Rose, and Susan Marsh. *Saving Wyoming's Hoback: The Grassroots*

Movement that Stopped Natural Gas. Salt Lake City: University of Utah Press, 2017. An important book that won the Wallace Stegner Prize in Environmental Humanities tells the story of the 2012 efforts to prevent industrialization of the Hoback and Noble basins in northwestern Wyoming.

Taylor, Tory. *On the Trail of the Mountain Shoshone Sheep Eaters; A High Altitude Archaeological and Anthropological Odyssey.* Scotts Valley, CA: CreateSpace Independent Publishing Platform, 2017. Taylor masterfully combines his own explorations in the high mountain backcountry and his narrative with the history of the Mountain Shoshone who lived in Wyoming's Wind Rivers and Montana's Absarokas before the arrival of Europeans.

Trenholm, Virginia Cole. *The Arapahoes, Our People.* Norman, OK: University of Oklahoma Press, 1986. First published in 1970, this compelling history of the Arapaho tribe follows their ways of life from prehistoric Minnesota and Canada through the 20th century in Montana, Wyoming, and Oklahoma.

Urbanek, Mae Bobb. *Wyoming Place Names.* Missoula, MT: Mountain Press Publishing, 1988. This is the best guide for those who want to know the stories behind names like Bessemer Bend and Tensleep Canyon.

LITERATURE

Ehrlich, Gretel. *A Match to the Heart: One Woman's Story of Being Struck by Lightning.* New York: Penguin, 1995. A masterpiece from Ehrlich, this is a memoir about her near death and subsequent reawakening.

Ehrlich, Gretel. *The Solace of Open Spaces.* New York: Viking Penguin, 1985. Arriving in Wyoming to work on a PBS film in 1976, Gretel Ehrlich could barely extricate herself from the independent and hard-won life she created for herself there. This collection of essays is one of the best ever written about Wyoming's landscape, people, and culture.

Forbes, Jamie Lisa. *Unbroken*. Greybull, WY: Pronghorn Press, 2011. An award-winning novelist, Forbes writes about the harshness of Wyoming ranch life.

Fuller, Alexandra. *Quiet Until the Thaw*. New York: Penguin Books, 2017. Though Fuller is better known for her memoirs set in Africa, her Wyoming stories are just as powerfully written. Her first novel tells the story of two Lakota cousins who choose different paths in a complex tale spanning generations and geography.

Galvin, James. *The Meadow*. New York: Henry Holt & Company, 1992. Part novel, part natural history, this poetic book tells the 100-year history of a meadow in the arid mountains that bridge Wyoming and Colorado.

Harrison, Jim. *The English Major*. New York: Grove Press, 2008. Perhaps known more for his poetry and dramatic fiction—like *Legends of the Fall*—Harrison's comedic novel about a 60-year-old, sad sack of a man traveling cross-country is a delight.

Proulx, E. Annie. *Close Range: Wyoming Stories*. New York: Scribner, 2000. Pulitzer Prize-winning Proulx is among the state's best-known writers, and for good reason. The tales are dark and the landscape unforgiving, but the characters in this collection are sublime. "Brokeback Mountain" is just one of the stories in this collection.

Schaefer, Jack. *Shane*. New York: Random House, 1949. It just doesn't get more Wyoming than this cowboy classic.

Shay, Michael. *Deep West: A Literary Tour of Wyoming*. Greybull, WY: Pronghorn Press, 2003. This anthology brings together 19 writers with roots in the state, including Annie Proulx and Robert Roripaugh.

Spragg, Mark: *Where Rivers Change Direction*. New York: Riverhead Books, 2000. A profoundly compelling memoir by one of Wyoming's most beloved contemporary authors, this book tells the story of Spragg's coming-of-age on a Wyoming dude ranch.

Twain, Mark. *Roughing It*. Mineola, NY: Dover, 2013. Published originally in 1872, this nearly 900-page work is an account of Twain's six years in the wild, woolly West.

Wister, Owen. *The Virginian*. Mineola, NY: Dover, 2006. This classic 1902 novel put Wyoming on the map.

RECREATION

Birkby, Jeff. *Touring Montana and Wyoming Hot Springs*, 2nd edition. Guilford, CT: Globe Pequot Press, 2013. A comprehensive guide to public and private springs across the region.

Downing, Paul. *Fly Fishing the Southern Rockies: Small Streams and Wild Places*. Fountain Hills, AZ: Majestic Press, 2016. This comprehensive guide by a longtime editor for *Fly Fish America* offers advice on where to fish and what to use, and includes waters in Wyoming, Colorado, and New Mexico.

Graham, Kenneth. Rockhounding Wyoming: A Guide to the State's Best Rockhounding Sites. Guilford, CT: Globe Pequot Press, 2017. Covering 75 sites from the red desert to the Wind Rivers, this former hardrock miner covers the popular and hidden dig sites.

Dawson, Ben, and Roxy Dawson. *Hiking Wyoming*. Guilford, CT: Globe Pequot Press, 2022. One of several state hiking guides series, this one carefully outlines 48 of Wyoming's best hiking trails.

Keffer, Ken. *Hiking Wyoming's Bighorn Mountains: A Guide to the Area's Greatest Hiking Adventures.* Guilford, CT: Falcon Guides, 2017. Another in the state hiking guides series, this book lives up to its name with great coverage of dozens of trails, both for day hikers and backpackers.

Lewis, Dan. *Paddle and Portage: The Floater's Guide to Wyoming Rivers.* Douglas, WY: Wyoming Naturalist, 1991. Intended more for less experienced boaters, this book gives an overview of various waters around the state.

Logue, Terrence, and Maria Katherman, Peggy Knittel, Beecher Ed Strube, and Dana Van Burgh Jr. *A Field Guide to the Casper Mountain Area,* 2nd edition. Casper, WY: Endeavor Books, 2017. A wonderful handbook covering everything from geology, plants, and animals to local history. There are maps, mileage markers, and color photos.

Lomax, Becky. *Moon Montana, Wyoming & Idaho Camping.* Berkeley, CA: Avalon Travel, 2014. The best guide for camping in the region.

MAGAZINES

A longtime literary publication covering Montana, Wyoming, and Idaho, *Big Sky Journal* (subscriptions 800/731-1227, www.bigskyjournal.com) is published five times annually and includes special issues devoted to fly-fishing and the arts. Regular features by well-known writers focus on ranching and rodeo, hunting, fishing, art, and architecture.
   The Open Range (www.openrangemagazine.com) touts itself as a gritty publication devoted to the realities of living and working in the West, with stories about everything from night calving and blacksmithing to working in the oilfields.
   Wyoming Magazine (www.wyomingmagazine.com) focuses on adventure

and travel opportunities across the state, with stories about communities, entertainment, and outdoor pursuits.
   Wyoming Wildlife (subscriptions 800/710-8345, http://wgfd.wyo.gov) is an award-winning publication of the Wyoming Game and Fish Department.

MAPS

Wyoming Atlas & Gazetteer. Yarmouth, ME: Delorme Publishing, 2013. The most indispensable map book you'll find, these topographic maps cover roads and trails all over the state.

GRAND TETON AND YELLOWSTONE

History

Betts, Robert B. *Along the Ramparts of the Tetons: The Saga of Jackson Hole, Wyoming.* Boulder, CO: University of Colorado Press, 1991. This history goes back to the first human habitation in the region and covers Native Americans, mountain men, and pioneers.

Black, George. *Empire of Shadows: The Epic Story of Yellowstone.* New York: St. Martin's Press, 2012. Black offers a fascinating look at the gripping and unexpected history of our first national park.

Clayton, John. *Wonderlandscape: Yellowstone National Park and the Evolution of an American Cultural Icon.* New York: Pegasus Books, 2017. Using iconic figures—including painters, naturalists, and entrepreneurs—as the storytelling mechanisms, John Clayton paints a fascinating cultural picture of the park.

Everts, Truman, and Lee H. Whittlesey. *Lost in Yellowstone: Thirty-Seven Days of Peril.* Salt Lake City, UT: University of Utah Press, 2015. This book captures one of the most remarkable stories of survival in Yellowstone's history.

Gourley, Bruce T. Historic Yellowstone National Park. Guilford, CT: Globe Pequot/Lyons Press, 2021. Bruce Gourley captures the most interesting moments in the park's history.

Haines, Aubrey. The Yellowstone Story: A History of Our First National Park. Yellowstone National Park, WY, and Niwot, CO: The Yellowstone Association for Natural Science, History, and Education and The University Press of Colorado, 1996. This comprehensive volume tackles the park's early years, from primitive exploration to early development.

Righter, Robert W. Crucible for Conservation: The Struggle for Grand Teton National Park. Moose, WY: Grand Teton Natural History Association, 1982. This gripping history makes one grateful that things worked out the way they did.

Righter, Robert W. Wind Energy in America: A History. Norman, OK: University of Oklahoma Press, 2003. Righter gives readers an excellent, in-depth look at the saga of wind energy across the West.

Saunders, Richard L., editor. A Yellowstone Reader: The National Park in Folklore, Popular Fiction, and Verse. Salt Lake City: University of Utah Press, 2003. This volume offers a core sample of historical literature that spans the late 19th century through the 1980s.

Whittlesey, Lee H. Death in Yellowstone: Accidents and Foolhardiness in the First National Park. Lanham, MD: Roberts Rinehart Publishers, 1995. Who doesn't love reading about a little gore and some good old-fashioned stupidity when traveling through Yellowstone?

Natural History

Blakeslee, Nate. American Wolf: A True Story of Survival and Obsession in the West. New York: Crown Publishing, 2017. There's nothing like a good wolf story, and Blakeslee portrays Yellowstone alpha female O-Six against the backdrop of conservation politics.

Johnsgard, Paul A., and Thomas D. Mangelsen. Yellowstone Wildlife: Ecology and Natural History of the Greater Yellowstone Ecosystem. Boulder, CO: University Press of Colorado, 2013. With stunning images by Mangelsen and detailed natural histories of the animals that call the park home, this is an outstanding book for wildlife lovers.

Mangelsen, Thomas, and Todd Wilkinson. Grizzlies of Pilgrim Creek. New York: Rizzoli, 2015. The project of famed photographer Tom Mangelsen and environmental writer Todd Wilkinson, this gorgeous, oversized book tells the story of grizzly bear #399, one of the most beloved and oft-seen bruins in Grand Teton National Park.

Murie, Margaret, and Olaus Johan Murie. Wapiti Wilderness. Boulder, CO: University Press of Colorado, 1985. A magnificent read by two of the region's now deceased but beloved conservationists, the chapters alternate between his work studying elk and her descriptions of their fascinating life together.

Phillips, Michael K., and Douglas W. Smith. The Wolves of Yellowstone. Stillwater, MN: Voyageur Press, 1996. Told with fabulous color photos and intimate details by the two men who oversaw the project, this book tells the story of the wolves' reintroduction to Yellowstone in 1995.

Riis, Joe, with contributions from Arthur Middleton, Emilene Ostlind, Gretel Ehrlich, and Thomas Lovejoy. Yellowstone Migrations. Seattle: Mountaineers Books, 2017.

This marvelous photographic exploration of the last great migrations of elk, pronghorn, antelope, and mule deer features rich, meaty essays by some wonderful writers.

Schreier, Carl. *A Field Guide to Yellowstone's Geysers, Hot Springs and Fumaroles.* Moose, WY: Homestead Publishing, 1999. This slightly larger-than-your-pocket book is the authoritative guide to Yellowstone's best-known thermal features, with information about the origin of their names, regular and irregular activity, statistics, and anecdotal histories.

Schullery, Paul. *Searching for Yellowstone: Ecology and Wonder in the Last Wilderness.* Helena, MT: Montana Historical Society Press, 2004. A fascinating and compelling environmental history of the world's first national park.

Schullery, Paul. *Yellowstone Bear Tales.* Boulder, CO: Roberts Rinehart Publishers, 1991. Read this for hair-raising accounts of bear encounters by one of the park's most respected natural historians.

Wilkinson, Todd. *Yellowstone Wildlife: A Watcher's Guide.* Minocqua, WI: North-Word Press, 1992. This is an excellent guide for where to see wildlife, with fascinating must-know information about each creature.

Recreation

Henry, Jeff. *Yellowstone Winter Guide.* Boulder, CO: Roberts Rinehart Publishers, 1998. This full-color guide is a must for travelers seeing Yellowstone in its quietest and arguably most magical season.

Lilly, Bud, and Paul Schullery. *Bud Lilly's Guide to Fly Fishing the New West.* Portland, OR: Frank Amato Publications, 2000. Written by the father of Western trout fishing and one of the West's most respected natural historians, this book weaves Lilly's personal history as an angler, guide, and conservationist with the history of fly-fishing in the region along with sage advice.

Lomax, Becky. *Moon Best of Yellowstone & Grand Teton: Make the Most of One to Three Days in the Parks.* Berkeley, CA: Avalon Travel, 2021. This is the ultimate guide to what to see and how to see it in these two national parks.

Marschall, Mark C. *Yellowstone Trails: A Hiking Guide.* Yellowstone National Park, WY: Yellowstone National Park Association, 2008. Another great hiking guide, this one includes descriptions of more than 100 trails ranging from day hikes to backpack trips.

Nystrom, Andrew Dean, Morgan Konn, and Tim Cahill. *Top Trails Yellowstone & Grand Tetons: Must-do Hikes for Everyone.* Berkeley, CA: Wilderness Press, 2009. This book covers 45 wonderful hikes from 0.5-mile (0.8-km) jaunts to 30-mile (48-km) treks.

Schneider, Bill. Best Easy Day Hikes Grand Teton National Park, 4th edition. Guilford, CT: Globe Pequot Press, 2018. The descriptions are concise and the maps are accurate. What more could you want?

Schneider, Bill. *Hiking Yellowstone National Park,* 3rd edition. Guilford, CT: Globe Pequot Press, 2012. This excellent hiking guide offers short, moderate, and long hikes throughout Yellowstone.

Watters, Ron. *Winter Tales and Trails: Skiing, Snowshoeing and Snowboarding in Idaho, the Grand Tetons and Yellowstone National Park.* Pocatello, ID: Great Rift Press, 1997. This book intertwines guide advice with great stories—you'll wish Ron was along for the trip.

Internet Resources

All You Can Read
www.allyoucanread.com/wyoming-newspapers
This site brings together a variety of news sources from around the state.

Atlas Obscura
www.atlasobscura.com/things-to-do/wyoming
From the fun to the funky, this site offers 44 unusual attractions across the state.

State of Wyoming
www.wyoming.gov
Wyoming's official website offers a wealth of information about the state and its government.

Wyoming Travel and Tourism
www.travelwyoming.com
The state's comprehensive offering for visitors, this is a great place to find information on towns, accommodations, travel ideas and itineraries, shopping, and dining.

Wyoming State Parks, Historic Sites, and Trails
www.wyoparks.state.wy.us
Useful information on parks, recreation, and historical preservation.

Wyoming Travel Information
www.wyoroad.info
Up-to-date road information provided by the Wyoming Department of Transportation.

National Park Service
www.nps.gov
The NPS website is helpful for making plans to visit any of the national parks.

Recreation.gov
www.recreation.gov
This government-run site allows visitors to make reservations at public campgrounds.

Wyoming Game and Fish Department
http://wgfd.wyo.gov
The website offers much of what visitors need to know about fishing and hunting in the state.

U.S. Forest Service
www.fs.usda.gov
The Forest Service website is helpful for pursuing recreational opportunities—including multiuse trails, campgrounds, and cabin rentals—throughout the eight national forests, recreation areas, and grasslands in Wyoming.

Wyoming Outfitters and Guides Association
www.wyoga.org
A fantastic resource for planning guided outdoor adventures.

Wyoming Dude Ranchers Association
www.wyomingdra.com
An excellent place to look for dude ranch vacations.

Index

List of Maps

Photo Credits

Title page photo: Wyoming Office of Tourism/Peter Adams; page 2 © Wyoming Office of Tourism; page 3 © Wyoming Office of Tourism; page 8 © (top left) MOTBD/Donnie Sexton; (top right) Carbon County Visitors' Council; (bottom) Haveseen | Dreamstime.com; page 9 © (top) Glenn Nagel | Dreamstime.com; (bottom left) Sheridan Travel & Tourism/Shawn Parker; (bottom right) Wyoming Office of Tourism; page 10 © Henry Turner | Dreamstime.com; page 13 © (top) Stevehymon | Dreamstime.com; (bottom) Maragans | Dreamstime.com; page 14 © (top) Wyoming Office of Tourism/Andy Austin; (bottom) Wyoming Office of Tourism; page 15 © (top) Coltonstiffler | Dreamstime.com; (bottom) Wyoming Office of Tourism/Jason Lindsey; page 16 © Wyoming Office of Tourism/Eric Lindberg; Jesse Kraft | Dreamstime.com; page 18 © (bottom) Bbeckphoto | Dreamstime.com; page 20 (left) © Lorpic99 | Dreamstime.com; (right) courtesy Linda Mohammad; page 25 courtesy Linda Mohammad; page 26 © (bottom) Scukrov | Dreamstime.com; page 27 © Wyoming Office of Tourism/Martin Ruegner; page 28 © (top left) NPS/Neal Herbert; (top right) Montana Office of Tourism and Business Development (MOTBD); page 38 © Linda Bair | Dreamstime.com; page 47 © (top) NPS/Neal Herbert; (bottom) NPS/Jacob W. Frank; page 50 © (top left) NPS/Neal Herbert; (top right) NPS/Jacob W. Frank; (bottom) NPS/Neal Herbert; page 58 © NPS/Jacob W. Frank; page 63 © NPS/Jacob W. Frank; page 65 © (top) NPS/Jacob W. Frank; (bottom) Wyoming Office of Tourism; page 67 © NPS/Jim Peaco; page 75 © (top) Montana Office of Tourism and Business Development (MOTBD); (bottom) Montana Office of Tourism and Business Development (MOTBD); page 79 © F11photo | Dreamstime.com; page 80 © (top left) Johan Elzenga | Dreamstime.com; (top right) Filip Fuxa | Dreamstime.com; page 87 © Silksatsunrise | Dreamstime.com; page 90 © Wyoming Office of Tourism; page 93 © (top) Randy Harris | Dreamstime.com; (bottom) Steven Hardin | Dreamstime.com; page 96 © Wyoming Office of Tourism; page 100 © (top) Wyoming Office of Tourism; (left middle) Kwiktor | Dreamstime.com; (right middle)Papabear | Dreamstime.com; (bottom) Wyoming Office of Tourism; page 104 © Jackstraw22 | Dreamstime.com; page 107 © Wyoming Office of Tourism; page 108 © (top left) Wyoming Office of Tourism; (top right) Wyoming Office of Tourism; page 111 © Wyoming Office of Tourism; page 115 © (top) Wyoming Office of Tourism; (bottom) Acoyster | Dreamstime.com; page 118 © Michael Turner | Dreamstime.com; page 125 © (top left) Wyoming Office of Tourism; (top right) hmanlic via Wyoming Office of Tourism; (bottom left) Wyoming Office of Tourism; (bottom right) Wyoming Office of Tourism/Tristan Greszko; page 134 © (top left) Wyoming Office of Tourism/Andy Austin; (top right) Wyoming Office of Tourism; (bottom) Stevehymon | Dreamstime.com; page 145 © Wyoming Office of Tourism; page 155 © (top) Visit Cody Yellowstone Country; (bottom) Jimsphotos | Dreamstime.com; page 163 © Richard Collens | Dreamstime.com; page 164 © (top left) Wyoming Office of Tourism; (top right) Wyoming Office of Tourism/Jason Lindsey; page 170 © (top) Wyoming Office of Tourism/Jason Lindsey; (bottom) Wyoming Office of Tourism; page 173 © David Burke | Dreamstime.com; page 174 © Sandra Foyt | Dreamstime.com; page 182 © (top) Wyoming Office of Tourism; (left middle) Wyoming Office of Tourism; (right middle) Visit Gillette-Wright; (bottom) Onesmallsquare | Dreamstime.com; page 195 © Wyoming Office of Tourism/Jason Lindsey; page 199 © (top left) Alexey Kamenskiy | Dreamstime.com; page 206 © (top) Wyoming Office of Tourism/Jason Lindsey; (left middle) Wyoming Office of Tourism; (right middle)Samsherman | Dreamstime.com; (bottom) Wyoming Office of Tourism/Jason Lindsey; page 216 © (top) Rolf52 | Dreamstime.com; (left middle) Wyoming Office of Tourism; (right middle) Wyoming Office of Tourism; (bottom) Wyoming Office of Tourism; page 229 © (top left) Benkrut | Dreamstime.com; (top right) Bdingman | Dreamstime.com; (bottom) Littleny | Dreamstime.com; page 230 © Wyoming Office of Tourism; page 240 © (top) Wyoming Office of Tourism; (bottom) Wyoming Office of Tourism/Andy Austin; page 243 © Wyoming Office of Tourism/Andy Austin; page 247 © Wyoming Office of Tourism; page 250 © wilderness_john via Wyoming Office of Tourism; page 254 © (left middle) Montana Office of Tourism and Business Development (MOTBD); (right middle) MOTBD/Donnie Sexton; (bottom) MOTBD/Donnie Sexton; page 269 © Wyoming Office of Tourism; page 274 © Jchutch | Dreamstime.com

Get inspired for your next adventure

Follow @**moonguides** on Instagram or subscribe to our newsletter at **moon.com**

#TravelWithMoon

ROAD TRIP GUIDES

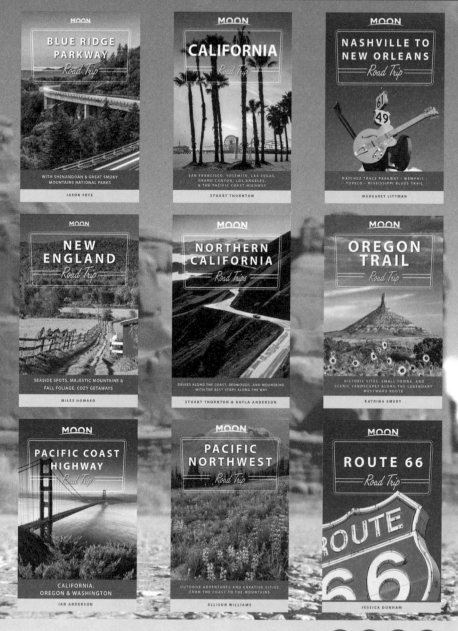

MOON

BLUE RIDGE PARKWAY
Road Trip

WITH SHENANDOAH & GREAT SMOKY
MOUNTAINS NATIONAL PARKS

JASON FRYE

MOON

CALIFORNIA
Road Trip

SAN FRANCISCO, YOSEMITE, LAS VEGAS,
GRAND CANYON, LOS ANGELES,
& THE PACIFIC COAST HIGHWAY

STUART THORNTON

MOON

NASHVILLE TO NEW ORLEANS
Road Trip

NATCHEZ TRACE PARKWAY · MEMPHIS ·
TUPELO · MISSISSIPPI BLUES TRAIL

MARGARET LITTMAN

MOON

NEW ENGLAND
Road Trip

SEASIDE SPOTS, MAJESTIC MOUNTAINS &
FALL FOLIAGE, COZY GETAWAYS

MILES HOWARD

MOON

NORTHERN CALIFORNIA
Road Trips

DRIVES ALONG THE COAST, REDWOODS, AND MOUNTAINS
WITH THE BEST STOPS ALONG THE WAY

STUART THORNTON & KAYLA ANDERSON

MOON

OREGON TRAIL
Road Trip

HISTORIC SITES, SMALL TOWNS, AND
SCENIC LANDSCAPES ALONG THE LEGENDARY
WESTWARD ROUTE

KATRINA EMERY

MOON

PACIFIC COAST HIGHWAY
Road Trip

CALIFORNIA,
OREGON & WASHINGTON

IAN ANDERSON

MOON

PACIFIC NORTHWEST
Road Trip

OUTDOOR ADVENTURES AND CREATIVE CITIES
FROM THE COAST TO THE MOUNTAINS

ALLISON WILLIAMS

MOON

ROUTE 66
Road Trip

JESSICA DUNHAM

MOON.COM | ROADTRIPUSA.COM

MAP SYMBOLS

═══ Expressway	○ City/Town	✗ Airport	⌁ Golf Course
═══ Primary Road	◉ State Capital	✗ Airfield	P Parking Area
∿∿∿ Secondary Road	⊛ National Capital	▲ Mountain	≜ Archaeological Site
┄┄ Unpaved Road	✪ Highlight	✛ Unique Natural Feature	▲ Church
----- Trail	★ Point of Interest		
·········· Ferry	• Accommodation	⟦ Waterfall	▯ Gas Station
✛✛✛✛ Railroad	▼ Restaurant/Bar	▲ Park	Glacier
▒▒▒ Pedestrian Walkway	■ Other Location	⬤ Trailhead	Mangrove
▮▮▮▮▮ Stairs	Ⓐ Campground	⛷ Skiing Area	Reef
			Swamp

CONVERSION TABLES

$°C = (°F − 32) / 1.8$
$°F = (°C × 1.8) + 32$
1 inch = 2.54 centimeters (cm)
1 foot = 0.304 meters (m)
1 yard = 0.914 meters
1 mile = 1.6093 kilometers (km)
1 km = 0.6214 miles
1 fathom = 1.8288 m
1 chain = 20.1168 m
1 furlong = 201.168 m
1 acre = 0.4047 hectares
1 sq km = 100 hectares
1 sq mile = 2.59 square km
1 ounce = 28.35 grams
1 pound = 0.4536 kilograms
1 short ton = 0.90718 metric ton
1 short ton = 2,000 pounds
1 long ton = 1.016 metric tons
1 long ton = 2,240 pounds
1 metric ton = 1,000 kilograms
1 quart = 0.94635 liters
1 US gallon = 3.7854 liters
1 Imperial gallon = 4.5459 liters
1 nautical mile = 1.852 km

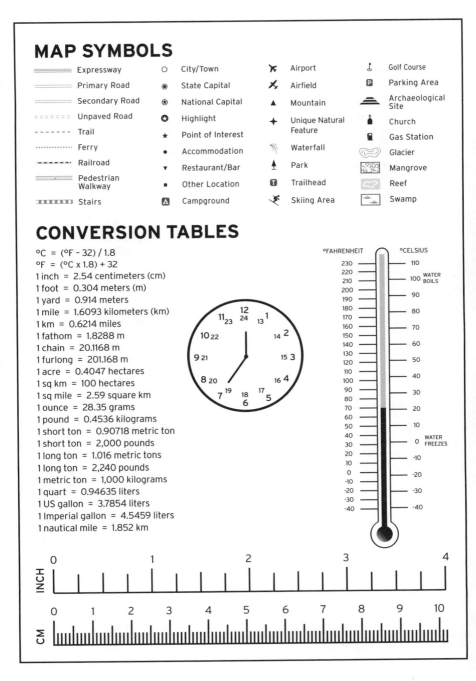

MOON WYOMING

Avalon Travel
Hachette Book Group
1700 Fourth Street
Berkeley, CA 94710, USA
www.moon.com

Editor: Kimberly Ehart
Acquiring Editor: Nikki Ioakimedes
Series Manager: Kathryn Ettinger
Copy Editor: Deana Shields
Graphics and Production Coordinator: Ravina Schneider
Cover Design: Toni Tajima
Map Editor: Albert Angulo
Cartographers: Erin Greb and Karin Dahl
Indexer: Greg Jewett

ISBN-13: 978-1-64049-720-7

Printing History
1st Edition — 2015
4th Edition — February 2023
5 4 3 2 1

Front cover photo: Grand Prismatic Geyser, Yellowstone National Park © kwiktor | Gettyimages.com
Back cover photo: bison in Grand Teton National Park © Linda Bair | Dreamstime.com

Printed in Thailand for Imago